Gavin + Cynthia Richmond.

Something to R...
South Africa
Few Laughs

LAUGH, THE BELOVED COUNTRY

Laugh, the Beloved Country

A Compendium of South African Humour

James Clarke & Harvey Tyson

DOUBLE STOREY
a juta company

First published 2003 by Double Storey Books,
a Juta company, Mercury Crescent, Wetton, Cape Town

ISBN 1-919930-32-9

DTP by Claudine Willatt-Bate
Cover design by Toby Newsome
Repro by Virtual Colour, Cape Town
Printing and binding by ABC Press, Epping, Cape Town

Contents

Foreword

Archbishop Desmond Tutu

I could not stop laughing virtually from the very first moment I started reading the manuscript of *Laugh, the Beloved Country*. People seeing me doubled over, say on a plane, saw this as proof positive of what they had always believed – that there was a screw loose somewhere in the Tutu cranium.

As is well known, I am very restrained, speaking only in cultured and quiet tones especially when addressing a huge rally. I am renowned for not being strident or even garrulous (although the late Minister of Police, Mr Louis le Grange – not a very reliable judge of such matters – complained that 'Bishop Tutu talks too much' and my wonderfully supportive spouse remarked that it was the first time she had felt she could concur with a Nationalist Cabinet Minister).

I do not normally indulge in hyperbole, being famous for my understatements. Thus, when I say that here in this volume, the reader is being served up a most delectable confection, it is not said lightly. This anthology is a splendid, indeed a glittering, array of talent possessed by those in our country (quite a few seem to have been born elsewhere) who have the gift to tickle us.

As is also common cause, as our learned friends in the legal profession might venture to say, I am not jingoistic at all, nor am I chauvinistic (though I did get into hot water with the ladies when I held forth that Madiba needed someone to bring him his slippers), so it must be taken seriously when I say that this collection demonstrates, beyond reasonable doubt, that as a nation we actually do have some remarkably talented people. Without even trying to be politically correct, the collection by that witty duo Harvey Tyson and James Clarke manages remarkably well to be marvellously representative of the demographics of our rainbow nation. (I had in all humility to get that in somewhere.)

I discovered a long time ago that humour is a serious business. It certainly helped many of us to survive the idiocies and the humiliations of our unlamented former apartheid dispensation – a dispensation which, extraordinarily, continued for decades despite the fact that nobody (as far as I can tell today) ever supported it. The 'Nats', as they were popularly known, were returned to power repeatedly with increased majorities by non-existent South Africans.

If we did not laugh so much, we would have been crying. Perhaps we were crying when we were laughing. The two are so close.

Taking the mickey out of someone, even out of oneself – and not taking ourselves too seriously – helped us not only to survive, but to make the kind of transition from repression to freedom that still leaves the world open-mouthed.

Why was the transition relatively peaceful? I think in part it was that we eventually learned to laugh at ourselves. Laughter certainly helped me to defuse somewhat tense situations on one or two occasions. There were very angry crowds at Chris Hani's funeral and at that of the victims of the Boipatong Massacre. On those occasions I told a story I used often – it was to illustrate the utter absurdity of reserving universities for specific ethnic groups by asking, 'What about a university for large noses only?' If you were afflicted with a small nose you would have to apply to the Minister of Small Nose Affairs for permission to attend the university for large noses. And the crowds relaxed as they guffawed.

Thank God for satirists, cartoonists and humorists of all shapes and sizes, of all races, ages and genders (I suppose I should add, of all sexual orientations), such as are represented in this collection, for keeping us sane and human, and for Clarke and Tyson for producing this collection.

Buy it and read it. You are in for a treat.

Preface

Bring together a French explorer, a Scottish engineer, a New Zealand-born TV presenter, a murderer, a medical writer, an international tennis star, a professor, a judge, an Australian-born farmer, an Afrikaans playwright, a Jewish diamond prospector, a frantic mother, two famous African writers, a variety of white and black novelists, editors and journalists – and something amusing should result. These men and women of different races, different centuries, different cultures (ranging from American-Irish to Zulu) have one distinction in common – each has been identified as among the most entertaining writers of English-language humour in South Africa in the last 200 years.

The essences of humour arise from the boiling pot of human experiences. Humour's light but potent essences increase during anxious times to mask fears and raise the spirits. They combine in a form of nitrous oxide – to dull any pain and to produce a giggle.

South Africa – a boiling pot if ever there was one – has produced an unusual number and a cultural variety of these essences, from bitter satire to wild farce; from sharp wit to gentle good humour.

We have tried to display them here – the brave if heavy satire of Thomas Bain two centuries ago; the quiet charm of Sol Plaatje and Louis Leipoldt a century later. There's the sharp wit of writers such as Pieter-Dirk Uys and Christopher Hope; the elegant good humour of Gordon Forbes and A.B. Hughes; the pungent, sardonic – yet caring – words of Zakes Mda. These are among the surprising number of writers of South African humour who have international reputations.

Then there are the sad ironies of Nat Nkasa; the cynical ridicule of Richard Rive; the sparkling mirrors held up to an anxious community in the immediate post-apartheid period by Gus Silber. We have also collected the farce and satirical antics of a whole mockery of columnists who greeted the anxious dawn of African democracy in the 21st century.

To identify and assemble the best of laughter of this country would take about six weeks, we estimated. That knowledge gave us the strength to tackle the project. We discovered immediately, however, that it might take at least six months. In fact it took nearly three years of labour, much of it taken up by the excitement of the chase. But we had forgotten the really bad news: the amount of time wasted through the mischief of our two distantly connected personal – very personal

– computers which malignantly scrambled everything we sent each other and devised major misunderstandings and daily chaos.

The good news was more significant: nearly every author, columnist, copyright holder and publisher we could trace gave us instant and enthusiastic cooperation. For this we thank them greatly. You will find our acknowledgements at the back – easily accessible for reference whether you are reading straight through the book or dipping and skipping at whim. If there is any interested party we have failed to acknowledge, it is by accident or through lack of clues for tracing them, and we apologise and ask forgiveness.

Three omissions from this anthology are worth mentioning: 'Thomas Equinus, the defrocked priest' who emigrated to Australia and could not be traced; satirist Robert Kirby, who in his inimitable style demanded fees and threatened us with lawyers; and – more seriously – we omitted a local talent who, outside of his country, was perhaps the most internationally famous South African light writer. He was Noel Langley of Natal, and his light novels, such as *Cage Me a Peacock*, were on bookshelves around the world in the 1930s and 1940s. His comedies became West End plays and Hollywood films. He was prominent, for instance, in the team which made *The Wizard of Oz*. Langley was an artist as well as author, and he wrote children's books whose latest editions are still being sold world-wide. Regrettably, we could trace nothing worthwhile of his humour about his beloved country.

Nobody, of course, can be totally satisfied with our selections. Humour lies near the elbow of the beholder, and every funny-bone is peculiar unto itself. There can never be full agreement on what is actually funny, and every individual will have his or her own set of favourite funny writers.

Who are we, then, to decide what is the best of humour? The editors of this selection claim, between them, more than a hundred years of mock-serious study of the elusive subject, but this has merely increased their own prejudices and funny peculiarities. You are at liberty to judge their judgements.

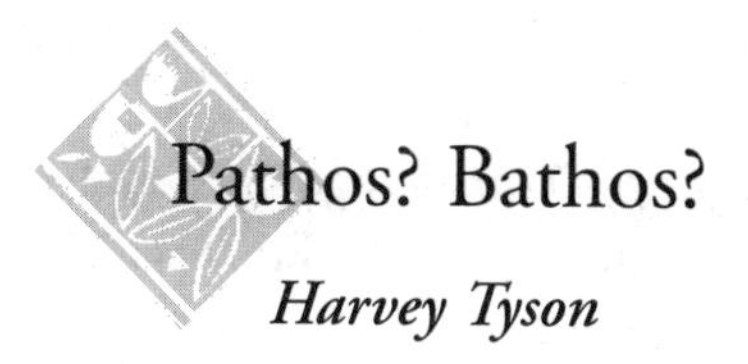

Pathos? Bathos?

Harvey Tyson

Not knowing whether to laugh or cry is one of the most subtle – and often intense – emotions of which a human being is capable. We know of no place where this mixed emotion has been so prolonged, in such complex situations and in so mixed-up a society as in South Africa.

At first James Clarke and I set out ambitiously to review the written humour of the entire English-speaking world. But we were not sure where to begin. In the end we decided to focus on a polyglot people in just one turbulent corner of this planet, and see how they used humour to help them survive or at least cope with harsh reality. We discovered, right beside us, samples of most of the gems of humour one could hope to display. South Africa's history contains such a richness of racial types, raconteurs, political experiences, cultural differences and misunderstandings; such a muddle of mischief, horror, oppression, tragedy; so many elusive rainbows – it's enough to make you cry … er, laugh.

We all know too that laughter is an essential survival mechanism. *Time* magazine, for instance, reporting on Zimbabwe in February 2003, recalled an incident recounted in Doris Lessing's *African Laughter*. At a meeting a story was told 'of cruelty, of official stupidity. The whole room was laughing … I said to the man next to me, "Why are you laughing? That's a terrible story."

'"That's why we are laughing," he said.'

As South Africa had to live with apartheid for much of the last century, the laughter wore a little thin and our humour was appropriately black in places. However – even if most of us forgot to laugh for a while – the country and its people remain remarkably sunny. And often quite funny.

Where's the Action?

Though people perceive humour differently, it is universal. It can be found in the skin of a banana, and wrapped in enigmas. It lurks in funerals, love affairs, domestic tiffs and in all the absurdities of life and death.

James Thurber, that amusingly chronic worrier, claimed that humour was 'emotional chaos remembered in tranquillity'. Which is another way of saying that humour exists only when you can afford to laugh. But I don't believe this is true. I believe we often laugh when we can least afford the luxury of it. Remember all those famous figures who cracked jokes on the way to the gallows, thereby hanging some great tales?

With humour – like hanging – everything depends. It depends not on where you are going but from where you are coming. From which culture. Which period in time. Which set of beliefs and values. Which country. From which democracy or from under which tyranny. Humour adapts, and allows us to adapt, to change.

The first question raised in our earnest research into humour was: Where are all the great English-speaking humorous writers? Dead, most of them. Even my co-editor, James Clarke, doesn't look too healthy. (The late comedian Vic Oliver, son-in-law of Winston Churchill, used that line 50 years ago – and *he* borrowed it from a philosopher writing in the 18th century!) Although James Clarke is the author of about two-dozen books, many of them dealing with vital global environmental issues, he is one of those extremely rare people who are regarded by most readers as an expert on humorous writing – even though such an animal cannot possibly exist. He ceaselessly engages in his column thousands of readers who have thousands of different senses of humour. He interacts with them in wit and laughter. The result, a zany brand of good humour. His humorous books have an appeal that is astonishingly broad, extending beyond this continent.

Broad Vision

James, therefore, may not agree with me that humour, as a *literary* art, is sadly shrinking. The art may have reached its apogee in mid-20th century, when those of us born in the first half of it could rattle off the names of so many universally known authors of humour – French, Russian, Italian as well as English. I was teethed on Mark Twain, W.W. Jacobs, Jerome K. Jerome, P.G. Wodehouse, Robert Benchley, Ring Lardner, Dorothy Parker, Damon Runyan, James Thurber, Evelyn Waugh … the list goes on and on. And on.

As a schoolboy at Kingswood College in Grahamstown, the Eastern Cape's 'City of Saints', I broadened my vision, literally, by reading the great humorists. I taught myself to read Stephen Leacock's hilarious essays at arm's length and at an angle of 90 degrees, while directly facing the maths master in class. ('But sir, the author is a professor of mathematics' was my prepared excuse – fortunately never used.) And in church, during an endless sermon, I could read a book by that genius of the English language, S.J. Perelman, carefully placed and 'carelessly' open among the hymnals a metre to one side.

Written humour is highly educative, yet one has only to look back at the reading matter of the mid-20th century to see how it is diminishing. Before and after

World War II, for instance, almost every newspaper in the English-speaking world had its resident or syndicated humorous column. There was J.B. Morton's famous Fleet Street 'Beachcomber' column, which was read throughout the Commonwealth. Other exponents, such as Bennet Cerf, Art Buchwald, Michael Frayn and Russell Baker were read around the world. But, of course, each community, each region, each nation, each international culture had its own favourites, just as each individual has his or her own favourite brand of humour.

My favourite, I suppose, was Patrick Campbell of *The Observer* in London whose weekly column of Irish wit was syndicated from Britain to Africa, Australia and America. His was a gentle, erudite, deprecating style that made even his occasional schoolboy farce seem elegant in retrospect. I wonder how he would be read today? I cannot tell because – although I used to read and re-read a book of his marvellous reminiscences – some bloody swine 'borrowed' it.

But I stray.

As fashions, technology and the century changed, the numbers of well-known 'funny' writers seemed to dwindle to a distant, somewhat shaky mirage. Offhand I can think only of Irish-American P.J. O'Rourke, of Englishman Alan Coren; of Bill Bryson and of Jewish-American, latter-day-Damon-Runyan, wild-cowboy Kinky Finkelstein, and Dave Barry of the *Miami Herald*, the most syndicated humorist in the US and possibly the most popular in the whole English-speaking world at the start of the 21st century.

There are, of course, many whom I have momentarily forgotten, mislaid or never known. But even a full roll-call will, I believe, suggest that current humorists are unable – in numbers if not in quality – to fill the thinning, laughing, literary ranks. Today the funny people appear to be all scriptwriters or professional performers on TV. Television sitcoms, unfortunately, are sucking up some, if not most, of the best writers of humour. And, incidentally, stand-up comedy in theatre and TV around the world is becoming stronger – and sometimes quite brilliant – after a century dominated by print. Now literary humour is shrinking in the face of the electronic media and their commercial or data-dominated styles.

Getting it Together

All the more reason, we thought, for re-examining what written English words of wit we could salvage from an exceptionally fertile field in one corner of the globe. In drawing on 200 years of comic and light literature from this multi-cultural society, we were able to see how a new, collective sense of humour shows first signs of beginning to evolve in a place where so many tragically funny things happen, and so much humour (and ill humour) abound.

There are 11 official languages in South Africa, as well as communities whose language and culture originate in half a hundred countries ranging from Portugal and Pakistan to Bali and Belgium. So, to claim that our selections provide a perfect and balanced panel representing all these cultural styles – even limited to written English – is, well, laughable. South Africa is simply too rich in funny moments and human folly, too rich in experiences that cry out to be laughed off, for us to give a precise and balanced picture.

And when one confines oneself to 200 years of written English humour out of Africa, historical circumstances dictate that one restricts the choice to mainly English-speaking, mainly white, males. Funny that. But times are changing, and so are the ratios between male, female, white and black writers of humour.

We abjure political correctness (as humour demands). Balance of any kind is not our main objective. Laughter is. We have presented samples of the significant forms of humour written over the past 200 years, and then each of us has simply chosen the light writing that appeals to us (sometimes that which neither of us liked) and thrown in some of our own contributions (which we loved).

Style and Sequence

Our saddest discovery in assembling this anthology was the damage which ageing does to even the best and lightest of light writing. It applies not only to the need for the topicality on which satire and some other forms of humour feed, but also to style and fashion and the reasons why people smile. Thus we have felt constrained to sum up rather than publish extracts of some historical wit.

It would have been historically interesting to have published our selections in chronological order. We considered tracing the progress of humour – or possibly the lack of its development – among writers of English in southern Africa from pre-colonial times to the latest post-democratic tendencies. We would have begun this book with a French botanist of the late 1700s and ended with a black playwright who observes the early 2000s. But history adds little to laughter, and we decided that the random laughs that arise out of alphabetical order, though disjointed, are, funnily enough, more fitting. You may find that the overall result is less an anthology than an anatomy – or rather a jumbled collection of the funnybones – of a society that is often at war with itself.

We believe that humour played a significant role on the road to peaceful change. It has helped 40 million people survive the chaos that inevitably followed an unprecedented political *volte-face*. Some of the laughter you will find on these pages definitely helped get us through – assuming we are through!

If we aren't, there'll be some more laughs coming.

Hermanus

INTRODUCTION

Satire vs. Smiles

James Clarke

Against laughter nothing can stand – Mark Twain

I shall confess, right here, up front, that I am an Englishman by birth and was, to use that unfortunate expression, 'brought up' in London and the English Midlands. I am, in fact, a Cockney and, as such, genetically programmed to see the funny side of almost anything – even if it's a traffic cop demanding I wind down my window.

I began my writing career on daily newspapers in Birmingham and Wolverhampton, but I have been in South Africa on a permanent basis for almost 40 years, so I am now irredeemably South African and, therefore, the possessor of a licence to laugh with, and sometimes at, South Africans.

My co-author is a dyed-in-the-wool South African and one of South Africa's most famous editors. Harvey Tyson, as editor-in-chief of *The Star* in Johannesburg, fought in the editorial trenches throughout the worst of the apartheid years. He was often in court – charged by the State police with various forms of subversion relating to his newspaper's stand against apartheid, or else supporting one of his staff who had run foul of the government. He saw apartheid come and he helped it go. There were some very tense times – his phone was tapped, he discovered police spies on his staff, the cops often called on him – yet in our 40-year association I never knew an instance where Harvey's sense of humour failed him.

Harvey Tyson has written some very grown-up books in his time and many seminal articles on politics as well as on the press and on travel. He is a respected literary critic and he has written a lot of humour – he rather modestly agreed to only three pieces appearing in this book. I am not famous enough to be modest, so you will find I have six.

In 1992, after Harvey's retirement and at the start of South Africa's transition to majority rule, violence increased and people seemed to become afraid of reading newspapers. *The Star*'s circulation fell. I was asked … no, I was *ordered* by Harvey's successor, Richard Steyn, to inject humour into the paper on a daily basis. This led to the most enjoyable period of my 50 years in daily newspaper journalism.

Harvey and I debated this book over many memorable (and some rather hazy) lunches in Johannesburg as well as along the beautiful Cape coast where he now lives looking out over Walker Bay with its leaping whales and crashing seas.

A Funny Country

Jointly writing a book when the co-authors are 1 200 km apart has its difficulties but, finally, we decided we would concentrate on revealing the funny side of South Africa. What made South Africans laugh, and what still makes them laugh?

We decided that, first and foremost, this must be a fun book to read. There's more than enough serious stuff available about South Africa. Fortunately South Africa can be a very funny country. We mean really funny. Most of the time there may be no intention to be funny, and this usually makes it funnier.

One thinks of broadcaster Pip Freedman's story of his friend Charlie, an old 'Kapenaar' who sold crayfish (rock lobster) on the streets in Cape Town. They'd scuttle around his feet, and when you bought one he'd drop it into boiling water and the steam would escape from under the shell – 'Chee, chee, chee'. A woman – an English tourist – bought one and Charlie popped it in the pot. The crayfish, one hopes, died instantly but 'Chee, chee, chee' went the steam. The woman said:

'You're boiling it!'

'Yes, lady.'

'But you're boiling it alive!'

'Correk, lady.'

'But that's cruel!'

'Nay merrem, is not cruel,' said Charlie, who'd been boiling crayfish for years. 'Dey's used to it!'

Good Humour

Most of this book contains the works of those whom we are tempted to call 'the pure humorists' as opposed to the political satirists, who dominated the field in the last third of the 20th century.

Really good humour should be gentle and make everybody feel good.

Satire needs victims.

I have been privileged to witness a miracle in this country in recent years. I don't think the world appreciates the magnitude of what has happened here. A tough white-dominated government stepped down in favour of a group of preponderantly black greenhorns. That took great courage on everybody's part. Things have not gone smoothly as this book will reflect but – hallelujah – we're on our way … somewhere.

As the most notable of the transition humorists, Gus Silber, put it: 'South Africa isn't what it used to be. It isn't what it's going to be, either.'

The absolutely last thing we wanted this book to be was political and we also decided we would not bend over backwards to be PC – politically correct. Yet to avoid politics when writing about South Africa would be like writing about the life cycle of *Oryx gazella* without being zoological. After all, take South Africa's equivalent of James Thurber – Herman Charles Bosman. He's very funny. No, let me rephrase that: he *was* very funny in mid-century. No, no, I must be honest – he is still very funny to me. You will detect I have a problem saying this. This is because some of Bosman's writing, in today's context, appears to be insensitive. But there was very little venom in Bosman's writing – mischief, yes, but rarely open scorn. Afrikaner politicians wanted his work banned because it seemed to mock the Boer. Some black politicians now want him banned because he uses 'the *K* word' as we in polite circles now refer to that taboo word, 'kaffir' (the equivalent to 'nigger' in the US). The word is now more taboo in our educated white society than 'the *F* word' used to be. It is an interesting indicator of the changing South African mindset. But one cannot honestly reflect the evolution of South African humorist literature while fiddling with its words, and so 'the *K* word' had to stay. In other words this book is, by default, something of a political or sociological review.

Funny Thing, Humour

I have never really been able to define humour. Somebody asked Charlie Chaplin: Why, when somebody slips on a banana peel, do people find it amusing? He didn't know, but said it was even funnier when somebody spotted the banana skin and, with a knowing little smile, carefully stepped over it only to fall straight down an open manhole.

The truth is, we don't know what makes people double up and expel air, convulsively, through open mouths as if they have just been punched in the breadbasket.

Humour is often used as a means of questioning some of society's basic dogmas, not necessarily to destroy them but to provoke thought about them. Humour, like 'protest poetry' and ballads, is used for ridiculing the establishment, and this comes out in this book.

A famous black journalist, Nat Nakasa, said: 'I shudder to think what would happen to us if apartheid did not have some comical aspects to it.'

There's a lot of philosophy in humorous writing. Mainly one is laughing at the foibles of the world's funniest animal, *Homo sapiens*. A lot of the time humorist writers are really laughing at themselves, but they do so with the comfort of knowing that most of those who read their words are in the same boat – confused by the world, perhaps amused by their own ineptitude in dealing with it, but determined not to let it get them down.

Speaking for myself, I can only take so much reality.

As a humorist I have no deep philosophical goal. I really just want to make people laugh … and, maybe, think a little.

To my simple mind, humour should leave one smiling. But here we come back to the old bogey that Harvey has already alluded to: that which made us laugh 25 years ago often no longer does. The world has changed. South Africans, even more so, have changed. And so have their humour writers.

Lone Hill, Sandton
Greater Johannesburg

APARTHEID

AT FIRST *sight it seems tasteless to begin this alphabetical collection of laughter with apartheid. And worse, boring!*

Not a bit of it. Here is a collection of gems of real humour, with belly laughs as well as ironic smiles. These gems, put together in 1990 in a book called Apartheid, the Lighter Side, *belong to all of South Africa, and are unlike any other collection in the world. They include magnificent examples of delicious self-parody.*

'I laughed, and laughed, and laughed,' said Athol Fugard, one of South Africa's most insightful playwrights, when asked to preview the collection of contemporary news reports on apartheid. This was because apartheid's laws and the tortuous explanations of its proponents out-satirised the sharpest satirists, as many satirists in this book have complained – not always in jest.

It took a straight news agency man and parliamentary reporter, Ben Maclennan of the South African Press Association (Sapa), to gather in, from apartheid's darkest and ugliest days, the contemporaneous ridicule of apartheid. He appreciated that, for more than 40 years, the English-language press – apart from fulminating daily in its editorials – had been documenting in its news columns the absurdities which apartheid produced all by itself. Reporters sought out all the idiotic consequences of segregationist laws that they could find, and their newspapers avidly published them.

Maclennan's collection of these reports proved that the proponents of apartheid, not the satirists, were South Africa's best – and worst – comedians. Here was proof that, when it comes to the absurdity of human nature, satirical hyperbole is sometimes outmatched by ridiculous reality.

Ben Maclennan was born in Scotland in 1956, eight years after apartheid became the law in South Africa. He was raised in Grahamstown in the Eastern Cape, where he studied journalism and wrote books on East Cape frontier history. During the final years of apartheid he was posted by his news agency to parliament's press gallery where he listened to the last of the ravings of pious racists. He sorted through old Hansards and newspaper clippings to collate material for his book Apartheid, the Lighter Side *(Chameleon Press in association with Carrefour Press, Cape Town, 1990). Though he took most of his news reports from the* Cape Times *library files, many of the reports had originated in other newspapers across the country and were passed on to the* Cape Times *via various agencies.*

We have selected the best of these straight-faced, hard news reports (many of which we remember reporting ourselves, or commenting on, in the newspapers), and we have categorised them here under new headings.

Seeking Clarity

The chairman of the Group Areas Board, Dr van Rensburg, explained the law on race classification thus:

The Group Areas Act defined three races: 'White (hitherto known as "Europeans"), Native and Coloured'. All those who fell between White and Native were regarded as Coloured. But the Act allowed the Coloured group to be subdivided into Indian, Chinese, Malays and those commonly known as Coloured people. The Malays were regarded as Malays only as long as they lived in their own group area of Schotsche Kloof. If they moved into another area, even across the road, those Malays became Coloureds, he explained.

Cape Times, March 2 1961

Eleven-year-old Sandra Laing, who was White, then declared Coloured and has now been classified White again, does not quite understand what has happened to her ...

Sunday Times, August 6 1967

Jan Smuts Airport, in common with the Union's other ports of land, sea and air, will soon amend its apartheid applications. The words 'European' and 'Non-European' will be replaced by the words 'Whites' and 'non-Whites' over appropriate doors and entrances. The reason is that foreigners, particularly Americans, confuse the issue – and the exit – by tending to use doors that seem to distinguish them from people who originate from Europe.

Cape Times, February 24 1959

A Coloured taxi-operator told the local Road Transportation Board in Cape Town yesterday that if he were forced to convey only non-Europeans in his car he would not be able to carry his own wife and mother in it – because they were White.

Cape Times, August 29 1959

A new bus apartheid system of seating will come into force on some routes on Monday. In the new system the front four rows of seats and the longitudinal seats over the off-side wheel in the lower saloon are reserved for Europeans, and the long seats over the near-side wheel for non-Europeans. The rest of the seats in the lower saloon and all seats in the upper saloon are for all classes. The system changes slightly on Sundays when non-Europeans have both of the long seats over the rear wheels, the Europeans having the first four rows. The trunk-route from Wynberg to Sea Point will be segregated only between the city and Sea Point, conductors changing the boards before reaching the city stop at the Waldorf.

Cape Times, August 18 1959

(In an interview the manager of City Tramways denied passengers were confused.)

Stringent government tests to ensure that White couples adopt only White babies include a check to see if the nappies are hiding dark patches – what nurses at Mowbray Maternity Hospital call 'blue bums'. It is claimed that most Coloured babies have these dark patches on their bottoms when they are born.

Sunday Express, May 18 1975

A European child, deeply sunburnt after a month's holiday at Muizenberg, was ordered out of a 'European only' coach by a train conductor this week.

Argus, January 14 1956

Seeking Diplomacy

There was no definition for Japanese under the Group Areas Act, said the chairman of the Group Areas Board, Dr van Rensburg. A Japanese, as far as the Act was concerned, was 'Coloured' because by definition he did not fall into any other group ... But Japanese living here could get permits to live as Whites, buy houses in White areas, and attend White cinemas and restaurants. But any Japanese tourist would technically be Coloured. However, he could once again be treated as a White and book in at the best hotels for a maximum period of 90 days.

Cape Times, March 2 1961

'We have not discussed the matter in Council, but I am certain that Beaufort West as a whole would be only too pleased to throw the municipal bath open to the Japanese, particularly in view of the government decision that they be regarded as Whites. The value of a visit from a world-class Japanese swimming team would far outweigh any race prejudice there might be. Besides, this is a big wool-growing area and the Japanese are very interested in our wool,' said Mr R.V. de Villiers, Mayor of Beaufort West.

Cape Times, February 1 1962

A municipal bus driver with 20 years' service, who refused to stop for a Japanese passenger because he thought he was Chinese, was suspended yesterday by the Pretoria City Council.

Cape Times, February 13 1962

Seeking Morality

There was a great danger that African girls were trying to get Whites in trouble, said Mr S.J. Erasmus in the Regional Court yesterday when he was acquitting a Pietersburg church elder and Sunday School teacher of two charges under the Immorality Act [for having sex across the apartheid-defined colour lines].

Cape Times, December 3 1959

A Constantia housewife, Wilhelmina Sophia Giliomee, of Alphenplaas, yesterday told Mr G.S. Frank in the Wynberg Regional Court that for three hours she watched three Coloured men and a European woman commit an offence under the Immorality Act in a field near her home on January 22. Mrs Giliomee said she did not wish to interfere but after three hours it was 'too much.'

Cape Times, June 4 1959

An eighty-year-old man in whose cupboard two Bantu girls were found, this week appeared in the Bloemfontein regional court on a charge of immorality. He denied guilt and said he had shut them in the cupboard 'for fun'. – And was acquitted.

Die Beeld, October 18 1970

Just when Smythe was about to commit the offence [under the Immorality Act] the policemen entered the room. Smythe, who was startled, said: 'Oh dash it.'

Cape Times, March 12 1963

Seeking Justification

Dr D.F. Malan [apartheid's first prime minister] told an Opposition member who questioned legalised race discrimination on trains: 'Does he not know that the question is so acute that large sections of the European population refuse to travel in the trains or buses any longer simply because frequently Natives and Coloured people deliberately seat themselves next to the white women, and next to other Europeans, simply to show that they stand for absolute equality and social equality?

'This intolerable state of affairs had led to European women resorting to the use of motor cars on account of this intermingling ... That has not only imposed a large additional burden on their shoulders but has contributed and contributes today to the traffic congestion in Cape Town.'

House of Assembly, September 21 1948

Dr Hendrik Verwoerd [apartheid's third prime minister] said yesterday it was necessary to take action to deal with these people who took pleasure in defying social convention in their homes and flats. Not only did White and non-White meet, but they sought to provoke the neighbours by hanging out of their windows ... There were neighbourhoods where just a single Liberal did that sort of thing, deliberately. This was the sort of complaint that had compelled him to come forward with the Native Laws Amendment Bill.

Cape Times, March 22 1957

Mr B.J. Vorster [apartheid's fourth prime minister]: 'I say that I draw a distinction between personal relations and inter-state relations. To illustrate it even further to the Honourable Member, it is not our policy that there should be social mingling of whites and non-whites in South Africa, but because I was dealing with an inter-state relationship in that instance, I could receive the Prime Minister of Lesotho as I did, because it was not a personal relationship but an inter-state relationship.'

House of Assembly, April 11 1967

Pres. P.W. Botha [apartheid's fifth political leader] admonished the nation to 'ride the waves, remembering at all times to stay on their feet and sit firmly in the saddle, to avoid being unseated.'

Cape Times, October 8 1988

'We do not want chaos in South Africa.' – Mr P.W. Botha explaining why cinemas will not be opened to all races.

House of Assembly, April 21 1983

Mr F.W. de Klerk [apartheid's last ruler] said: 'The government has no intention of putting each race into a separate compartment. However, we would never accept integration.'

Speech in July 1975, quoted in the Weekly Mail, August 8 1989

'I've been in Parliament for 17 years, and I have never defended the concept of apartheid.'

State President Mr F.W. de Klerk, House of Assembly, March 27 1990

In the past the torch of civilisation had been kept burning in the country because 'among other things our forefathers were such good shots'.

– Minister of Defence Mr Jim Fouché, opening the new rifle range of the Klerksdorp Commando.

Sunday Times, November 19 1961

People who argued in the name of Christianity that any person in South Africa should be able to live, work and vote where they wanted to and marry whom they wanted to were dangerous and should be resisted, the Deputy Minister of Bantu Education, Dr Andries Treurnicht, said yesterday.

Cape Times, May 11 1976

'The word apartheid does not exist.'

Mr D. Christophers (National Party, Germiston), Parliament, April 10 1989

Seeking Purer Sport

'To us in South Africa, rugby is really our god with a small letter, and to be defeated like that ... it was abnormal. God spoke to us. The people of South Africa are sinning against God by these shameful dresses ... God took the matter up and He is punishing us. Mini-skirts are the outstanding sin in South Africa.

'The fact is that they disclose their thighs, which is sexually mingled up in a man's mind with the private parts of a woman. If you see the upper thighs of a woman you are struck, sexually struck. And the worst part about it is that when these ladies sit next to a man driving a car they can see almost up to their private parts. What man can withstand that? And my main point is that God came from Heaven. When Adam and Eve fell into sin, they covered themselves in leaves, they made a kind of mini-skirt; and God came down and He had animals killed and He took those skins and He made proper dress for them.'

– Mr Gert Yssel, schoolmaster and lay-preacher, on a defeated Springbok rugby team in the United Kingdom.

Sunday Times, June 14 1970

The application to play a multiracial match – a match between racially mixed teams – was rejected when what was being sought was in fact permission to stage a 'multinational' match – a match between a white (local) team and a coloured (local) team.

Cape Times, September 24 1977

Seeking Sanity

Two Chinese women are being bleached white at the Sterkfontein Mental Institution, near Krugersdorp, to prepare them for transfer from non-White wards to the White section. 'Chinese are now entitled to treatment in White wards, but before we can move the women we must prepare them for the tremendous change ...'

Cape Times, December 18 1964

A former Cape Town magistrate, Josephus Johannes Ferreira, 37, was ordered to undergo at least two years' psychiatric treatment after he was found guilty in the Goodwood Regional Court yesterday of contravening the Immorality Act.

Cape Times, December 10 1968

It has long been a sore point that the municipal employees forced to evict black people from Durban's two remaining 'Whites only' beaches are themselves black, and are not allowed to frequent the beaches they patrol.

Sunday Times, August 13 1989

Seeking in Vain

When [ultra-rightwing] leader Mr Eugene Terre'Blanche arrived for yesterday's meeting with Law and Order Minister Mr Adriaan Vlok, his khaki-clad bodyguards mistakenly led him into the adjoining post office. Mr Terre'Blanche – who arrived in a gleaming white stretch limousine – was overheard telling his bodyguards, 'Guys, you will have to do better than this,' before they regrouped and entered the right building.

Cape Times, May 15 1990

'There are women who are members of the AOK [an Afrikaans teachers' 'cultural organisation']. We all know that women cannot be members of secret organisations. How can an organisation be secret if women are members of it?'

– Verwoerdburg school principal Mr Willem de Vos of the *Onderwysers-kultuurorganisasie* rebutting accusations that the right-wing Afrikaner group was a secret body.

Die Burger, November 10 1987

Christmas specials: 12 gauge Atis riot pump action shotguns R975. Rossie .38 Special snub nose R575. Beretta .22 pistol R310.

Gun shop advertisement, Argus, November 28 1985

Angry artiste Jeanette Ginslov [has been] banned from Rand Afrikaans University for dancing to a recorded speech of the State President.

'... I went ahead ... topless, and dressed only in a skin loincloth with potter's clay in my hair. I also painted my body to link up with the art theme. I stood stationary in a balletic pose [when] the State President ... said he wanted to maintain law and order in this country.'

Sunday Times, April 24 1988

Red shoes and other bright colours on their feet are the in-thing for the women of the Free State Women's Agricultural Union, it was decided in Welkom at the Union's yearly congress. Dull colours are out. And also those little shoes with the terribly sharp points. A proposal on the footwear was unanimously accepted by the congress and will now be referred to the national congress of the Women's Agricultural Union.

Die Burger, September 20 1988

The Minister of Public Works, Mr F.W. de Klerk, has decided to instruct his department to remove the sculpture by Moses Kottler at the National Register Building here [Pretoria] because of the representations received from a large number of objectors. The work shows a young man and a young woman, almost nude, looking up at the South African flag, their hands clasped. One of the objections, apart from portrayal of nudity, has been that the semi-nude man appears to have his hand on the nude breast of the woman. The sculptor, Moses Kottler, has denied this. The hand, he has said, was not on the woman's breast, but clasped her hand above the breast, which was where her hand had to be to clasp his. (Mr Kottler also declared that the couple was married anyway, and that the objections were therefore of no consequence.)

Cape Times, July 31 1957

English news reports coming into the news department – about 75 per cent of all reports – are first translated into Afrikaans by senior editors and then translated back into English for the English broadcasts.

– Former SABC news reporter Mr Robin Whitehead on the broadcasting corporation's policy.

Sunday Times, November 12 1961

Seeking Justice

Bloemfontein's African traffic constables can give Whites tickets only if they are not in their cars at the time, it was decided at a meeting yesterday.

Cape Times, December 19 1973

'Sir, when a man is detained under a state of emergency then it is likely that a charge will not be preferred against him, for he is being detained to stop him from doing harm. He is being detained to prevent him doing the harm he was intending to do. No charge is going to be preferred against them now, but they are not going to be permitted to continue their subversive work.

'Now what does a person under such a state of affairs want with a legal representative?'

– Mr G F Froneman (National Party, Heilbron), debating the emergency regulations. *House of Assembly, May 18 1960*

'I want to put it clearly today: it does not matter whether limitations are imposed on the freedom of the Press; nor does it matter whether there is a degree of control over the Press; nor does it matter whether action is sometimes taken against the Press. The Press is free in principle.'

Mr Louis Nel (National Party, Pretoria Central), *House of Assembly, January 27 1981*

Seeking the Solution

'I will have to check whether he is still in jail.'

– Department of Prisons official, responding to a press query on whether Mr Nelson Mandela was about to be released.

Financial Mail, February 21 1986

'We are not going soft on the ANC. In fact, the ball is on the other foot.'

– National Party Director of Information, Mr Con Botha.

Weekly Mail, July 21 1989

LES AUPIAIS, *born in New Zealand, was educated in Natal, where she joined the* Natal Witness *after university. She moved to* The Star *in Johannesburg in 1983. Three years later she was head-hunted by* Cosmopolitan *to be the magazine's bureau chief in Johannesburg. By 1993 she was managing editor of the magazine in Cape Town. She later became head of Independent Newspapers' magazine division, where she launched the award-winning magazine* Sunday Life.

But TV beckoned in the form of M-Net's Carte Blanche. *She is currently a presenter on South Africa's premier actuality programme and also contributes to Radio 702 on Saturday. As if that were not enough, she has launched her own media company and coaches in communication.*

Aupiais has won two international awards for investigative and medical reporting. She is also consulting editor on quarterly magazines and has somehow managed to raise teenaged triplets, although she is unsure how this all happens.

The following three items are from her column in Sunday Life, *which appeared in the* Sunday Independent *in 1996.*

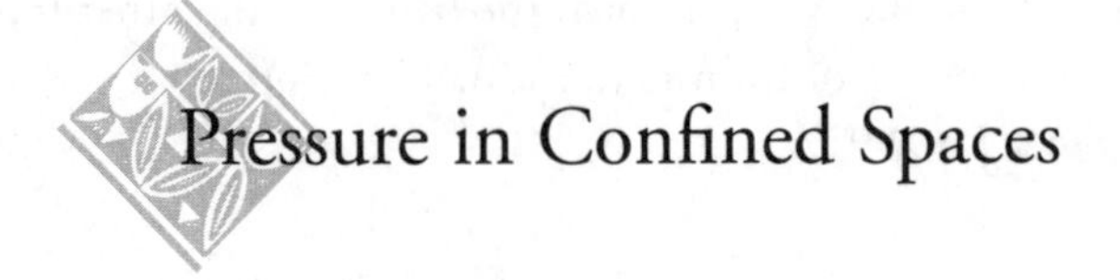

Pressure in Confined Spaces

There is something terrifying about pressurised lavatories on planes. All that corrosive blue gunk swirling about and the sound they make when they flush; like the hydraulic brakes of a pantechnicon during an emergency stop. And when you're on board ship, all that pitching and rolling makes the U-bend gurgle like someone dying by slow strangulation. Somewhere at the back of your mind, the place where logic evaporates, lurks the idea that one day there'll be a pressure surge and your butt will be sucked tight to the seat and the only way to release the pressure would be to flush. The blue dye is sure to be indelible. How mortifying.

I was in the South of France last week. I got there via three flights and a short cruise. Consider this a short thesis on confined spaces.

It was quite by chance that I saw the sign in the park. It was on the side of a brushed steel bunker about 2 metres high and 2.5 metres long. The sign on the side said something in French about '*automatique*' and curt instructions to stick two francs into the slot. The curved side of the lozenge hissed open. I climbed in, thinking that it would be bloody funny if this was the way the aliens captured specimens from earth for the planet Zog. The French would collude of course.

The door slid shut. Inside, the capsule was wet from floor to ceiling. It smelt of a corrosive disinfectant. The plastic toilet bowl was moulded to the wall and had no seat. Where the cistern should have been was a hole and a stream of water. The toilet roll was encased behind steel with a barely discernible piece of damp tissue paper sticking out of a slit. No handles. No sign of anything to be pushed or levered. There was a sign on the door that, roughly translated, gave you 15 minutes to use the capsule. Or … ? It didn't say.

I stood and thought about dropping my trousers but they'd absorb the water on the floor. I decided not to drop my trousers. I stood a while longer. Then, careful not to lean against the wet wall, and balancing on one leg, I climbed out of them. I was half naked in a futuristic French *pissoir* and I still didn't know how the thing worked. If aliens did carry me off to ravage me on Zog, I'd look as if I went willingly, dressed for impregnation. I sat on the moulded plastic thingy. It was freezing. Trying to pick out 10 centimetres of damp toilet tissue took three minutes. *Papier mâché* is a difficult medium with which to work. I made a last and desperate attempt to find a flushing lever, climbed back into my trousers, and slid open the door.

The panel hissed shut behind me. And then, with a sound like sluice gates opening on a dam, the capsule roared. Water thundered off the steel interior like a tidal wave smacking into the hull of an empty oil tanker. It went on and on as if the Japanese hysteria for hygiene and German obsession with technical perfection had combined to provide the French with an extraordinary spectacle: *Le Loo Plus Sportif.* Judging by the force of the flush, the pathetic little puddle of recycled Perrier that I'd passed was now half-way to Barcelona via the Med. It shook me, I can tell you. Not so much because of the violence capable by something as benign as a public loo, but because of what I'd nearly done to my fellow South African traveller. The rand being in such poor shape, I thought I'd save him a few bucks by letting him slip in during my two-franc 15-minute slot. A right shock he would have got when the door closed and the thing went '*automatique*'.

Just then, an elderly man walked through the park trailing a small dog. It squatted and performed on the grass, kicked back with its hind legs scattering a few blades of grass over the deposit and stalked on. For the locals, it was business as usual.

Breeding Discontent

I was looking at a schematic drawing of two rabbits in a book about suitable family pets. We have come to that, my family and me, the crossroads between guardianship of an elderly mongrel and the need for something new to nurture and observe. We eliminated the fragile and exotic, the highly-strung and the vet's-bill-waiting-to-happen, but were caught somewhere between cerebral ganglia and the dim-witted and warm. Fish were given the boot. Fur triumphed.

The diagrams in the Junior Pet-Keeper's library book on rabbits were headlined 'Determining the Sex'. I would not, on inspecting the tiny hairline fracture under the doe's tail, have called it a 'vulva'. It was rather too voluptuous a word for that. Just above the tail line of the prostrate buck was a tiny circle no bigger than a pinhead labelled 'penis'.

There was little chance that I would frighten off the family with this artwork. I would have to read out loud an extract, especially the warning bits in italics that read 'Do not breed rabbits unless you are sure you can find good homes for them'. And then in short, rather brutal sentences, what lay ahead if you did allow the hairline anywhere near the pinhead: 'A rabbit may have up to 12 babies. They will grow fur after 10 days. There may be too many for her to feed. You may have to find a foster mother. The babies may all die.'

There it was then. Procreation to possible cremation in 37 words. I balked at the thought of having to explain that although it could be hugely entertaining watching rabbits mate, the frantic bonding would be followed a scant 30 days later by a dozen small blind things that were bald and/or dead. The book showed so little detail of genitalia because there appeared to be no genitalia. Rabbits announced their sexual inclination by demonstration and by then it was all over.

There were other clues in the text about the pitfalls of rabbit-owning that wouldn't necessarily alarm a child, but would put adults right off. Like 'It may live to five years and older'. Purgatory. I cannot imagine going from Grade 1 to post-pubescence without the novelty and charm of two or three (or two or three hundred) rabbits wearing a bit thin. Virtual-reality raves will probably overtake the thrill of de-fleaing pelts.

As an adult, think of the ghastly responsibility of cage-cleaning and the ignominious task of hutch-lurking in order to catch them on the job. While we might easily conclude that 'sitting all hunched up, ears back and not interested in anything' applied to most partners after a long and dreary cohabitation and was good news when applied to rabbits, the book lists the behaviour under 'illnesses'.

A satirical yet percipient piece written in 1996:

Bob's Sec's Life

Last month Robert Mugabe married his secretary. On her wedding day, 31-year-old Grace Marufu climbed out of a cream Rolls-Royce, wearing a cream floral gown. Three hours later she was Mrs Mugabe. She already has two children, aged six and nine, by the man. Pretty smart work. Nice if you can get it.

For those of you out there who are 30-something and feel the need of a serious game plan concerning landing an elderly CEO, he of hefty political clout and/or power and money, and a fairly dodgy length of retirement, it might be worth noting that being geographically desirable is a good start. There are other pointers. First, visit your gynae and make sure your ovaries are in good nick so you can make an heir apparent – it's always a good legal complication should your CEO go off you. Next, learn Windows, how to type and file – this gives you access to all highly sensitive documents. Your system should be baffling to everyone except yourself. Finally, get signing power.

Should your little cash bull have any leanings towards socialism – any at all – take politics to bed. It's entirely circumstantial evidence but look at the example set by Bob and Grace. Bob's been an ardent Marxist man all his life, a collective socialist. Then in June he announced the formation of an African Capital Markets Forum. Grace (see file R: Rolls-Royce) is not a socialist. She is merely collective. It's hard to substantiate, but rumour has it that she had 'unit' inserted into the marital vows just prior to the 'trust, honour and obey'.

Plan a biggish wedding. Grace's list was anywhere between 6 000 and 40 000, depending on which report you read. The trick here is to begin in the manner in which you intend to continue – it is less of a shock to him later. Also, it is very public. Although it was officially Bob who slapped a criminal defamation suit on the three journalists who reported that the couple had married on the quiet, one can't help feeling Grace's chagrin here. It kind of takes the edge out of a designer wedding gown and a cream Rolls if the ceremony's a mock-up of the clandestine original.

In making social arrangements for your CEO, get a handle on his troubled psyche. You could blow your future right out of the water by, say, booking for the première of [the gay movie farce] *Priscilla, Queen of the Desert*, thereby releasing all sorts of latent this and that. Note: Grace would be sure to have done this. There was no way Bob was going anywhere near her La Perla bodice.

Insist on a modicum of privacy and your own territory. Recently a white Zimbabwean farmer who owns a 3 000-hectare farm adjacent to Bob's rural home whinged bitterly that his neighbour had a personal interest in nationalising his farm because the old boy wanted space around his property. New to the capitalist game, perhaps Bob does not fully appreciate that the farmer might want to be paid for several thousand hectares. But as he awarded himself a 133 per cent increase last month (Grace under pressure from the caterers?) it's reasonable to expect he might have an inkling of the meaning of suitable remuneration.

Finally, a four-decade gap between you and the bloke you've banked on almost guarantees that he'll nod off in the afternoon, after say a hectic cabinet reshuffle. You are free to shop. Again, returning to Bob and Grace: in May he was in a froth about the flood of South African goods pouring into Zimbabwe and South Africa's punishing 90 per cent duty on goods coming the other way. In August, Grace persuaded him to fly to Cape Town for part of their honeymoon and to shop in Adderley Street. It seems she has no problem at all about where her labels come from. Power's like that. It shifts. Best you're two metres from his desk.

ARNOLD BENJAMIN

ARNIE, *to use his real name, was one of those marvellous Woody Allen-type worrier-kings. He was born in Greater Johannesburg at the end of the 1920s and graduated from the University of the Witwatersrand, where, in between editing student publications, he 'incidentally' did a degree in law though he never practised. Instead, in 1952 he joined* The Star *in Johannesburg and from the 1960s began reporting extensively on emergent black Africa. He worked in* The Star*'s Nairobi bureau for three years before being posted to the London bureau and New York. In New York he developed an interest in graffiti and this resulted in three books on the subject, one with a seminal title that became the battle cry of the Great Perplexed –* Prune Juice Will Set You Free. *He wrote several books of humour – including the captioned, illustrated* Alternative Mandela Album. *Benjamin also published two scholarly books on the changing face of Johannesburg.*

Arnie was an Africa and foreign correspondent, but in the 1970s, on his way to take over The Star*'s Washington Bureau, he was badly injured by a taxi in Rio de Janeiro and forced to retreat back to Africa to become a leader writer and assistant editor. The change was a blessing for his readers because, almost as a sideline, he amused them with frequent columns under various titles for about 25 years.*

Perhaps his best known column was So It Goes. *The items below are from that column, as well as from an extant leader-page column called* The Little Spot.

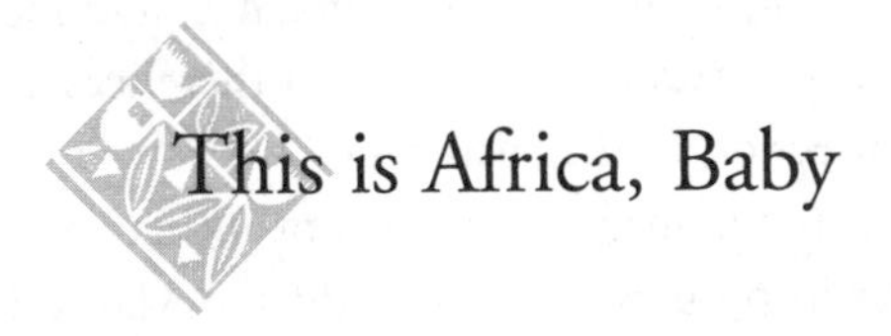

This is Africa, Baby

A lady wrote to *The Star* the other day to say she had waited 47 minutes while trying to phone a bank – and for 20 of those minutes she was told her call was next in line. While this was clearly a recording, a reader asks, is it a record?

Alas, no. A top-secret document in Telkom's archives states that the South African (and possibly world) record is held by Pasienza Potgieter of Parys who spent 75 hrs 43 min waiting to get through to Directory Inquiries. 'I had to do it,' she kept repeating obsessively. 'This voice kept telling me not to hang up or I would lose my place in the queue.'

Ms Potgieter died of shock when she finally found she'd been put through to the wrong extension. However, Telkom honoured her (posthumously) with its rare Albert Hertzog Award, named after a former telecommunications minister renowned for his dogged resistance to introducing television.

A happier story concerns the depressive who spent so many thoughtful hours being kept on 'Hold' by Suicides Anonymous that he discovered new meaning to his life. And Goodluck Khumalo spent 14½ hours trying to reach a police hijacking hotline. By the time he got a response his car had been recovered, stolen again, shipped out to Zambia, and seized by SA Customs when a Bulgarian syndicate tried to re-import it. With the insurance money he was able to buy it back on auction at a bargain price.

Rating the Robbers

Quite apart from the normal hazards of rip-off, poor service or food poisoning, possible attack by armed robbers is becoming one of the new uncertainties of dining out in Johannesburg.

The recent spate of restaurant hold-ups around here may add some element of spice to an otherwise dull meal, but who really needs this kind of excitement when you're trying to relax?

And just imagine what it might do to the restaurant reviewing profession:

'… I was just starting to enjoy the softly lit ambience, and looking forward to my *Sole Meunière au Sauce d'Homards Anciens*, when there was a sudden unseemly commotion from the direction of the cash desk.

'I soon established that the management was not to blame; it appeared some sort of armed robbery was in progress. To his credit the Maître D', Lucky Pierre Escargot, handled the unforeseen situation with all the aplomb which has made the smooth service in the *Coq Très Malade* a byword in this city.

'After assuring customers that all was under control, he very politely addressed the man who appeared to be in charge: "If you insist on robbing this restaurant, *M'sieur*, it would be helpful if you would choose a time which is not our busiest. Would you mind waiting in the bar until I can give your request proper attention? As it is I already have three couples there waiting for tables."

'Next, I noted that Maître Pierre was sinking to the richly carpeted floor, having been struck on the head by a bottle. From where I sat it was hard to be sure, but the label suggested it was the 1985 Ongeluksvlei *Grand Vin Ordinaire*, a modest if somewhat unctuous claret which I've often found to be a versatile all-rounder for most occasions.

'"A sensible enough choice by the robber for his particular purpose," I observed to my dining companion, "and one which Pierre and his sommelier would no doubt have approved had they been given any say in the matter."

'What happened next was more disquieting, though. Not content with emptying the till, the robbers started moving from table to table demanding clients' valuables in a most menacing manner. When it came to our turn there seemed to be little choice but to comply. However, my companion, a resourceful lady, asked if they could deal with her a little later as she was in the middle of her *hors d'oeuvre (Pommes Frites à l'Anglais avec Sauce Piquante à la Tomate)* which would quickly spoil if not eaten piping hot.

'Taking no notice, however, the crass intruder tried to snatch her gold ring – at which, throwing caution to the winds, she picked up a *baguette* of Pierre's excellent garlic bread and retaliated with a sharp blow to the man's head. The loaf must have been rather more *encroûté* than usual because the startled robber ran for the door crying out in pain, closely followed by his cronies.

'All in all, this unsettling experience left a disagreeable after-taste to an otherwise enjoyable evening.

'In normal circumstances I would not hesitate to confirm the four-star rating of the *Coq Très Malade*. One cannot give any kind of rating, however, to the type and style of the robbers the restaurant attracts.'

Back in the real world, this topic calls to mind something that happened while I was living in New York 20-some years ago. There were headlines one day about a classic old-style Mafia killing at an Italian trattoria in Queens.

Gunmen of one 'family' brazenly marched in and shot up a rival godfather and his henchmen while they were comfortably ensconced at dinner.

A good American friend of mine was unusually interested in the event; indeed began phoning old newspaper buddies for details. His major curiosity was not in the massacre itself, but to establish the name of the restaurant.

'If the Mafia eats there,' said this seasoned New Yorker and dedicated diner-out, 'it's just got to be worth trying.'

Apartheid: When Did It Go?

The Post Office is to carry out a high-level investigation into the racial situation at the Zeerust Post Office after the local National Party branch allegedly asked for the reinstatement of apartheid. – News report

We were sitting, as usual (Oom Schalk Lourens said), in the branch post office, which operates in Jurie Steyn's voorkamer while we waited for the post-cart to arrive from Ramoutsa.

We were discussing – as we feel we have to do, ever since that H.C. Bosman made our Zeerust district famous – the pressing affairs of the day. Meanwhile a bottle of Oupa Bekker's new vintage peach brandy was passed around.

'Have you seen what it says here, in this English paper that was wrapped around my copy of *Landbouweekblad*?' asked Chris Welman.

'That they're holding a high-level investigation into the Zeerust post office?'

'About time too,' someone put in. 'The last time I was there it must have been in 1953, to collect my rinderpest money – the place was in a real mess.'

'Ja, I remember that time well,' said Gysbert van Tonder. 'It was when young Alida van Niekerk was working there and she had stars in her eyes about that Oosthuizen boy. She was so *deurmekaar* that she couldn't even count out five tickey stamps, let alone cash a Union Loan Certificate.'

'And as for deliveries,' said At Naudé, 'they should appoint a commission of inquiry into the whole Marico ...'

'No man, it's none of those things,' said Chris Welman impatiently. 'If only you'd let a man finish ... It says here that people want apartheid reinstated at the post office.'

The gathering buzzed like bees when the *witgathaaksteekswartdoringboom* is in flower.

'Reinstate apartheid? When did it go?'

'Ja, when?' demanded Hermanus Immelman, who once stood for the Mealie Board and takes a keen interest in politics. 'And anyway, since when did a native need to use a post office?'

'Well, it seems things have changed a bit. And I must tell you they don't use that word any more either. You're supposed to call them Bantus now.'

'No, it's changed again, Now it's plurals. I heard Oom Connie Mulder say that at a meeting once.'

'Those liberals like him want to change everything.'

'This Zeerust post office business must be the fault of that young Hertzog – what's his name, Albert? Things have never been the same since they made him Minister of Posts and Telegraphs.'

There was a long silence.

'Anyway, pass the mampoer,' someone said.

Jurie Steyn sighed heavily.

'You know something, even Oupa Bekker's mampoer is not what it used to be.'

'I agree,' said Gysbert van Tonder. 'You remember how it was in 1948? Now that's what I'd call a good year.'

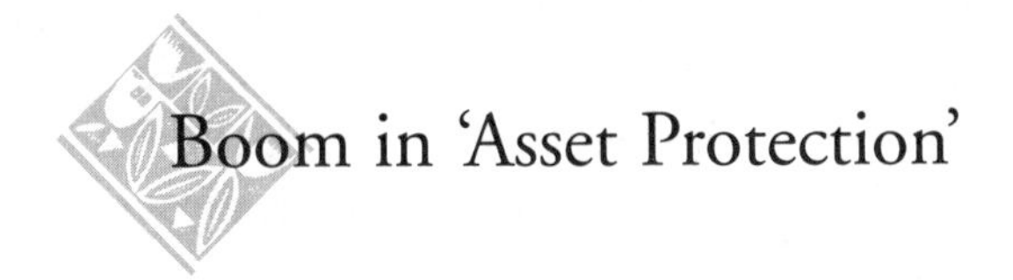

Boom in 'Asset Protection'

In my neck of the suburbs the security business is the hottest growth industry going. Every householder, fearfully contemplating burglary, car theft and worse, is obsessed with what one of the new guard firms calls 'asset protection'. Eventually I was badgered by the insurance people to get my own assets better protected too.

So I sat down and phoned some of the 12 Yellow Pages worth of listed services. It became clear that burglar alarms, screaming sirens, security guards, dogs, electronic gates and surveillance, special locks and razor-wire fencing are only a beginning.

It's also *de rigueur* to have your in-house panic buttons hooked up to 'armed response' patrols which cruise the streets, sometimes also offering help with medical crises. Their names alone, let alone the military-style vehicles and uniforms, are usually menacing enough to scare anyone off.

'Hello, Rambo Guards here. Yes, along with our special high-tension electrified fencing and 25-hour surveillance at a mere R750 a month we offer a personalised night bodyguard service. On request, one of our highly trained ex-Congo killer mercenaries will wait to escort you from your car right inside your house, liquidating anything en route that moves.'

'ExtermiWatch at your service. At any moment of the day or night we have 100 of our armoured vehicles constantly patrolling the mean streets of your suburb. What's that, why don't you see them patrolling? Ah, you do – but you don't realise it. We use unmarked vehicles. Even our killer dogs are undercover, disguised as Border Collies. Our philosophy is to take out the crooks in the act, not to scare them off so they can have another go at your assets.'

'Thank you for calling Medkill. Besides rushing out to deal with the immediate asset protection situation, we are geared to tend instantly to any casualties left alive. And we're the only service in town equipped with poison gas. No, of course we didn't sign the Geneva Convention. This is total onslaught, isn't it?'

'Yes, this is ParaZapforce. Our name denotes not only paramilitary and paramedical services, but paratroops. On receipt of your radio alarm call we send a first-strike commando of elite ex-Rhodesian psychopaths to deal with the immediate asset protection situation. If more help is needed we move in with airborne shock troops from searchlight-equipped helicopter gunships. We're offering a special on that for this month, a mere R499.50 per landing after your basic monthly R600.'

'What do we at Faststrike offer? A unique service of undercover hit squads or SAS-type storm troops who stage pre-emptive raids and hit the forces of evil well before they can get a chance to hit you. We're also doing a feasibility study on an amphibious Marine service, landing men from assault craft or submarines – just as soon as we find enough waterfront areas of the Transvaal.'

'Hello, Securicharge here, specialising in satellite surveillance of your home, debugging devices, and polygraph lie detection. Why Securicharge? Well, as a show of force we often do full commando-style charges to defend your assets. And everybody agrees we really know how to charge.'

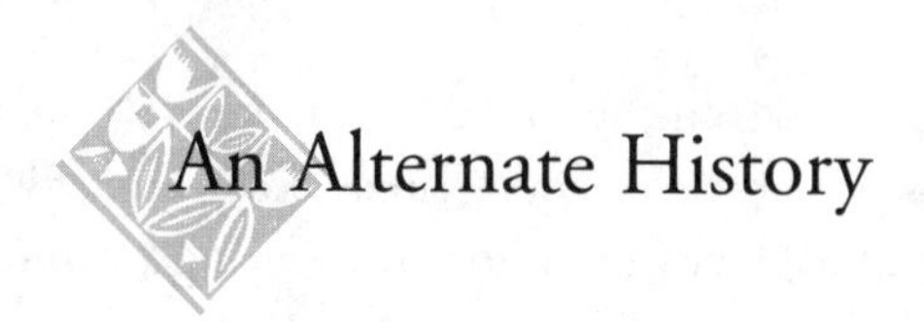

An Alternate History

In 1990 – the year Nelson Mandela was released from prison by President De Klerk; the year South Africa's course changed forever – Benjamin created a new version of South African history. It appeared in a publication titled *The Alternative Mandela Album*. He explained it thus:

'This compilation tells the story of Nelson Mandela and South Africa's watershed year, 1990, through pictures, cartoons, headlines, imaginary quotes and real ones, newspaper snippets and some of my own columns for *The Star*. South African public life usually suffers from excessive solemnity, and 1990 has been no exception. The aim is to introduce a little light relief at a time when it has never been more needed ...

'Our story really begins in April 1652 when the Founder of White South Africa, Jan van Riebeeck, lands at the Cape of Good Hope to set up a revictualling station for the Dutch East India Company's ships.'

Then follows the famous painting of Jan and friends greeting the locals – with Benjamin's marvellous, imaginary quotes. Regrettably, this and other of his historical illustrations have not reproduced well, and we can offer samples only in the quality in which they were published.

Benjamin continues: 'Later came more settlers, then the British, the Great Trek away from the British, the discovery of gold which brought the British back in pursuit, Frontier Wars and other conflicts of interest …

'... which finally resulted in a new word, apartheid, and the emergence of a charismatic leader of the African National Congress, Nelson Rolihlahla Mandela. The best thing to do with him, the White Government thought, was to jail him for the rest of his life.'

In an historic picture taken at Mandela's trial, one of his aides is pictured saying, 'He won't become a lost Xhosa.' And the relatively young Mandela announces: 'There'll now be a short intermission – maybe 27 years.'

A third of the way through the book appears the photo of Mandela emerging from prison under the headline FREE AT LAST – while the crowd enjoys Benjamin's wisecracks. His history continues: 'Amid scenes of huge enthusiasm, Mandela and his wife Winnie were on their way to Cape Town to address his first public meeting in 27 years.' Then appears Benjamin's version of what happened on that balcony of Cape Town City Hall when Mandela first addressed the nation – and the world.

The crowded events of 1990 are recorded in a context that ruins the facts, enhances the basic truth, and transforms most people's fears to laughter. Below is a sample of Benjamin making fun of some fairly justified fears:

'Johannesburg property developers kept on compulsively demolishing and rebuilding the city,' he wrote, and illustrated it with the newspaper photograph of the demolition of Johannesburg's once tallest skyscraper.

Johannesburg property developers kept on compulsively demolishing and rebuilding the city

'And so', says the author in his concluding remarks, 'South Africa wobbled on, teetering between hope and despair through the great year of destiny, 1990. Ahead lay the next year of destiny and of the amazing Mandela–De Klerk saga – and perhaps a few more similar years. Nothing was clear except that a lot was changing – even the traditional design of the country's banknotes.'

It meant that Van Riebeeck's face was vanishing from our rand currency. Benjamin visualised the result thus:

DOC BIKITSHA

IF YOU TRY *to get Doc Bikitsha to talk about his robust career in journalism, the conversation will be long and very amusing, but it will end up on the subject of the late Jim Bailey, co-founder, with Bob Crisp, of* African Drum *(later* Drum*). Jim Bailey, English public schoolboy, RAF fighter pilot and Oxford graduate – son of the flamboyant Rand pioneer, Abe Bailey – corralled the best of black writers and soon the magazine was as ubiquitous in black society as the Singer sewing machine. Doc Bikitsha says if it wasn't for Jim Bailey's* Drum, *South Africa would never have had that breeding herd of intrepid journalists – Can Themba, Lewis Nkosi, Arthur Maimane, Nat Nakasa, Peter Magubane. 'Even Ratau Mike Makhalenele, "our office teaboy", became an internationally renowned saxophonist and composer – the switchboard operator became the Pan Africanist Congress's lobbyist in the UN.'*

The journalists of Drum *became a brotherhood, and Bikitsha recalls the hard drinking and – in retrospect at least – the sometimes amusing battle of wits between black intellectuals and the ever-suspicious constabulary hoping to catch them out of doors without their 'passes' or, better still, with hard tack (blacks were not allowed to buy or drink spirits in those days – not that Doc recalls being handicapped by that law).*

He lived in Sophiatown as did many of his colleagues – 'it was good in Sophiatown with the gang' – until, in the 1960s, the apartheid government, to make way for cheap white housing, razed the place and shipped its population to the new township, Soweto. Bikitsha, like so many of his contemporaries, never lost his sense of humour, and the article below, apart from being typical of Bikitsha's humour, reveals a lot about life during the worst years of apartheid.

Doc Bikitsha was born in 1930 and is retired in Johannesburg. He began his adult life as a teacher, having studied at the 'Bantu Normal College' in Pretoria, where a fellow student was Desmond Tutu.

Bikitsha was fired as a schoolteacher, partly for being nonconformist – he encouraged his English class to read newspapers and report back on world affairs – the last thing the white authorities wanted. The government had even forbidden television in South Africa (it was introduced only in 1977) for fear whites would become liberalised.

After Bikitsha was fired as a teacher he walked into the offices of The Bantu World *where he became a reporter. This prepared him for* Drum *and later the* Rand Daily Mail, *for which he wrote from 1976 until it closed 10 years later.*

And despite being 'fired, suspended, gated, reinstated … you name it' for too much partying, he developed a great following and wrote for many journals including Bona, Golden City Post *and* The Star.

Naughty Days and Dog's Meat Nights

Many years ago we ate 'Dog's Meat' with a dash of adventure, romance and jail.

Dog's Meat – to you, and later generations, which may not know it – is or was the gentle art of sleeping at your domestic servant lover's quarters without the blessing of the employers or local authorities.

It was also the art of making use of the said employer's facilities with or without his consent.

'Facilities' meant the employer's larder, liquor cellar and other amenities; it was rare to have his approval.

Those who had it could be counted on the fingers during my days. If you were OK'd, it was usually on condition you did some gardening, car-washing and other menial chores about the house.

This pastime is called 'Dog's Meat' not because of the flesh of that animal or beast, but because of the flesh or meat bought for the dog to eat. Which was, in turn, eaten by servants because it was of a better grade than theirs at times.

In other words, the meat the white boss or madam bought for his or her pets was usurped by the servant for her own pots.

This pets' meat became a handy addition to the servant's 'boy's meat' rations when extra visitors called. The whole exercise is complicated because some whites reasoned their pets deserved delicate innards or offal and choice cuts for their sustenance, and their servants lesser cuts than their pets.

However, servants maintained it was their right by servitude to deprive the animals of these meats.

I don't know if that system still persists, but it was rife during my time in the Fifties and Sixties. It went to such an extent that servants at times deprived their employers of other delicacies from fridges and storage bins right inside the house.

Let me explain this meaty problem by going back in history.

Since the white man came in this country in 1652, some form of 'Dog's Meat' has existed. It was harsher for the Bushmen and Hottentots. As time went on, these white adventurers expanded and met with a fiercer opposition, which not only rebelled against forced labour but helped itself liberally to their cattle and goods. It began with the Xhosas and their historic wars.

With the discovery of minerals – gold, diamonds and others – established settlements mushroomed all over the country. The lure of instant riches was too much even for the pastoral and nomadic blacks. They were attracted to these settlements, worked and have since been battling for honest wages.

That is how township-beerhall, or 'university', sages describe the historic origins of 'Dog's Meat'. In the ghettos, beer-gardens or halls or pubs are referred to as universities because of the diversity of brains there. These teem with intellectuals from the hard school of life's experiences.

Now let's come nearer home on this subject. Those years when I was sprouting hair in strategic places and my voice was breaking, I noticed the gay blades of the times had a special fondness for domestic servants. I took pains to find out by listening in on adult conversation at shop-fronts or winter galley fires in passages. As much of it was whispered, at times accompanied with much laughter, I missed vital aspects, which I later made up for from personal experience.

If you've noticed, buses to Johannesburg's suburbs have always been packed with males. You can't exactly say they are scullery boys on a jaunt into town. They alight in dribs and drabs along the route and vanish into the shrubberies of those well-kept white homes.

There's nothing as possessive as a domestic servant, I learnt. They can be cool and detached with their bosses, but warm and responsive with their affairs.

Those days in winter, when you arrived at the girl's room (domestic quarters), a blazing open fire from a Falkirk stove welcomed you.

Still remember those trim round iron stoves, guys? Now they've given them a modern fan or built-in wall heaters and killed the romance of this venture.

What followed was a deep bowl of soup with fresh bread. I doubt if the owners of the house had the same fare.

After a hot bath it was supper in bed under snow-white sheets with the evening papers and a half-jack of the master's best brandy or whisky. Include his fags if you want to.

Now there are beds of all sorts in this world. Our domestics beds are unique and different.

They propped them up with bricks, empty tins or drums. I don't know why they loved those dizzy heights, but I can tell you one thing, it was a feat getting atop one. And what comfort!

Same routine in the morning. Many of us learnt to savour cornflakes, rusks, bacon and eggs and other outlandish dishes here.

Cripes! The parties these dolls used to throw. I still remember them with fondness.

The whole kitchen fraternity would turn up dressed to the ears. With or without their madam's 'Jewish' (fashionable dress) and jewellery.

A weekend at your doll's was an experience and a half. She'd dip generously into her savings to entertain you.

If she had no means, she'd borrow from the main house. Normally, the master and madam were away and the children also learnt to love and respect nanny's brother, hubby or uncle.

At one joint of mine in Craighall Park, the kids got so fond of me that they told their father there was somebody cleverer than him at Nanny's room.

I got them to call me 'Bra Doc', which is equivalent to calling somebody Sir or Your Lordship.

Later, when the cops raided (I knew at whose tip), my Press card came to the rescue. The white rookie cop saw the South African Police stamp on it and thought I was a gendarme.

Why, those years I even used my Press card as a season ticket on the trains. It was during my naughty days and I expected nobody to take offence. Not even the police.

For many these trysts ended up at the maternity clinics and the Commissioner's Court. A sad way to end such a beautiful relationship.

In any case, I don't see any change in the situation. But perhaps I'm wrong and they don't even call it 'Dog's Meat' anymore.

HERMAN CHARLES BOSMAN

SOUTH AFRICA *has given its most famous humorist a bad time. In the 1960s the then Transvaal director of education, Dr A.L. Kotze, banned some republished works,* Bosman at His Best, *from the school curriculum. The official cited the author's use of the words 'syphilis' and 'donder' as the major reason for the book not being suitable for children. He did not mention the word which Bosman used to describe black Africans. His main reason was undoubtedly because Bosman's short stories tend to show rural Afrikaners as narrow-minded and hypocritical – like so many rural communities the world over. By contrast, in 1999 a post-apartheid education authority spoke of banning Bosman in schools because officialdom objected to the word 'kaffir'.*

Despite official objections, Bosman is to South African literature what James Thurber is to American literature. Roy Campbell, the South African poet, said Bosman was 'the only literary genius South Africa had produced'. Bernard Sachs, author and newspaper editor who knew Bosman when at Jeppe High School in Johannesburg, said that Smuts and Bosman were the 'two outstanding brains' produced by the Afrikaner (in The Star, *March 3 1966). Sachs says that Bosman 'was totally indifferent to politics and even looked down with contempt on the whole political landscape. This included the racist mythology which is a way of life, and death, for the Afrikaner.' This much was true – nearly all of Bosman's stories hold up for derision the unshakeable racism of the bushveld. He does so with a satire that even Swift might have envied. Bosman uses Oom Schalk Lourens, a bigoted old boer, to narrate his yarns, which are, in effect, parables. In* Funeral Earth *he writes, 'We had a difficult task, that time (Oom Schalk Lourens said) teaching Sjefu's tribe of Mtosas to become civilised. But they did not show any appreciation. Even after we had set fire to their huts in a long row round the slopes of Abjaterskop, so that you could see the smoke almost as far as Nietverdiend, the Mtosas remained just about as unenlightened as ever.'*

Bosman's irony is best appreciated when you are acquainted with the tough backvelders *of the Groot Marico district in the dry western bushveld. Bosman was one of South Africa's first writers, white or black, who saw racism as immoral and who chipped away at it relentlessly. There can also be no argument that if he belittled any group it was his own.*

Bosman's personality is perhaps the most enigmatic of all South Africa's 20th century writers. He was born in Kuils River near Cape Town. His mother, Elisa Malan, had an unusually close relationship with her younger brother, Charles Malan, a brilliant lawyer. And there's a suggestion that Herman Charles Bosman was the result of an incestuous liaison between the two. In 1904 Elisa, an intelligent and academically minded woman, suddenly married a mineworker, Jakobus Abraham Bosman, and soon afterwards Herman was born (Valerie Rosenberg, Sunflower to the Sun, *1976).*

*At the age of 20, Bosman was sentenced to death for shooting his half-brother in Yeoville, Johannesburg. It seemed a casual shooting, the result of a brief but charged altercation (the victim was on a bed at the time in the modest family home) and Bosman behaved equally casually in court, even to the extent of winking at some girls. It is impossible to say whether it was cold-blooded murder or a crime of passion (which seems the more likely). Either way he was in a death cell in Pretoria Central before being reprieved. He was in prison for almost five years but it took another 25 years before he could bring himself to write about life behind bars, and he did so with little amusement (*Cold Stone Jug*, 1949). He became a journalist on leaving prison and set up many independent journals, all commercial failures.*

He published his own books initially, the first being a slim volume, Mafeking Road *(1947), a collection of some of his best short stories. It propelled him to fame. Johannesburg* Sunday Times *book reviewer, Mary Morison Webster, who knew the man and found him a bit of a reprobate who smoked dagga and mixed with drop-outs (a 1940s 'hippie'), recalled her 'strange elation' (*Sunday Times, *5 May 1971) as she read* Mafeking Road *and realised here was a genius.*

His last recorded words came after being asked by a doctor where he was born. He replied: 'Born in Kuils River. Died in Edenvale Hospital.' And that is what happened.

Bosman's dark and his sunny sides; his reckless rebelliousness and his sly cunning; his crude cruelty and his touching tenderness – all revealed in his poetry and prose, and in the tempestuous life he led – indicate that here was a man of bewildering complexity; a writer of wild, often sublime, inspirations which place him far beyond the average artist. He joined the Communist Party in the Stalinist age, for instance – but seemingly only to mock the Comrades. In Britain, he taunted Mosleyites – yet seemed attracted to Hitlerism. He was a romantic, steeped in English literature and a deeply perceptive critic – yet he could not abide T.S. Eliot, and venomously attacked his Murder in the Cathedral. *(After Bosman's death, when his 'Oom Schalk' stories were widely published, T.S. Eliot was among the first to praise them.)*

Time has been unusually kind to his light writing because of his skill in this. Long may it last. In wishing so, we must appreciate what time does. It not only changes humour, it also changes meanings, even values.

A case in point is the way Bosman's characters casually use the word 'kaffir' – a word that over the course of the last century became a derogatory word and later an unpardonable racial insult and, if used pejoratively, a criminal offence. In many of Bosman's published works the word is spelt 'kafir'. Bosman vigorously defended the use of it. His logic, and his other etymological defences of the word, are weak. Obviously what he was really doing was reflecting accurately the (translated) true-to-life speech of his characters, and he wasn't going to pollute that. His vehemence notwithstanding, he too abandoned the word eventually – most notably in the so-called 'Voorkamer' series, which are stories he wrote right at the end of his life.

Bosman's short stories are available today in many published forms, and his popularity continues to grow decades after his death. One of his tales, Mafeking Road, *is so well known that many people can quote phrases or passages from it as they might Shakespeare. We have selected two other pieces to represent the author here. Both show Bosman looking back in time ... yet they are stories which mirror, not the sentiments of the 19th century characters he portrayed in the early 20th century, but indirectly some of the philosophical views of 21st-century Africa. For instance, the first tale we have chosen, about the mystique and efficiency in communication of African drums, has ideas which are more acceptable to the world of e-mail and the internet today than to the world of stamps and telegraphs of which Bosman wrote 60 years ago.*

The Kafir Drum

Old Mosigo was the last of the drum-men left at Gaberones when they brought the telegraph-wires on long poles to this part of the country (Oom Schalk Lourens said). You can hear some kafir drums going now, and down there in the *vlakte* – there they are again ... tom-tom-tom-tom-tom. There must be a big beer-drink on at those huts in the *vlakte*. Of course, that's all the kafirs use their drums for these days – to summon the neighbours to a party. On a quiet night you can hear those drums from a long distance away. From as far as the Bechuanaland border sometimes.

But there was a time when the voice of the kafir drum travelled right across Africa. I can still remember how, many years ago, the kafirs received messages from thousands of miles away with their drums. The tom-tom-men in every village understood the messages sent out by the drums of the neighbouring villages. Then in their turn they spread the message further, with the result that, if the news was important, the whole of Africa knew it within a few days. The peculiar thing about this was that even when such a message originated from a tribe with a completely strange language, the drum-man of the tribe receiving the message could still interpret it. In the old days there were two drum-men in each village. They were instructed in the code of the drum from boyhood, and then in their turn they taught the art of sending and receiving messages by drum to those who came after them.

No white man has ever been able to learn the language of the kafir's drums. The only white man who ever had any idea at all of what the drums did – and even his knowledge about it was of the slightest – was Gerhardus van Tonder, who regularly travelled deep into Africa with his brother, Rooi Willem.

Gerhardus van Tonder told me that he had asked the drum-men of several tribes to teach him the meaning of the sounds they beat out on their tom-toms.

'But you know yourself how ignorant a kafir is,' Gerhardus van Tonder said to me. 'I could never understand what the drum-men tried over and over again to explain to me. Even when a drum-man told me the same thing up to ten times I still couldn't grasp it. So thick-skulled are they.'

Nevertheless Gerhadus said that, because he heard the same message so often, he was able, later on, to make it out whenever the drums broadcast the message that his brother, Rooi Willem, had shot an elephant dead. But one day an elephant trampled Rooi Willem to death. Gerhardus listened to the message that the drums sent out after that. It was exactly the same as all those earlier messages, Gerhardus said. Only, it was the other way round.

Even in those days the prestige of the drum-man had fallen considerably, because a mission station had been started at Gaberones, and the missionaries had brought with them their own message which came into conflict with the heathen news from Central Africa. But when the telegraph-wires were brought up here from Cape Town, taken past the Groot Marico and into the Protectorate – then everyone knew that, so to speak, the days of the kafir drum-man were numbered.

Yet on one occasion when I spoke to old Mosigo about the telegraph, what he had to say was: 'The drum is better than the copper wire that you white men bring on poles across the veld. I don't need copper wire for my drum's messages. Or long poles with rows of little white medicine bottles on them either.'

But whatever Mosigo thought, the authorities had had the copper wires brought as far as Nietverdiend. A little post office had then been built on Jurie Bekker's farm, and a young telegraph operator from Pretoria appointed to serve as postmaster. This young man had arranged for a colleague in Pretoria to telegraph to him, from time to time, items from the newspapers. By means of these telegrams, which were pinned up on a notice board in the post office, we who live in this part of the Bushveld kept in touch with the outside world.

The telegrams were all very short. In one of them we read of President Kruger's visit to Johannesburg and what he said, at a public meeting, about the Uitlanders.

'If that is all that the President could say about the Uitlanders,' said Hans Grobler, 'namely, "that they are a pest stop and that they should be more heavily taxed stop and that a miners' procession threw bottles stop," then I think that at the next elections I will simply vote for General Joubert. And why do these telegrams always repeat the world "stop" so monotonously?'

Those of us who were in the post office at the time agreed with Hans Grobler. Moreover we said that not only did we need a better president, but a better telegraph operator as well. We also agreed that extending the telegraph service to Nietverdiend was a waste of hundreds of miles of copper wire, not to speak, even, of all those long poles.

When we mentioned this to the telegraph operator, he looked from one to the other of us, thoughtfully, for a few moments, and then he said, 'Yes. Yes, I think it has been a waste.'

Thereupon At Buitendag made a remark that we all felt was very sensible. 'I can't read or write,' he declared, 'and I don't know what it is, exactly, that you are talking about. But I know that the best sort of news that I and my family used to get in the old days was the messages the kafirs used to thump on their drums. I am not ashamed to say that I and my wife brought up seven sons and three daughters on nothing but that kind of news. I still remember the day old Mosigo – even in those days he was old already – received the message about the three tax-collectors who got eaten by crocodiles when their boat was upset on the Zambesi ...'

'And that sort of news was worth getting.' Hans Grobler interrupted him.

'I don't mean that we would be *pleased* if three tax-collectors got eaten by crocodiles' – and we all said 'Oh, no,' and guffawed – 'They are also human. The tax-collectors, I mean. But my point is that that sort of news was news. That is something that we understand. But look at this telegram. About "the fanatic who fired at the King of Spain stop and missed him by less than two feet stop." What use is a message like that to us Bushveld Boers? And what sort of a thing is a fanatic, anyway?'

As a result of the conversations at the post office I decided to look up Mosigo, the last of the drum-men at Gaberones.

I found him sitting in front of his hut. The wrinkles on his face were countless. They made me thing of the kafir footpaths that go twisting across the length and breadth of Africa, and that you can follow for mile after mile and day after day, and that never come to an end. And I thought how the messages that Mosigo received through his drum came from somewhere along the farthest paths that the kafirs followed across Africa, getting footsore on the way.

He was busy thumping his old drum. Tom-tom tom-tom, it went. It sounded almost like a voice to me. Now and again it seemed as if there floated on the wind a sound from very far away, which was either an answer to Mosigo's message, or the echo of his drum. But it wasn't like in the old days, when you could hear clearly how the message of one drum was taken up and spread over koppies and *vlaktes* by other drums. Anyone could see that there were not so many drum-men left in the Bushveld, these days. And the reducing of their numbers wasn't because the chiefs had had them thrown to the vultures for bringing bad news.

It could only be due to the competition of the white man's telegraph-wires.

I carried on a long conversation with old Mosigo, and in the course of it I told him about the King of Spain. And Mosigo said to me that he did not think much of that kind of news, and if that was the best the white man could do with his telegraph-wires, then the white man still had a lot to learn. The telegraph people could come right down to his hut and learn. Even though he did not have a yellow rod – like they had shown him on the roof of the post office – to keep the lightning away, but only a piece of python skin, he said.

And looking at Mosigo's wrinkles I considered that he must have more understanding of things than that young upstart of a telegraph operator who had only been out of school for three or four years at the most. And who always put the word 'stop' in the middle of a message – a clear sign of his general uncertainty.

Even so, although I did not myself have a high opinion of the telegraph, I was not altogether pleased that an old kafir like Mosigo should speak lightly of an invention that came out of the white man's brain. And so I said that the telegraph was still quite a new thing and that it would no doubt improve in time. Perhaps how it would improve quite a lot would be if they sacked that young telegraph operator at Nietverdiend for a start, I said.

That young telegraph operator was too impertinent, I said.

Mosigo agreed that it would help. It was a very important thing, he said, that for such work you should have the right sort of person. It was no good, he explained, having news told to you by a man who was not suited to that kind of work.

'Another thing that is important is having the right person to tell the news to,' Mosigo went on. 'And you must also consider well concerning whom the news is about. Take that King, now, of whom you have told me, that you heard of at Nietverdiend through the telegraph. He is a great chief, that King, is he not?'

I said to Mosigo that I should imagine he must be a great chief, the King of Spain. I couldn't know for sure, of course; you can't really, with foreigners.

'Has he many herds of cattle and many wives hoeing in the bean fields?' Mosigo asked. 'Do you know him well, this great chief?'

I told Mosigo that I did not know the King of Spain to speak to, since I had never met him. But if I did meet him – I was going to explain, when Mosigo said that was exactly what he meant. 'What is the good of hearing about a man,' he asked, 'unless you know who that man is. When the telegraph operator told you about that big chief, he told it to the wrong man.'

And he fell to beating his drum again.

From then on I went regularly to visit Mosigo in order to find out what was happening in the world. We still read on the notice-board in the post office about what had happened in, for instance, Russia – where a fanatic had opened fire on the Emperor 'and missed him by one foot stop'. We began to infer from the telegrams that a fanatic was someone who couldn't aim very well. But to get news that really meant something I had always, afterwards, to go and visit Mosigo.

Thus it happened that one afternoon, when I visited Mosigo on my way back from the post office, and found him again sitting in front of his hut before his drum, he told me that there would be no more news coming over his drum, because of a message about the death of a drum-man that he had just received.

It was a message that had come from a great distance, he said.

Still the following week I again rode over to Gaberones. It was after I had read a telegram on the notice-board in the post office that said that a fanatic had missed the French President 'by more than twenty feet'.

And when I again rode away from Gaberones, where, this time, I had not seen Mosigo but had seen instead his drum, on which the skins stretched across the wooden frame had been cut, in accordance with the ritual carried out at the death of a drum-man – I wondered to myself on my way home, from how far, really, had it come – farther than France or Spain – that last message that Mosigo received.

Unto Dust

I have noticed that when a young man or woman dies, people get the feeling that there is something beautiful and touching in the event, and that it is different from the death of an old person. In the thought, say, of a girl of twenty sinking into an untimely grave, there is a sweet wistfulness that makes people talk all kinds of romantic words. She died, they say, young, she that was so full of life and so fair. She was a flower that withered before it bloomed, they say, and it all seems so fitting and beautiful that there is a good deal of resentment, at the funeral, over the crude questions that a couple of men in plain clothes from the landdrost's office are asking about cattle-dip.

But when you have grown old, nobody is very much interested in the manner of your dying. Nobody except you yourself, that is. And I think that your past life has got a lot to do with the way you feel when you get near the end of your days. I remember how, when he was lying on his deathbed, Andries Wessels kept on telling us that it was because of the blameless path he had trodden from his earliest years that he could compose himself in peace to lay down his burdens. And I certainly never saw a man breathe his last more tranquilly, seeing that right up to the end he kept on murmuring to us how happy he was, with heavenly hosts and invisible choirs of angels around him.

Just before he died, he told us that the angels had even become visible. They were medium-sized angels, he said, and they had cloven hoofs and carried forks. It was obvious that Andries Wessels' ideas were getting a bit confused by then, but all the same I never saw a man die in a more hallowed sort of calm.

Once, during the malaria season in the Eastern Transvaal, it seemed to me, when I was in a high fever and likely to die, that the whole world was a big burial-ground. I thought it was the earth itself that was a graveyard, and not just those little fenced-in bits of land dotted with tombstones, in the shade of a Western Province oak-tree or by the side of a Transvaal koppie. This was a nightmare that worried me a great deal, and so I was very glad, when I recovered from the fever, to think that we Boers had properly marked out places on our farms for white people to be laid to rest in, in a civilized Christian way, instead of having to be buried just anyhow, along with a dead wild cat, maybe, or a Bushman with a clay-pot, and things.

When I mentioned this to my friend, Stoffel Oosthuizen, who was in the Low Country with me at the time, he agreed with me wholeheartedly. There were people who talked in a high-flown way of death as the great leveller, he said, and those high-flown people also declared that everyone was made kin by death. He would still like to see those things proved, Stoffel Oosthuizen said. After all, that was one of the reasons why the Boers trekked away into the Transvaal and the Free State, he said, because the British Government wanted to give the vote at any Cape Coloured person walking about with a *kroes* head and big cracks in his feet.

The first time he heard that sort of talk about death coming to all of us alike, and making us all equal, Stoffel Oosthuizen's suspicions were aroused. It sounded like out of a speech made by one of those liberal Cape politicians, he explained.

I found something very comforting in Stoffel Oosthuizen's words.

Then, to illustrate his contention, Stoffel Oosthuizen told me a story of an incident that took place in a bygone Transvaal kafir war. I don't know whether he told the story incorrectly, or whether it was just that kind of story, but, by the time he had finished, all my uncertainties had, I discovered, come back to me.

'You can go and look at Hans Welman's tombstone any time you are at Nietverdiend,' Stoffel Oosthuizen said. 'The slab of red sandstone is weathered by now, of course, seeing how long ago it all happened. But the inscription is still legible. I was with Hans Welman on that morning when he fell. Our commando had been ambushed by the kafirs and was retreating. I could do nothing for Hans Welman. Once, when I looked round, I saw a tall kafir bending over him and plunging an assegai into him. Shortly afterwards I saw the kafir stripping the clothes off Hans Welman. A yellow kafir dog was yelping excitedly around his black master. Although I was in grave danger myself, with several dozen kafirs making straight for me on foot through the bush, the fury I felt at the sight of what that tall kafir was doing made me hazard a last shot. Reining in my horse, and taking what aim I could under the circumstances, I pressed the trigger. My luck was in. I saw the kafir fall forward beside the naked body of Hans Welman. Then I set spurs to my horse and galloped off at full speed, with the foremost of my pursuers already almost upon me. The last I saw was that yellow dog bounding up to his master – whom I had wounded mortally, as we were to discover later.

'As you know, that kafir war dragged on for a long time. There were few pitched battles. Mainly, what took place were bush skirmishes, like the one in which Hans Welman lost his life.

'After about six months, quiet of a sort was restored to the Marico and Zoutpansberg districts. Then the day came when I went out, in company of a handful of other burghers, to fetch in the remains of Hans Welman, at his widow's request, for burial in the little cemetery plot on the farm. We took a coffin with us on a Cape-cart.

'We located the scene of the skirmish without difficulty. Indeed, Hans Welman had been killed not very far from his own farm, which had been temporarily abandoned, together with the other farms in that part, during the time that the trouble with the kafirs had lasted. We drove up to the spot where I remembered having seen Hans Welman lying dead on the ground, with the tall kafir next to him. From a distance I again saw that yellow dog. He slipped away into the bush at our approach. I could not help feeling that there was something stirring about that beast's fidelity, even though it was bestowed on a dead kafir.

'We were now confronted with a queer situation. We found that what was left of Hans Welman and the kafir consisted of little more than pieces of sun-dried flesh and the dismembered fragments of bleached skeletons. The sun and wild animals and birds of prey had done their work. There was a heap of human bones, with here and there leathery strips of blackened flesh. But we could not tell which was the white man and which the kafir. To make it still more confusing, a lot of bones were missing altogether, having no doubt been dragged away by wild animals into their lairs in the bush. Another thing was that Hans Welman and that kafir had been just about the same size.'

Stoffel Oosthuizen paused in his narrative, and I let my imagination dwell for a moment on that situation. And I realised just how those Boers must have felt about it: about the thought of bringing the remains of a Transvaal burgher home to his widow for Christian burial, and perhaps having a lot of kafir bones mixed up with the burgher – lying with him in the same tomb on which the mauve petals from the oleander overhead would fall.

'I remember one of our party saying that that was the worst of these kafir wars,' Stoffel Oosthuizen continued. 'If it had been a war against the English, and part of a dead Englishman had got lifted into that coffin by mistake, it wouldn't have mattered so much,' he said.

There seemed to me in this story to be something as strange as the African veld. Stoffel Oosthuizen said that the little party of Boers spent almost a whole afternoon with the remains in order to try to get the white man sorted out from the kafir. By the evening they had laid all they could find of what seemed like Hans Welman's bones in the coffin in the Cape-cart. The rest of the bones and flesh they buried on the spot.

Stoffel Oosthuizen added that, no matter what the difference in colour of their skin had been, it was impossible to say that the kafir's bones were less white than Hans Welman's. Nor was it possible to say that the kafir's sun-dried flesh was any blacker than the white man's. Alive, you couldn't go wrong in distinguishing between a white man and a kafir. Dead, you had great difficulty in telling them apart.

'Naturally, we burghers felt very bitter about this whole affair,' Stoffel Oosthuizen said. 'And our resentment was something that we couldn't explain, quite. Afterwards, several other men who were there that day told me that they had the same feelings of suppressed anger that I did. They wanted somebody – just once – to make a remark such as "in death they were not divided." Then you would have seen an outburst all right. Nobody did say anything like that, however. We all knew better. Two days later a funeral service was conducted in the little cemetery on the Welman farm, and shortly afterwards the sandstone memorial was erected that you can still see there.'

That was the story Stoffel Oosthuizen told me after I had recovered from the fever. It was a story that, as I have said, had in it features as strange as the African veld. But it brought me no peace in my broodings after that attack of malaria. Especially when Stoffel Oosthuizen spoke of how he had on occasion, one clear night when the stars shone, to pass that quiet graveyard on the Welman farm. Something leapt up from the mound beside the sandstone slab. It gave him quite a turn, Stoffel Oosthuizen said, for the third time – and in that way – to come across that yellow kafir dog.

DARREL BRISTOW-BOVEY

DARREL BRISTOW-BOVEY, *a young writer who is going far – one hopes it is not Australia or Canada – was born on the Bluff just across the harbour from Durban in 1971. He studied law at Cape Town 'primarily as a way of avoiding the army', but switched to English Honours and Masters under André P. Brink and J.M. Coetzee.*

He worked for three years as the editor of English fiction at Tafelberg Publishers in Cape Town, where he was responsible for, among other things, reading and evaluating submitted manuscripts. 'The main thing I learnt there was that not everyone has a novel in them. Most people barely have a note to the milkman in them.'

In 1997 he was invited by the Sunday Independent *to review a play by André P. Brink, and it so impressed the 'Indy' that the Sunday newspaper offered him a column. He chose television as a subject, and the column became one of the pillars of that newspaper. He also writes a weekly sports column in* Business Day, *a weekly radio column on SAfm radio station, and writes monthly columns in* Marketing Mix, Style *and the* MTN Consumer Magazine.

As a post-apartheid writer he is able to write sardonically without bitterness and without guilt. He believes 'people find writing funnier and more interesting when they haven't met the person who writes it. Being a humour writer is like being a radio personality: the illusion is everything.

'Also: being a humour writer is like being a speaker at a wedding reception. When you've made them laugh once, they're likely to carry on laughing, whether you're funny or not.

'A drawback is that people expect you to be funny in real life. And one soon realises that the bits people laugh at most are the bits you didn't find funny at all.'

Bristow-Bovey's ambition is 'to write a long and stirring and utterly unfunny novel – and to see the day when the seventh trumpet sounds and all sub-editors spontaneously burst into flames and perish screaming.'

Currently his main task as a freelance writer is to watch and review television, but he seeks relief from this by going down to the local pub and writing about the boys in the Chalk 'n Cue. Occasionally, to escape the awful reality of soap operas and other television junk, he brings the Chalk 'n Cue into his television reviews. Here are some examples. But, before you start reading, be warned. He has a weakness for puns.

The Penis Mightier than the Sword

'We encourage our men to write a letter to their penis,' said the woman with the complexion of an unpeeled potato. She said it without smiling.

'I call mine George,' said the man clutching the teensy tiny hand-written letter. He said it without blushing. It was a bad moment to be a man.

Personally I don't pursue a more formal acquaintance with the wee fella than a gruff 'Hey, you', but there's no accounting for taste. I have known men who have called their better halves by a variety of endearments – Excalibur, El Chunko, the Mighty Thor … one irretrievable degenerate even called it André Agassi, I suspect as a tribute to Mr Agassi's preference for the double-fisted backhand – but 'George' just seems defeatist. Not even King George, or George of the Jungle – just George. George for short.

George's owner was visiting the Institute for Internal Caring and Sensual Awareness. That might sound swish to you, but it was really a double-storey bungalow in a back suburb of Dorchester. The garden was well-tended, but the guttering needed work, and that, in a way, was the whole message of *The Truth About Sex* (TV channel SABC3; Monday; 9.30 pm).

I'm not sure that sex has a truth to be revealed, but I am sure that the more you talk about it, the further it recedes. Sex is, on the whole, nasty, brutish and short, as Hobbes never commented, and therein lies all of its charm. Much like contemporary art or the wine served at a dinner party, the more you talk about sex, the less appealing it becomes. Curiously, I have precisely the opposite experience with cricket, but that is another column. What everyone on Monday's show seemed broadly agreed on was that the comic potential of discussing sex largely resides in having a good chuckle at the blokes.

Working on the assumption that utter humiliation before a world-wide audience is the surest cure for impotence, George's owner read out his intra-trouser memo: 'Dear George,' he intoned earnestly, 'I feel I've put too much pressure on you lately …' I couldn't listen. As one Frenchman said to the other, there's nothing worse than a second-hand letter.

We were introduced to the unlovely David, making his appearance at a group-therapy session. 'I'm David,' he boasted, leering around the room, 'and I'm a sex addict.'

'And how do you feel about being here?' asked the therapist, like the straight man in a comedy routine.

'Oh, very excited,' said David, right on cue.

Sex addicts, who I believe exist as much as I believe that Felicia's show gets South Africa talking, are the true heroes of our society. They combine all the modern virtues – the celebration of weakness, the triumph of victimhood, the limp abnegation of personal responsibility – and present them with a gleam in the eye that suggests they might be persuaded to tell all if the right book deal comes along. Or even if you just ask them nicely. Even if the genuine sex addict exists, he should be slapped, not simpered over.

David tried to drum up some sympathy. 'I've tried to quit my sexual obsessions by watching television instead,' he confessed tearfully, 'but I just grew addicted to watching television.'

That wasn't so much a confession as it was a plea to be punched in the kidneys, but the snivelling git did inadvertently make an important point – addicts of that sort are generally not as enamoured with the object of the addiction as they are with the swooning pleasures of weakness itself.

Justine also considered herself a sex addict, but all the mocking laughter was reserved for her boyfriend Johnnie, who sat about looking hollow-eyed while she appropriated parts of his body to assist her in exercising her constitutional right to have an orgasm five times a day. If sex addicts have orgasms. Finally, unimpressed with Johnnie's flagging devotion to duty, she started inviting strangers home to share her addiction. Johnnie, burden eased, looked even more gaunt. He looked like a bundle of cling-wrapped sandwiches from which the sandwiches had been removed.

'Justine's a happy woman,' he said in a haunted voice. 'She just likes to spread her happiness.'

All in all, the men made a poor showing of it. To be fair, we don't make it easier for ourselves. As long as we continue to throw up individuals like Nick, who has gathered together a discussion group for men who want to discuss the size of their penis, we deserve all the ridicule coming to us. All the Charlize Theron ads in the world won't ever make me as ashamed to be a man as the sight of those seven tossers sitting around a living room, surreptitiously eyeing the front of each other's chinos and saying in voices overly loud, 'Well, sometimes I wish mine were a bit smaller, know what I mean?'

Still, to laugh at humans in a sexual context is a cheap laugh, because it's such an easy laugh. A key component of humour is the gap between expectation and reality, and with all the piffle and poppycock that surround human sexuality, it's set to be a source of low-maintenance yuks and titters for a good long time to come.

('Hot Medium', Sunday Independent, 2000)

All That Sparkles

When I was small my father would take me on his knee and share the accumulated wisdom of his years. 'Never mix your drinks', he would say, 'when there's a barman to mix them for you.' Also: 'Never order a drink that is served with a straw. Straws are for men who can't hold their liquor.' Although he stopped saying that one after Uncle Chad lost both hands in the unfortunate Xerox incident of '77.

Regarding romance, Pop was adamant: 'Never, never come between a woman and a diamond,' he would whisper hoarsely, a shadow passing across his face.

I tried to tell Eddie Prosser that, down at the Chalk 'n Cue, but of course he wouldn't listen. There was small chance of Eddie Prosser listening to good advice. Eddie Prosser was too large to be comfortably taken on my knee. Worse still, Eddie Prosser was in love.

'Fellows, tonight I'm asking Eva to marry me,' he announced. We glanced at each other. We weren't fond of Eva. She had the annoying habit of finishing people's sentences. 'Joost's eyes are …' Porky Withers would begin. 'Blue!' Eva would say. Porky Withers would frown into his drink. We all knew that Porky Withers was going to say 'the same colour as my underwear', because that's what he always says after the fourth gin on a Thursday, but there was something about Eva that discouraged argument.

'Eva', Eddie had explained proudly, 'is a modern woman'. She believed in equality and independence. Once he had opened a door for her, and she had punched him in the throat. She always insisted on splitting the dinner bill, which was a relief to Eddie, because Eva's tastes ran to lobsters and champagne. Even though he was only paying for half her lobster, Eddie told us confidentially, he could still only afford to order a small garlic pita bread for himself. It's lucky she's a modern woman, we agreed.

Still, we wished Eddie well. We became alarmed only when he showed us the ring. It was a simple band of yellowish metal that might have been gold but more likely wasn't.

'Where's the diamond?' we asked. Eddie smiled like a man in love.

'No diamond,' he said happily. 'This symbolises our bond, it doesn't need a flashy stone. I'm pledging myself to her, not buying her.'

We looked at each other again. 'What does Eva think?' asked Karl the barman.

'She agrees!' cried Eddie joyfully. 'When her sister got engaged and had a great big ring, Eva said, "Love is in the heart, not on the finger." She said it quite sharply, too. She almost snarled.'

'Has she ever specifically said', I asked slowly, 'that she does not want a diamond ring?'

'Well,' said Eddie, 'not in so many words. But I know my Eva. Diamonds are for sparkling, boys, wedding rings are for love. Plus I've written her a poem.'

I shan't repeat the poem Eddie Prosser recited to us. Afterwards, we all drank heavily to forget that poem. You'd be surprised how many words don't rhyme with the name Eva Grobelaar. And you'd be surprised at the words that do.

We all pleaded with him. 'Buy a diamond, Eddie,' we begged. 'You don't know what you're doing. You're tampering with a powerful force of nature: do not trifle with the strange lunar mysteries of a woman and her diamonds.'

But Eddie became angry. He accused us of coming between him and his modern woman. He used some ugly words. They didn't rhyme, but they still weren't pleasant to hear.

We didn't see Eddie for a long time after that. Of course rumours filtered back. Short Dave said that Eddie had sold his car. Someone's wife saw Eddie pressing his nose to the window of a jewellery store in Rosebank. Sad Henry heard that Eddie had taken a night job.

Then one day Eddie Prosser shuffled into the Chalk 'n Cue. He looked thin, and his hands shook, even after the third rum and ginger ale. When I put some shredded lettuce from my Chalkburger on my upper lip and pretended to be Groucho Marx, he hardly even smiled.

'Can't stay long, boys,' he said. 'Eva will be wondering.' Then he told us his story. Apparently Eva hadn't been charmed by the plain band of yellowish metal and the poem. Apparently Eva had raised questions concerning the depths of Eddie's love, if he couldn't even spring for a lousy solitaire diamond, or perhaps a tasteful cluster. Apparently Eva had said that if after such an insult Eddie wanted her to believe that he loved her, well, he was really going to have to prove it. And not just some dinky little ring, either.

Eddie sighed, his eyes like empty mine shafts. 'You were right,' he said softly. 'Wedding rings are for love, poems are for romance, and diamonds ...' he drew a deep breath, 'diamonds are for Eva.'

(Femina magazine, 1999)

The Height of Stupid Courage

If you are reading this, and I fervently hope you are, you are almost certainly an adventurous person. You are of that blessed breed that craves white knuckles and clenched jaws; you do not sleep easy until you have stared a white-water rapid in the eye without blinking or until you have rassled a grizzly in the wild. You probably own a compass and your own small tent, and I wouldn't be surprised to learn that you know what a crampon is.

I salute you. I, by contrast, am not adventurous. I am more fond of ice-cream than adrenaline. My idea of the great outdoors is a McDonald's drive-thru, and whenever someone mentions crampons in mixed company, I blush and change the subject. I admire you, but I am not of you. I am fearful, you see.

At the merest suggestion that I might be placing myself at risk of serious bodily mutilation or nosebleed, I start snuffling and whining. I would call myself a coward, except I'm afraid the real cowards will take offence and beat me up. I am a rung below a coward. Only after enough bourbon do I scrape together the courage to be a coward. Which is not to say that I never do anything adventurous, but whereas you fine *OutThere* readers risk your bodies and expensive gear for the sake of living life more keenly, only one thing can make me defy nature and put myself in peril: a woman.

A young lady of my acquaintance recently invited me to fly in a modified stunt biplane, doing loop-the-loops and other unspeakable aerobatics in the thin air above Gauteng. 'Why?' I scoffed.

'Are you afraid?' she replied.

'Yes,' I said, but not out loud. Out loud I said: 'Of course not. When do we go?'

Next day we were in Germiston, which is frightening enough, inspecting two red-and-yellow Smirnoff Pitt Special biplanes. Have you ever seen a stunt biplane? They are about the size of an Opel Corsa, and made from the kind of thin aluminium that Isabel Jones cuts through with a Ginsu knife on infomercials. Did I want to be upside-down in mid-air inside a vehicle that could be eaten by Isabel Jones? I did not.

There were two consolations. One was a leather aviator's helmet that made me feel like Biggles. The other was a cold supply of the sponsor's product. The true adventurer doesn't drink before adventuring, but I did. I sat in the two-man cockpit in front of the pilot.

'Buckle up!' he yelled.

That made me weep. Under what circumstances would a seat-belt help? In case we abruptly come to a halt in mid-air? In case we accidentally reverse into a mountain?

'Shouldn't I have a parachute?' I demanded.

He laughed in a mocking sort of way. I looked around for the black box. The aeroplane's black box is always a source of comfort to me: an object that can't be destroyed, even in the worst disaster. Perhaps I could hide underneath it. I always wonder: if the material in a black box is so damned indestructible, why don't they make the whole plane from it?

As the propellers spun and we started taxiing for take-off, I noticed the young lady beside the runway.

'Aren't you coming?' I screamed hoarsely.

'No,' she yelled, 'I'm afraid of heights.'

The next forty minutes passed like a blur, or like my life rushing before my eyes. We rolled and somersaulted, we climbed and stalled, we fell from the sky like a piano. Far below, motor-cars crept along the M1. For the first time in my life I wished I was down on a South African road, where it's safe. I had been provided with a sick-bag, and I would have used it, if I could have figured out which way gravity was working.

Back on the ground, I walked unsteadily. I seemed to be walking very slowly. Then I realised I was crawling. But it was all worth it to impress the young lady. I lay at her feet and suavely waited for the dry heaves to stop.

'So, how did you know about these planes?' I asked.

She smiled sympathetically. 'My boyfriend is the pilot.'

(OutThere magazine, 1999)

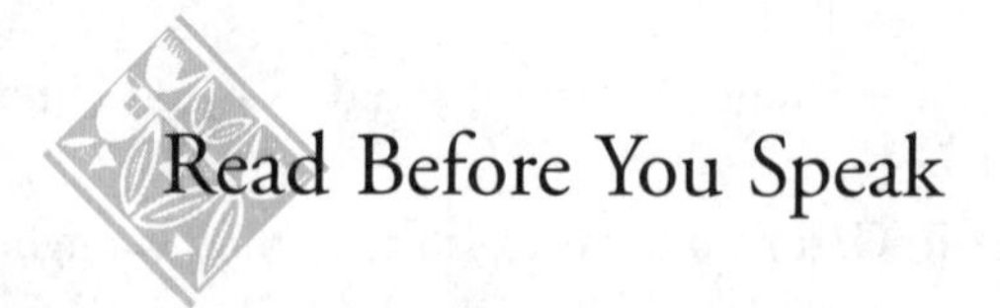

Read Before You Speak

For many years I was convinced that I am the Jonah – or do I mean the Ishmael? No, I'm pretty sure I mean the Jonah – of conversation. I was aware that there were such things as good conversations, and I was led to believe that people around me were having them, but they never seemed to be happening anywhere I was. What sex was for me as a teenager, conversations were when I became an adult. (Sex too, to be honest, but sometimes it's better not to be honest.)

I would find myself at the apex of a three-way conversation about the cost of buying a house in Cape Town, or how difficult it is to finance a local feature film, or conceptual art, and I would think to myself: 'I am the black cat of conversation. I am the unlucky charm. I am the ladder under which conversations wander. If I weren't here, these people would be talking about something interesting.'

It was only recently that the thought occurred to me that perhaps it is not all my fault. Maybe – just maybe – people don't know how to talk any more. Certainly they don't know how to listen. Even Oscar Wilde wouldn't cut much mustard at today's dinner party. Try it for yourself: pick a conversational quote from Oscar Wilde (oh, go on, do: no one in your circle is going to recognise it). Wait for the right moment, then say, in a voice clear and dry:

'The only difference between a caprice and a life-long passion is …'

You will get no further. The brunette at the bottom of the table will interrupt to tell her neighbour in a voice like a paper bag being crumpled about the Thai restaurant in Illovo she went to last Saturday.

To be fair, it wouldn't be a picnic to have Oscar Wilde at your dinner party. The great conversationalists of yore were really monologists. For them the opposite of speaking wasn't listening, it was waiting, but no one even waits nowadays. When they're not tripping over themselves to spill the kind of conversation that clatters to the floor and rolls about like loose change, they are volunteering the unwonted and unwanted information that in more civilised societies would have them burnt at the stake. I was recently at a party at which a stranger wandered up, clutching an Amstel. She said, and I am not making this up:

'I shouldn't drink beer. It's the very worst thing for a yeast infection.'

How would you respond? Is there a reply that would neither involve a foolish gabble about the difficult life of farmers, nor leave you feeling dirty in the morning? What would David Niven have said? Would he have launched nervously into an anecdote about a porn actress he'd once met named Candida Camera? Further proof, if proof were needed, that I am not David Niven. That is the tragedy of being a poor conversationalist at a party – you are like an iceberg drifting toward the equator. Not only do you diminish yourself with each passing moment, but you sink those with whom you come in contact.

Are you unsure whether or not you are a poor conversationalist? Ask yourself: 'Have I in the past month discussed the value of the rand, the crime rate, motor cars, my garden, my gym? Have I told an anecdote involving my children, or the last time I was in London? Have I told a joke at the dinner table? Have I ever quoted phrases from *Who Wants to be a Millionaire?* in the belief that I was being funny?' I think you know the answer.

But fear not, gentle reader. As ever, I have suffered that you may thrive. Herewith, please find the Guide to improving your conversation. The list is not exhaustive. Let the same not be said about your conversation.

- Just because it happened, doesn't make it interesting. If it will help the story, lie.
- Great people talk about ideas; average people talk about things; small people talk about the wine.
- If your sexual fantasies were of the slightest interest to other people, they wouldn't still be fantasies.
- Think before you speak. Read before you think. Wash your hands before you read.
- Only a cad says everything he means, and only a bore means everything he says.
- Unless you are Joseph in the court of Pharaoh, or Dorothy in *The Wizard of Oz*, and I would venture to suggest that you are not, that strange dream you had last Tuesday is of interest to precisely no one.
- Gossip is only really interesting when it is about yourself.
- And most importantly: Always leave the party five minutes before you run out of things to say.

(Style magazine, 2000)

DAVID BULLARD

THIS SATIRIST *and author of a weekly column of humour was born in Surrey, UK, during the great smog of 1952.*

David Bullard began his career with his father's stockbroking firm and became a yuppie living in outrageously fashionable London suburbs long before the species was officially identified by anthropologists.

In 1981 he was headhunted by a South African financial institution and 'after passing the rigorous South African immigration examination (Question 1. Are you white?)' settled in the country and eventually starting his own company (trading bond options). He did well enough to be able to indulge in journalism. He writes a quirky weekly column, Out to Lunch, *in the* Sunday Times *in Johannesburg, where he lives.*

Out to Lunch *embraces anything from politics to sport, and has the distinction of having attracted the attention of the Human Rights Commission when it was cited as a fine example of white racism. All the same, the President of South Africa apparently enjoys the column so much that the head of state security snips it out and files it for him whenever the President is out of the country.*

Apart from the Sunday Times, *Bullard writes regular columns for a variety of magazines on a number of topics, including motoring.*

(In 2002 Jonathan Ball and the Sunday Times *published* Out to Lunch *– a collection of Bullard's columns.)*

How Not to Run 'The Comrades'

I am not running the Comrades marathon for the 10th time this year. While others set off on this suicidal mega-jog at some unearthly hour, I will still be tucked up in bed awaiting the welcoming smell of fried bacon and eggs and freshly brewed coffee, which serves as my normal wake-up call.

Then, after breakfast and an invigorating shower, I shall put on one of Wagner's lighter albums and settle down to my morning cigar and a good book while I contemplate which wine to open at lunch.

This strikes me as a much better plan than spending most of the day running from somewhere you didn't want to be, to somewhere you don't want to go, on the off-chance that you will get a medal to commemorate this folly.

The conscious decision 'not' to run the Comrades for the 10th consecutive year is not at all the same as simply having no interest in running the race. Rather, like training for the Comrades itself, it is something that needs to be worked at.

Long ago I started training on the shorter races and the so-called 'fun runs'. I would get an application form, fill it in and deliberately not submit it, knowing that if I could somehow avoid the smaller and less important races I could surely strive for greater things.

It's surprising how, with the right training and a positive mind-set, the body can tolerate the pain and disappointment of not being at the starting line on the morning of a long, boring road race. I was fortunate enough to be able to afford the services of a superb personal trainer who insisted that I stick to his rigorous programme. 'You're never going to run the Comrades if you don't do exactly what I tell you,' he explained in what I assumed at the time to be a solecism.

On the first morning of the training he turned up with two six packs of beer, a bag of beer-flavoured chips and a couple of raunchy videos. He then announced that if he couldn't get me into shape not to run the Comrades then his name wasn't Arnold Schwarzenegger, which it definitely wasn't anyway.

Apart from making me lie around on the couch doing strenuous beer-opening exercises for what seemed like hours on end, my trainer also insisted that I learn to 'hop'. He would toss me the TV remote control and when he said the word 'hop' I had to switch channels.

I became aware that correct eating habits were an essential part of my training if I was to not run the Comrades competitively. Carbo-loading is vital to build up the necessary flab, but all the advantages of a good carbo-load are completely wasted if you walk to the takeaway, so we used Mr Delivery to send the pizzas.

This year I am in peak form, and I know I will walk, not run, in my 10th Comrades. After all, I already have the Two Oceans and The Argus under my belt, so what's a piddling 90 km?

('*Out to Lunch*', *Sunday Times, Business Times*, 14 June 1999)

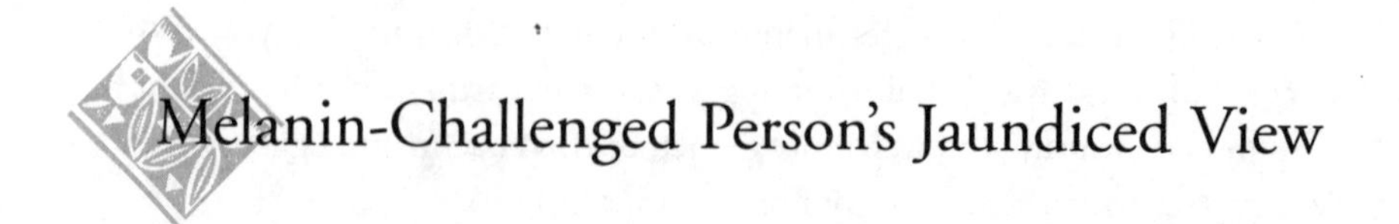

Melanin-Challenged Person's Jaundiced View

All this political correctness is getting me down. For example, why on earth should we call black people 'people of colour'? You might as well call the starving 'people of calorific deficiency' or people who live in places like Bosnia 'people of imminent shrapnel recipiency'. While the use of politically correct euphemisms may be amusing because they are so ludicrous, they are mostly pointless and insulting because they highlight what well-meaning liberals perceive as human deficiencies and invite ridicule. The Black Panthers would have looked pretty ineffectual had they been called the Melanin Enriched Panthers. The next thing you know they'd be giving up the black power salute in favour of a limp-wristed wave.

Does it really help to call a midget 'vertically challenged'? It isn't going to make him any taller and everybody knows what you really mean is, er … a person of restricted height. And why the hell should fat people get on the bandwagon with 'circumferentially challenged' and 'persons of size'? Fat people are always moaning about how they want to be accepted simply as normal people who have been bulk packed, so why do they attract attention to themselves by hiding behind politically correct shields? What about us thin people? You don't see us consulting lawyers because somebody comments on how slim we are instead of calling us 'persons of off-the-peg size'.

Curiously the people who refer to themselves as the gay community, a term no doubt intended to conjure up agreeable images of cohesion and good neighbourliness, have moved in the opposite direction. Today the love that dared not speak its name shouts it from the rooftops. Gays make no demands for politically correct euphemisms now; on the contrary, many have chosen to return to the abusive terms of their closet days and be known as queers and dykes. Presumably it has now become so acceptable to have an alternative sexual lifestyle that, with the shock element no longer present, most of the fun and gaiety has gone out of it. Nobody gives a damn about gay parades any more except to see them as an entertaining spectacle, not unlike your average Rag Day float procession, except for the fact that the queen is a man.

Why before we know it, the word gay will mean happy and cheerful again.

South Africa has embraced the concept of political correctness with the enthusiasm you would expect of a country previously denied these things. Along with cellular phones, satellite dishes and hardcore pornography, political correctness is proof of at least being part of the real world. A mad world possibly, but at least a real mad world. We have pinched affirmative action from the Americas. All this meant, in the US, was that political parties realised that once they had given the Negro the vote they had better be nice to him because he could sure as hell jerk the politicians' snouts out of the trough at short notice. Not enough black people were getting good jobs for them to be a malleable voting force, so the idea of affirmative action came in, which was simply a quota system intended for whitey to prove he actually recognised that slavery had been abolished.

We have exactly the same thing here and I have often wondered how much trauma counselling black employees will need in the future when they realise they were only employed because of the colour of their skins and not because anyone actually thought they could do the job. All this has achieved is to suggest that any black appointment must be a result of affirmative action irrespective of the person's qualities.

Thus racism is kept alive and well in the workplace.

Empowerment is another favourite pc term. It's similar to affirmative action in that it is part of the instant gratification sop to the masses. Sufficiently vague, it promises jam tomorrow, but never jam today. It has a suitably punchy, no nonsense sound to it and the message is that even if you find it difficult to write your name, you can rise to the top of the corporate ladder. Providing, of course, that you regularly attend Cosatu rallies. It's a cruel prank, but the proletariat, with their skimpy knowledge of Karl Marx, believes it because there is nothing else to believe in.

Much of this silliness started with the loony left-wing London boroughs who spent vast amounts of ratepayers' money inventing and advertising jobs which could only be filled by minority groups. The physically handicapped, ethnic minorities, and about everybody else with a suitably large chip on the shoulder just needed to wait for the appropriately advertised job vacancy to appear. Again, instead of helping the situation, the plight of whichever unfortunate group was flavour of the month was highlighted and ridiculed. Single parent, lesbian, one-legged, whale-loving drug abusers became the laughing stock of Camden. Even if they had wanted to apply for a job they could actually do, how would anybody ever take them seriously?

Of course, the only people for whom politically correct labels have not been devised are the army of bureaucrats and crazies whose job it is to think up these titles. How about 'circumlocutionarily advantaged persons' or 'bovine excrement verbalisers'. The whole thing is enough to turn you into a person of 'differing sobriety'.

('Off the Wall', Style, 2000)

CARTOONISTS

THEIR WIT DOWN THE YEARS

SO. *You're wondering how 'media art' qualifies as light writing.*

The wit in a cartoon balloon and the wit in a columnist's column are relatively close. Cartoon wit can flow purely from within the artist's talent, but it can be conjured up between artist and writer – an amalgam of journalism and graphic artist's chemistry. There are also cartoonists who write lightly, just as there are literary humorists who draw cartoons. James Thurber's highly simplistic cartoons are the most famous of the latter. Few writers draw well and, in Thurber's case, that was the charm of his illustrations. When Thurber – surprised by the popularity of his cartoons – told his publisher he was going to take art lessons to improve them, the publisher told him, in effect, 'You do that and you'll have to look for another publisher!'

Back in the 19th century, cartoonists were often explorers, painters, engineers, hunters and chroniclers. Two such men who relished the opportunity to be caricaturists were Thomas Bowler and the cabinet-maker turned painter, Thomas Baines. Baines is often confused with his equally famous contemporary, Thomas Bain, the surveyor-geologist. In modern times there was Wynand Claassen, a Springbok rugby captain, who caricatured his whole team in full colour, while Donald Kenyon, brother of another Springbok rugby captain, was a cartoonist for the Daily Dispatch *for nearly 50 years.*

There was Charles Evenden, a Cockney-born newspaper seller who, aged 12, gave up school and his part-time news pitch to work in a London factory, where he lost three fingers. As a teenager he migrated to Australia and became a farmhand, woodcutter, sailor and soldier. He suffered shell shock at Gallipoli and eventually in 1925 reached Durban, where he became the Natal Mercury*'s cartoonist, known as 'Evo'. His drawings were simple – yet often extraordinarily subtle. He is best known – internationally known – as the founder of the MOTHs (the Memorable Order of Tin Hats – an ex-servicemen's organisation) as well as for his cartoon which inspired his editor, Kingston Russell, to back his vision of the MOTHs as an organisation honouring the fallen and fostering comradeship.*

Then, spanning the mid-20th century, there was a generation of cartoonists who campaigned against racism, oppression and authoritarianism, and became giants in their profession. Events made them so.

We who worked with them remember instantly the work of eight of their number in the English anti-apartheid press: David Anderson (who uses the name Andy), Abe Berry, Bob Connolly, Dov Fedler, John Jackson, Jock Leyden and David Marais.

Bob Conolly: Self-caricature

New Jersey-born Bob Connolly, who was recruited in 1937 in the Bronx by I.W. Schlesinger to be a cartoonist on the latter's short-lived Johannesburg Daily Express, *became Johannesburg's most popular cartoonist soon after he joined the* Rand Daily Mail *a year later. There was a touch of Low about Connolly's humour but it was always gentle – too gentle, some might argue, for the apartheid years. He wrote two books, and in the wise-cracking* The Bob Connolly Story *(Howard Timmins, Cape Town, 1958) he said: 'Down through the cartooning years I've found that cruelty in an editorial cartoon and irreverence, too, are forces I can do without. Ridicule, I discovered, is a deadly and potent weapon; destitute of humour, it is a waste of time.'*

Connolly was not the first – and certainly not the last – cartoonist to use a 'Little Man' to make a comment within a cartoon's comment. His was a wartime figure in a steel helmet. Fedler introduced a news-seller (as did Jackson); others used unique devices of their own, whether a man or a boy, a dog or even a worm.

A number of South African cartoonists, including Abe Berry, who drew for The Star *for 40 years, and David Marais of the* Cape Times, *were published around the world over many years and appeared in* Punch. *Perhaps the funniest of that generation, even when he was making a major political statement, had to be the gentle John Jackson of the* Cape Argus. *Dov Fedler* (The Star) *is another who prefers laughter to satire, but a cartoonist who skilfully used both was Andy, a 'farm boy' from Natal who drew for several South African newspapers before emigrating to Canada before apartheid ended. He continued to produce cartoons for* The Star *until 2002.*

The 'big eight' grew into media institutions over the years because of the roles they played in attacking apartheid and overcoming censorship.

Cartoons enjoy a relative immunity, no matter how blunt or razor-sharp their criticism of policies and politicians. Newspapers were able to use the invulnerability of the cartoonists' wit in the darkest days of authoritarianism and censorship in South Africa. Thus cartoons provided an effective means of free expression at a time when government restrictions sought to gag newspaper opposition. The State failed to block the instant punch of a political cartoon, or to counter its stiletto thrusts. Of course, if it had been Nazi Germany, the newspapers would simply have been closed down or taken over. This did not happen under apartheid, because the apartheid state was not a true police state, and though it feared the mockery of caricature, it was more fearful of being laughed at by the world if it were to censor cartoons.

Once again, humour triumphed over political arrogance.

David Marais: Self-caricature

In a remarkable book on South African cartoonists which took 19 years to research, two academics, Murray and Elzabé Schoonraad, authors of The Companion to South African Cartoonists *(Ad Donker, Johannesburg, 1989), identified more than 500 known (and some hitherto unknown to us) caricaturists, cartoonists and illustrators working in Africa between 1830 and 1990.*

The 21st century's first crop of cartoon commentators are as sharp and as witty as their predecessors. The new post-apartheid school of cartoonists, such as Zapiro, Stephen Dugmore and Rico, have brought an original and entertaining touch to the art.

How do these sometimes earnest jokers contribute to society? In describing the role of a cartoonist, the authors of The Companion *state: 'While the dialectic journalist sometimes finds it difficult to circumscribe his ideas aphoristically, the graphic journalist has an excellent opportunity and an instrument of unequalled effectiveness by means of which he can convey his message simply and directly.'*

Quite so.

'A further important aspect of media art', according to another academic quoted in the book, 'is reporting on … the political history of a country … and to train the pupil to see connections between various elements in the drawing and the world … and to introduce to pupils in an interesting way such concepts as … metaphor … symbol … analogy … allusion … implication … inference … attitude and intention … interpretation … fact and opinion.'

What these academics are saying (we think) can be summed up in the words of a former editor of Die Burger, *Prof. Piet Cillié: 'In immediacy and direct impact a drawing can surpass the text.'*

Probably the first professional cartoonist in South Africa's history was Frederick I'Ons, a British settler who lampooned the British colonial government in the Eastern Cape. He savaged Sir Andries Stockenström and his Lieutenant Governor in a series of famous (or infamous) cartoons which were undoubtedly slanderous. But the colonial government realised that authoritarian action might backfire, so they silently endured the insults.

Strangely, the only cartoon we know of that caused the closure of a newspaper in South Africa was the first one published by The Star, *which, incidentally, later became the first newspaper on this continent to employ a full-time cartoonist.* The Star, *publishing in the Transvaal Republic before the Anglo-Boer War (27 February 1887), portrayed President Paul Kruger having his head read – literally. Kruger promptly banned* The Star. *The next day a strangely familiar newspaper appeared on the streets called*

The Comet – *and its readership soared.*

Dr Franco Frescura, when still an architectural student at the University of the Witwatersrand in the 1960s, drew a cartoon in a student publication of a man looking into a lavatory bowl and asking, 'Are you our Prime Minister?' B.J. Vorster, the uncompromising Prime Minister of the day, seized the publication and confiscated Frescura's passport so that for years he was unable to travel. Frescura later said he was not proud of what he'd done, for it was not in his nature to be so unsubtle but, career wise, it cost him dearly in his younger years.

These two instances are the exception that proves the rule regarding the traditional invulnerability of cartoons in the more civilised countries. The root of this invulnerability can be found in the word 'caricature', taken from caricare, *an Italian word meaning, loosely, to overload your vehicle and thus metaphorically to over-emphasise reality. A caricature, through its exaggeration, hammers home its point – and at the same time allows a publisher to shrug his shoulders and remind the wounded victim, 'It's only a joke.' Thus, the press is fairly immune to libel suits from politicians and public figures who accuse them of publishing cartoons which distort the facts and give 'the wrong' perspective.*

That's one of the ironies. Even when a cartoon portrays a tragedy, or social ill, or a political crime against humanity, exaggeratedly and with dramatic overstatement or gross simplification, it contains the seeds of the indomitable humour which lies in the cartoonist's 'lack of perspective'. A fundamental humour of hyperbole underlies most of the blackest or most propagandistic of cartoons.

The histories of cartooning and of humorist writers have much in common, not the least being an historical lack of women protagonists. Elzabé Schoonraad and her husband, though they spent nearly two decades tracing every cartoonist in southern Africa, could identify only one woman in those 200 years who became a leading political cartoonist. Out of more than 500 names listed in their directory, only 20 are women, and nearly all of them are graphic artists rather than caricaturists. The imbalance in media graphics, as in so many other fields, has been due not to a lack of talent so much as to the world's historical structure of political and economic institutions, social customs, and media organisations.

But all of these obstacles facing black aspirants and women everywhere have been overcome. A handful of black artists has appeared in recent years to join the two-centuries-old list of cartoonists.

'Guduza' entertained the readers of Ilanga *for many years with his smooth talk and clever Zulu sayings. But Guduza was a caricature created by George Muller, a multi-talented white South African trained in London. Muller was a reporter, sub-editor and then assistant editor who worked all his days as a scribe, and seemingly all his nights, at least during the 1970s and 1980s, as a cartoonist. He provided daily front-page pocket cartoons ('By George') for major dailies as well as political caricatures for*

various journals, including the bi-weekly Zulu newspaper, Ilanga.

A famous African cartoon commentator was 'Jojo', who distributed wisdom as well as wisecracks to Sowetan *readers, and to hundreds of thousands of others across Africa. Many of his fans would have been amazed to know that Jojo's creator was not from Soweto – he was a white boy named Len Sak from the Eastern Cape. Sak, a quietly spoken man who is in total empathy with black South Africa, freelanced for (black)* Golden City Post, The Star, The World *and* Drum *(the last two journals being essentially black), in Nigeria and Ghana as well as locally; for the Jewish press worldwide (sometimes with Yiddish captions); and for several Afrikaans newspapers.*

Constance Penstone

Australian-born Constance Penstone (1864–1928) was the female pioneer in South Africa. She was not only the first, but is still the best-known of women political cartoonists. Constance and her husband, Charles Penstone, were co-owners of The Owl *magazine in the late 1890s. Both were journalists as well as cartoonists. As they had the same name and initials, he signed as 'C. Penstone', and she had to be content with the by-line 'Scalpel'. She worked often with D.C. Boonzaier – perhaps the most famous of all Afrikaans caricaturists, and she acted simultaneously as political cartoonist of the* Cape Times *under the equally well-known editor, Edmund Garrett. Shortly before her death she told* The Argus*:*

'Those were the old days through the Boer War when there was an abundance of dramatic copy ... It was all remarkably interesting work; but as I know now, too strenuous – always that printer's devil [we think she must have been referring to deadlines] ... waiting inexorable and implacable around the corner.'

And that is a tension editors often share with cartoonists ... waiting anxiously to see whether the cartoonist will meet the daily deadline, fill the empty, waiting space – and hit the bull's eye. Will readers see the humour? Or will they see only a crudely wielded axe? Will the axe strike down the intended target?

Editors know that, skilfully handled, the cartoonist's axe, or rapier, simply has to be mightier than the pen.

JAMES CLARKE

HE WAS A MAN *with a very serious mission, until he focused on the funny side of life. His mission was to save the world … Clarke's environmental campaign, CARE, in* The Star *(Johannesburg) was one of the first of its kind in the world when it was launched in daily news headlines 30 years ago. At that time surprisingly few people were concerned about environmental threats. He set out to popularise the scientific and highly relevant, if unperceived, issues. The campaign certainly did change things in South Africa but, five years before his retirement as one of the senior editors on his newspaper, he was asked 'to be funny' in print – every day. Suddenly all his readers loved him for making them forget their problems. This irritated him immensely.*

James Clarke was born in London in 1934 and, after a few years as a daily newspaper reporter in Britain, settled in South Africa. He has written and compiled 24 books on widely different subjects including a bestseller, Man is the Prey *(André Deutsch, London, 1968; Stein & Day, New York, 1969), which was a 'personal investigation into the methods and motives of man-eaters and man-killers'.*

He wrote a comprehensive book on South Africa's environmental situation, Back to Earth *(Southern Books, Johannesburg, 1991) and updated it in 2002 for the Earth Summit (as* Coming Back to Earth, *Jacana, Johannesburg, 2002). Clarke's first love in writing appears always to have been humour. It was a field in which he had dabbled for years, sometimes under an assumed name. Then, in 1992, his daily humour column,* Stoep Talk, *and leader writing became his fulltime occupation and led to four books of humour.*

The characters created in Stoep Talk *include the flamboyant Soweto taxi-driver, Togetherness Amadeus Tshabalala; Threnody Higginbottom (pronounced Smith) who is Clarke's imaginary secretary; and the institution called Densa, which he founded for those too dumb to be admitted to Mensa, the international club for the highly intelligent.*

James Clarke does not ridicule the targets of his humour, he hardly even pokes fun at people. He prefers to laugh with *them. While he seldom resorts to satire, his irony is sometimes made of steel.*

– H.T.

Taxi-ing to a Dead Stop

A London Transport consultant says Johannesburg's 'township taxis' could easily serve the preponderantly white suburbs. – Report

Togetherness Tshabalala jinks his Toyota mini-bus taxi (with BMW hubcaps) through the rush-hour traffic.

He is a confident man of high spirits, as evidenced by the stickers on his rear window:

'God loves Taxi Drivers' and 'Defeat Constipation – Travel by Taxi'.

On the front of his taxi, in the folds of a dent which, ominously, is in the shape of a large traffic cop with his arms out, is a lurid notice reading:

Jukskei Park Express

Inaugural Flight

Using the word 'flight' is Togetherness' little joke.

We are witnessing (dear reader) the inaugural journey of a township taxi which hopes to establish a daily service between the quiet far northern suburb of Jukskei Park and Johannesburg – a 25 km journey which takes Togetherness 8.5 minutes if it's not too busy and assuming he can occasionally use the pavements.

The percussion waves from Togetherness' powerful radio cause the vehicle's sides to rhythmically flex.

He hoots as he drives. Togetherness hoots at anything he sees – including trees – as is the custom of taxi drivers.

Aboard the taxi are a dozen white people. They do not come whiter. Their whiteness is not due to fear, it is due to stark terror. Take John Hilton. Never in his life has he done zero to 100 km/h in six seconds – not in heavy traffic. Denise Smith's colour had changed to green-white as quickly as the last traffic light changed to red – a colour which, as is traditional among taxi drivers, Togetherness ignored.

He looks over his shoulder – for a full minute – asking passengers their destinations. Elsbeth Brown, sitting right at the back, says Randburg centre. She really wants to go all the way to Johannesburg centre but, suddenly, Randburg seems preferable.

She worries about how she will make her way from the backseat, but only fleetingly because the taxi has now reached Randburg and has stopped as suddenly as a plane might stop up against a mountain.

Now everybody is in front in a warm, intimate heap.

Elsbeth alights as gracefully as anybody can with one knee locked behind the other. She is vaguely aware of passers-by loosening her clothing and shouting: 'Give her air!'

Togetherness bowls happily along Jan Smuts Avenue, overtaking a police car that is chasing a getaway car. Then he overtakes the getaway car, exchanging boisterous greetings with the driver whom he appears to know. Togetherness is steering with his elbows because he needs his hands free to check the morning's takings and to wave to girls.

He announces: 'Ladies and gentlemen, this is your captain. We will shortly be landing in Johannesburg. Please make sure your seatbelts are fastened and your seats are in the upright position. Thank you.'

Piet Smit is chewing on a seatbelt that is made of leather. Togetherness had them specially made because he noticed how passengers often like to bite on something.

A passing taxi fires a brief but inaccurate burst from an automatic rifle in Togetherness' direction as he merges with the streams of in-bound traffic. Togetherness merges with the other traffic in much the same way his ancestors merged with the British 24th Regiment at the battle of Isandlwana.

He stops at his usual disembarkation point in the middle of a busy intersection and picks his teeth, patiently, while people sort out their legs and teeth before groping their way towards a street pole around which they can throw their arms.

By the time his passengers' eyeballs have settled back in their sockets, Togetherness is halfway back to Jukskei Park.

The dramatic eclipse of the sun in the Northern Hemisphere in 1999 reminded Clarke of an eclipse in South Africa in 1994 – that year of radical change …

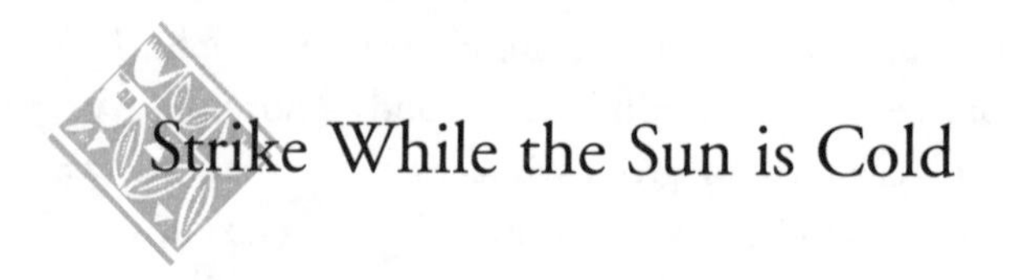

Strike While the Sun is Cold

The Old Testament says, 'And it shall come to pass in that day, saith the Lord God, that I will cause the sun to go down and I will darken the earth in the clear day.'

And it came to pass that one Jan of Swartruggens, who was ignorant of the forthcoming eclipse, was in the field.

He spake loudly unto Phineas: 'Go thou at once and fetch the butylphenoxyacetate that we may administer to the beasts against the pox.'

Jan never saith 'please' or 'thank you', not in any of the 11 official languages of his land. He saw his workers as the sons of Ham, hewers of wood and drawers of too much in wages.

Now it had come to pass in the land that the leaders had declared all men equal (and women nearly so) and there were to be free and almost fair elections but Jan knew not of it.

Phineas returned with the butylphenoxyacetate and Jan admonisheth him for being slow.

Phineas saith unto him, 'Lo, I can go no faster carrying 100 kg of butylphenoxyacetate because, after 87 summers and almost as many winters, I am a little halt.'

But Jan heeded him not and made as if to smite him.

Phineas rose up and spake in a voice of righteousness saying, 'The Lord shall punish thee for thine political incorrectness. Verily, even this day the Lord will send a sign.'

Jan spatteth upon the ground.

Phineas saith, 'Even this hour!'

(Phineas had been listening to the radio and knew that the Moon and Sun were to meet at the 9th hour and that the Moon would take away part of the sun for a while.)

The sky darkened as advertised. Jan looked up for a cloud but the sky was clear even unto the Dwarsspruitrand.

The heavens grew darker and Jan again cast his eyes up. Verily, even as he looked, the sun, though high in the firmament, was being consumed, and Jan was sore afraid.

Believing dusk was nigh, the birds of the air began returning to their roosts and the cattle began to move back to their kraal and the sunflowers scratched their heads.

All these things Jan saw and he fell upon his knees and spake unto Phineas saying 'Verily, thou art right. I have sinned all my days.'

'Verily indeed,' saith Phineas.

Jan smote his forehead and rent his raiments and cried out, 'Wilt thou forgive me, a worthless sinner?'

Phineas smiled and made an affirmative action with his head.

Jan rose saying, 'Behold, I have a bottle of *Oudies* in the bakkie, let us drink to our new-found understanding that passeth all understanding.'

And the sun came out and Jan gave thanks unto the Lord and went to his house with his arm round Phineas and the two men drank the brandy even unto the last drop.

Jan's wife, Marie, entered the house and saith, 'My husband, what is this? Hast thou taken leave of thine headfiller?'

Jan spake unto Marie: 'Lo, woman, this is my friend, Phineas Ndlovu. Rejoice! The Lord sent me a sign. Didst thou not see the sun disappear?'

'Verily,' saith Marie, 'today I have seen everything.'

Moral: Make hay when the sun doesn't shine.

Despite the political transition in 1994, a die-hard conservative group in South Africa, known as the AWB, mourned the passing of apartheid. The neo-Nazi group was led by a strident leader, Eugene Terre'Blanche, who in 2000 was sentenced to six years for assaulting a black man. The AWB's main objective was to establish a white 'homeland' where blacks would be welcomed – but only as 'temporary workers'. In May 2000 Clarke found the ideal spot.

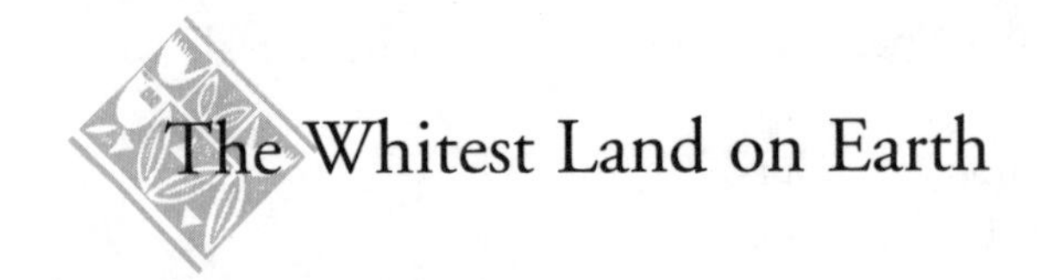

The Whitest Land on Earth

11 000 sq km – this is the area of an iceberg that last week broke away from the Antarctic's Ross Ice Shelf. – Time

Koos van Jaarsveld, an AWB *oberdammengruppenführer* and veteran of the World Trade Centre attack of April 1993, opened the letter with some astonishment. There was no doubt whom (or even who) it was from – the deeply embossed South African Presidential Seal said it all.

The letter read:

Dear Sir,

In the absence of your leader who, currently, we are caring for, I am addressing you in the hope that you will make known the contents of this letter to your comrades (if you will forgive the expression). My colleagues and I in the Cabinet believe we have found for you just what you have been seeking – a land fit for your Volk.

No, it is not in the Karoo and nor is it in the Kalahari desert. On the contrary, you could not hope for a cooler place, nor, now I come to think of it, whiter. In fact it is an island – an island almost 300 km long and 40 km wide! As big as Israel!

You will want to know where, I am sure. The fact is YOU CAN CHOOSE where you'd like it to be! Yes indeed, it can actually be towed anywhere – and you'd get fishing rights for 200 nautical miles around. The subsoil is somewhat thin. In fact, we are talking of an iceberg, but don't worry, it can be covered with an insulating layer of topsoil and we already have a mission in Alaska studying how Inuits grow their mealies and pumpkins in permafrost. Wildlife, in the form of seals and penguins, abounds. We can tow this island, using the *Wolraad Woltemade* tug, anywhere you want.

When he comes out of jail your leader can become President Eugene Terre'Blanche of Oranje Groenland. The island's name is just a working title, you understand. You may name it anything you like.

Ah, how grand it will sound – 'President Terre'Blanche', the only president in the world whose Presidential Seal can be trained to balance a ball on the end of its nose!

If you choose to be anchored off Africa, then you could stage Africa's first Winter Olympics! The games could legitimately be an all-white affair because the people of Africa are not wildly enthusiastic about bob-sledding, ski-jumping, ice-hockey, etc. and it is therefore unlikely that black competitors will want to come to your island. (But please try not to raise this issue.)

Should you not want to anchor off Africa, our technical boys (Phineas Ndlovu and Gabriel Mtata down in the Government Garage) say they could easily put an engine behind your island so it could be manoeuvred to constantly follow the summer season around the world, or towed into a parking position off, say, Australia or Chile. Yes, indeed, anywhere. ANYWHERE! Anywhere.

The project would need R10 billion, but don't worry, all parties and institutions who were approached were spontaneous in agreeing to donate, and within days we were oversubscribed 17 times.

Where you eventually anchor would, of course, be (as your apartheid government used to put it so elegantly) an 'own affair'.

What happens, I hear you ask, when the Volk begin to slide into the sea as the sun begins to reduce your homeland to the size of an ice cube? This will not happen for 150 years – which leaves time enough to meet The Challenge of Afterwards. (That, naturally, will also be an 'own affair'.)

Think about it. Yours etc.

Marking Secretaries' Day

What with the strike in the public service and Secretaries' Day coinciding last week, business fizzled and telephones went unanswered throughout Gauteng.

It was no different at the headquarters of the Stoep Talk Organisation. Threnody, my private secretary, had conspicuously circled Secretaries' Day on her desk calendar when it was still barely mid-August outside. I pretended not to notice. I like her to think I can remember special days unaided.

Halfway through Wednesday I said, 'Happy Secretaries' Day!' and from behind my back I brought out a surprise in an envelope. She opened it and exclaimed, 'But it's a Christmas card!' That was the surprise, I said. Oh my, how we laughed.

Well, I certainly did.

It's always nice to give a little surprise on Secretaries' Day. Last year I surprised her with an expensive (and hardly used) 'Get Well' card. The year before it was a birthday card.

I fully realise it is also incumbent on the boss to do something bordering on the generous on Secretaries' Day, otherwise you get tea slopped in your saucer for months afterwards. So I took Threnody, once again, to lunch at Bobo's, where, I was pleased to see, they'd installed seats at last. It made it a lot more comfortable than having to stand at the counter admiring the back-lit blown-up photographs of sausages and chips.

'This is your day,' I told her, 'and you may order whatever takes your fancy! Spare no expense! Even the "Special" – a ladies' steak and chips, if you like.'

To be frank, this annual lunch requires a very real sacrifice on my part. It's not just the money, it's that Threnody is so very reserved. She sits up very straight and tense while I tend to be an exuberant eater, waving my fork around and dropping things down my tie which, when I get home, I often dig straight into the compost heap.

I allow her to drop the 'Mr Clarke' and just call me 'Sir'. I call her 'Threnody', although in the office I never address her as anything but 'Miss Smith'. Her real surname, as you know, is Higginbottom. I cannot bring myself to say this.

Threnody ordered a small hamburger, with chips. I ordered just a cold drink for myself but told her not to worry about me. 'Just relax,' I said. To show her that I was perfectly at ease and that there was no need for her to hurry the meal, I tapped a little tune on the table with my fingers.

The conversation, as always, comprised mainly little fits of coughing.

Cough, cough, cough, she went and then she said how long it had been since she'd had a rise. Naturally, I was curious. 'How long?' I asked.

'(Cough. Cough.) Four years.'

She confessed she'd actually prayed for a rise. I was shocked that she should have gone above my head and said if she wanted a rise she must say so.

'(Cough. Cough.) Well, I do!' she said.

Then I too went into paroxysms of coughing and subtly changed the subject:

'How's your mother?' I asked. (A lot of bosses don't care about their secretary's family.)

'Fine,' she said.

I asked her if she liked my 'surprise' card. She said 'yes'. Then I reminded her of last year's 'Get Well' card and we had another jolly good laugh.

No Such Thing as a Free Lunch

It was Bosses' Day on Friday. I'd never heard of it until I sensed Threnody, head secretary of the Stoep Talk Organisation, hovering near my desk.

'What is it, Threnody?' I asked rather testily which, on a Friday, a boss is entitled to be. 'Can't you see I'm busy?'

She looked at my screen for a second and said, '(Cough. Cough.) If you move the four of clubs over to there it will release the five of hearts, which can then go up there and then that one ...'

'I was about to do that,' I said.

Those who have played solitaire on their computer, and get it to work out, will know the glow of satisfaction, the burst of pride, the ecstasy, that overpowering feeling of having mentally triumphed over mankind's most complicated and daunting piece of machinery.

'(Cough. Cough.) Do you know what day it is?' Threnody asked a little hesitantly.

'I suggest you consult the nearest calendar,' I said drily.

'(Cough. Cough.) It's Bosses' Day!'

'So?'

'Well, in September, on Secretaries' Day, *you* took *me* to lunch, so my mother said I (Cough. Cough) should take *you* to lunch!'

I swivelled my boss's chair around and tilted it in an executive-like way so that I could see her more clearly. I noticed, for the first time, that she was wearing quite a snazzy dress and had had her hair done. I was, to tell the truth, quite taken aback.

'YOU? Take ME to lunch?' I said. Then, a little suspiciously I asked, 'Where?'

'Well, not that hamburger place that you took me for Secretaries' Day. When I told my mom I was thinking of taking you there, she nearly had a fit. She said I should take you to La Maison Cuisine.'

'But that's very expensive!' I said.

'My mother gave me some money.'

'Well then, have you booked? I mean, what are you waiting for? They could be full!'

And so it was that I found myself walking into La Maison Cuisine and ordering extra large *huîtres* and *roti canard à l'orange* with *une bouteille de vin rouge* and waving *la fourchette* as I told Threnody my life story. I told her how I had started out in adult life with just a bicycle (albeit a three speed one with drop handlebars and quite a snazzy bell) and how, over the years, I became an intrepid reporter until one day I was able to buy myself a 12-speed bicycle …

'What year was that?' she asked.

'You tell me,' I suggested.

'1916?' she said.

'What!' I said. 'My gosh! How old do you think I am?' (I was barely 50 at the time.)

She thought for a long time and said at last: 'Sixty?'

'What!'

'Sorry, sir, am I a bit out?'

'A bit? You're 10 years out!'

'You're 70?'

This greatly curbed the appetite, which, up to that point, had been shouting up from below that it wanted *crème brûlée*. Although Threnody only sipped her wine and was still on her first glass, the first bottle, miraculously, was empty. I ordered another and solemnly toasted her dear old mum.

Threnody ate with surprising energy while I traced my writing career from standard 2. I had barely reached my prize-winning composition (well, third prize) in fifth grade when the bill came. Threnody, without looking at it, folded a R50 note inside it and placed it back in the folder.

'That won't be sufficient,' I said, thoroughly alarmed.

'That's all my mother gave me! My mother said "R50 should be enough for that old skinfli … for your dear old boss."'

I had to pay the R325.45 balance and part with a 20c tip.

Back at the office I looked in vain in the dictionary for the word 'skinfli'.

It was quite some time before my colour returned.

Threnody, on the other hand, was uncharacteristically chipper and hummed a little tune. Obviously the *vin rouge*.

Ancient Egyptian Airlines

I have always enjoyed history. If you think history lacks humour, then you haven't heard of 'feel-good history'. Feel-good history is a branch of history where the authors set out to make people feel good about their past. I was taught it at school in Britain during and after World War 2. We were told that the dense smogs which settled over Britain and brought its traffic to a standstill for days on end were a sign of Britain's industrial might and how it was this that had enabled us to buy up whole countries in Africa, freehold, for vast sums of beads.

Sometimes beads were not enough and so gunboats were used. But as kids we felt good about it.

Every community has its own version of history; some are dafter than others.

But in the United States, the Portland Public Schools Board was recently censured for going too far in its African-American Baseline Essays. Its version of history claimed that black people in Africa invented the aeroplane 4 000 years before the Americans.

Where the Portland essays were accused of going overboard was in giving the impression that, first, the Ancient Egyptians were all black and, second, that they invented the aeroplane. The essay claimed a 14 cm model glider was, at some stage, unearthed somewhere in Egypt and quotes an obscure British authority saying 'the Ancient Egyptians used their early planes for travel expeditions and recreation …'

Personally I was surprised that there should be any controversy.

It is common knowledge in the circles in which I move – mainly tight circles – that the Ancient Egyptians had aeroplanes and flew them all over the place. These planes were originally called Pharaoh-planes in honour of the 18th dynasty of Pharaohs, who financed their research and development. After the Pharaohs died out the 'ph' was dropped and the machines were simply called 'araoh-planes' and, later, 'aeroplanes' (Annals of Heavier-than-Air-Machines, Tablets III–IV. 3/7/1999 BC).

A pharaohdrome was recently unearthed near Cairo (op cit).

The first Pharaoh-plane was developed at Luxor by none other than Damocles Caliph III and was named the DC3 in his honour. It was known as a heavier-than-air machine on account of its being made from the same type of stone as the Pyramid of Khufu (sit op).

It was not terribly successful as aircraft go (el cid).

Few Egyptologists have been prepared to admit that the pyramids were designed not as tombs but as launch pads for the Mark 1 Pharaoh-plane. Slaves would drag it to the top, pour honey down the sides for lubrication, and release the aircraft down the slope. There were lots of accidents. How do you think the Sphinx lost its nose? The first planes simply speared into the sand but Thutmose IV ordered a lighter and more porous stone from Thebes and this led to the first reported flight by Mentuhotep II (none other) in 1286 BC at Kittihorus (ibid., op cit, sit op).

Many who witnessed its flight over the First Cataract thought it was a swan and cried out, 'A swan! A swan!' From this incident the city of Aswan, just below the cataract, derives its name.

Eurocentric history books deliberately do not record that Nefertiti began her career as an airhostess with Ancient Egyptian Airlines (Annals of Ramses II, 1174 BC, Tablets IV–VII). The general manager was the up-and-coming Tutankhamen. It is also not widely known that another great Egyptian queen began her career as an airline hostess (op cit, El Al) – Cleopatra herself. Cleopatra eventually founded Cleo's Air Operations, abbreviated as C-AIR-O. The name was eventually adopted by Egypt's capital.

Nebuchadnezzar of Babylon, after defeating the Egyptians by verily smiting them with large catapulted rocks, took over the airline and unwisely started a price war with the Bedouin caravans, whose camels were in fact lighter and faster than even the later Bronze Age aeroplanes, weight still being a problem.

The last Ancient Egyptian Airlines plane to fly had none other than the Roman, Pontius Pilot, at the controls. The plane crashed in the desert near A-syut in the Lower Nile Valley. According to legend, the name A-syut is derived from Pontius Pilot's last words before he hit the ground.

Aircraft made a brief comeback in the Early Iron Age but again the material was unsuitable. It was left for Wilbur and Orville Wright to re-invent the plane in the 20th century.

CHRIS ELLIS

CHRISTOPHER R. ELLIS *is a general practitioner in Pietermaritzburg in KwaZulu-Natal and is one of a rare breed of medical writers (category: serious).*

He was born in 1944 in Gloucestershire, which he recalls as 'a very jolly county full of horsy people'. He was educated there and at medical school in London before being 'sent to the colony of Natal to check that standards were being maintained and that the colonials were dressing properly for dinner'.

He attributes the two great successes in his life to perseverance. 'After 25 years of intense practice, lessons, videos, scheming and rigorous intellectual analysis of technique at the country club bar, I have achieved a handicap of 17 at golf. This is still below my full potential, and I am now concentrating on keeping my approach shots to the 18th hole out of the car park.

'My latest and perhaps greatest life success is that my wife, Nicky, has just bought an enormous fridge for the kitchen and that I have been given the old one. I am steadily filling it with alcohol of an amazing variety. In moments of depression I open the door (a light comes on automatically and I am considering installing music of a soothing kind to come on at the same time) and gaze, and wonder how this was all achieved in one lifetime.'

Chris Ellis has produced a number of books, including one for the guidance of doctors with Zulu patients – whose language he speaks and whose customs he has grown to respect. His first book, The Soft Edges of Family Practice *(Premier Book Publishers, Johannesburg, 1991), was awarded the Noristan Prize. He has also published an anthology of poetry, a monograph on hypertension as well as many papers on a wide range of health topics in South African and in international journals. Ellis, father of four sons, is a regular contributor to* diversions, *a Johannesburg-based leisure magazine for the South African medical, pharmaceutical and other health-care professionals.* diversions *published, as a series of monthly articles,* Despatches from the Last Outpost *(later published by Sue McGuinness Publications, Johannesburg, 2000, as a book) – the 'Last Outpost' being the jocular South African term for the Pietermaritzburg region of Natal.*

Ellis, who refers to KwaZulu-Natal as 'the Colony', has become something of a James Herriot in the medical world. His humour is of the old school, gentle and mocking.

Small Black Dogs and the House Call

I have always taken a sneaking enjoyment out of doing house calls. They get me out of the surgery and I can drive around the village inspecting the gardens. The drive may sometimes be diagnostic, as I can see who is coming out of the pub or watch the workman I signed off yesterday on workmen's compensation vigorously digging his potato patch.

The drive may sometimes give me more unexpected diagnoses. On driving to a patient's house I once diagnosed another patient's problem. The other patient was a man of 25 whom I had seen in the surgery three times for a tight chest and difficulty in breathing. I suspected that he was hyperventilating but he had said that he had no worries. I found out the cause of his hyperventilation because I took the longer and rougher road that is seldom used, behind our local golf course. As I came round a corner I saw his wife in a car parked off the lane and she was in an embrace with a man who was not my patient. It was that most feared diagnosis: *in flagrante delicto*.

House calls, apart from revealing the village wildlife and being a pleasant drive, can also have their dangers. The general practitioner often finds himself treading cautiously as he opens the garden gate. Like the postman and the milkman, he shares a common enemy: the much-loved family dog.

These come in two varieties, Canis major and Canis minor. In my nightmares they are, for reasons which will become apparent, always black in colour.

Canis major appears as a great flapping bloodhound with a bark like a blow torch being turned on and off, while Canis minor is a small black dog of hysterical disposition whose cries are aimed at the higher ranges of auditory nerve damage.

Thus I find myself walking down the garden path, holding my medical bag in front of that portion of the anatomy which all GPs fear to be bitten on: the tender part. The dogs are usually on edge and doing some furious pacing up and down, as someone inside is sick and they know that something is wrong.

Locking the dogs up doesn't seem to help my fear much either. It's the incredible crashing and clawing as the splinters come off the outhouse door to the accompaniment of anguished howls of canine frustration that worry me.

Just as I am bending over the patient I imagine them breaking through the door and two Dobermanns, like Higgy Baby's Zeus and Apollo, leaping onto my back as I palpate Miss Threshbold's spleen.

The reason for my paranoia is that I have, to date, been bitten twice on house calls.

The first was a call at the end of a tiring day to an imposing suburban house. As I walked down the pathway, two small black dogs silently appeared around the corner of the house. I think the two of them must have been planning their strategy for days. I rang the doorbell. A few seconds later the wife of the house opened the door. It was then that they struck. I felt this excruciating pain in my right Achilles tendon and turned to see the pair of them hightailing it around the corner of the house. I was actually unable to exclaim because my tongue had got wedged between my front teeth in surprise.

I limped into the house like a tendon-strung bull, trying to control my anger. This was made worse because the wife addressed me in a voice that implied that I must have provoked them.

'They've never bitten anyone before,' she admonished.

I was starting to choose some descriptive words for her dogs, but became overtaken by self-pity and hopelessness. I examined her daughter's tonsils, standing on one foot and then, having unstuck my tongue, gave some instructions in a lame voice. I then silently left to do some serious psychic bleeding.

The second occasion was a house call I had made many times before and this had obviously lulled me into a false sense of security. I didn't even know they had a dog. Amanda, the 12-year-old daughter, let me in, as her mother was in her customary state of fugue under the bedclothes. I went into a routine where I talk and examine at the same time. Asking some perfunctory questions to which I knew the answers, I started to listen to her chest with my stethoscope. It was then that he bit me and in the same right ankle. He must have been secreted under the bed all the time.

The same excruciating pain gave me such a surprise that I forgot what I was doing. Startled, I came up with a jolt but the bell of my stethoscope caught in her brassière. As the tubing took up the slack I found myself thrown back on top of her by my ear-pieces. It was almost *in flagrante delicto* again.

I started to feel overwhelmed with self-pity again and became petulant and complaining but the fugue had not noticed anything was amiss and was in fact still answering my questions with a long list of complaints.

I cautiously looked under the bed, to be met with a small growling black dog, obviously trained in the same school of perfect timing.

I think I have the answer to dogs and house calls now, following a call I made last week. I have found out that it's not the size that matters, it's the colour.

I was asked to drop in, on my way to work, on a patient who was feeling unwell with flu. The front door was open and her calls from the far end of the house indicated the venue. As I entered the bedroom I saw that she was in bed wearing a diaphanous nightie and twinkling eyelashes.

Unfortunately, on the bed was the dog I dread most, a Manchester bull terrier. It is what the Zulus call the white pig. It was the biggest I'd ever seen and appeared to occupy half the double bed. I believe in my paranoia that when they bite they go into masseteric spasm and hang on for days until the body of the visiting doctor has stopped twitching. It didn't help when she said, 'He's never bitten anyone before, doctor.'

I very slowly sat down on the bed and asked her what the matter was. I had to restart as, at the first attempt to speak, the words came out in a strangely high pitch. The thing never moved and everything seemed to be going well until the examination. As my hand approached her bosom, he started to throw his tonsils around in the back of his throat, somewhat like the sound of distant thunder. The thunder died down when I took my hand back but restarted as soon as I approached again. I could see that his pink eyes had now started to cross and uncross. I was busy assuming that he was judging the distance to my radial artery when she gave him a terrific kick onto the floor and sent him scurrying out of the door. So maybe it's the colour after all and the big white ones are alright, but take my advice and watch out for the small black ones. Their timing is perfect.

From the same work come the following piece, in which Ellis lampoons his favourite characters, the eccentric 'colonials' who live Gilbertian lives inside their personal suburban stockades around Pietermaritzburg, the prim, still rather Victorian, city, which Tom Sharpe parodied so well.

Open Gardens

I am beginning to think that there are more eccentric Englishmen and -women per square foot in Pietermaritzburg than anywhere else in the English-speaking world. I have written about the condition of advanced eccentricity before but we seem to have entered the ridiculous section of life here on planet Earth.

I seem to see patients who come out of the hills of the Drakensberg and have barely touched down in this century. The continually changing climate of four seasons in a day must help loosen one's ties with reality. And who needs reality anyway?

I am fairly used to all this, having looked after ONFs for some time (ONF = Old Natal Family). One OMA (Old Maiden Aunt) of an ONF used to come down from the hills wearing three hats, one on top of the other, to see me. I never had the courage to ask her why she had them stacked up on her head like a pagoda. Probably expecting unseasonable rain. In fact, on further consideration, I think she must have been expecting bad weather because she also wore two flapping raincoats and gumboots. She did, indeed, look very much like a walking clothes'-horse.

Anyway, she had a lot of other business to discuss. She always asked me at each consultation, 'You're from England, aren't you?' and I would reply 'yes' and then she would fix me with a meaningful look and say, 'You do know that my brother knew the British ambassador in Casablanca?'

I'm not sure what effect she expected this statement to have on me. It was almost given out as a challenge that we were both connected to the right sort of people. I would answer each time, as it was a routine exchange, with a deferential 'no' and with, I hope, the right amount of awe at knowing someone with those sorts of connections.

I am glad to say there are plenty more like her still driving around in a carefree manner, obviously born before such tiresome things as indicators were invented, or, for that matter, traffic lights. (I'm sorry, in South Africa that should read 'robots'.)

Our eccentrics have a Saturday afternoon sport here in the Natal Midlands that fits in well with the colonial loss of reality ties. It is called Open Gardens. It is played mainly by ladies, with the odd male in a very secondary role as sweeper–driver.

They are FF events (that stands for Frightfully Floral) because not only are the gardens magnificently bedecked but so are the visiting teams, dressed in floribunda and straw hats, wide brimmed with bands or decorations optional.

There is a general air of peace and tranquillity until one ONF meets another, and then there's a lot of hallooing and jolly greetings among the Hilton rhododendrons.

A real plus for the sport of open gardens is the continuous tea-time. I try and eavesdrop at tea in the conservatory. It does not take much effort because everyone seems to talk as loudly as they can about the British ambassador in Casablanca. This is not really absolutely fabulous country, it is more absolutely splendid with a touch of spiffing and, oh, what a lovely garden.

The other common subject at tea is the gardener, who always seems to have AIDS. This is divulged in quieter tones by the OMAs over the scones and greengage jam and, my dear, he's been with us simply ages.

AIDS seems to be part of the job description for the Natal gardener if you listen in on these conversations. It used to be drink, which has now taken a back seat, although the combination of drink and AIDS will do. I'm not sure on what clinical signs the madams base their diagnostic powers. Fading away during pruning time, perhaps.

While this is all going on, the menfolk are either watching the Natal Sharks on the telly or playing golf at the Maritzburg Country Club, which has now been renamed the Victoria Country Club. This is because the Victoria Club in town was sold and the regimental sergeant-major gave orders to re-form ranks at the country club, for the last stand of Empire and for the last rounds.

The bar is lined with life members swapping stories about their war wounds with their hearing aids switched off. Some of the more senior members (colonels and flag officers) set off early in the mornings before the heat of the day starts. Wide-brimmed straw hats can be seen zigzagging over the fairways and a few happy hours are spent pootling around in the rough and giving parade-ground orders to their caddies.

The time that worries me most is when these chaps get back, almost on their last legs, and get into the shower room. Desiccated colonels appear swaying out of the steam of the shower like shrunken plucked chickens with dripping military moustaches. The eyes are glazed and staring straight ahead in a sort of walking hypotensive coma. The only thing that keeps them going seems to be the thought of the final destination: the bar. Apparently to die before you've got to the bar is considered very bad form and, what is worse, you forfeit your money in the ball pool.

There is something else about all this that worries me. I have recently bought a wide-brimmed straw hat.

The following article is from The Humerus – *the humour section of* diversions *magazine (and later reprinted in* Despatches from the Last Outpost*).*

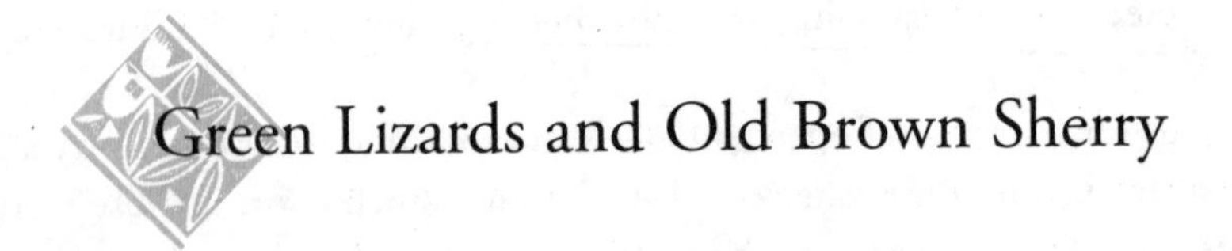

Green Lizards and Old Brown Sherry

I have to get a green lizard today. Apparently one doesn't need a special licence to keep them. It's because we are going up to the cottage in the Drakensberg for the weekend, and a green lizard is the only thing that will work, dad. We've had quite a lot of success with the little Tasmanian Devil but there's a lot of weed in the dam and apparently a green lizard is a large-mouth bass's equivalent of *fillet mignon à la crème* with *chasseur* sauce. So we are off fishing, which is a sport, a patient of mine tells me, for those who are not allowed to drink at home.

Much of the fun of fishing is cruising around in fishing shops, of which there is quite a choice here. Up and down the aisles of rods and between the trays of lures one can acquire a whole new vocabulary without even catching a fish. There's even a small fishing shop to visit on the way up to the Berg. It's at Rawdon's at Nottingham Road and we try and stop for tea. It's a sort of 'must' on our list. It is almost my idea of heaven: carrot cake and lemon meringue pie under the trees. Dennis Thatcher used to say that his idea of heaven was sitting in the garden on a warm summer evening with a glass of chilled champagne and with Margaret in a reasonable frame of mind.

My idea of heaven is tea at Rawdon's, then a wander over to the fishing shop and then a visit next door to The Last Outpost's own brewery to get a litre or two of Whistling Weasel. The brewery is called the Nottingham Road Brewing Company and they brew Whistling Weasel, which is a pale ale, and Tiddly Toad, which is a lager. You can also buy Pickled Pig and Pye-Eye Possum, both of which sound dangerous to know.

It is then off to the cottage for fishing and walking and reading and drinking. And talking. And eating from the *braai*. And plenty of sleeping.

Now there are some rules to fishing in the Last Outpost, and we were discussing some of them in the Country Club last night. Mind you, at the end of the discussion, and the evening, the rules had been adjusted somewhat.

Sea fishing from the beach should, it was decided, involve an early rise with two of the farm lads loading up the bakkie or 4x4. On arrival at the beach there should be a fair amount of manoeuvring to get a good spot and then the chairs are set up on the beach. The lads bait up, walk down to the water's edge, cast out and walk up the beach and hand you the rod. They then get the beers out of the cool box and we start a hard day's exercise. This is preventive medicine at its best with chops and *wors* on the *braai* for lunch. One should try and get the pulse rate up into the 80s, if possible.

Dam fishing, on the other hand, is altogether another game. Before setting out, some planning has to be done. Someone has to go down and buy a bottle of Sedgwick's Old Brown Sherry. And not the small bottle. It has to be the two-litre bottle with the little ring handle at the top. And it should be put in a brown paper bag. This is almost all the extra equipment one needs.

On arrival at the dam, the bakkie should be parked near the water but the fish must not see the sherry. Apparently they instantly go off the bite. It has to be consumed, still in the brown paper packet, sitting up against one of the back wheels of the bakkie. Fishermen can take it in turns to sit and check the level of the sherry. One can have some fairly philosophical thoughts, sitting up against the back wheel of a bakkie, watching the level of the sherry going down.

One such philosophical thought came from Henry David Thoreau, who said 'Many men go fishing all of their lives without knowing that it is not fish they are after.' Now *there's* a man who must have leant up against a few bakkies in his time.

GUS FERGUSON

A GREATLY *undervalued humorist is Gus Ferguson, a Scots-born pharmacist living and practising in Cape Town. He is by world standards a brilliant writer of comic verse (with eight volumes published), and he is known mostly through his whimsical and sometimes hilarious verses about snails.*

We resolved not to touch poetry in this anthology, but confronted with the elegance of Ferguson's rhyming wit, what could we do except break our rules to include him?

Gus Ferguson was educated in Durban and at the University of Cape Town and, as a very athletic sixty-something, is a familiar figure in South Africa's most popular annual marathon cycle race – the Argus – where he has done well in more than 20 annual races.

Among Ferguson's published works is Love amongst the Middle-Aged *(Queillerie, Cape Town, 1997), containing a collection of his Thurber-like cartoons and drawings. He says in its introduction, 'Over the decades I've learned to hide my lack of talent under a bushel ... Fortunately for me, recently bad drawing has evolved into an art style that signifies sincerity and a demotic rejection of privilege.' He quotes a friend of Thurber's, who, having looked over some of Thurber's work, said, 'You know, if you could get good at that, you would be mediocre.'*

Ferguson's poignant haiku, below, is from Stressed–Unstressed *(David Philip, Cape Town, 1978), as are all the verses quoted here, and it is a lament with which most poets will identify.*

Today I took books
To the pulpers but sadly
They don't do poetry.

Elitist

Many poems I have writ
Extolling snails and I admit
I might have rambled on a bit.
But now my conscience tugs,
Would I have done the same for slugs?
They're both molluscans, both pathetic
But the snail is more aesthetic.

Quarry Pond Samsara

i
I come to fish here all the time,
The fish are only five.
I know them, each one, personally
And catch them all alive.

Of course I use fine hooks and bait,
Good line takes the strain:
But since they are inedible
I let them go again.

ii
To eat to suffer is our lot,
It pierces lips and gums
And rips us from our element
Until our saviour comes.

He mercifully slacks the line,
Unhooks and sets us free;
His infinite compassion is
Our sacred mystery.

Sailing Alone around the World

In Cape Town many years ago
There lived a snail called Dallio.
'Though slow as often molluscs are
He yearned and burned to travel far.

He had no kids, he had no wife
And travelled all his live-long life.
His meals he took while on the hoof,
His shell, a backpack and a roof.

He tacked in six years all the way
From Rocklands Beach to Bantry Bay.
Long-suffering, with motives pure,
He learned while living to endure.

Then, on his death his soul was told:
'Obsessive snail, since you were bold,
The doughtiest of all your nation,
Choose a re-incarnation.'

'Ironical,' old Dallio said,
'Alive I had no choice, but dead
An option looms. I'll be a man,
A great explorer if I can,

And circumnavigate the Earth,
Around its plumply massive girth
I'll sail, alone, by night and day
Through wave and wind, through storm and spray

In a solo sloop of wood and oakum.
And can I be called, please, Joshua Slocum?'

Carpe Diem

A goldfish in a goldfish bowl
Surveys the world outside
And feels completely in control
Of everything he spies.

He thinks: 'I'm in my element,
My glass a faithful lens
That shows a foggy firmament
That wobbles and distends.

'An ever-shifting universe
Of ectoplasmic forms
Beyond all known parameters
Of finite fishy norms.

'And yet, this mystic interplay
Does serve me with such love
That I am blessèd every day
With manna from above.'

On the Death of an Old Computer

Ascii to Ascii,
Dos to Dos.

LEONARD FLEMMING

THIS AUSTRALIAN-BORN, *British-educated South African was an archetypal Englishman; a product of his period and of the British Empire at its height. His life and his work exemplify, more than most, how a man may be imprisoned by time – not only in his sense of humour, but in his entire attitude to life. His writing reflects his unquestioning belief in hard work, service, honour, good humour, humility – and the arrogant belief that Britons and even their colonials were superior to all other people.*

His light writing – though not as urbane and whimsical – is reminiscent of Edwardian favourite Jerome K. Jerome. His first book, A Settler's Scribblings, *was published in 1910 and his most popular book,* A Fool on the Veld, *appeared in 1916. But reprints of these came out often over the years, right until the end of World War II, which is about when he died (1946).*

Flemming was born in 1868 and raised on a farm in South Australia, but followed his father, a would-be actor, to London and then Cape Town. After leaving school he served throughout the Anglo-Boer War and afterwards was rewarded with a thousand acres in the Orange Free State. At night he wrote, and his work became known to readers of the London Magazine, *the London* Daily Mail *and publications around the Commonwealth. He was enthusiastically dubbed 'the Mark Twain of South Africa' and lavishly praised by, among others, General Smuts and John Galsworthy (famous author of* The Forsyte Saga, *who thought he would never be as well known as his colonial acquaintance!). The London* Sunday Times *said at the time: 'There is no finer tonic to be found in literature than that which breathes from the pages of Mr Leonard Flemming'.*

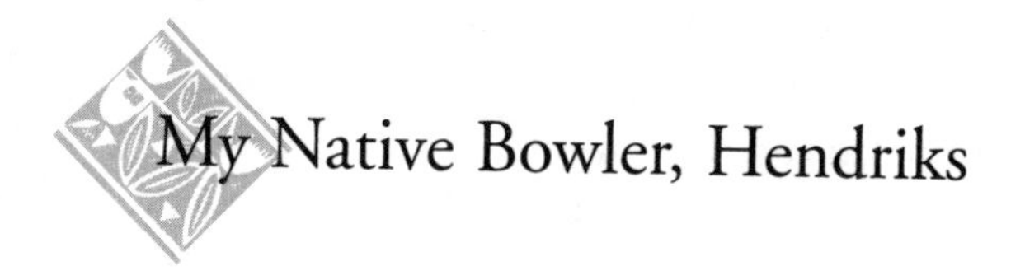

My Native Bowler, Hendriks

When we backvelders have our game of cricket, we get to the field, one may say, straight from the plough.

What cricket is in us we brought to the country years ago from the second or first eleven of our old school in England.

With the handle of a bat in our hands we are a little bit 'out of it'; the plough handle is what we are familiar with, and yet when you get hold of your bat there is some latent instinct lurking away in the background of the memory that prevents one making an absolute fool of oneself. For all that, you feel 'out of it', and when you stand up to face the first delivery from the young enthusiast of a distant *dorp* who has for years attempted to bring to perfection some patent 'googlies', you wish that you had had a little practice before you went in to meet him.

As a great lover of the finest game in the world, it seemed to me more than a little hard luck to go to the wickets in a match – you will only play four or five in the year – and, because the bat is a strange thing in your hands, get out for a 'blob'. This after you have travelled about thirty-odd miles by road, for a game, and dreamed for weeks of making a big score.

So before the season had commenced, and some months previous to the first match I would play in, I decided to work into the daily strenuous round of the farm, twenty minutes' cricket practice.

Let me stand at the wickets, I said to myself, for twenty minutes every day for a month or two, and surely when I play in a match I shall feel very much at home; at any rate, the fact of having to hit at a ball will not terrorise me.

My nearest cricketing enthusiast lives hours from my estate, and it was rather too much to expect to get my daily practice with any help from him.

More than anything I wanted to be bowled at, and bowled at regularly and well, and good bowlers do not grow in profusion on farms in the middle of the Orange Free State.

Poor in bowlers, then, but rich in enthusiasm, I was determined to make an experiment. I have a large staff of trusty and faithful natives, and though I know none of them had ever seen a cricket match, much less handled a bat or ball, I determined to single out the most active of the bunch and get him to throw, or, if he could manage it, bowl at me every day until I felt the old confidence, or supposed confidence, returning to my long-neglected 'cricket muscles' and the little 'cricket cell' of the crowded brain.

His name is Hendriks. When I first broached the subject of him bowling to me his face expanded, a row of very white teeth showed up against a jet black face, and his eyes fairly twinkled with merriment.

He was, at the time, modest enough to say that he did not think he would be able to do what I wanted, and seeing that he had never in his life had a cricket ball in his hands, this unusual modesty scarcely surprised me.

But he was very willing to try, and I was very willing to show him how; so I got the ball and an empty paraffin tin, and took my pupil down to a very hard threshing-floor some fifty yards from the house.

This threshing-floor is surrounded by wire-netting 4 ft high, to keep the fowls and larger stock from eating grain that the floor sees about once in seven years, and it seemed a very useful enclosure now to knock a ball about in.

I put the paraffin tin up, measured out the 22 yards, drew the creases, explained that one foot must be behind the line before the ball leaves the hand

and, as a guide for the native youth, sent down a few overs, more or less on the mark, and told him to 'have a shot at it' himself, just as I had done.

He was rather inclined to throw, which he did well, but he showed ambition and a certain amount of initiative, and when I found him getting somewhat into the 'hang of it', I told him to practise for a few days by himself, and as soon as I thought he was even a little efficient I would don the pads one day and 'have a whack'.

He enjoyed this pastime beyond words, and the next day invited his three-year-old brother and six-year-old sister to stand some way behind the paraffin-tin with a large wool-sack and stop the ball.

Sometimes in my lunch-hour, while I was having my smoke, I could hear the paraffin-tin being bashed about most unmercifully, and occasionally, when I looked out of my window after a particularly lengthy cannonade, I would see the tin turning somersaults, and two tiny ones running hard after a ball that had jumped the netting and whizzed away for some few miles behind.

I began practising on the Sunday. I could have a couple of hours, I thought, and with pads on and bat in my hand, I, for the first time, faced my native bowler.

I had some little difficulty in explaining to him what 'centre and leg' was, and after he had grasped the situation and given it to me, I got him to hold the bat where I had made the mark, and went up to the bowler's end to see how near he had managed to get to 'centre and leg'. I was delighted to find his eye true, and that he had given it to me within a fraction of an inch.

Thinking that it would repay him for his past (and future) efforts, and at the same time make me play carefully, I promised Hendriks three-pence every time he hit the tin with the ball. His pleasure at my proposition was immense, and there was a gleam of expectant fortune in his eye.

I have seen this same gleam in my own race, but never with such pronounced anticipation as on this occasion.

I was making 'the block' a little more distinct with the bat, when I heard a swift whizzing sound, and then with a crash saw the paraffin-tin spinning round some yards from its original position.

To this day, I am sure Hendriks thinks that I have done him out of three-pence, but I mildly suggested that it would be much more satisfactory for us both if he waited until I looked at him before he bowled. Hendriks understood, and waited, and with his first ball knocked the paraffin-tin about one yard and a half away. I think it was the fastest ball I had ever seen in my life – not that I saw very much of it at all, but it came like lightning, a perfect length, and got the tin bang in the centre. I could see that by the dent the ball had made.

It was a most extraordinary half-hour's practice – for me and for Hendriks. I know at the end of it I owed Hendriks three and three-pence. Hendriks had never before earned so much money in such a short space of time – I had never been bowled so often either.

The next day's practice was not quite so remunerative to Hendriks – I began to understand him a little better, but for all that he managed to get the ball past the bat into the paraffin-tin fairly often.

Pay a native well and you'll get any amount of good work out of him; consequently, I was getting, after a few weeks, some of the best bowling I had ever had, and, moreover, at a less extravagant outlay than at first, for, as I say, I began to understand Hendriks and his method better each day. This by no means disheartened him. Rather did it help to make him keener – so keen, in fact, that often when I had to leave the farm, and Hendriks was given a spade to dig the garden with, I would return to find Hendriks still digging the garden, but a paraffin-tin close by with a very different shape to that I had last seen it with, told me that Hendriks had not worked all the time with a spade. And every time I went away I returned to find a paraffin-tin with its shape completely altered – and Hendriks digging hard in the garden.

Hendriks was secretly perfecting other methods of earning three-pences – but never a word did he say about it, nor did he ever let me think that he had any interest in anything but the garden.

For about a fortnight I had no time to practise. Hendriks had, I know, for I was away a good deal, and one Sunday, when I said, 'You can come and bowl at me a bit, Hendriks,' Hendriks merely said, 'Yes, Baas,' aloud, and 'You got bloomin' poor chance,' inwardly.

That Sunday Hendriks bowled me twenty-one times in half an hour. He bowled the most terrific breaks I have ever played against. He bowled leg-breaks, he bowled off-breaks, he bowled 'googlies,' and he 'swerved'. He altered his pace and he altered his action, and altogether he gave me the most astonishing half-hour's cricket any man ever had. The garden may have suffered in that fortnight, but Hendriks had become a marvel.

I haven't told him that there is a big future for him as a cricketer and 'plenty much money' attached to it. He digs my garden well (when I am not away), and is very content with his salary, ten sheep a year, but I know I have got one of the best bowlers in the world.

GORDON FORBES

GORDON LOVELL FORBES, *on the strength of two books published 17 years apart, rates among South Africa's best humorists. He was born in 1934 and raised on a Karoo farm near Burgersdorp, which, most unusually, had a first-class tennis court. Forbes and his three siblings became superb tennis players. Gordon and his sister, Jean (later Jean Drysdale), became Wimbledon stars in the honest-to-goodness days of amateur tennis. Forbes, a tall, gently spoken man, was in the South African Davis Cup team in 1955 and 1963. With his long-term friend Abe Segal, he reached the men's doubles semi-finals at Wimbeldon and played in many other grand slam tournaments.*

Encouraged by his sister Jean, he wrote a book about his years on the tennis circuit and of his hilarious travels with the streetwise, straight-talking Segal. Segal in so many ways was the antithesis of the younger player, yet under Segal's rough, tough exterior there beat a heart of pink marshmallow. He took the nervous teenager under his wing after Forbes was catapulted into international tennis.

Forbes's book A Handful of Summers *(Penguin, London, 1978) came to be published across the world to enormous acclaim.* The Times *said it was 'the funniest tennis book ever written', as did Mark McCormack. It was still being reprinted 20 years later. It was not until 1995 that Forbes brought out his second book, another winner entitled* Too Soon to Panic *(Viking/Penguin, London, 1995). Forbes had a triple bypass in 2000, but three weeks after the operation he was back at Wimbledon – as a spectator, mark you. He rarely misses Wimbledon.*

The following extract from Too Soon to Panic *illustrates his genius when it comes to plausible dialogue.*

When the Bed Fell on Segal

Abe and I, ensconced in the splendour of a suite at the Grand Hotel, Oslo, were rooming together for the first time. I had always been a bit nervous of Abe and had delayed thinking about the possibility of sharing a room with him for as long as possible. But, in Oslo, it was unavoidable. Firmly he picked up my bags, calling over his shoulder, 'Get your ass along here, Forbsey. Seymour is psycho and Vermaak snores.' The die was cast. I gave a nervous start. Here was Abe, fondly thinking that I was a farm boy who slept without stirring. It was only after dinner, and when we were at last inevitably going to bed that I decided to give him some kind of warning. Even then I waited until I was brushing my teeth before I spoke, half-hoping to sound casual, and half-hoping he wouldn't hear.

'Abe,' I said, my mouth full of toothpaste, 'Listen. I, er, sometimes do things in the night.'

'Oh,' he said. 'You do things in the night.' He looked at his reflection in the mirror and said to it: 'He does things in the night. That can't be a problem. I mean, what can a man really do in the night that could be that bad?' He looked at me in a kindly way. 'Don't worry about it, pal. Listen, we all do things in the night. Sometimes.' He looked at me sharply. 'Like what, for instance?'

'I might leap,' I said sheepishly, 'or shout out.' I felt a bit of a fool. 'Sometimes I walk about quietly for a while, or unpack my case. I never know until I've done it.'

'Bullshit,' said Abe. 'You're puttin' me on. Don't give me that kind of crap just when I've got rid of Vermaak and Seymour. I can't be the only guy in this team who's normal!'

I left it at that. After all, I told myself, I didn't do things every night, and I had warned him. And so it was. For three nights I slept like a child. Abe had obviously forgotten my warnings and I began to hope that the mere magnitude of his presence had flushed the evil spirits from out of my nocturnal id. On the Wednesday of that week, the cold snap came, coinciding, as these things often do, with the collapse of the hotel's central heating system. Snow fell, and things became generally below zero. Simultaneously, I was told that I might have to play the singles, if Seymour's flu persisted. My nervous juices, I suppose, began to act up. That night we went to bed shivering in an icy room, creeping under the huge feather quilts with a sigh of relief.

Disaster struck at about midnight. I awoke, I was cold, and convinced that Abe had taken my quilt. 'That bastard,' I thought, with subconscious courage, and proceeded to remove his feather quilt, carefully laying it on my own bed, and going back to sleep. Five minutes later, inevitably, Abe awoke, frozen to a palish blue. Rapidly he searched around, under, over, behind his bed. The quilt had gone. To all intents and purposes, vanished literally into thin air.

'I couldn't figure it out,' said Abe in one of his many explosive subsequent musings. 'Holy shit, I say to myself, I have got to be losin' my mind. Maybe I dreamt that it was a huge marshmallow and ate it! So, I start gettin' nervous and feel my stomach. By now I'm startin' to get stiff. I figure I've got about ten more minutes before I get that stuff called Rigor Mortis.'

I, meanwhile, perfectly comfortable beneath my double layer of feathers, was oblivious to Abe's torment until I was awoken by the light being put on and Abe's voice.

'Forbsey! God all-bloody-mighty. Singles or no singles, this is beyond a joke.

Look at me. It'll take me a week in the sauna to get my blood movin'. They're gonna need a blowtorch to get me out of bed!'

It was a heavy week for me. Although I was spared the opening singles match, the mere thought of it must have set my nerves on edge. The following night I saw a desperate-looking man put his head around our door, produce a hand grenade, pull the pin out with his teeth, count slowly, then roll the smoking thing under Abe's bed. In a flash I'd leapt out of bed and sped to the bathroom where I crouched, holding my ears. Suddenly I remembered that Abe was still in deadly peril. Dashing back into the bedroom I grabbed him by the arm and heaved him out of bed. One is extraordinarily strong at these times.

'Get to the bathroom,' I shouted, 'there's a grenade under your bed!'

In a moment we were both in the bathroom, crouched down, holding our ears and waiting for the holocaust. Nothing happened. Presently Abe looked at me in a strange sort of way.

'Forbsey,' he said releasing his ears, 'what's happening?'

'There was definitely a grenade,' I said, beginning to feel the first stirrings of doubt. 'Under your bed. Absolutely definitely.'

Abe's position of refuge was low down beside the bath, next to the full-length mirror. He turned and regarded his tousled reflection.

'It's me all right,' he mused. 'Definitely me, lyin' next to the bath, holdin' my ears, waitin' for a grenade to go off.' He turned to me and asked in a kindly voice, 'What kind of grenade?'

'Just an ordinary one,' I muttered, feeling a fool, furious with myself, but still under the influence of the nightmare.

'Just an ordinary grenade,' Abe said. 'Not an unusual one.' He gave a shaky snort of laughter. 'Just a run-of-the-mill kind of hand grenade.'

Letting up, he peered round the edge of the door, entered the bedroom and looked under his bed:

'Jesus, Forbsey!' he said, 'I mean, Jesus!' His voice carried a finality beyond exasperation. 'You're not for real. With you, every night's like bein' in a movie. First I think I'm Titus Oates, or that Scott guy, then I'm at Omaha Beach in a shell hole. If this goes on, in a week I'll be the world's only double VC, and clean off my head.'

Forbes provides a useful lesson for would-be writers of humour: keep a diary; record thoughts and conversations – not just the unfolding of events …

Diary Notes: Copenhagen 1955

Now there's this thing about chatting up girls. New sort of art form. Abie's the best at it. The top seed and also impatient as hell. Things have to happen immediately. If it suddenly comes to him that girls are needed, you have to galvanise yourself into action. Broads. If I ask him where to find them he gets scornful.

'Jesus, Forbsey, go out an' make the right noises, buddy, an' they come out of holes in the ground! Listen! You think they don't want a bit of action?' He gives a snort of laughter. 'The world's full of broads, buddy, an' the only time they're not lookin' for a bit of action is after they're dead!' And if I still look dubious he goes off and hunts for both of us. Once he even unearthed girls for the whole team, like a bird dog.

Meanwhile, in his rough way, he's an expert at it. Like in the queue at the airport, waiting to get on the plane. I'm right behind him, and in front of him is this girl – great, with all kinds of eyes and legs. Abie takes one look at her and goes into action. He starts to sniff and sniff, turning his head this way and that. 'God damn,' he says. 'Somebody around here smells like Christmas!' The girl immediately turns, and he pounces. 'Oh, it's you,' he says, 'that figures. I knew it couldn't be the idiot behind me!' And she starts to shake with laughter.

Now if I'd done that, she wouldn't have turned round. I'd have had to keep on sniffing and saying, 'God damn, somebody around here smells like Christmas,' about five times until the security people came and took me away.

Last night, after our meal, we walked in the Town Gardens. They have an amazing stall there, full of white china crockery. You pay a bit of money and get six wooden balls to let fly with. I never missed – an orgy of shattering. I picked off all the teapots with the first six throws. Because of all the practice I'd had throwing stones at things in the Karoo. As I turned to buy more balls, Abie, who was watching, said: 'God Almighty, Forbsey! You just stay here an' keep on crackin' their teapots an' I'll go and nab us a couple of broads.' He was back in a few minutes with Ushi, and I was told to 'keep her while I go find another'. Ushi. Absolutely Scandinavian. She knew about twenty English words to my Danish 'Tak', and although she had a bit of a hook in her nose, she was not bad for a three-minute foray.

We smiled at each other, and six teapots later, Abie reappeared with Heike. Dark-haired, this one. Definitely an older woman. Black sweater, bulging with sharp pointed equipment. 'She's a dancer,' said Abie, explaining everything. 'Great legs, Forbsey. With legs like hers you don't need arms!'

He was carried away by his success and was raving on a bit.

An important tool of the humorist is understatement. Readers do not laugh at one's words so much as at the images they themselves are forming in their own minds. One simply has to set them off.

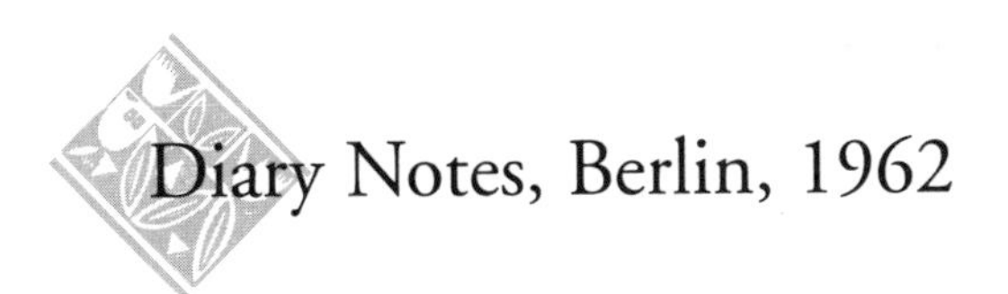

Diary Notes, Berlin, 1962

It's a Monday and we're at the Rott-Weiss Tennis Club in Berlin. Davis Cup vs the Germans. The place smells of coffee and cigars. Abie wears his raincoat all the time as though he's one of Smiley's People. He'd love to be a spy except he doesn't know exactly who to spy on. Drysdale keeps disappearing in search of women, and neither seems concerned that I am still in shock after nearly losing the deciding match against the French.

We have the centre court at twelve for practice, and as we arrive the German team is just coming off, relaxed and laughing as though they have already won the match. Bungert, Kuhnke and Buding and about twenty coaches carrying water jugs.

'Not the world's worst team,' I say. Davis Cup nerves sometimes make me gloomy.

'Bunch of wankers,' says Abie.

He gives the trumpet blasts, but it is Drysdale and I who have to play the singles. *We* have only *one* coach, who also acts as manager, travel agent, doctor, physio, psychiatrist, ball boy, etc. Claude Lister of Bathgate Road, Wimbledon SW19, cheerful, courageous and British to the core – which is just as well. Stability is what we need.

We started out with drills, all three of us, then Drysdale collapsed in the shade and had to have milk to drink, which means that he's been doing things in the night. So Abe and I played singles, and it turned into one of those days. Heavy, humid and windy. The balls felt like lead and two of them fluffed up so much that Abie threw them at Claude and told him to get others as we weren't playing 'friggin' badminton'. I had no centre to my racket, thus no touch, thus waves of irritation and bad behaviour. Also, there are these poplar trees behind the courts that give off fluffy seeds.

'Friggin' things float about like they own the place!' says Abie. 'A man goes up for a smash and ends up hittin' a floater …'

'Come on, chaps,' says Claude. 'Everything's going to be all right.'

When Abie won the set I threw my racket at the fence, which, at that precise moment, seemed to be a reasonable thing to do. Because it was *that* kind of a day, the racket hit a pole and fell to pieces.

'Crap-almighty, Forbsey!' said Abie. He came over to my side and took me by the shoulders.

'Listen,' he said. 'What day is today?'

'Monday.'

'Right,' he said. 'Monday. The match starts Friday.'

'So what?' I said.

'So it's too soon to panic,' he said. 'Just be with me. I'll tell you *exactly* when to panic.' And somehow after that I began to play better.

Tuesday: Better balls and more strings in my racket. Even *more* seeds today. 'It's the mating season for trees,' says Abie. After we practised, he announced that he wanted to see the Berlin Wall.

'You want to hit against it?' Drysdale wanted to know.

'Take him away,' Abie said to Claude. 'Put him in his cage and feed him.'

Abie regards Cliffie as a minor and usually talks to him via someone else. If Cliffie said, 'You want to hit some balls at three?' Abie will say to me: 'Tell him I only play with juniors in the mornings.' Meanwhile Cliff is getting tougher and tougher to beat, and Abie knows it.

Wednesday: Lost a practice set to Drysdale. Then Drysdale lost to Segal. Then Segal lost to me. 'That means that you're *all* in good form?' said Claude Lister, although I'm not sure how he works *that* out. My forehand is still playing up. Abie says it's still too soon to panic (and *still* the seeds come down).

Thursday: Beat Drysdale. *Killed* Segal, 6–2. ('Frig you, Forbsey,' he said. 'You're supposed to be crappin' yourself, remember?') My whole game has come back by some miracle – a huge turn-around. But can it *last*? ('Of course it can,' says Claude, but how does *he* know?)

Friday: We're bitterly disappointed. 'Now I've seen everything!' was all that Abie said. Drysdale leads two sets to love against Buding and loses in the fifth. I lead 4–3, 40–30 in the fifth against Bungert and lose. Too cautious. A precious point that could have changed everything. Claude says we put up a jolly good show. 'They had the run of play on the day,' he says. Meanwhile we're down two to nothing, with three to go. A miracle is needed, and miracles are in short supply.

Saturday: The doubles. Abie and me against Bungert and Kuhnke. In the locker room Abie adopts his philosophical attitude. 'What can I tell you, Forbsey?' he says. 'A man can only do what he can do,' but I'm as scratchy as the devil. A strange mood. I'm prepared to try my guts out, except I don't feel a win in the air. Later, just before we walk on court, he stops me and grips my shoulders, again.

'Listen, Forbsey,' he says. 'Listen. So what's the worst thing that can happen today? What's the worst, most crap-defyin', shit-forsaken thing that can *possibly* happen to us? We could lose the match, right?'

'Right,' I mutter.

'So we've lost matches before, right?' he asks.

'Right.'

'So we'll have a glass of beer,' he says. 'It's not like they don't make beer in Germany, is it? And we won't actually get the death sentence, will we?' And he lets go of my shoulders and picks up his racquets and walks off.

Play starts at three. The court is packed with spectators come to witness our demise. By quarter to six it's two sets all. A saga.

'Like the book that Russian guy wrote,' mutters Abie at changeover, when we're standing next to the umpire's seat, towelling off. 'Who was that Russian guy again, Forbsey?'

'Tolstoy,' I reply, a bit absently.

'Right, Tolstoy,' he says.

The fifth set goes on dead even, at 4–3 for us. On Bungert's service, out of the blue we find ourselves with a break-point at 40–30, same situation as in my singles. I'm on the left court and I realise that I have to make a return, and what flashes through my head is the return I made in the singles that was too careful. So I walk in a bit of a circle, hoping for a mental glimpse of something more attacking while the crowd quietens down.

Bungert gets ready to serve and the court goes dead quiet. As he's about to serve, Abie holds up his hand and stops play. Bungert waits, and Abie walks over to me and puts his lips right next to my ear.

'OK, idiot,' he says, 'panic *now!*' and in spite of everything I have to laugh.

The Germans think we've got some terrific play figured out, so that when my return goes down the middle they're busy watching the lines.

'Game, South Africa,' says the umpire.

In later life Forbes wrote from time to time for various journals in South Africa – it was more of a hobby than an attempt to make a living from writing. This thoughtful piece was published in the Rand Daily Mail *in 1980. It was a particularly miserable time in South Africa's history. John Vorster had lied in Parliament and was forced to resign as State President and an unsmiling P.W. Botha had taken over. As cracks appeared in the Nationalists' granite façade, black organisations – deemed illegal by the government – became emboldened and the secret police began a counter-reign of terror. The country's liberals felt powerless and South Africans looked to the future with foreboding. Forbes reflects the mood and the ironies in his short story* The Three Ronnies …

The Three Ronnies

If you take the Durban highway and turn right at Villiers you go southward, across the soft plains of the Eastern Free State, until you get to Bethlehem, where the mountains begin. Then, if you have some time and like to wander you can detour through the scenery via Clarens and the Golden Gate before arriving at Ficksburg. From there it is fairly plain sailing until you get to about Zastron, where you will find a change in the mood of the country. It gets drier, and seems older and, somehow, more lonely. At Aliwal North you cross the Orange River and turn right on the Burgersdorp road. The winter scenes unfold like watercolours, solitary landscapes of washed beiges, browns and slate; sharp horizons, shallow ribs of cloud, climbing gradually to the cool winter blue.

It's a moody and marvellous road, nearly all the way. Finally you reach what John Buchan called 'The Old Country', a veld of rocky hills and koppies – sparser grass with the resinous broom brushes and grey 'rapijs'. Here the Boers rode about like mad while the British built stone blockhouses and made numerous bivouacs. This is the land of the Lee-Metford, the blesbok, the merino sheep and the farms with their lines of bluegum and poplar, with willows near the dams. Syferfontein, Soetwater, Mooivlei, Kommandantskop – and sometimes, marvellously different, an Ellismere, or a Craigievar, or simply a gate in the endless roadside fence with a signpost that says 'Success'.

Our old farm is called Dunkeld. It is near the town called Burgersdorp, and it is the reason we have made this journey. By the time we arrive it is sunset – a short, crisp dusk changing quickly to the winter night, which will settle down and lock the landscape in what my brother Jack has always called 'a dark and icy grip'. Ever since our lonely childhood on this old farm, my brother tends to get a bit carried away in midwinter.

We get out of the dusty car and suddenly it is back to the past – the log fire, the gun racks; pine floors and old leather; a piping dinner of soup and roast lamb and the red wine which I always bring – all by now tradition. After supper we will sit around the fire as we always used to do as children, remembering the endless evenings with books, conversations, games of cards or chess or playing the same old records on the gramophone. I from the city, Jack from the farm. All the old questions – rain, the price of wool, the whites, the blacks, the state of the nation. What will become of us, what is to be done?

Down here, it seems they are all simply waiting.

Waiting for what?

'Man, just waiting, I suppose. Waiting to see.' We shake our heads and stare at the fire.

'I've got something for you!' Jack says suddenly with a twinkle in his eye. 'Something nice and symbolic for that damn diary of yours. Give the whole damned lot of them something to think about!' He pauses, gives a short laugh, then adds: 'A sort of third dimension to our favourite problem.'

Now more logs must be put on the fire and a little more brandy applied.

'Your old friend, Ronnie Roberts,' says Jack. 'It's all his doing. His youngest son is now five. He's also called Ronnie – did I ever tell you? I'm sure I did. Anyway, you should stay more in touch.'

He kicked at the fire and unwrapped a caramel toffee, peering through his brandy at the light.

Ronnie had indeed been my closest friend for quite a few years, while we were young and wondering whether to be farmers. He had become one and I had gone off to other worlds, and now we had all but lost touch. Ronnie had married young and they had had five children in four years.

'A Catholic girl,' my mother always used to say with gentle emphasis. The eldest boy was called after his father, and to distinguish between father and son, and because Afrikaans is so much a part of farm life in Burgersdorp, the son became 'Klein Ronnie'. Virtually simultaneously, Ronnie's most senior farm 'boy' also had a son, whom he called Ronnie in honour of the Boss.

With further confusion in the offing, the little black boy became 'Swart Ronnie' and for a while everything went very well.

Here Jack paused for a moment, and I sensed a new development coming up. 'One day,' he went on, 'the Ronnies captured a day-old baboon baby whose mother had been shot in a hunt. Quite a commotion, I might add, what with the troop roaring and barking and so forth, and more shots going off. Anyway, the boys took the baby baboon home and in a burst of affection they called it "Ronnie" as well. So it became "Bobbejaan Ronnie," and is mostly just BR because the Ronnies are always in a hurry.' He stopped, and when he resumed he was in the present tense.

'You mean to say they've still got him?' I asked.

'Absolutely,' said Jack. 'The three Ronnies are inseparable. They swim, eat and even bath together – that is, if Sheila [Ronnie's wife] doesn't catch them at it. Bobbejaan Ronnie sleeps on Klein Ronnie's bed, but sits on Swart Ronnie's knee while he has his lessons with Klein Ronnie. He even seems quite interested. Of course he can't quite cope with the arithmetic yet, but he's only about two. Give him time. As it is, they've all got their strong points. Klein Ronnie is best at tennis and Swart Ronnie kicks soccer balls all over the farm, but neither can hold a candle to BR when it comes to mountaineering and tree climbing. They're trying to teach him to get eggs out of birds' nests in high trees, but so far he usually eats them on the way down the tree. Stupid animal.'

He pauses thoughtfully again for a while.

'Oh, and they all love taking swigs of Ronnie's beer,' Jack is saying, 'but Bobbejaan Ronnie can't hold his liquor. After only a mouthful or two, he tries to leap from chair to chair, but often misses!'

Another chuckle. It is one of those priceless moments which you hope lasts forever. Jack is busy remembering more things. For example, Father Ronnie dare not punish Klein Ronnie, without having his ankles bitten, but Bobbejaan Ronnie appears to have no objection to the odd cuff being handed out to Swart Ronnie!

'A whole new kind of discrimination!' he says. 'How will we ever cope?'

I listen delightedly, as he talks, while all the time odd thoughts keep flashing through my head. Will we, for instance, be needing yet another homeland in South Africa? And if so, is this not perhaps an opportunity to get rid of some of our steeper and more stony regions? And supposing Bobbejaan Ronnie turns out to be a world-champion high jumper or fantastic at pole-vaulting, can he leap for his country? Can he become a Springbok? And, if so, can he wear the magic blazer? My word, what a puzzle!

But the best is yet to come and Jack knows it. 'The other day,' he says, 'they all three went with Ronnie to deliver the cream cans to the passenger [railway] station because the cream has to get to Queenstown before it goes off. Too sour, that is. Anyway, at the station, Klein Ronnie decides he has to go to the toilet, so he sets off with BR on his shoulders. Then Swart Ronnie decides he also has to go, so he follows. Klein Ronnie and BR are allowed into the "whites only" toilets but when Swart Ronnie tries to follow, the stationmaster stops him and points towards the *other* toilets. Now what do you make of that?'

'It's a real puzzle,' I said.

'A proper mystery,' Jack agreed.

'But where will it all lead?' we ask ourselves.

'We'll simply have to wait and see,' says Jack.

(Rand Daily Mail, 1980)

Lovers of the Long Shot

'It's very pleasant to dine with a bachelor,' said Miss Mattie softly,
'I only hope that it is not improper. So many pleasant things are.'
– Sylvia's Lovers (1863)

While the bachelor population of the northern suburbs ebbs and flows ('mostly it ebbs', a bachelor girl told me the other day) there is a handful of eligible chaps whom I suppose one could call 'professional' bachelors. They work at staying single, seem to enjoy their state, and with just a hint of superiority smile down upon those of their friends who, as one of them put it, 'toil in the chains of matrimony'.

They never seem to toil – in spite of the fact that remaining a bachelor, they say, is not easy. All the currents of life nudge them towards the shores of matrimony. In order to stay single, they have to be permanently on guard; and become expert not only at ending relationships, but at knowing *when* they must be ended. Lovers who seem on the verge of penetrating their independence must regretfully be ditched.

'Relationships are like yoghurt,' one of them told me recently. 'They should be date stamped "Best before end of June," or something like that.'

The ditching process can, they say, be very sad. But the pain is usually eased by the start of the next liaison, which, if it is successful, will bring its own seasons of novelty, excitement, rapture and then, finally, demise, and the next bout of pain, and so forth. A sort of cyclical agony and ecstasy!

They are a cool group, these bachelors. They become mature rather than middle-aged; interesting rather than worn out; purposeful rather than finicky; and they live in pads rather than in other forms of accommodation. And in spite of their lofty 'I can take it or leave it' attitudes, they are nearly always on the lookout for pretty women: new stock; fresh mice; exciting jumps; game birds; or, in fact, any new ports in the storms blown up by new romances.

In the long term, though, they yearn for a truly fine romance – something so rare and true, so far removed from anything plebeian, so one-in-a-million that it exists only in their imaginations; yet presents, none-the-less, the perfect quest. Their lives, they say, are unencumbered. They are free to move and frequently talk of 'jaunts' – excursions to such places as The Winkler, the Swamps, Clifton, Gstaad, Las Vegas, San Tropez or Wimbledon. The term 'first class' is often let slip. Although sometimes free for lunch on Sundays or supper on Tuesdays, they keep their options open, hinting at a rendezvous – of picking up someone 'after her show' or 'when her plane gets in'. They must constantly be on the alert for anything major.

It is difficult for us encumbered people with wives, families, etc. not to be wistful in the face of such visible independence. 'Just how exciting is it all?' we ask ourselves. 'Do they really do all that? And are the women always there, with their little overnight bags, their secret smiles, their savage scents and sophisticated shoes?'

I sat recently by the side of the Umhlanga Rocks sea in the company of one of my bachelor friends. It was one of those perfect seashore days – brilliant sky, light breezes and the waves just turning over. Gulls, dolphins, etc. The Natal coast, at its best, is nearly unbeatable. We were on a jaunt. Not quite Gstaad, but a definite jaunt none-the-less, complete with sleepers on the Trans-Natal and new bathing suits. My friend was, for the time being, alone – meaning that he had not brought with him an in-house companion, but instead had opted for the nod of the gods who deal in chance meetings. This was a jaunt where the long shot, that most elusive but, when achieved, most priceless of all romantic encounters, was to be give its opportunity. Deep in the mind of every professional bachelor lies the yearning to come upon, by some amazing twist of fate, the ultimate soul mate. At dawn perhaps, by the water's edge, disillusioned by a hundred empty affairs; or late at night in a small café, alone, reading; or simply walking on some windy shoreline, with blown hair and moody eyes. And beautiful, always beautiful. A succession of troubled and misunderstood Julie Christies. Heavens alive! In the mind lie waiting a hundred possibilities.

The first sightings; the distant scrutinies; the meeting of eyes; the instinctive recognition of another heart, also empty, also with open options. Pieces falling into place. Names murmured above sea sounds. Names with the ring of forever. Samantha Ogilvy. Andrea Sykes. Inclinations revealed – and when revealed, found to coincide. Mahler. Salinger. The prose of Oscar Wilde. Two people, for once not passing in the night, but stumbling upon one another. The touch of hands. Long, artistic fingers, thought-provoking … The meeting of minds!

There are few things more hankered after by these timeworn fellows than the truly successful long shot.

So far on this weekend, however, not only had no long shots found their marks, targets had not even been sighted. My friend's romantic horizons were totally uncluttered, his inclinations mocked by the brilliant skies and by the empty chair beside him. And on the third day of a five-day jaunt, I detected a sour note in his musings.

'Umhlanga,' he said pulling a face into his drink. 'A desert in the world of romance. Barren soil if ever I saw it.' He cocked an eye at my wife dozing by the poolside. 'You don't realise how lucky you are,' he said.

'Be just!' I replied. 'You above all people should know by now that the price of flirting with the possibilities of a wild romantic storm is that you may well become stranded without finding a suitable port.'

'Well,' he said drily, 'such is the intensity of this storm that at present any port will do!'

At that moment, as if God-sent, a lady approached. Her face was carefully arranged and she was dressed in a beach outfit, through a slit in the skirt of which a slender thigh emerged. Selecting a suitable spot close to where we sat, she shook out a large beach towel, arranged herself upon it, applied oil to her limbs, and then, with studied rapture, turned her face toward the sun.

'There', I said carefully, 'is a possible anchorage.'

'For how many years', said my friend, 'do you suppose it has harboured ships?'

'About 38,' I said.

'Many ships?' he enquired.

'Perhaps,' I said, 'but older ports are often more interesting than new ones.'

Just then our 'port', as if aware of our attentions, directed at my friend a hooded look which for a long moment met his eyes.

'My storm', he murmured, 'is getting worse. I need refuge. Shall I ask it to lunch?'

'That seems a good plan,' I said. They were busy with a barbecue by the pool and I tried to imagine those carefully painted lips closing around a large sausage.

'I shall approach her boldly,' said my friend 'and say – "are you hungry?"'

'That might work,' I said.

He took a deep breath. As he rose to his feet a large brown man and two children ran out of the surf and threw themselves down upon the sand beside our harbour. We looked at one another.

'So much for that long shot,' I said.

But the eyes of my friend had already narrowed and I followed his gaze. In the distance a girl approached. She was accompanied by a large shaggy dog. She wandered rather than walked, and often paused to look seawards while the breeze lifted her silver-blonde hair.

From Laughing Through the Turmoil *(Johannesburg, 1990)*

HERE IS *an author of a new and rare breed: one of those modern journalists who is known for his creative writing and also respected for his insight into the application of hi-tech communication technology in business. There certainly aren't too many around. Arthur Goldstuck, who lives with his young family to the north of Johannesburg, has a light pen, plus expertise in information and communications technology (ICT). He lectures at universities and other institutions on the role of new technologies in business strategy.*

He wrote The Hitchhiker's Guide to the Internet *in the 1980s (a definitive guide to the Internet in South Africa) as well as* The Art of Business on the Internet. *In the 1990s he compiled* Never Play Leapfrog with a Unicorn *and* Money Talks but Mine Just Says Goodbye *(both being collections of bumper sticker and T-shirt sayings) and he collaborated with cartoonist Rico of* Madam & Eve *on a satirical post-apartheid work* Going, Going, Gone. *Goldstuck has written four books on South African urban legends, including* The Rabbit in the Thorn Tree *and* The Leopard in the Luggage.

As a humour writer Goldstuck was at his most creative as a postgraduate in the 1980s, from which period the first article is taken. Times have changed so quickly that the questions he poses in this satirical 1980s quiz create almost a nostalgia for those crazy times. (Quiz: Who remembers the bumbling Chris Heunis? The very reverend Allan Hendrickse? Or the exchange rate when the rand was worth one-and-a-third US dollars?) In reality, Goldstuck's student days were tense times when many organisations and political parties were banned, Nelson Mandela was still imprisoned and the press was under restriction.

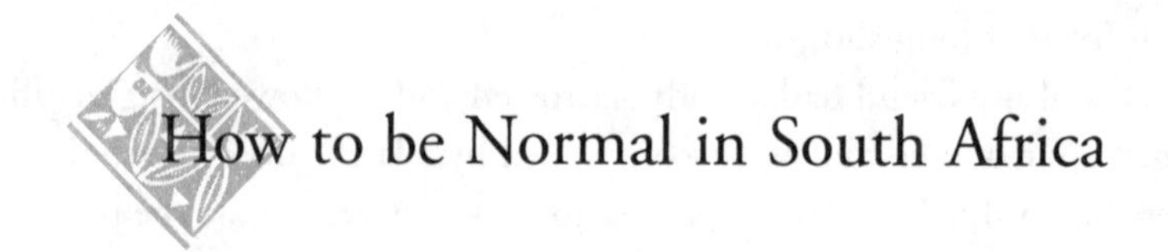

How to be Normal in South Africa

The concept of normality has become so warped in this country that it is the unusual, the bizarre, and Eugène Terre'Blanche which are regarded as normal.

It all goes back to 1652, when a well-known vegetable farmer, Jan van Riebeeck, established South Africa's first refreshment station at the Cape. He charged exorbitant prices to foreigners, so that even today it is normal for Cape Town restaurants to overcharge visiting holidaymakers.

Meanwhile, along came the Dutch burghers, the French Huguenots and the British Settlers. Without exception, they complained about the hired help, the government and the weather. This led to such historic events as the Great Trek, the Anglo-Boer War and Plettenberg Bay. And today, it is still regarded as normal, when the going gets tough, to emigrate, or to start a war, or to buy a holiday home with money you don't have.

Normality took a great step backward in 1948, when the newly elected National Party Government announced that black was no longer a normal colour, and had to be kept in quarantine in case it corrupted other colours. This went hand in hand with the Separate Representation of Normality Act and the Suppression of Normality Act, both of which have left South Africa's sense of normality well and truly warped.

The effect, 40 years later, has been that there is no specific normality that is normal throughout the country. Every area or city interprets normality differently. For instance, in Pretoria everyone wears a moustache. While this would be regarded in Cape Town as a sign of strangeness or of a policeman or even a boxing champion, it is perfectly normal in Pretoria.

In Bloemfontein, it is normal to be brain-dead. Those who are abnormal there, and can actually think, flee to Johannesburg. Here, everyone is on Valium, cocaine, or on good terms with a stockbroker. Those who can't accept this awful reality skip to Durban, where they quickly learn to cope with large cockroaches and vicious curries.

There are a few aspects of normality that do apply to all of South Africa.

For instance, 40 years ago, only half the population wore shoes. Today, half the population eats shoes. Further, most South Africans share an irrational fear that the hideous people they swapped addresses with on holiday will actually turn up. This is also normal.

Obviously, then, this normality business can get pretty confusing. So, to help you decide whether you can take your normal place in society, we provide this handy quiz. Please attempt to answer all the questions before checking your score.

Being South African means:
– Never having to stand in line for a Russian visa
– Never having to buy cheap goods overseas (with the exchange rate and all)
– Never having to say you're sorry

Growing up is the most traumatic time of a South African's life because:
– You're not allowed to think about sex
– You're not allowed to think about politics
– You're not allowed to think

When the going gets tough the tough ...
– Get going
– Go shopping
– Go to Australia

When travelling overseas and someone asks you where you're from, you say:
– 'Please don't hit me'
– 'You treat your minorities far worse!'
– 'Kenya'

Normal South Africans have a deep understanding of their politics. Prove your normality by selecting the correct statements (tick three):
– The Government knows what it is doing
– Chris Heunis understands his own speeches
– Chief Buthelezi is to modesty what Isaac Newton was to gravity

Does your pulse rate speed up when you are:
– Lying down?
– Lying down underneath someone?
– Lying in Parliament?

Do you prefer your sexual activity ...
– On a desk in the office?
– On the kitchen table?
– On your own?

Your favourite reading is:
– Wilbur Smith
– The *Sunday Times* back page
– The Personal Services in *The Star* classified

What is your most important source of calories?
– Boerewors
– Provita
– Fingernails

What is your favourite hobby?
– Shopping
– Getting a tan
– Getting arrested

What is your favourite weaponry?
– Something large enough to make an obvious bulge under the armpit
– Something small to slip through supermarket security checks in your purse
– A bodyguard equipped with both

In rush-hour, bumper-to-bumper, snail's pace traffic, do you:
– Make new friends
– Make new enemies
– Shoot people who cut in front of you

Your hear of another coup in the homelands. Do you:
– Load a truck with emergency supplies and drive through the night to assist refugees?
– Fall asleep from sheer boredom?
– Blame it on the Press?

Do you think Allan Hendrickse ...
– could be our next State President?
– would make a super lifeguard?
– would have a decent shave?

The Pope announces a visit to South Africa. Do you:
– Boycott the church?
– Bid for the souvenir franchise?
– Invest in anti-Popemobile landmines?

You're invited to talk to the ANC. Do you:
– Demand immunity from a customs check?
– Demand protection of yuppie rights?
– Demand to see your return tickets?

You've cut down on travel because:
– Air flight isn't safe any more
– Airline food isn't safe any more
– Customs checks aren't safe any more

Which of these is correct? (tick one):
– Everything I see on TV is true
– Everything I read in the newspapers is a lie
– Pik Botha has the most sincere moustache on television

When newspapers quote you as 'a resident who asked not to be named', is it:
– For fear of reprisals?
– For fear of being asked to lead a new political party?
– For fear?

HOW DID YOU SCORE?
(1) I skipped the questions and came directly to the scores.
You are a normal South African, i.e., you are impatient, disobedient, and too lazy to even read through 20 simple questions. We have ways and means of making you obey instructions …

(2) I scored by underlining the answers in ink pen.
You are a normal South African, i.e., you are selfish, destructive and exhibitionist. At the drop of a pen, you are willing to deface an expensive product, just to make sure no one else can use it again. Even worse, you do not hesitate to stamp your identity on everything you touch, just in case someone fails to notice your existence.

(3) I scored on a separate piece of paper, which I immediately threw away.
You are a normal South African, i.e., you are shy, introverted, and easily embarrassed by any display of being alive. You probably apologise to civil servants sitting behind counters when you disturb their sleep and you have nightmares about being mauled by a Maltese poodle.

(4) I was able to answer at least one question.
You are a normal South African. Not only are you bigoted, gullible, guilt-ridden and in big trouble, but you are willing to tell total strangers the most intimate details of your sexual hangups, your political misdemeanours and your strange feelings for small, furry animals.
(Style magazine, 1988)

The story below, written twenty years later in the new era, provides a very different kind of quiz and shows a different style, more sophisticated and more elegant. Goldstuck's co-author in the second article, Dr Jeff Zerbst, was one of South Afrcia's most unusual horseracing columnists. He posed as Thomas Equinus, a defrocked priest leading a life of debauchery. He wrote a successful play, and in the short-lived satirical magazine Laughing Stock, *he wrote 'The Diary of Piet Retief' (the Boer pioneer leader slaughtered by the Zulus) – a parody of the Voortrekkers, which led to death threats from right-wing Afrikaners. Zerbst has a doctorate in theology (his thesis was on comparative religion) and now lives in Australia.*

Mind Games: The True Confessions of a Mental Mutant

Ever since a cigarette stain changed the number on his IQ bar from 230 to 280, 'Spiro the Whiz' Archimedes has become a pain in the lobe. Now, inevitably, he is at my elbow in the pub.

All of 1.2-metres high, bald all the way from the back of his neck over his crimson cranium and down to his eyebrows, he wears large black-rimmed spectacles. A Mensa 5-star Order of Merit bar glitters on his lapel.

The Oscar Wilde Boar and Brain Ladies Bar falls silent as Spiro downs an ouzo and shouts: 'I've heard you're pretty good, kid, but are you ready for a 280?'

Several people gasp and drop their calculators. A kid in the corner, about to checkmate a genius-level chess computer, sighs and faints.

'Best of three,' I retort arrogantly, and do a quick warm-up by using trigonometry to calculate the angle of a roof beam.

Spiro whistles nervously while he concentrates on his ouzo, obviously engaged in a complex profit margin calculation.

Our audience can see that we're engaged in brilliant cogitations and breaks into applause every time one of us leaps up and shouts, 'Of course! Ha, ha! I have it now. QED.'

But things move fast in the Boar and Brain. The barman and referee, Jimmy 'The Schnoz' Durante, calls 'Time, Gentlemen'.

He produces Eysenck's *Limbering Up for Intellectual Giants, Volume 17: Number Games* from under the counter. With a quick flick of the wrist he opens the book on problem 186.

A very basic sequence problem:

'Insert the missing number: 7 49 441 __'

I see it in a flash. Multiply 7 x 7 to get 49, multiply 49 x 9 to get 441. Therefore, multiply each number by its last digit.

I shout out 'Four forty one' before Spiro has translated the integers from Greek.

The crowd goes mad. Three skinhead intellectuals go into a frenzy and scrawl the 173-times table on each other's craniums.

Silence falls as the Schnoz flips the pages once more. Question 79. Another easy one: 'Find the odd one out: SIR MAN FIG TON HOG.'

Inexplicably I waste 0.75 of a second mulling over the meaning of the words instead of analysing the relationship between the letters. As suddenly as I see the solution, Spiro's foreign accent shatters the intellectual silence: 'TON! Ha, ha! I have it now, QED.' He does too – in every other word the consonants are next to each other in the alphabet.

One all. Spiro has the psychological advantage. I'm sweating. The skinheads are beating up a professor of physics who has been unable to calculate on demand the maximum velocity of a Harley-Davidson on a macadam surface at sea level.

Never before has my reputation been so terrifyingly at stake. I quickly estimate getaway routes at premium velocities in case of defeat. The Boar and Brain does not suffer defeated genius easily. Last month a scatterbrained doctor of quantum mechanics was drowned in a vat of rum for being unable to resolve Zeno's paradoxes or spell his own name. I know the feeling.

Terror envelops my psyche as the Schnoz produces the final question. It is problem 56:

Driver = 7

Pedestrian = 11

Accident =

Spiro's eyebrows cross. I realise he is assigning numerical values to the letters. Desperately I take another route, counting the letters instead – the discredited high school novice path, but it sometimes pays off. Dimly I note the alarm on Spiro's face as he realises his terrible mistake.

Voila! Each number equals the number of letters plus 1. Its very simplicity is the catch!

'Nine!!!' I scream.

The Schnoz nods and Spiro Archimedes runs for the door.

Too late. He's miscalculated the shortest route and runs straight into a skinhead with a Ph.D. in Torture Implements of the Spanish Inquisition. As I down my first celebratory glass of champagne I hear Spiro screaming in the toilets. An isosceles triangle is being inscribed on his midriff with a blowtorch.

Two hours later, drunk with success and champagne, my intelligence and common sense almost nullified, I try walking home.

Before I know where I am, I've strayed onto foreign turf. I am standing outside the yumpby (young upwardly-mental prodigy brats) hangout, the Cerebral Steakhouse.

And how am I supposed to know the dreaded Mensa Rebel Alliance is having their merger talks with the Mensa 200 IQ-plus Separatist Fringe inside? Next thing I know, I'm surrounded by a dozen skinny runts drinking milkshakes and wearing the trademark of the rebels: Woody Allen spectacles and Einstein wigs.

With a shiver of shock I see the cranium-and-crossbones medallion hanging from their leader's neck. It is Freddy 'The Egg' Wittgenstein. Cruellest mind in town.

'Think you're a regular old bard's brain, don't you?' he squeaks with a sneer.

His 9-year-old lieutenant, Donovan 'The Leech' Heisenberg, dashes forward and chants right in my face: 'He's got muscles for neurons, muscles for neurons.' He jumps back to the protection of his pals without spilling a drop of his double-thick malted chocolate.

I know their kind. I spread my legs and stab my finger in the air in the classic Philosophers' Stand.

Two or three of the gang shift uneasily on their feet. Another takes an involuntary step backward. You can cut the tension in the air with Occam's razor.

'It was the best of times, it was the worst of ...' I begin. A snort from 'The Egg' stops me dead.

'Effing 19th-century social fetishist,' he sneers.

'Yeah!' one of his cronies spits. 'Pre-modern effing moral propagandist!'

Damn. I hadn't taken them for intellectual retro-modernists.

Quick as a back-flash, I hit them with the essential contradiction in Anselm's ontological argument for the existence of God.

'The Egg' opens his mouth, then closes it again, speechless. I step forward, wagging my finger.

'That's only the Kantian critique,' I thrust out. 'Wait till I give you Russell's linguistic analysis!'

As the gang starts shifting backwards, one of them makes a last-ditch comeback.

'Sturgeon's law! 90 per cent of everything is crap!' he shouts desperately.

You always get the odd street-fighter in these gangs. No cognisance of empirical evidence. No respect for sophistry.

Now, I may walk with mental giants, but I can still rough it up with the worst of them ... I bark back: 'Dicks's corollary! Anything you can imagine must effing well be real.'

At that, they turn on their heels and run.

Intoxicated with success, I realise I am near the Grey Cell-A-Go-Go, and I decide to put myself to the ultimate test. There is someone there I'd been cogitating on for a while.

I walk to the door, solve the elementary conundrum the bouncer spits at me, and enter.

She is sitting alone in the corner, watching herself in the wall mirror and calculating the diffraction factor caused by the tilt in the ceiling fluorescence. She has a beautiful mind and a mainframe to match.

I sidle up to her. The Mensa card is lying on the table in front of her, face down. As open an invitation as one can ask for in public.

'How would you like to come play with my gigabytes?' I whisper invitingly.

Without blinking, she murmurs: 'Show me your IQ and I'll show you mine.'

'380,' comes a high voice from behind me.

She looks up sharply, and I whirl round, angrier at her reaction than at the interloper.

It is Spiro Archimedes, back from the dead, smelling of burnt flesh, a new Mensa rating coated in Tippex on his lapel, and a huge bulge in his forehead.

I quickly calculate the volume of his intellectual desire and decide he is desperate. I strike hard:

'Did the little Sophist get burnt at the Boar and Brain? Take a hike, chrome dome.'

But she isn't listening. Her eyes are locked hard on the 3–8–0 and I can see she is calculating the genetic potential of children thrown by the Mediterranean midget.

Suddenly she turns to me and hisses: 'Does your motherboard know you're here?'

She turns back to Spiro: 'Ever had your mind blown, sweetie?'

It is too much for me. I wrench away Spiro's Mensa card, scratch off the Tippex and hold it up to the light. She screams as the digits 2–3–0 appear. I glow triumphantly, pinning my 255 rating proudly to my philosopher's tunic.

Spiro is on his feet, shadow-thinking and very aggressive.

'Let's duel for her,' he says. 'Eysenck – best of three.'

'Talking of best of three,' she interrupts coldly, 'I think I see him now.' We both turn and look into the glazed eyes of Barry 'Moron from Outer Space' Fripp, local basketball hero. He was once beaten at noughts and crosses by a stuffed parrot which had hypnotised him with its gaze.

'How did you get in here?' I demand.

He thinks for a few minutes.

'Eiuuum, errrr, I – am – friend – of – doorman … duuuh.'

'Ooooh, isn't he cute,' giggles the female, surreptitiously sweeping her physics calculator and Mensa card into her handbag.

She looks at us coldly. Her eyes say: Go home to your software simulations.

She grabs Barry's bulging wrist muscle.

'Come, my Neanderthal playmate. Let's go find the secret of fire.'

Without another syllable, he scoops her into his arms and lurches out, snorting loudly and spitting iron filings as he goes.

Three days later Spiro, Freddy 'The Egg' and I turn ourselves in at the Max Planck Home for Chronic Over-achievers. We ask for the full-frontal.

Now we all teach high-school maths.

We're not particularly happy, but at least we don't think about it much.

HISTORICAL HUMOUR

HUMOUR IS *like a butterfly. Sometimes you appreciate it as it flits lightly by, but sometimes you don't catch it at all. And its life can be very short.*

Even the best of light literature is subject to ageing and oblivion. However, if it is well written, you can still enjoy its designs, colour and form when it is pressed between pages such as these. But we need to approach it obliquely, for the tragedy of humour is that what was satirical last month, or hilarious two decades ago – let alone two centuries ago – may be embarrassing today, even when read in private in a locked room.

The extent of the damage which time and distance can cause literary wit is appreciated when one compares the swift shelf-life of light writing with the remarkable longevity of serious essays. One can select essays written over three centuries – Addison, say, or Steele of the eighteenth, Haslett of the nineteenth and A.P. Herbert of the mid-twentieth century – and find that their styles, their thoughts, their elegant prose differ only in theme and a few ageing phrases. They remain in context and can still live in our memories. Humour, however, is inclined to fade into incomprehensible nonsense, as ageing copies of Punch *cartoons remind us.*

Longstanding humour has to go outside of the written page to find modern audiences. While clowns, mimes, Charlie Chaplin and the enactment of parts of Shakespeare's plays may tickle the funny bone of much of the world for generations, no book of humour remains funny for very long, with obvious exceptions such as passages of Jane Austen and slabs of Henry Fielding – except that his Tom Jones was resurrected mainly through film.

There are always exceptions. For some of us, for instance, the humour of Charles Dickens still lives, as does the comic philosophy of the parson masquerading under the name Lewis Carroll. With all these exceptions, doubts and qualifications in mind, it seemed to us to be an interesting exercise – a bit of a laugh – to test the English-language life-forms of light writing in darkest Africa over the past two centuries.

François le Vaillant (1753–1824)

This famous author and pioneer ornithologist should not by rights be appearing in this selection of English-language humour, for he was a Frenchman. And far from writing in English, he didn't even write in French. Yes, his accounts of his travels in southern Africa (the first published in 1790) were translated into English and also into German, Dutch, Danish, Italian, Russian and Swedish. But it is now known that he employed ghost-writers. We owe to them the bombastic and romantic style of prose, which still amuses us today.

One has to browse through acres of print to find the little gems such as we found here in this greatly summarised account of his first few adventures during his *Voyage … dans l'interior de l'Afrique*.

Le Vaillant's first adventure – even before his great *voyages* – involves a 'tyger' (a leopard), and it is pure farce recounted in straight-faced, florid verbiage.

Accompanied by Dutch farmers, Khoe hunters, horses and dogs, he sets out to shoot a leopard discovered hiding in a bush. After Le Vaillant fires three shots the animal emerges, bleeding, and runs to another bush. The local farmers, according to Le Vaillant, retreat in fear. But our hero rallies the Khoe, fires 40 rounds into the bush, and tells his servant: 'Come, get on your horse and go and see what condition he is in. I'll guard the entrance, and if he tries to escape I shall shoot him at once, without the help of these cowards.' The Khoe goes in, and finds the leopard dead. Thus, one of Africa's earliest Great White Hunters is able to bask in tales of the 'tyger' hunt in which his 'great courage' is contrasted with the cowardice of the 'peasantry'. However, according to another traveller, John Barrow, who passed that way shortly afterwards, the leopard had already been wounded by a trap-gun set by one of the Khoe, and it was dead when Le Vaillant shot it.

Later, far on his travels and deep in a forest, he lost track of a beautiful, raucous, green and purple bird – a Knysna loerie – which he had shot. He stamped his foot in exasperation and struck the ground with his gun. The gun went off, the earth collapsed, and he found himself in a deep hole. He had fallen into an elephant pit dug by the Khoe. Unfazed, Le Vaillant went elephant hunting. After three days, having failed to see any tuskers, a Khoe took him up a tree and pointed to one.

'There it is! There it is,' the guide kept calling with increasing impatience. Only when the creature moved and waved its trunk did the explorer realise what he was looking at.

'I could not believe that the prodigious mass beneath me was the animal I had so wished to encounter,' he explained.

Early in his travels he bagged a hippo, but only after 30 shots – plus a fatal one fired from the opposite bank of the river by his Khoe servant. The White Hunter reserved for himself some hippo fat, to cure 'all disorders of the breast', and the hippo's teeth because 'by the aid of art they supplant nature and figure admirably in the mouth of a pretty (French) woman'. Unlike elephant tusk, hippo molars did not turn yellow, he explained, and could be made into wonderful false teeth for fashionable ladies.

And so did the reputation of Great White Hunters quickly grow in Europe.

Le Vaillant set another precedent in Africa. Though he was a lone white man venturing into the interior and avoiding all contact with civilisation, he made sure that he changed his clothes and his linen three times a day. He set the tradition of keeping up standards. Each night, among the mosquitoes, snakes and occasional roar of a lion, he would dress beautifully for dinner.

'I never assist at those dinners where etiquette and tediousness preside, but the disgust at the occasion brings to my remembrance my charming African meals, where my honest Hottentots provided a banquet for their friend,' he wrote. Or rather his ghost-writers wrote.

There is no doubt that he was a marvellous eccentric. He took with him on his journey, lasting no less than sixteen months, a single companion to share his tent and his experiences. They hunted together and they shared their different kinds of food, whether it be plant roots or venison stew. His companion was named Kees, a young baboon. Also, with his vast cavalcade of Khoe went a white cockerel, whose duty it was to awaken Le Vaillant each morning.

Not that he was unsociable. Le Vaillant genuinely loved the people who accompanied him on his first expedition. He encouraged them with generous distributions of brandy and tobacco to join his feast. One night he produced numbers of Jew's harps, and endeavoured to teach all the Khoe – hunters, wives and daughters – to play harmoniously in the veld. Meanwhile Kees, the baboon who loved brandy, drank so greedily from the passing cup that he sucked it up his nose. Le Vaillant cured Kees, first by giving him a separate plate to drink from, then by setting his plateful of brandy alight as he was about to sip it. Oh, such party games!

When Le Vaillant met a beautiful maiden of the Gonaqua tribe, the games grew more serious. So charmed was he with her comeliness and modesty that he gave her everything her heart desired. A girdle, a bracelet and a necklace of small white beads. A red kerchief and a mirror. He promised her more – anything if she would stay. When she asked for his knee-buckles he observed that 'the most sparkling gems were not so brilliant as her expressive eyes', and he would fain have stripped the buckles from his legs, letting his breeches hang loose. But he had to say no. They were the only pair he had. 'How much did I wish at that moment for the most miserable fastenings to supplant this useless luxury!' he opined.

He followed her to a pool, sat on her clothes and playfully aimed his gun at her while she and the other young Gonaqua women bathed. (The embarrassment of the naked ladies caused him 'to blush for having sported with their delicacy', he confessed.) Nonetheless, he persuaded his chosen one to go hunting with him and to fetch the bird trophies he shot, even those that fell in the water, for he had no bird-dog, could not swim, and no doubt craved her nudity, despite his blushes.

Le Vaillant had been instantly smitten. He wrote of his Cape beloved: 'Her figure was charming, her teeth beautifully white [no need of artful aids from the hippopotamus], her height and shape, elegant and easy. She might have served as a model for the pencil of Albane … She was the youngest sister of the Graces.'

And he boasted: 'After the prodigality of my gifts paid deference to the power of her beauty the young savage and myself were soon acquainted.'

He made her dispense with her cosmetics – grease and animal fat smeared on her face – and he named her Narina, the Khoe word for 'flower'. He presented her with a badly stuffed kingfisher, which she prized, but it is unlikely that she appreciated that he also bestowed on her a form of immortality.

He named a beautiful bird – with the finest *oiseau* breast in all Africa – after his Gonaqua girl. Today birders from around the world search the forests of central and southern Africa for the sumptuous plumage of the Narina Trogon.

This true tale, and others told by Le Vaillant, are so good, it is a pity he bothered to invent a few fables. Even so, the volumes on his travels in Africa are well worth reading, not only for the unconscious (or is it conscious?) humour and the baroque language, but also for his views on his discoveries and on life in the wilds. The texts contain many exaggerations and errors, but these in themselves are interesting as well as amusing.

We should add that Le Vaillant, as a great pioneer ornithologist, was not terribly successful at preparing bird specimens, and when chests of his packed bird skins arrived in Paris they had often fallen apart, and so the head, tail and torso from three unrelated birds were sometimes fitted together, with bizarre results.

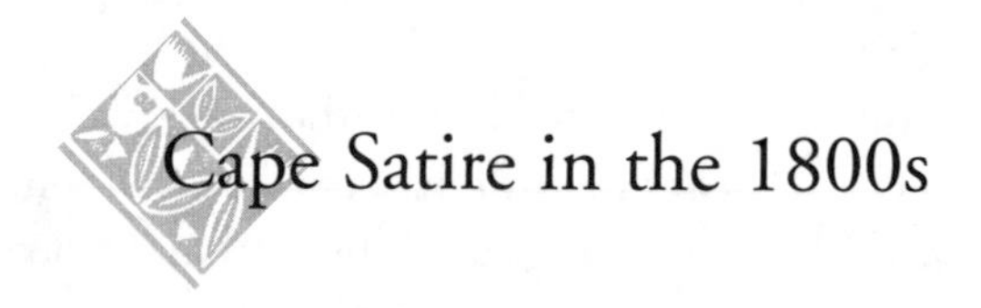

Cape Satire in the 1800s

The early 1800s saw the rise of an ungainly breed of doggerel whose discordant bark was decidedly worse than its bite. It led to the appearance in Cape Town in 1825 of a quarterly publication which announced itself as:

SOUTH AFRICAN GRINS
Or the
QUIZZICAL DEPOT OF GENERAL HUMBUG
Published by
Q. IN THE CORNER ESQ
disciple of Momus &c. &c. &c.

(Momus, in Greek mythology, was the personification of mockery and of grumbling.) Q. mocked everything, including books published by William Burchell and other explorers and hunters in search of fame. Q., in his awful verse, often mocked the Cape's newspapers

> which are to accommodate the Capers
> Printed in Dutch and English half and half;
> 'Tis true, tho' possibly you may laugh.
> A free press in Cape Town is not permitted
> Which is a thing much to be pitied.

But most of all, Q. (the pseudonym of Frederic Brooks) satirised the habits and behaviour of Cape Town's leading citizens. So when Brooks sailed away from the Colony, there appeared in the *South African Chronicle* a 'Friendly Adieu to Humbug Q.' signed by 'Hans Caper', who wrote:

> By vulgar rhymes and dirty jokes
> You would fain quiz the good Cape folk ...
> 'Tis plain to trace in all your books,
> The fountain head of filthy BROOKS.

Thus was the humbug exposed, and thus did the little doggerels snap and snarl.

Countless wags continued to poke fun in the papers at everything from the manners of the 1820 Settlers to the female fashion of women in trousers, known in 1835 as pantalets. The bite came when Andrew Bain started to mock broader targets.

Andrew Geddes Bain (1797–1864)

Here is one of the most robust satirists in English colonial history. Though the central character in his writing is a slovenly, drunken Khoe whore, his targets are the highest authorities in Whitehall and in the Cape Colony – the very people he was totally reliant on for employment.

Bain's own high status made him highly vulnerable. And the non-status of his co-author, son of George Rex – falsely rumoured to be the bastard son of King George III – hardly helped.

Bain was neither a writer nor a campaigning journalist like his contemporaries Pringle and Fairbairn, who fought for a free press in the colony. He was first and foremost a Scottish roads engineer, later an explorer and geologist under commission from the colonial government. His fame rests on his and his son's major public works – great mountain passes still in use after 150 years; on his explorations into the interior, and on his work *Geology of South Africa*.

Bain was a pioneer in almost everything he did, so that, despite relying on government funding for most of his activities, he was a free spirit who could not resist biting the pompous hands that fed him. It would have been a risky business – a government contractor satirising the government – even under a pseudonym. When he wrote his best-known piece, *Kaatje Kekkelbek* (Katie Chatterbox), he used the pseudonym 'Klipspringer' (an African antelope rather like a chamoix).

But he was never over-cautious about the anonymity of his satire. For instance, on the same sheet, watermarked 1838, on which 'Klipspringer' wrote the first verse of *Kaatje Kekkelbek* – and in the same handwriting – is scribbled a satirical verse over his real signature. The verse refers to Colonel John Hare, installed as Lieutenant Governor of the Eastern Cape in succession to Andries Stockenström, and to Sir George Napier. It also refers to the missionary Dr John Philip and to John Fairbairn, poet and newspaper editor. The doggerel bites thus:

The Swearing In

I, John, do solemnly swear
That the people of Albany I'll never spare
But of all the black tribes take special care.
(By the doing of which I'll be doing no more
Than Stocky and Nap … here have done here before.)
I swear too, like them, to attend to the nod
Of Philip or Fairbairn – so help me God!
Of each Kafir grievance be ope to conviction
And Colonists' plaints treat as matters of fiction.
But now I'm installed let the public beware!
Not to hunt with the hounds but to side with the Hare.

He not only mocked the colonial administration, he allowed his characters to ridicule the Supreme Court judges of the Colony. In the first performance in Grahamstown of *Kaatjie Kekkelbek*, for instance, Kaatje says in an aside to an appreciative audience of 1820 British settlers:

So the Judge he thinks he's clever and educated, sitting there with what looks like a mop on his head and his cloak and bib just like a preacher – but, believe me, we Hot'nots are far smarter – we know when old Kekwis [the Hon. Justice George Kekewich] is on Circuit – then we steal the most, because his punishment is always 'Six months hard labour' (which means 'six months good living'), but the bad-tempered one, with the red phiz, called Menzie [William Menzies 1795–1850, Senior Puisne Judge] … he gives us two years in the convict cells, and lashes, as in old Breslaar's time [F R Breseler, appointed to Court of Justice in 1822]. We don't give a damn for the long speeches of Seur Jan Wyl [Sir John Wylde, Chief Justice of the Colony]. But they dismissed old Kekwis for being too kind to us, and replaced him with Muisgraaf [William Musgrave, a second Puisne Judge]. There was also Montakee [John Montagu, Colonial Secretary], who was more or less Governor in Capetown. No-one could diddle the fellow. He made all the Hot'nots work on the Hard way [the 'Hard Road' constructed across the Cape Flats by convict labour] …

Merely questioning the judgments of Their Lordships in Britain and in South Africa could result in heavy penalties – even today, as some journalists and writers know to their cost. [As a newspaper editor under the apartheid regime one of us was found guilty of contempt of court after publishing an article that showed the racial disparities of a judge's sentences on white and black accused. Yet our carefully researched newspaper article, written by a legal expert, looks like an official law report in comparison with the wild satires of the judiciary which were performed and published in the mid-1800s.]

While penalties were more harsh a century or two ago, the press, generally, was more robust, declaring its prejudices, its racism and its politics frankly and without regard to balance. South Africa's first professional cartoonist, Frederick I'Ons, a British settler in the Eastern Cape, impugned Governor Stockenström with his savage caricatures at this time, without being prosecuted for libel. Sensitivities were blunter then.

Nor did the public demonstrate any sensitivity about chauvinism or racial discrimination. In this context it needs to be pointed out that while the word 'kaffir' is legally offensive today, it was used then to describe Xhosa speaking people living in the Cape.

This is not to say that Bain, and nearly all settlers everywhere, were not strongly prejudiced. The white colonials hated the missionaries for their interference – as many black politicians tend to blame missionaries in reverse and in retrospect today. A settler audience would have loved the following aside from Kaatje:

Right, jong! I wish the missionary society would send me to speak the truth as oom Andries [Andries Stoffels] and Jan Tzatzoe [taken to England by Dr Philip to give evidence before the Aborigines Committee] did in Exeter Hall, where all the English came with open mouths to swallow what we Hot'nots had to say. I don't want Dr Philip to whisper sweet things in my ear and tell me what to say, as they did with the others. Katie Chatterbox has her own tongue … I shall tell how the Boere and the Settlers cheated and oppressed us, and that they want to establish a Temperance Society to stop us drinking brandy, then I shall get plenty of tobacco and dagga and brandy and half-crowns; because if you want to be rich all you have to do is run down the Dutch people; but they'll never let me go because they are afraid of Katie Chatterbox! But I will have my rights! I'm going to the Governor!

It is probable that Fred Rex took the part of Kaatje, the chatterbox, adding to the amusement of the 19th-century audience. He was the son of George Rex, whom many accepted (incorrectly) as the illegitimate son of George III and Hannah Lightfoot, dispatched to the far end of Africa, to Knysna, in 1803. It was also thought, incorrectly, that Fred was the co-author of the famous, or infamous, political skit, but it seems he merely provided Bain with some help with colloquialisms. We shall not reproduce the work, for the extracts quoted above should convince you that the satire is hardly funny today. But *Kaatje Kekkelbek* is important to the history of English-language humour out of Africa – despite the amount of *taal* it contains – the 'Cape Dutch', which was to develop into Afrikaans in the 20th century.

It is significant that Bain's satirical character lived for more than a hundred years. After appearing on the amateur stage in the capital of the 1820 British Settler country in the Eastern Cape, Kaatje reappeared soon afterwards in print in Cape Town's *South African Sentinel*, and again seven years later in *Sam Sly's Journal.* A century later she was revived as a coarse and witty commentator in a radio programme shortly after World War II, and surely she will reappear in the 21st century as a modern miss with a sharp eye and tongue to be feared by all pomposity.

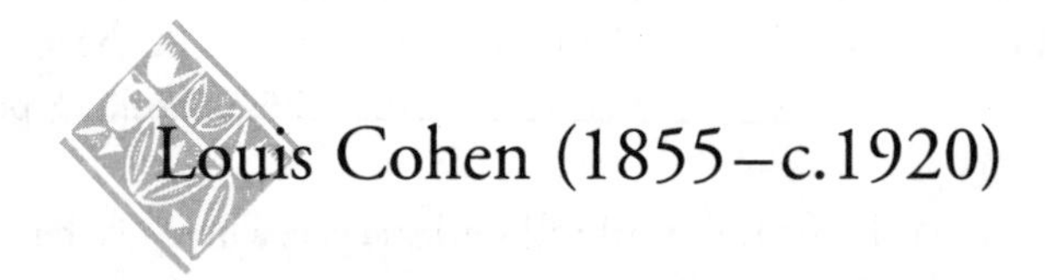

Louis Cohen (1855–c.1920)

With a revolver, a tent and 25 gold sovereigns given him by his relieved father, Lou Cohen set off at the age of 17 to join a thousand other adventurers, romantics, rogues and black sheep to make a fortune, one way or another, in the Kimberley diamond rush. His satirical eye and acidulous pen prevented him, however, from attaining his goal – even as his closest friend, Barney Barnato, reached for his first million pounds. They met in the Scarlet canteen in Kimberley, where Barney choked on his soup and spattered the patrons.

'Excuse me,' he told Cohen, 'a fly fell on my nose.'

So began an early friendship and erratic partnership, which broke up when Cohen mocked Barnato's rapid rise to riches. Cohen went on to libel most of the diamond tycoons, and was sued by J.B. Robinson, who tried to stop the publication of Cohen's *Reminiscences of Kimberley* (London, 1911). Fortunately Robinson failed, for Cohen's account of the great diamond days is as amusing – if dubious – an historical document as you could hope to read.

He lampooned everyone, not only the rich. For a while, for instance, he lived dangerously as a theatre critic. He recalled in his *Reminiscences* a critique he wrote of a performance by the actress Miss Flora Miller. 'The lady, who was very tall and muscular, announced to her friends and admirers, after she had read the notice, her fixed determination to thrash me at sight.' She came in sight that very morning, and the 'Junoesque goddess of war' charged at him with an umbrella which, he claimed, he dodged 'with great elegance like a matador'. But the attack was so formidable that he bolted – 'with the Amazon in full chase' – into the auditorium of the Theatre Royal, where he knocked down a cleaner, scattered chairs, tripped over a poodle and 'by the skin of my teeth' reached the stage, where the 'fair artiste' engaged him in battle once more … 'holding her petticoats with one hand and beating nothing in particular' until 'almost at the last hurdle, when victory was in her grasp, the huntress fell … displaying a lavish amount of hose and lingerie'.

Cohen made things worse by gleefully reporting the incident in his newspaper column. An angry member of the theatre staff stormed into his office and challenged him to a fight. 'I fought him without much damage to myself,' Cohen boasted, 'but while I was engaged with the man, a parcel of diamonds worth seven hundred pounds, which I carried in my back pocket, fell to the ground. I saw Barney Barnato – who was seconding me – pick them up, and recovered them politely from his hands.'

It can be seen, from what he omitted from that last passage, that he was becoming less rash and more adept in his sharp attacks. He was also a great raconteur, and a hundred years and more have not entirely destroyed his style of humour. Here is a single sample, admirably brief despite the deliberately oratorical style:

Often undesirable ladies who, all the same, were most desirable, made their appearance on the Diamond Fields, to the great delight of those men who had something human in their hearts, and something tangible in their pockets. One day, a plump, nicely-dressed, bright-eyed, young woman jumped from the post-cart when it arrived from Cape Town. Sa Singularité was well-known, and did not conceal the fact she desired to be better known … And at Graybittel's canteen she was. Quiet men got restless, restless men got thirsty, vain men posed, and quarrelsome men fought – but the saffron-coloured woman drank with all … She frolicked with the lot … Everybody present wanted to be her knight – all creeds and denominations – until at last the delightful creature … demanded to be put up for auction. Amidst intense excitement the South African octoroon was offered for sale – not for life, of course. As she stood upon a champagne case she beamed on all. The bidding commenced at five pounds, and ultimately the erring one was knocked down, after a keen and heated competition, to Mr. John Swaebe, for twenty-five pounds and three cases of champagne. With a soul on fire Johnny departed with his bargain, to the envy and disappointment of many of his rivals. Now, Johnny had a framed canvas abode across the road, and to this humble dwelling he escorted his bride. But after half an hour had elapsed, 'the boys' got round the tent and carried it bodily away, thus exposing to view the amorous pair – and the honeymoon was over.

That report of the auction is today firmly fixed, in various guises, in all versions of 19th-century history. What a fine, modern-day tabloid reporter Lou Cohen would have made. He names and gives details, right down to the numbers of bottles of champagne included in the price. When he recounts the scandals of diamond mine financing and politics, he is equally confident of his 'facts' – even when he is incorrect, or his version heatedly denied.

His most amusing tales, however, belong to the early days of the raucous Kimberley camp. There is the story, for instance, buttressed with the names of a number of witnesses – all renowned, respected local gentry in later years – about Nelly Maguire. 'This merry flame was a well-known character on the Diamond Fields, and she gloried in her red hair and a brogue you could cut with a knife.' Nelly 'mingled with her contempt for virtue a decided liking for Ireland's national drink …'

It is one of the many tales you might wish to enjoy, if you are ever able to trace a copy of Louis Cohen's classic autobiography. This Liverpudlian is one of the colourful fish in the small pool of English-recorded 19th-century humour out of Africa.

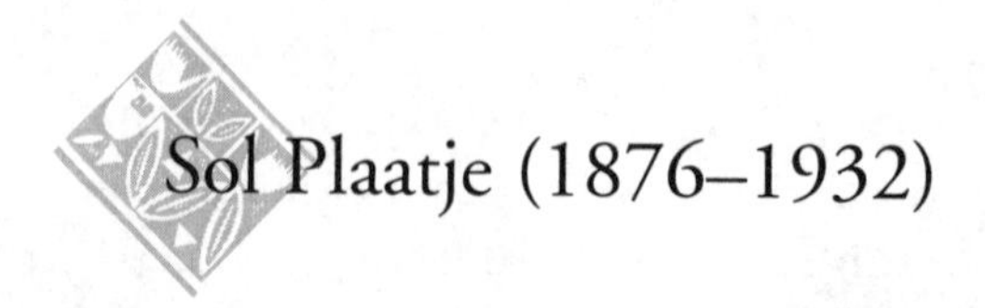

Sol Plaatje (1876–1932)

No review of humour out of Africa can ignore the name of Solomon Tshekisho Plaatje, son of a dispossessed chief of the royal house of the Barolong.

All his formative years were spent on mission stations, where he learned English, German, Dutch and several African languages as well as literacy in his own Setswana. He was brought up on the Nelson Royal Reader, a textbook series used across the entire English-speaking world in the late 1800s. He spent several years in London, and in the USA and Canada.

His writings are truly prodigious, for he put pen to paper most days of his adult life – Sundays and Christmas Day included. He wrote newspaper editorials, articles, letters to the press, political speeches, evidence for government commissions, many autobiographical pieces, and countless letters to people and politicians in South Africa and abroad. He wrote three important books, and he translated four of Shakespeare's plays into Setswana.

Time, circumstances and wider exposure of his works are giving Sol Plaatje in the 21st century the important status he deserved at the end of the 19th century. But time has almost destroyed the reputation he had as a man of humour. His writing causes fewer laughs today than Colonel Baden-Powell's recorded military orders at Mafeking.

Nonetheless, Sol Plaatje's *Mafeking Diary*, penned throughout the siege in 1899, reveals 'an intriguing sense of humour, and an ability to describe not only the hardships of life under siege but also its moments of humour, the incongruities of a daily life that fluctuated between the banal and the tragic,' writes Brian Willan, who did a superb job in collecting the African journalist's written words from a thousand sources, and publishing *Sol Plaatje: Selected Writings* (edited by Brian Willan, Witwatersrand University Press, 1996).

Here are two samples of the humour in war a hundred years ago. Sol Plaatje absorbed much of his laid-back, offhand style from the garrison defending the former mission station during the Boer siege. Perhaps, as an 'outsider' he would have enjoyed the solemn antics of Robert Baden-Powell, defender of Mafeking, founder of the Boy Scout movement, and soon to be knighted, then created a Lord. Plaatje certainly joined most Mafeking residents in learning to joke about 'Au Sanna', the 94-pounder siege-gun that shelled them regularly, day and night, but seldom on Sundays.

Saturday, 9th December (1899)

Too little, if anything has been said in praise of the part played by that gallant Britisher – the Barolong herdboy. Cattle are now grazing on what may be termed 'disputed' territory, just where the Dutch and English volleys cross each other; and it is touching to see how piccaninnies watch their flocks, and how in the bright sunshine along the wide plain south and west of the stadt – especially when after filling his belly with a lunch of black coffee and beef – the Dutch artillerist would turn his attention to them, and sate his iniquitous whims by sending a shell right into the midst of a group of them. God would guide it flying over their little heads and it would kindle a mortal fire near them: it is an imposing sight to see them running after a fragment and picking it up.

Two other herds(men) went out last night. They went out as far as Jackal Tree where they lay down on the grass near the Boer camp when the enemy were busy outspanning. It was raining at the time and the oxen were tied up to the yokes ... They successfully loosened four of the oxen without detection. One of the smart thieves led them away by their *riems* (leather thong harness) while his confederate drove their loot behind.

There is a regiment composed of a mixture of Zulu, Shangaan, Tembu and other Transkeian breeds under one McKenzie, styled the Black Watch ... Some of these fellows on sentry duty saw their Barolong brethren advancing with their highly prized but *nqabile* (scarce) possessions. The party was made, and an eruption such as nearly started a revolution in the whole place, ensued. Their row was such as could have attracted considerable attention if 'Au Sanna' was not the lawful claimant of our attention. The case was 'sticking up' (robbery), and the Colonel judged against the Transkeians, as the Barolong could substantiate their claims by the *riems* they carried in their hands. The Zulu swore that they bought the cattle from the Boer laager. The Colonel gave the Barolong the third ox and as they were abnormally fat animals he bought the others off them.

Thus was justice done by honest thieves.

Sunday 29th October

... Mauser bullets were just like hail on the main road ... One flew close to my cap with a 'ping' – giving me such a fright as caused me to sit down on the footpath. Someone behind me exclaimed that I was nearly killed and I looked to see who my sympathiser was. When I did so another screeched through his legs with a 'whiz-z-z-' and dropped between the two of us. I continued my journey in company with this man, during which I heard a screech and a tap behind my ear: it was a Mauser bullet and as there can be no question about a fellow's death when it enters his brain through the lobe, I knew at that moment that I had been transmitted from this temporary life on to eternity. I imagined I held a nickel bullet in my heart. That was merely the faculty of the soul recognising (in ordinary post-mortal dream) who occasioned its departure – for I was dead! Dead to rise no more. A few seconds elapsed after which I found myself scanning the bullet between my finger and thumb, to realise that it was but a horsefly.

Plaatje's biographers are much enthused about these displays of humour, but the judgements come from the politically academic and are hardly concerned with laughter.

Nor was Sol Plaatje, for that matter. His *Mafeking Diary* allowed him to explore style and to experiment with writing in English. His manuscript was recently found stuffed in the binding of an old book and may never have been intended for publication. However, it demonstrated Plaatjie's excellent sense of irony, which grew up with him, providing him with a perspective that helped him become what Tim Couzens of the University of the Witwatersrand described (in an introduction to a new edition of Plaatje's historical novel *Mhudi*) 'one of the most remarkable men Southern Africa has produced'.

Sol Plaatje was a journalist, an editor, a political leader and an intellectual who kept his feet on the ground. He was a founder of the African Native National Congress, but in 1917 turned down the offer of presidency of the ANC, the political home 50 years later of Nelson Mandela. Instead, Plaatje wrote what is claimed to be the first African novel, followed by a slashing attack on colonial politics in a book titled *Native Life in South Africa*. He produced the *Sechuana Dictionary* and a book of African folktales, and he translated Shakespeare because he saw how close those pre-industrial stories were to the rural myths of Africa. Of the four Shakespearian plays which he rendered in Setswana to ensure the relevance of his native tongue, it is fitting that the first and only one 'the man of humour' was able to publish turned out to be *A Comedy of Errors*.

C. Louis Leipoldt (1880–1947)

Louis Leipoldt and Sol Plaatje represent almost two extremes of the life-styles of the people of South Africa at the dawn of the 20th century. Their cultures, their backgrounds, their experiences and their perspectives were as contrasting as black and white. Yet they had an extraordinary amount in common.

Both were brought up by missionaries. Both were phenomenally prolific writers. Both achieved their best work in a language which was not their mother tongue. One came to be regarded as a founding spirit of the Afrikaans language, the other a founding spirit of the African National Congress. Both had visions of a unified land of diverse peoples. Both wrote deeply on these subjects.

More relevant in our context: both authors exhibited a sense of humour. Humour gave each of them an equable perspective on a torrid political scene. But their humorous writing did not appear in print until long after their deaths.

Writing in 1930, Leipoldt used the values of a rural community living on the Cape West Coast a century earlier to counter the Voortrekker myth of white superiority propagated by Nationalists. His liberal thesis was that many of those Afrikaners who chose not to trek stayed behind to fight for a wider future with a wider (non-racial) franchise. But at first Leipoldt, the famous poet, turned to fiction in Afrikaans, including a comic tale about Widow Priem's Cow.

'It is the first funny story I've tried,' he noted. 'It is not satisfactory.'

Widow Priem grew instead into one of the characters in his serial comedy *Galgsalmander*, about the rural community of the Clanwilliam district. That wasn't very satisfactory either, so Leipoldt began a more significant trilogy in English, using the theme, and the translated title, *Gallows Gecko*, as the first of three novels. This introductory light satire to the 'Valley Trilogy' was written in weeks, but not published until the year 2000, more than half a century after his death. The manuscript was retrieved from the Jagger Collection at the University of Cape Town, and edited by Stephen Grey (*Chameleon on the Gallows*, Human & Rousseau, Cape Town), to whom we are indebted for its publication. It is the tale of a French-speaking strolling player and lover who wreaks havoc when he settles in a strongly conservative Namaqualand village.

If the shortened extracts lead you to read the full story, followed by Leipoldt's second in the trilogy *Stormwrack*, you will have come to know an author who – like Sol Plaatje – has been hailed by some critics as one of the most significant writers in English-language literature in South Africa.

But first of all, enjoy a gentle smile.

Our extract begins after Pierre Mabius, known as 'Blikkies', arrives in The Valley; charms the farm labourers with his music; impresses the intelligentsia with his masterly chess play, and is taken on trial as the schoolteacher. Then the school committee meets to discuss a complaint from Widow Priem ('implicitly dissociating herself from any criticism of the methods of our teacher') but taking up the case of her only son, his dire punishment, and his coming home very late from school …

'Your reverence,' said Blikkies, rising respectfully and bowing first towards the head of the table and then right and left, 'that garçon of the douairière, Priem – its name, gentlemen, is Frikkie … Of a stupidity and laziness incroyable, not to be believed, gentlemen. I set him a fair copy. I wrote for him an exhortatory sentence, "Regard the ant that is not sluggish and be like unto him," and I say, I order, gentlemen, the young man to copy it four-five times. I attend to the other children, who are not cigales – grasshoppers, gentlemen – and when I turn to Frikkie, I find he has not done a line, not a letter, not a comma. Do I lose my temper, gentlemen? No! You would not like a teacher who loses his temper. You would say – quite rightly, gentlemen – this person is unfitted to teach our children how to control their tempers. I say, briefly, "Boy, you will write those lines four-five times if you sit here until we see the cross shining in the sky." I do that one day; I do that two days; I do that the third day, and each day Frikkie goes home a little earlier. And each day I have four-five copies of Frikkie's writing, the second better than the first and the third better than the second.'

'You have heard the meester's explanation – sit down, Meester,' said the parson, 'and the matter is now open for discussion' …

'I am of the opinion', said Brother Martin precisely, tendering his snuff box to the senior elder, 'that the complaint may be dismissed. We should, as committee, uphold the authority of our teacher … but … Is it, I ask you, brothers, a fit punishment for disobedience that a boy should be kept in? I speak under correction, but my own view is that the application of a quince stick to the lad's seat would be much more efficacious, and would at the same time serve as a wholesome example to the class.'

'Therein I wholly support you, brother,' said Uncle Dorie. 'We have repeated scriptural authority, as his reverence will bear me out in saying, for what you have just said. In the thirteenth chapter of Proverbs is written, "He that spareth his rod hateth his son, but he that loveth him chasteneth him betimes." Nowhere in the Good Book, so far as my memory serves me, are we bidden to keep a child in for disobedience. I, too, do not wish to criticise our teacher, but I cannot refrain from expressing my conviction that scriptural methods such as those you have alluded to, brother, are more likely to conduce to good upbringing and the eradication of sloth and disobedience than these new-fangled ways. If,' concluded Uncle Dorie vigorously, 'my son refuses to do what he is told, I lam him, and I have found that he does not repeat his refusal.'

'The widowed Sister Priem', remarked Brother Mias, in a voice as if he were intoning the litany, 'has nothing whatever against corporal punishment. In fact, she confessed to me that she would thank the Meester if he administered a proper thrashing to the lad, he being now grown beyond her capacity to hit him forcibly enough to inspire contrition' …

Thus do the loving, pious parents and the brotherhood guide the foreigner into civilised ways. Leipoldt's gentle satire of contemporary morals is masterly, even today. Though the period of his tale is nearly as far back as Queen Victoria's coronation, the sexual *mores* which he teases belong to a rural society of the mid-20th century. It is almost breathtaking to compare his satire of rural morals with the satire appearing later in this book poking fun at astonishingly different city morals only five decades later. (See Richards's *A Dip in the Gene Pool*.)

In the following extract, Pierre Mabius, known as 'Blikkies', goes on holiday to the seaside with his employers and becomes the hero of the Bay's youth, which in return for the pleasure and entertainment that his gifts of drawing, dancing and flute-playing give them, try to teach him to swim.

He has no notion that bathing and bare flesh will soon carry him towards an unforeseen deep end. He is troubled, instead, by his fear of water …

The community took … things, philosophically. But one thing it deemed it its duty to criticise adversely and, for so mild-mannered a community, strongly. It tolerated Blikkies's Roman Catholicism, for as a matter of fact that deviation from established convention did not obtrude itself. Blikkies attended the communal services, sang with the rest and in good tune, and made no parade of his different faith, although he crossed himself on occasions and everyone knew that he had not been admitted as a communicant. But the pastor, and the church council, apparently, had vouched for him, and that, the Bay community felt, as the Valley had already felt, was quite sufficient.

But when it came to drawing naked youths in pencil on paper – why, that was a matter altogether different. 'Do you know', Uncle Dorie asked Everardus, with more surprise than annoyance in his voice, 'what Teacher has done? He has drawn young Matie Kromhout – you know, Ebenezer's boy, the fourteen-year-old who is with his father and the rest of his family – he has drawn the youngster standing on a rock. Naked, so that you can see the lad's posteriors. Just like a Bushman painting on a cave wall. It is wholly indecent, Nephew Evrard, and the people have spoken to me about it.'

'Then you had better talk to him,' said Everardus with a smile, although, knowing the community, he realised what a gross impropriety Blikkies had been guilty of.

'Ach – talk to him. It is easily said. But the fellow twists everything one says and, really, Nephew Evrard, I don't quite know what to say. You see, it is a good picture. I would not say it is a bad one. You can tell it is Matie – it is a wonderful likeness of the boy. But naked, nephew! Ah, here you are, Teacher. I was just saying to Nephew Evrard here that you really must be more discreet. You must not bring new-fangled fashions into our little world, and we expect, Teacher, we expect that our – a teacher, should have some regard to decency and what is befitting.'

'It is to me astounding, messieurs,' said Blikkies, shrugging his shoulders and twirling the ends of his little black moustache, 'that monsieur le doyen should accuse me of a thing so degradant. I cannot see that I have merited a charge of a nature so monstrous.'

'Here, Teacher,' said Everardus quickly. 'It is only that you have drawn young Matie without any clothes on. Which you mustn't do, Teacher.'

'Certainment I have drawn the little fellow,' expostulated Blikkies, energetically, pulling from his side pocket a mass of crumpled papers and sorting one from the rest. 'I have it here – Meneer Nolte can see for himself.' He handed the sketch over to Everardus, who saw it represented a boy – in that interesting stage between boyhood and adolescence, when every line and curve hints at a maturity yet hidden by a youthful softness – poised on the edge of the bathing pool, with arms outstretched above his head, preparatory to dive. It was a part-profile view, and the excellence of the line drawing, and the boldness of the pose, appealed to Everardus, who found Uncle Dorie peering over his shoulder as he studied the sketch.

'Meneer Nolte can see for himself,' resumed Blikkies. 'The garçon is of a shape most beautiful – alas that his face is not that of a Narcissus, but le bon Dieu does not give all at once. But his proportions ... Look, if you please, Meneer Nolte, at the buttock-curve, at that body; they are for the sculptor to chisel in marble, gentlemen. And my poor sketch, it wants the colouring; it is altogether a poor thing.'

'It is altogether an indecent thing, Teacher,' said Uncle Dorie severely. 'If you wish to draw the lad – and none of us has any objection to your doing that, aye, even his parents would, I daresay, like to have a sketch of him, and Nephew Ebenezer is well enough off to pay you a riksdollar for it – then draw him, in heaven's name, decently clothed.'

'But it is his body I wish to draw,' exclaimed Blikkies. 'What is there indecent in the young man's body? He is clean – he swims daily in that pool, even as I do and the rest, though dabble, I cannot yet swim, nor am ever likely to. But I do not want his clothes. They make him laid, ugly. But deshabillé he is of a beauty to make one want to draw him. I have watched all the others but there is not one to compare with him. I have here – see, the men, and the garçons too, but look, Meneer Nolte, look meneer le doyen, there is not one to be compared with him.'

'I don't want to see them,' said Uncle Dorie, taking nevertheless the sketches that Blikkies handed him, 'and I must say that I do not think you should watch a fellow creature's nakedness. It is not good. It is forbidden in the Book.'

'Will meneer le doyen', riposted Blikkies sharply, 'give me the citation in the Book where it is forbidden?'

'Hey? The text?' said Uncle Dorie, taken at a disadvantage. 'I do not at the moment remember the exact reference. It is somewhere in Isaiah where the prophet tells us to cover the naked.'

'But that is to inculcate our duty towards the poor,' remonstrated Blikkies. 'The prophetic gentleman tells us to take the poor into our house – as Meneer Nolte has done unto me, for which I am eternally his debtor – but he in no ways enjoins us not to draw a youth so gloriously proportioned as the fils of Meneer Kromhout.'

'I do not know if your and my Book agree,' said Uncle Dorie, taking refuge in the difference of faiths, which showed that he was by no means sure of his ground, 'but there are other texts apposite to the occasion. But text or no texts, Teacher, we cannot have you drawing the boys with nothing on. Why, the women may come to see it, and I ask you, what then?'

'And I answer, Meneer Van Aard, that if the women cannot see how beautiful it is, that young man's body, then they are indeed devoid of any soul.'

'But man, seriously, it is indecent. You surely do not mean to tell me that it is anything but gross to show that sketch to any woman?'

'They have all seen us naked, and they know what we look like. And when we are sick, does anyone care if we are naked when the women minister to us?'

'That is altogether something different, Teacher. You twist my words. I cannot pin you down. I say it is indecent, and there is an end to it. Why, if the thing becomes known – and many of us have already seen it, for you drew it openly, publicly, at the pool, and the other lads saw it.'

'I did so, meneer le doyen. Why should I not? Look you, I have a proposal to make. Let us take my poor sketch to his reverence, and abide by what he says. It was my intention to show it to him in any case.'

'Certainly,' said Uncle Dorie with alacrity. 'His reverence is just across the way. I know how he will take it, and I am quite content to leave the matter in his hands.' But to Uncle Dorie's huge astonishment the Rev. Sybrand, after a cursory glance at the sketch, looked sharply at Blikkies, and then concentrated his attention on the drawing. He held it at arm's length; he peered at it through his horn-rimmed glasses; he took the glasses off and looked at the sketch at close range, and he nodded his head vigorously. At last he spoke.

'Teacher,' he said, with real feeling in his voice, 'let me congratulate you. It is a little masterpiece. The curve of that shin – now that might, I think, be a little less hard. But it is altogether a beautiful piece of work, worthy of so beautiful an object. What a pity it is that the boy, Matie, has not a mind to correspond with so well formed a body.'

'But your reverence,' exclaimed Uncle Dorie, appalled that his arbitrator had so suddenly and unconditionally surrendered to the enemy, 'it is monstrously indecent. Impure, if I might say so.'

'I do not see why you should say that, Brother Doremus,' said the pastor mildly. 'There is nothing indecent about it. You would not call God's handiwork indecent, would you, now?'

'Bis, bis, your reverence,' exclaimed Blikkies, marvellously delighted.

'To be pure,' went on the pastor, disregarding the Teacher's enthusiastic approval, 'all things are pure, as the Good Book tells us through the lips of the apostle. And nowhere in holy writ, brother, will you find that man's body is regarded as otherwise than something to be looked at with reverence and to be wondered at. Is it not made in His image? I know what is in your mind, brother, and I will not say that it is fitting, at present, that these things should be publicly exhibited, as they are in other countries, where such a sketch would be extolled as the work of an artist. Indeed, it were perhaps better that our friend should keep them for such as can understand and appreciate them.'

'Will your reverence favour me by accepting the lad's likeness as a gift from the humble artist?' asked Blikkies quickly.

'Gladly and with gratitude,' said the pastor, pocketing the sketch. 'I will have it framed and hung up – not in my study-chamber, Teacher, for there are many among us who think not as we do. And you, my good friend, must favour me by following Brother Doremus's suggestion, and refrain from publishing your sketches, even though they are of youths so marvellously well formed as this lad appears to be.'

With the pastor's tact and common-sense way of looking at the incident, the affair was settled, but Uncle Dorie was not altogether satisfied …

JENNY HOBBS

JENNY HOBBS *was born in Durban on the day of the* Hindenburg *disaster in New Jersey. Despite this unpropitious beginning, she says she has had a happy and productive life as a journalist turned novelist 'with diversions into humour along the way'.*

After university in Pietermaritzburg she served as a supply teacher in one of the toughest school districts in London and, following a spell of travelling, married an engineer, settled down and had four children. She now lives in northern Johannesburg.

Hobbs began writing for popular and literary magazines 'only after my children were more or less off my hands', and one of her notable creations was Blossom Broadbeam, the 'Johannesburg chick from Bez Valley' (Bezuidenhout Valley being, then, a working-class suburb).

Hobbs' four novels have all done well, especially Thoughts in a Makeshift Mortuary *(London, 1982). She has written non-fiction too, including an amusing compendium on lavatories (with Professor Tim Couzens) titled* Pees and Queues.

The following was published in Darling *magazine and later appeared in book form –* Darling Blossom.

Excuse the Patrons, Please

There's this time my friend Charmaine and me, we get jobs as usherettes there by the Plaza Bioscope so long. We check this advert in the paper, it says: 'Usherettes Wanted, Evenings and Saturdays Only, No Experience Necessary.'

'That's the job for us, man, Bloss,' Charmaine reckons. 'Lay around in bed all day, graft for a harf a hour at night and catch all the latest fillums for free. Safe!'

I've jis given ou Gerrie the push then and I'm getting the morbs in the evenings what with no sporting events to screech at, so I reckon OK and we rock along next day for this interview.

The Manidger is a little thin grey-haired okie dressed in a greeny-black tuxedo what's seen better days. He's parking off there in he's office chewing on a stuk of biltong what looks like it's been hanging from a bit of krom wire for ten years minimum.

'You girlies looking for a easy job, hey?' he susses us. 'Well you got another think coming if you scheme usheretting's a walk in the park.'

'Is it?' Charmaine tunes him, grinning. She knows better, as per ushal. Charmaine can be a *moer* of a pain sometimes.

He only shrugs he's shoulders, shaking loose all the dandruff. 'You all the same, you young people today. You want the least work for the most cash.'

'So what's wrong with that, mister?' I reckon. 'It's a free country.'

'Nothink wrong,' he sighs. 'Only that you all seem to have these funny ideas about usheretting being easy money not to menshun the free uniforms. But don't let me stand in yore way. Come and try out the job by all means. Jis don't say I didn't warn you, OK?'

We leave him picking out the bits of biltong what've got stuck in he's teeth with he's little fingernail.

'Encouridging okie, hey?' Charmaine says. 'Trying to put us off like that. I mean, reely.'

'We got the job, tho,' I tune her back. 'Usherettes, *ek sê*. Look out, Paul Newman, Robert Redford, Al Pacino – yere we come!'

Monday morning we've got to be at the bioscope bright and early to get our uniforms fitted etsetra. It's a smart maroon skirt and jacket with gold piping, flat black shoes, 'And no beehives, unnerstand?' the Manidger reckons, chucking this *skeef* look at our hairstyles.

Shame, and we spend all the day before setting and back-combing and spraying them with lacker so as to get them to stay up high enuff. Do it proper and sometimes it larsts for two weeks, a good beehive. Every morning you only have to mos lift up the flat bits you slept on with a knitting needle and spray on more lacker, it's dead easy.

Charmaine gets all *woes* then. 'Don't try and be funny with us, mister! We wear our hair the way we like, *jong*.'

'Zat so? I don't serpose it's occurred to you, my girl,' snaps the Manidger, 'that the patrons might have some trouble seeing parst a moving haystack. Hey? It's flat hair or no job. Finish and *klaar*.'

Well even Charmaine can't argue with that, so harf-past six we back at the Plaza and standing by our places near the door curtins in the foyer, looking like blerry school-teachers with our hair plarstered down and carrying these *moer* of a long black rubber torches. Charmaine's on the Stalls downstairs with two chicks called Betty and Petronella and I'm on the Circle upstairs with Hettie. Each one gets a pile of *Stage & Cinema* to flog as well, you get paid 2c extra for every copy you get rid of. It's sort of like the cherry on the top, some cherry ha ha.

Then it starts. And s'true's bob, fans, if you ever scheme showing people into they seats is easy, let me tell you it's not. No ways. I never had such a terrible time in my whole entire life as that first night usheretting. Sigh. And we think it's gonna be a piece of ole tackie.

I mean, first of all, the types you get! The worst are the Stragglers: they keep you sommer standing there in the isle pointing yore torch at this row of empty seats feeling like a spaz, whilst they meantime chat in loud voices or take larst drags at they stompies in the foyer or argue about whose gonna sit where.

Then you get the Shufflers, what creep and slide they feet slowly along in the darkness, nipping straws in case they'll trip. Sometimes you wonder whether you'll be there until next Christmas hanging around waiting for a Shuffler, no word of a lie. There's also the Gapers too, what are so busy goggeling at the screen not wanting to miss they money's worth that they fall over everythink, steps, feet, empty cooldrink cups, full popcorn cartons, the lot. The mess under the seats after the show is worse then a pigsty.

And it's fantastic too what people bring with to the bioscope! No kidding, we've found false teeth, babies bottles, bunches of dead flowers, broeks, rubber snakes, odd shoes, a doek full of curlers, comics for Africa, a waspie and even a genuine glass eye once, I arsk you. How did the patron even see the movie with he's eye out, hey? Not to menshun the bubblegum what's forever sticking to yore shoes from off of the floor where people spit it out in the dark, *sies*.

Talking about the dark, then there're the Dirty Ole Men. Some nights I get home black and blue from being grabbed from out of nowhere when I wasn't looking. No kidding. Even the Manidger use to try it sometimes in the staff seats. I mean, he only takes me up to *yere* by my chin and he's old enuff to be my blerry great-grandpa even, but I reckon he had the farstest pair of hands in town, that oke. And he's breath always ponging of biltong what's more becorse he never could get all those bits out from between he's teeth.

Charmaine could sort out a Dirty Ole Man double quick, tho. She use to shine her torch in he's face and screech, '*Los my uit, oupa!* Hands off, mister!' and ushally after that he's ole lady would give him stick much better right throu the fillum.

You get all characters coming to the bioscope too. There's this intellekshul-looking ou always with a pile of heavy books under he's arm what takes in all the skop-skiet-en-donners, larfing like a drain. Then there's this ouma from the old-age home what sits in the same seat every Saturday arvey to check what's going on in the big wide world: sex, murder, vilence, drarma, romance – it's all the same to her. She's about ninety in the shade, deaf as a post and mad crazy about Steve McQueen, *nog*. And there's this fat *ou* too with chorbs what the other usherettes reckon comes to every singal showing of Julie Andrews fillums: he saw *The Sound of Music* fifty-seven times, no less. I arsk you!

And that's the other thing about being a usherette what you scheme's gonna be safe. Catching all the latest fillums. OK so maybe you smaak them the first time or even the second or third, but after that they give you the stone needle, s'true's bob. Same scenes, same words, same people pulling the same faces over and over and over – it works on yore nerves, man.

The thing is, see, juring performances somebody's got to sit upstairs and somebody down so as to keep a eye on the patrons in case there's any trouble. *You* know – heavy smooching going too far in the back row or kids chucking popcorn around or the chancers hasseling chicks on they eis. So we gotta take it in turns standing gard whilst the other usherettes *sluk* coffee and put they feet up in the rest room, otherwise we'd go *darem* looney on a long run, believe yore ou pellie blue. I once saw John Wayne climb in the saddle and reckon out the side of he's mouth 'Let's go get 'em, boys' about a thousand times until I could of been sick on the spot every time he started to lift he's leg. Genuine.

Flogging the ice-creams and cool-drinks at harf-time's another drag. You have this little like plastic tray hanging by a strap behind yore neck and everybody crowds around soon's the lights go up and for ten minutes they give you a hang of a hard time all wanting they stuff first. Eskimo Pies, Twistees, Fanta, you name it. Not to menshun the little kids at matineys what hang off the edge and try to mountin-climb up yore shins, screeching and dribbling so long …

I wouldn't wish working as a usherette on my worst enemy. *Nooit.*

CHRISTOPHER HOPE

THE INDEPENDENT *in London found in novelist Christopher Hope's later works 'a blend of devastating satire and gruesome humour to counterpoint the banal with the fantastic'. Scathing was one of the dominant moods in his earlier books about apartheid in South Africa, but Hope is not a bitter man by nature, and his writing – especially since the death of apartheid – carries understanding and sympathy as well as sharp wit. The* Financial Times *summed it up as 'crispness of wit, keenness of observation'.*

Even without those talents, Hope's plots guarantee mirth. One of his later novels, Darkest England *(Pan Macmillan, London, 1996), has a representative of a San (Bushman) community sent by his family elders to explore the land of the Great Queen. The intrepid explorer discovers some astonishing things, and encounters extraordinary experiences. The customs of British Customs officers, for instance, he finds inexplicable. The behaviour of English residents he finds quaint and sometimes barbaric. His observations lead him to believe that the institution known as the Church is devoted almost full-time to raising money, and that another institution known as the Banks is focused on communications and culture.*

When a group of British women discover that it is normal for a fine upstanding Bushman to have a constantly erect penis, they are so intrigued they demand a serial sex session, and Hope's hero has no alternative but to lie back and think of Bushmanland.

In the following extract he finally gets to see the Great Queen by the simple expedient of buying a ticket for a public tour of Buckingham Palace, then hiding there by posing in a dark corner as another of those pageboy ornaments – a blackboy statuette holding a platter of fruit. Then the Queen herself wanders in, after hours, bearing a duster …

Darkest England

She stopped dabbing at me with the infuriating feathers, pressed her ear to my chest for a moment, leapt back a step or two, very slowly retreated to the window and then, in a moment I shall savour for the rest of my life, the Queen of England addressed her loyal servant, David Mungo Booi.

Her voice, I should say, was regal; being high, small and taut like fencing wire, bending under the pressure of her queenly enunciation, it resembled the cry of the fish-eagle.

If I had come about taxes – Her Majesty declared – I was wasting my time. She had paid what she could. I would not get blood from a stone.

I said I had not come about taxes.

She put down her duster. Had I come to tell her that another of her Palaces was on fire? Well, she had this to say. Let it burn! She had only recently effected repairs to a burnt Palace: every tapestry, suit of armour, picture, she had paid to have restored without a penny from the public purse and precious little sympathy from her subjects. Despite appearances to the contrary, she was not made of money.

I expressed the hope that her Palaces would endure for a thousand years.

In that case, said the Monarch wearily, there could be only one explanation for my visit. What had her children done now? Hanky-panky? Kiss-and-tell? Secret phone calls? Bare-breasted shenanigans? Well, she was just not, repeat not, interested. And I would not have a penny from her. The royal offspring were old enough and ugly enough to look after themselves. Enough was enough!

I said I wished her family nothing but long life and many children.

I thought she rather flinched at this and I hastened to reassure her that my embassy had nothing to do with the matters she had been kind enough to mention; rather, it was my privilege to come to her as the first ambassador of her loyal Red People.

Her manner changed remarkably now. Declaring this to be fascinating news, and taking a little pair of silver scissors from her handbag, she snipped the white tape that protected the chairs and, patting a seat, pink as sunset and deep as an elephant's yawn, she invited me to sit beside her and tell her where in her former empire her Red People resided.

Back in the ages when my people were, I replied, we lived in the north-western reaches of the Cape Province of South Africa.

Cries of delighted recognition greeted my reply. She too had been to the Cape. And it was in the Cape that her great-great-grandmother had fought the 'Bores'. (Her tongue had difficulty – as ours does – in saying the names of our enemies, the Boers.) Her family had happy memories of these fellows, as they did of all the peoples they had fought and crushed. She had met several Bores while on her visit to my country as a young princess. Sadly, she had not met any of my Red People, who, she was sure, were absolutely fascinating.

She had a great gift for making one feel oneself to be the centre of her undivided attention. Her comments, warm and flowing, effortlessly relieved one of the responsibility of saying anything in reply. She pronounced herself absolutely delighted to meet a Red Man who could tell her more about the tremendous advances in my country. The black chaps and the Bores had hated one another, had they not? Yet now they were the best of chums. Wasn't that tremendously encouraging? And soon, she heard, everyone would be living in houses with four bedrooms and free telephones. Wouldn't that be tremendous encouragement to the rest of the world? She could not imagine how I had managed to tear myself away. How very, very touched she was by my gift of a hatful of fruit.

Did I plan to stay long in England? And had I brought other gifts, for her royal collections?

My answer dried in my mouth; the memory, still so raw, of my lost suitcase, and its treasures, assembled with such devotion by my trusting people, cut me to the quick. What I had brought, I said, was a great gift of her great-great-grandmother to my people. What I had lost, alas, were the gifts of my people to Her Majesty. I listed the treasures I had hoped to lay at her feet: a bow of the finest gharree wood, strung with sinew cut from the eland's hide; reed arrows, beautifully light, their heads of flint and iron bound with grass; a pair of ceremonial fire-sticks, so ancient it is said they were made in the First Times, when animals were still people, and had belonged to Kaggen himself; and the chief of music, the singing string, the Bushman fiddle, called the gorah, whose song is as sweet as she-rain after long drought; a rich necklace of ostrich-shell beads, threaded with ant-bear hair, fit for a royal throat; and two dozen copper leg-bangles that women prize; three of the choicest poisons in the world; as well as hides, honey and cups of tortoise shell. Lowering her voice, she urged me to think no more of my loss. What she was about to confide was not to go beyond the palace walls – but my lack of native gifts came as a relief.

Mr Booi, murmured the Sovereign, we own more mummies, bottled infants, golden death masks, pickled hearts, Attic marbles, sacred phalluses from a dozen extinct tribes than we know what to do with. Not to mention axeheads, arrowheads, maidenheads, shrunken heads, assegais, wampum belts, khukris, feathered headdresses, jade daggers and assorted yellow idols, saved from their owners' ignorance and brought home for safekeeping, often at great expense, in our Royal Museums.

It had been the enlightened policy of her missionaries, she graciously explained, and her explorers, soldiers and traders, to remove native artefacts to England, where they might properly be appreciated. That policy had been all very well at the time. But unscrupulous peoples, she feared, had taken advantage of this enlightened policy by encouraging her missionaries, explorers, soldiers and traders to take entire temples and tombs home with them.

Such objects were all tremendously interesting, of course, but those who had forced on her representatives tomb and temple, and seen them crated home to England, had not thought about costs. Now, had they? Frankly, if she saw another shrunken head, she'd scream. And who was expected to pay for it? In reply she tapped the Royal Breast with her wand of feathers.

Her collection of flora and fauna, arrows and earrings, from distant, darker parts of the globe were the envy of the civilised world, but the wretched things were frightfully delicate, and (between herself, myself and the gatepost) not always very well put together. They travelled so badly. Then the mist and the damp ravaged them, and they fell apart as soon as one looked at them. Since – blessedly, then – I had not added to her Royal Collections, what had I brought her?

Opening my quiver, I took from it the Paper Promise of the Old Auntie with Diamonds in Her Hair, and read it aloud:

'We, Victoria, by the Grace of God, of the United Kingdom of Great Britain and Ireland, Queen, Defender of the Faith, Empress of India, to our Trusty and well-beloved San People, of the Cape Karoo, Greetings. We, reposing special Trust and Confidence in your Loyalty, Courage and Good Conduct, do by these Presents Constitute and Appoint you to be a Favoured Nation and send you Our Sign of Friendship – wherever you are. From the Snow Mountains to the Sourveld. From the Cape even to the Kalahari. Assuring you of Our Patronage and Protection in Perpetuity. Like a Lioness her whelps, so do We, Queen and Empress, draw Our Red People to Our Bosom. Let no one molest or scatter them.'

Her Majesty listened intently, nodding her head from time to time when she recognised a phrase. At the end she said, yes, that was Great-Great-Granny's Promise. Make no mistake.

My heart was glad to hear it. Dropping to one knee, I beseeched her to make good her great ancestor's promise to her well-beloved San people. For indeed we had been molested. We had been scattered. My people were crying. They cried to the Great She-Elephant for help. Either to ride to their rescue or to let them come to her, where they might crouch like ants beneath her generous ears, guarded by her tusks. And let her stamp to death our enemies beneath her great feet. She gave a wan smile. The Old She-Elephant was no longer what she had been. She took her tusks out at night; her great ears were torn; and she stood on her feet, all day long, and they were in no condition to stamp anyone to death. More was the pity!

As for the Promises passed by the Queen Empress, well, she would like to show me something. With that she rose to her feet and crossed to a cupboard, opened it and there spilled on to the carpet roll after roll of parchment bound in ribbon, emblazoned with great red wax seals. All of them, every last one, cried Her Majesty, another Promise to another far-flung people. Picking up one at random, she settled a pair of glasses on her nose and read aloud.

'As we looked after you then, I beseech you, please look after your subjects now. Show us you are prepared to spill your blood for us – your Maori people.'

What could one expect, after one's relatives had dished out paper Promises all over the world, as if there were no tomorrow? Well, today was tomorrow. And the sooner far-flung nations in the back of beyond recognized it, the better. Some recipients of dear Great-Great-Grandmama's Promises often made very unreasonable demands. One of her ancestors had dispatched a sea captain to discover these very supplicants, and they had repaid the Royal Kindness by killing and eating the Royal Ambassador. If they were not eating visitors, then they were eating each other. And now they were calling on her to spill blood!

Children! For all their war paint and the funny faces they pulled. When they did not get their own way, they were quite impossible! A great fuss followed by a sad case of the sulks; and then they thought nothing of lifting grass skirts and presenting their naked BTMs to all and sundry. On her last royal visit, posteriors had dominated every walk-about. It did not strengthen a relationship if you began by eating the Queen's representative and ended by mooning at her when she took the trouble to visit you.

And, anyway, the shedding of blood was no longer in her gift. Normally one would have sent soldiers to do that. But now English custom demanded that the shedding of blood, wherever possible, should be left to others.

She was terribly sorry to hear that all was not well between the Red People and the Bores – particularly since they had seemed to be patching things up. But sending troops was just not on. Peace talks would be the most sensible thing. Perhaps one of her officials might act as intermediary and coax us to the peace table?

I said I was sorry, but that was not possible. Did the wild hare converse with the iron hook that rips out its throat?

The Monarch considered this and then munificently suggested that Her Government send a plane to drop food parcels on our remote villages and hamlets. She understood that this was increasingly the popular way of lending assistance in foreign conflicts in which one had no desire to become involved.

Alas, said I, my people did not live in villages; we moved continually in search of chance employment as fence-menders, hunters, tinkers, sheep-shearers, trappers.

Her Majesty now began to show small signs of vexation. If people could not be relied on to remain in one place but went walkabout at the drop of a hat, then they should not be surprised if the major powers did not shower food parcels on them. Aircraft cost the earth. Her own Royal Flight was seldom in the skies these days. Did I know that even her Royal Yacht was to be taken away? An elderly craft, which rolled badly in heavy swells but had given sterling service as well as providing less fortunate people in far-flung places with a glimpse of luxury they might otherwise never have seen. If those who planned this destruction could have seen the pleasure on the faces of simple people, as we steamed into some foreign port, they would think twice about scuttling our yacht.

But then her own people, she feared, had a positive genius for wrecking the very things they did best. Under pressure from impudent upstarts from distant lands, her deluded subjects were turning their backs on the sacred trinity that had made England great: Queen, Church, Currency.

Had I seen the paying guests traipsing through her Palace? Did I imagine she liked strangers in her home? And the mess they left behind?

But we ask you, Mr Booi, she said, gazing at me over her spectacles, what option does one have? How else are we to earn funds for our horribly depleted Treasury? We sweep and scrub and clear up after the visitors. Who else is going to do it for us?

Now she offered a gracious apology for mistaking me for a tax inspector. They had made her life a misery, sneaking in and totting up her riches and demanding she cough up, as they put it, her share of taxes. What riches? Had I any idea how much she spent repairing gutted Palaces, plus the hideous costs of maintaining her children, plus free housing for dozens of staff who had ideas not just above their stations but above hers as well? Had I any idea what a decent page cost? Or a brace of heralds? How hard she had tried to cut back on staff? Yet even now people complained and carped. The lowliest page threatened to go to the tax people. The very soldiers in their sentry boxes demanded that she pay their fox-hunting fees – it drove her into a slough of despond, a *vita horribilis!*

And now there was talk of evicting her from her home and sending her to live in a ghastly modern barn, resembling, no doubt, some hideous municipal public outhouse known as a People's Palace.

As springs bubble up out of sandy riverbeds where a moment before there has been no sign of water, two majestic globules rose somewhere in the deep wells of the Royal Eyes and ran down the proud cheeks in two straight lines, passing on either side of her thin nose and rather pinched lips. What discipline they showed! As if they knew – those regal tears – that they were coursing down the face of the Queen of England, two soldiers on parade, determined to put their best feet forward.

And then, with an offer which melted my heart, she dried her tears with the quiet observation that she would do her duty; however sharp the serpent's tooth of ingratitude. She insisted I join her in a cup of tea. She slipped off into the silent, darkened palace, apologizing for the gloom, but electricity was simply too expensive. I heard her fumbling down shadowy corridors, stumbling every so often as she collided with an escritoire, a commode or some other item of priceless furniture.

She was back, a few minutes later, carrying two steaming mugs of tea. All her fine china had been sold off, along with the royal silver. Even this line of royal merchandise, destined for the gift shop, where paying visitors snapped up souvenirs of their visit, had proved quite useless. The royal offspring, she explained, were given to separating or remarrying so unexpectedly that nuptial mugs were no sooner painted than they were out of date. The royal cellars were crammed with discontinued marital lines she could not sell for love or money.

Did the Red People, she wondered, also have large families?

Only when food supplies permitted, I explained. We had children in order to provide hunters as well as for the love and comfort they gave, especially when we grew old.

But when food was scarce and a baby was born, the mother might disappear into the bush with her new-born infant and return alone. Everyone understood what had happened; the child had been, as we said, 'thrown down'.

She allowed that this seemed to her a jolly sensible arrangement, and sighed so that I thought her heart must break …

… I saw before me an elderly lady in a headscarf, peering uncertainly at the world through a pair of thick spectacles, sipping a mug of cooling tea in a dark room. And I spoke in my heart this question: should the destruction of a Queen be any less tragic than the dying of the eland?

For what was Her Majesty but a member of a rare species? Whose natural habitat was being destroyed. Who faced prodigious odds in her struggle to preserve her ancient rites and customs. Royal numbers dwindled year by year, the few survivors of her line were harried from pillar to post. Her family band – attacked on all sides – faced a fate as cruel as anything we knew in the Karoo. After all, we had our donkeys at least. We had our zincs with which to build our overnight shelters. We had the sharp wind to lash us onward and a road that ran right into the horizon, along which we moved as we chose, when our blood was up and it was time to trek, asking nothing of anyone. Shearing done, fence poles sunk, goats slaughtered for a meal, and the five-man-can of sweet white wine, attended by its single cup, moving round the circle, pulling on black tobacco, we would dance until the white light came, and the dust itself sprang to its feet and danced beside us.

What had this poor woman to compare with that?

An idea took hold of me in the way the flames take hold of the candlebush on an inky night and it burns brighter than the evening star. For it took one to know one. But if our situation was bad, hers was infinitely worse.

I put down my mug; I doffed my hat, and, sinking now to both knees, I addressed her thus. Having seen how she and her family band had been molested and scattered, I could not but ask: if this was the way people of England treated their Queen, did they deserve her? Therefore I, David Mungo Booi, appointed representative of the Red People, formally offered her safe refuge and asylum in our lands.

We would build for her a Royal Hut on the banks of the Riet River, where all the maps and all the missionaries agreed there has been since the beginning the place called Bushmanland. From the First Times, when the animals were still people, ages before the coming of the visitors who stole our land.

Installed in her great place, with her firesticks she would kindle the first fire outside the hut and it would burn in the hearts of her Red People. And then all the travelling bands, now so long dispersed into the hot country and the high country and the far places, would come to take embers from the royal fire with which to kindle their own. All the Red People: the wanderers of the Karoo, the people of the Kalahari, Caprivi, Okavango and Angola; the People of the Soft Sand, the People who follow the Eland; the People from the East; the River Bushmen; the Basarwa and the Remote-area Dwellers of the deserts of Botswana. Not forgetting the #Haba; the G//ana; the !Kung; the G/wi; the !Xo. And she would be our headwoman.

We would sit by her fire.

We would listen to her stories late into the night.

We would play the foot bow and the mouth bow, the thumb piano and the one-string Bushman fiddle.

We would fight to ensure she did not go the way of the quagga, the black-maned lion and the wild horse.

And at her royal camp, near the place called Carnarvon, named for one who had been her relation, and not far from Calvinia, named for one who had been close to God, there would be singing and dancing until the dust danced with us and the world would know that, for the first time, the Bushmen had a Queen. And we would revere her until the end of time, even as her own people did not.

It was while still on my knees that I heard behind me hurrying footsteps, and into the room strode a quick fierce man carrying a riding crop. His hair had faded to the dull gleam of the golden double-daisy after cows have eaten it and their milk is already turning sour. He wore jodhpurs; he slapped the riding crop frequently against the side of his breeches with the flat retort of a rifle echoing across the veld when the Boers were shooting our springbuck.

The look of tender dismay that spread across the Sovereign's face told me at once that this person belonged to her family circle. It was also perfectly plain that she struggled to maintain her regal calm in the peppery presence of this quivery, irritable, sharp, barking man, who was now demanding, in a little voice, not unlike that of the jackal when it scents young lambs in the veld, to know if I was some sort of Chinese chappy.

Rising to my feet and replacing my hat, I replied that I was an ambassador of the Red People.

Was I not rather too yellow to claim that colour? came the response. And why the slitty eyes? Not another bloody foreign honour-guard? He touched a flat hand to the bridge of his noble nose, saying he had had them 'up to here'. More odd-bods from the four corners than he'd had hot breakfasts; little nippy wallahs with wavy knives, also blokes who'd barely taken the bones out of their noses or stopped eating their cousins; not to mention painted chappies from unpronounceable places who sported the most disgusting engine cowlings over their primary bits and pieces. Queuing up to clatter around the Palace courtyard. Didn't matter much any more – if only the poor buggers had known. There would soon be no one left to guard. Her Majesty was surrounded by enemies. They picked off her relatives one by one. Attacked their hunting rites. Jeered at their marriages. The great panjandrums of the press, not to mention the weasels among her Ministers; all determined to sink the greatest Royal House in the world.

Addressing the Sovereign directly, he asked if it was any wonder that so many of their family had gone to pot. Made foolish marriages. Tried to pass themselves off as entertainers, architects, photographers, even – God help him – soldiers or sailors. Anything at all but heirs to the bloody throne! Descendants of the great George and his Dragon, of Arthur, of Harold, of Hengist, not to mention Cnut. What good was I then, ambassador of the Red People? Red, green or yellow – it was yet another damn honour-guard of slitty-eyed pygmies wearing funny hats and not much else getting ready to slam the stable door after the horse had bolted. Unless something was done, and done pretty bloody chop-chop, she could kiss her throne goodbye; and she had that from the horse's mouth.

She lifted her nose as though assailed by the rank perfume of that noxious shrub we call the dog-shit-and-piss-bush. When she replied it was to introduce this individual as the Royal Consort; the royal Upper Lip was as stiff as a bow-string.

A.B. HUGHES

A.B. HUGHES, *or 'Barno' as he was known to many of his colleagues, was the archetypal columnist of mid-century – the sort who had his own peculiar cluttered offices filled with pipe smoke and who wrote mostly about the old days – essays headed 'Whatever happened to the old English breakfast?', and so on.*

Columnists in mid-century tended to dress in tweeds – even in Africa – and 'A.B.' was no exception. He sported the obligatory bristly moustache, horn-rimmed glasses and bald patch. He was friendly and his small talk was laced with good humour. At weekends he pottered about the garden – what else did you expect?

He had his serious side, and his one-time editor, Laurence Gandar, said he was one of the finest leader writers in the country – that, coming from Gandar, who as editor of the Rand Daily Mail *was probably the best, was praise indeed. Hughes's column,* Just in Passing, *ran in the* Mail *for ten years, mainly through the 1970s.*

Hughes was born in London in 1904 and educated at Merchant Taylors' and Jesus College, Oxford. He played rugby and rowed at college level. He was appointed tutor to the Queen of Albania's children and taught the classics in English prep schools before trying his hand at reporting.

He joined a paper in the Home Counties covering events in the Putney, Hammersmith and Fulham area. He was subbing on the Daily Herald *in London before emigrating to the* Natal Mercury *aged 26. Later he helped found the* Sunday Tribune, *which is still going strong. But most of his working life was with the* Rand Daily Mail, *where two of his tasks were writing the* Just in Passing *column, and the quaint* Passing Show *column in the* Sunday Times. *This was a good old-fashioned whimsical column, so typical of the type of gentle humour that was fashionable in newspapers after World War II. 'Barno' Hughes was rarely, if ever, political in his column – but as a leader writer he was powerful in his views about the inhumanity and fatal flaws of the apartheid policy.* Just in Passing *ran from the late 1960s through the 1970s and often reflected Hughes's great interest in natural science.*

Hughes created his last laugh in 1983, at his own funeral. During the funeral parlour service his coffin was, on cue, slowly lowered out of sight. Later, unexpectedly, it rose again. Everybody said 'Barno' would have loved that.

Hughes must have been one of the first columnists to poke fun at the computer and his fears are piquantly amusing all these years later. He reminds us how jokes have had to change. This is what he wrote in 1979, when the typewriter was reality and computers seemed like science fiction to most people ...

Horrible New World

I have warned readers many times that computers will eventually take over the world, and people will be phased out. But I didn't realise things had gone as far as they have.

Already machines exist that can distinguish between various voices and accents and respond to the right one, as a mother can distinguish her own child's cry from other cries competing for attention. For that matter a ewe can detect the cry of her own lamb out of hundreds, though I think you'll admit that it's another matter to have machines doing the same.

But there are more marvels. There are machines which can answer back. At present they have only a small vocabulary but before long they will be constructing complicated sentences and even reciting whole passages from Shakespeare.

You say to your computer, 'What's that bit about to be or not to be? You know. In *Hamlet*.' The computer gives a whirring noise and then out comes the whole thing.

All this will be possible if a giant American oil company called Exxon has its way. This corporation has been pouring money into systems which link the computer to the human voice. And a firm like that doesn't waste its dollars backing non-starters. Nor does it reveal in advance what it hopes to do.

But one of its projects is said to be a typewriter which obeys the human voice, so nobody has to sit down in front of it and bash away at the keys.

This seems to me utterly frightening. What is going to happen to all the shorthand typists? And all the jokes about the girl taking dictation while sitting on the knees of the boss? And the endless jokes about the dizzy blonde who gets the job and then says, 'You didn't really expect me to write shorthand as well, did you?'

This new kind of typewriter is going to ruin the joke factories and the huge industry turning out the kind of postcard known as a 'seaside comic'.

Another device, which is apparently already operating in Britain, is a means of speaking directly to a computer and feeding it with data.

Boss (to the switchboard operator): 'Put me through to our computer, please.'

Switchboard: 'You're going through now, Mr Splurge.'

Boss: 'Hullo, computer?'

Computer: 'Yes, sir. Computer here.'

Boss: 'Get an earful of this …'

If that doesn't frighten you, what does?

But that's not all. You know the problem that crops up when you ring an office and ask to speak to somebody and that blasted somebody is in another room or gone out shopping or something?

Delphi Communications Corporation, an offshoot of mighty Exxon (I wonder whether they know what Delphi was famous for?), can fix that. When the phone has been ringing in an empty room or on a desk where there is nobody to answer it, the computer lets it ring for a certain time and then chips in and asks the caller for a message, which the computer tucks away in its infallible memory, regurgitating it later when the absentee returns and picks up his or her phone. Clever, eh?

Provided you give it a drop or two of oil occasionally, the tireless computer works day and night, so you can ring your office from Miami any time you like to find out what they are doing and tell them not to.

Did you say that a brave new world is unfolding here? It seems to me a horrible world is in store for humanity and I want no part of it.

The only advantage I can see is that a great deal of petrol might be saved if businessmen stay at home and conduct all their office business from there. In fact, they could even stay in bed if they have a bedside telephone.

They need to go to the office only once a week to sign their letters. I don't think they have invented a computer yet which can do that little chore.

I Must Run

Christmas is the time of year when the art of getting away from parties assumes major importance.

Some people, experienced and accomplished leavers, make it look easy. Others never learn how to make a clean, smooth get-away and psychologists hint darkly that this is because these people are not really trying. Subconsciously they enjoy uproar, confusion and protests.

Most of the time-honoured departure phrases are useless in themselves. Nobody ever got away from a party by merely saying, 'I must run.' There must be a definite effort of the will, accompanied by action. Let us examine some of the cantrips that are supposed to have the magic power of getting you out of the front door.

Well, I think I …

This is a waste of time – everybody's time. It is immediately brushed aside and you are then in a weak position of having made a false start. Other false starts follow easily. In any case this phrase has been discredited since Stephen Leacock wrote his macabre story of the curate who couldn't go home.

Heavens! Look at the time!

If you must use this formula, be sure that there is a clock in the room at which you can stare with horror. It is silly to start shouting 'Look at the time' if there is nothing to look at. The weakness of this opening is that it invites the reply 'Oh, but it's early yet!' and you are immediately involved in an argument over the difference between early and late.

We mustn't keep you up.

This merely stimulates your hostess to say, 'We never go to bed before one o'clock.'

I've got to be up early in the morning.

This is useful – with one important proviso. You must have your lie ready. If you say that you have to be up early in the morning, your hostess may easily ask why and it is too late to start inventing a reason at that stage.

I always say firmly and gravely that I've got to leave for Mafeking at six in the morning. I use Mafeking because nobody has ever been there and nobody knows anybody there. It is a complete talk-stopper. And you don't argue with a man who says, with conviction, that he has to go to Mafeking.

Another good trick (for early parties) is to have a friend in a nursing home. A sad case. No, it isn't anybody your hostess knows. Just an old colleague and you must pop in and see how he is doing. Don't get carried away and tell them what he is suffering from. That will only start a flood of surgical gossip. *Just look wistful and go.*

Try to remember that putting out your cigarette and standing up is not the same as going. Many people – mostly women – think they have gone when they have stood up. This is a widespread delusion. You have not gone until the front door is shut behind you. I once timed a woman at a party. She came in late in a great hurry and said she could only stay a second. She then stood in the middle of the room saying 'Goodbye' for 47 minutes.

Try not to forget your hat, bag or cigarettes and then come rushing back a few moments after you have left. You might hear something to your disadvantage.

What's So Remarkable?

Scientists have an extraordinary eagerness to prove to themselves the existence of things which have been well known to the lay public for centuries.

They get state grants for this kind of work, so we can hardly blame them for doing it. But we don't have to burst into loud applause when they announce their discoveries.

Take these psychologists at the Wisconsin-Milwaukee University in America who have gone to great lengths to show that the human ear can pick up sounds, which it does not, in fact, hear and that the human brain can interpret them. Everybody knows that. We do it all the time.

The following conversation for instance is a typical example of communication in the Hughes family and, I suspect, in hundreds of other families.

ME: Owinsopsday?

WIFE: Mydno.

ME: Gemmeshavesopeya?

WIFE: Uh.

ME: Kewdling.

What these syllables really mean can be expressed in English as follows:

ME: Are you going to the shops today?

WIFE: I might be. I don't know.

ME: Get me some shaving soap, will you?

WIFE: Yes (if I can remember and it pans out that way).

ME: Thank you, darling.

A great deal of the effectiveness of this kind of communication is dependent on intonation. For instance the word 'uh' in that context carries a wealth of meaning. It implies that my wife is not committing herself because she has not yet decided whether she will go shopping or not. It also means that my wife has not consciously heard my request, but is willing in general terms to buy what I want if she can dredge it up from her sub-conscious if and when she gets to the shops.

You must bear in mind that during this so-called conversation I was reading the newspaper and my wife was worrying about the drain in the kitchen sink being blocked up. Nevertheless the shaving soap got bought somehow, so the dialogue was after all meaningful.

As I say, this sort of thing has been going on for centuries, probably millennia, but these scientists at Wisconsin-Milwaukee had to prove to themselves that the system actually works. And this is how they did it.

They took a sentence and recorded it on tape, secretly inserting a cough in the middle of one of the words. They then played the sentence over to a number of cooperative listeners and asked them to locate the cough.

Most of them never heard the cough and those who thought they did could not agree on where it came in the sentence.

The sentence chosen was: 'The state governors met with their respective legislatures convening in the capital city.'

It's a terrible sentence, just about as exciting as cold tapioca pudding. It sounds like the kind of thing that schoolboys are required to translate into Latin to show their mastery of the locative case.

In fact the cough, lasting for a tenth of a second, came in the middle of the word 'legislatures', but for all the attention it attracted it might as well never have been coughed.

These scientists also made another discovery that we ordinary people have known about all along. An unexpected silence, they found, is more startling than continued sound. They took the cough out again, leaving a gap in the sentence, and all the listeners spotted it at once.

This phenomenon is so old that some 2000 years ago the Greeks, as usual, had a name for it. They called it aposiopesis, or sudden stoppage in a speech. The schools of rhetoric regarded it as an infallible device for waking up a sleepy audience.

'J.D.'

THIS PSEUDONYMOUS *columnist, whose work was known to all Johannesburg in the mid-twentieth century, had a reputation which any writer would want to die for.*

As a tribute to his memory his newspaper colleagues volunteered to collate and edit his best columns. His typographer friends volunteered to set up, in their own time, his words in lead, and printers of the Sunday Express *worked after hours to print them. The* Rand Daily Mail *published the resulting book 'by public demand', and there was an immediate sell-out of* The J.D. Stories.

Oh, how we missed him in those uncomplicated days of 1950! Even the multitudes who did not know J.D.'s name mourned his passing.

His editor, Rayner Ellis, said: 'In the 25 years for which he wrote for South African newspapers, Jack Douglas, whom his readers knew as "J.D.," was more consistently amusing than any writer of the day ... It was his gift that, in whatever mood you were when you set out to read a "J.D." article, you were smiling before you had finished it. He taught us all to exercise our sense of humour and for this we remember him with gratitude.'

Outwardly, Jack Douglas seemed to take a pessimistic view of life. But the moment he sat down to write one of his leader page articles, he seemed to react to all that earnest editorialising around him, and effortlessly produced a witty piece on anything from Alaskan Indians (including Big Chief Sitting Pretty) to Zulu dancing.

One of Jack Douglas's ploys was to pretend to be the Walter Mitty of his age. He wrote about his career in the French Foreign Legion, in the fire brigade, in the bull ring and as a stage conjuror. He wrote about everything under the sun.

Here are two of his Mitty-style columns.

Going Slow

Browsing though my newspaper in the hope of finding an advertisement offering to adopt a mild-mannered Pressman with a strong anti-work bias, my attention was attracted by a statement that some body of workers intends shortly to stage a 'go-slow' policy; and as I read the announcement memory swung back to the time when I participated in such a movement.

At the time of which I am writing, I was an axlebox feeler's assistant groper on a British railway. In case the importance of my job may be overlooked, I should explain that an axlebox feeler is the man who squats alongside the wheel-tapper at every important station on any given route.

The wheel-tapper, as his title denotes, taps the wheels: although he has no idea why. The axlebox feeler, obviously, feels the axleboxes, and if he finds one that has grown hotter than he thinks it should be, he orders his assistant to mark an X in chalk on the coach concerned.

If it should happen that the axlebox feeler's assistant has forgotten to bring his chalk with him, he turns to the axlebox feeler's assistant groper and instructs him to make the X. Whereupon that latter official starts groping like mad through every pocket in the hope of finding a piece of chalk with which to make the X.

Well, at the time my story opens, as the women novelists say, we used to do our act at a very busy station indeed, a place you could, for instance, compare with Beaufort West. And being the leading axlebox feelers in the service, we were always given that side of the train which drew alongside the platform, for it is out of that side that the inveterate window-looker-outers used to hang. And, naturally, it was extremely soothing to have such a good audience every time a train came in.

One day, however, we were detailed to go and feel axleboxes on the 'blind side' of a train, a very mortifying instruction, as you can well imagine, for if anything is calculated to annoy your matinee idol it is having to act to an empty house, which was practically what feeling axleboxes on the blind side amounted to. So the head man told us we should enter a protest; which we did, and got transferred to the marshalling yard as a penalty.

Being in the marshalling yard meant that we were nothing better than a trio of shunters with nobody to see or worry about our art. Not that a shunter's art is anything to be sneered at. On the contrary, for there is a great deal to learn in that profession. First of all a shunter must know just how to signal to the engine-driver; and these signals are very complicated. To bring the engine up a bit closer a shunter waves his hands like this; to bring the engine up closer but more slowly he waves them like that; to tell the engine-driver to stop, the shunter moves his arms this way; and to tell the engine-driver that he has stopped he moves them that way.

My job was to move my arms that way. In fact, I used to feel that I was a tick-tack man at Epsom in slow motion. *(Pause here for explanation. Anybody who has been on an English racecourse will know exactly what I mean by a tick-tack man, and anybody who has never been on an English racecourse will not.)*

Any sensitive person will immediately grasp how wounded were the feelings of the head man in our trio of axlebox feelers, and therefore will sympathise with him when he gathered us around him and said, 'Chaps, there is only one answer to this indignity; we shall have to go slow.'

Neither of his two helpers having sufficient courage to inquire how we could go slower without becoming positively immobilised, we accepted his dictum. And here is one example of how slow we went.

We had to couple up the fast fish train to the south on to a special train that had been chartered by a travelling company of actors, and to do that you, if you are a shunter, pick up a coupling link, hold it between the buffers of two coaches, wait until your mate has waved the engine on to the job, slip in the coupling pin, and there you are. In slow time the job was done like this. The head man selected a coupling link and passed it to his assistant, the assistant examined it carefully for any flaws, and then passed it on to me, after which I fitted it between buffers A and B and called the assistant to come and inspect the effect.

The assistant said he thought the effect was perfect, but the head man didn't agree. Being scrupulously fair, he suggested we fetch the engine-driver and get his opinion. Good as that idea was, it wasn't good enough, because with the engine-driver we became a foursome, and the votes cancelled each other out; so the engine-driver went to call the fireman in order to have a proper quorum.

After we had arrived at a satisfactory conclusion, the driver and his fireman went back to their end of the train, only to find that the water in the engine had gone off the boil. Which was a nuisance. What is more, it brought along the guard, who wanted to know how much longer we were going to hold up his train. He became extremely annoyed about it and said our go-slow tactics were ruining the fish.

The head man, ever just, said he had sensed that something on the train had gone bad, to which the guard replied it must be the fish, for he had seen the actors on the stage the night before, and they could never possibly go any worse than they were then, and what with discussing Henry Irving and one thing and another, it was time to knock off before we remembered that the coupling link argument had still to be decided.

Not that that mattered much, because the driver and fireman had already gone to supper and taken their engine with them.

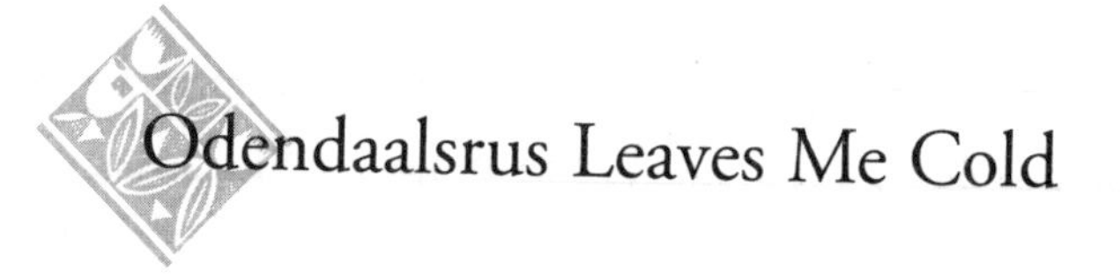

Odendaalsrus Leaves Me Cold

All this fuss about Odendaalsrus leaves me completely apathetic. And the talk about the money that changed hands over share transactions last week merely makes me laugh, for even if the suggested figure of £27,000,000 is correct it is just so much chicken feed by comparison with what I used to handle in the days when I dealt on the Stock Exchange.

The manner in which I became an operator in the market is almost a romance in itself.

I was talking to a man one day some years ago about stocks and shares and the fortunes people made out of them, when he said, 'Do you know that it is not so long ago that you could have bought the whole of the Blyforson mine for a song?'

'You don't mean that?' I gasped. 'The whole mine, eh?'

'Absolutely,' he nodded. 'And look at its shares to-day.'

Well, I couldn't exactly look at them, because I had none to do it with, but this man's remark set me wondering. A whole mine for a song, he said, so what I could have bought with a voice like mine does not bear thinking about.

However, the tales this man told me of the deals he had put through and the money he made decided me on my course of action, and as soon as I had got rid of him by lending him the half-crown he was so badly in need of I called on a stockbroker.

'I want to buy some shares,' I told the broker.

'Certainly, sir,' he said, because in those days a broker had time to call a client 'sir', and, what is more, to welcome him with a cigar and a whisky and soda out of the filing cabinet labelled 'Private and Confidential'.

'What particular stock had you in mind?'

'What stocks have you got?' I asked, not unreasonably, I thought.

'Gold, lead, silver, coal, almost anything you like,' replied the broker.

'Could I see one or two, do you think?' I put to him, for I was never one to rush in and buy anything without examining the article beforehand.

'We don't keep shares that way,' said the broker, a thought less affable than before. 'The procedure is for the client to instruct us about the name and number of the shares he requires and then we buy them on his behalf.'

'Oh, I see,' I said. 'Well, as I am more or less a beginner, how would it be if I bought one of each?'

'One each of what?' demanded the broker, this time with considerable irritability.

'One each gold, lead, silver and coal,' I answered. 'And I can pay cash for them, too,' I added, producing a pound note by way of good faith.

'You can't buy a single share of anything,' said the broker wearily, 'and there's no need to talk about paying cash.'

'Ah,' I exclaimed, 'now you're talking my language. If it isn't a matter of putting up the ante you tell me what you think I should buy and I'll do the ordering.'

In less than a week I had bought every available Upsit on the market; I practically controlled Teddies; nobody but I had a look in where Eastern Grips were concerned, and as for Cape Town Levels, if there was an odd one anywhere about I should like to know who had it.

I was a Bear in London and a Bull in New York. Financial journals offered fabulous sums to be allowed to write up my history. I offered them more fabulous sums to keep it quiet.

Mining groups all over the world sent me frantic cables imploring me to accept a seat on their boards.

Three brokers declined business from any other clients in order to devote their attention to me. Then the three brokers went broke.

But I didn't care, I still carried on, and engaged three new brokers, who also acted a charade on their titles in due course.

Then I decided to get rid of all my mining shares and go flat out for Industrials.

And that brought about Black Friday.

It made no difference to me; I was focusing my attention on a new hair restorer that was shortly to come on the market.

One of my brokers told me to step into Dandruff Deferred Ops. I told him to buy the lot. Then the company applied to some authority or other to issue another million of their Ops. I bought them, too.

A week later the company was declared insolvent, or had a winding-up order served on it, or something of the sort.

My broker rang me up in a panic and said he wanted the entire purchase price of my holdings immediately.

'Nothing of the sort, my good man,' I said to him. 'I've decided that I don't want them.'

'But you can't do that,' he wailed. 'You gave me a firm order to buy.'

'You told me', I pointed out, 'that what I was dealing in were Ops.'

'Quite right, I did.'

'And if I understand the word correctly,' I said, 'it means that it is optional whether I take them or not, and I'm exercising my option. Good-bye.'

CAROL LAZAR

CAROL LAZAR, *a long-established columnist and probably the country's best-known travel writer, produces a popular travel supplement in the* Saturday Star.

She has four grown-up children and is a keen photographer, scuba diver and pianist.

Lazar, daughter of an oncologist and a mother who escaped the Holocaust which swept away most of her family, was born in Northern Ireland when her parents were en route to South Africa from the ruins of mid-century Europe.

Lazar's outspoken mother appears often in her columns, as does Betty, one of Lazar's close friends (Betty Rajak of Johannesburg). In fact, '95 per cent' of the people Lazar writes about in her weekly column – Laser Beam – *are family and friends.*

Why Not a National Men's Day?

You might have noticed during the past few weeks a fair amount of correspondence in the newspapers, as well as heard in various utterings and protestations from males who felt they were being gender disadvantaged by the fact that they do not have a National Men's Day. This, of course, all in response to Monday's National Women's Day.

You may too have read or heard the debate about whether there should be a National Women's Day, the implication being by female purists that having such a day, instead of focusing on women to their advantage, denigrates them. Having a National Women's Day, they said, implied that women were lesser beings than men and came into their own only on one day of the year. Rather like Save the Whale Day, or HIV Day. Every day of the year, they felt, should be a National Women's Day.

Ag, ja, well, no, fine. There is validity in both schools of thought but the reality is that a national day for women creates an awareness, even if only temporary, of women's very real needs and aspirations.

Meanwhile, to get back to the original objections by men, my husband among them, they felt they were being discriminated against because they too did not have their day.

'If women, whales and a disease can have a day, why can't we?' he said from the comfort of the stoep where on this National Women's Day he was enjoying a beer with two friends and discussing why the Springboks had not won the test match.

My mother, who has her own opinion on why we did not win the test, the main reason being that the All Blacks fielded the stronger team, has never, in 85 years, let a good opportunity pass. Like a rocket launcher she blasted off: 'You and every other man in this country', she said, speaking generally but glowering at her son-in-law, 'celebrate National Men's Day every day of the year.'

'Ma, lighten up,' muttered my spouse as he removed himself to the safety of the three-metre flames blazing in the braai griddle. His friends moved with him. Momentarily it looked as if they were peering through hellfire, though I rather suspect that in my husband's mind Hades took the form of a diminutive octogenarian with strong views on life and even stronger vocal chords.

As the *wors* sizzled, my mother launched forth. 'Men have been having their day for centuries,' she said firmly 'and look where it's got us. Starting with God,' she continued. 'Only a male God would find merit in people spending all their time in strange buildings singing ridiculous songs and calling that worship. A female God would be far more pragmatic.'

'I say,' said Cyril who had recently become a reborn fish. 'That's blasphemous.'

'Nonsense, it's your mind that's blasphemous,' retorted my mother now in full spate.

At which stage, calling a truce, I dished up lunch.

'Ho, ho, I didn't know you were a hairy armpit,' said Cyril to my mother, attempting to make light of the previous conversation. It was an unfortunate analogy, being the pejorative description coined by patronising males of activist women in the '60s.

'My armpits were and are as hairy as my legs,' replied my mother, 'but, unlike you, there is no hair on my brain.'

Cyril, who at best resembled a kingklip, at worst a less than firm hake, choked on his *wors* and giggled nervously. 'Such a sense of humour your mother-in-law has,' he muttered to my husband.

I said nothing. This was not the time to talk of my mother's past. To tell of her courage, how during World War Two she left the country of her birth when her family were murdered and lived for many years as a refugee. How in South Africa, the country of the man she married, and the country of her adoption, she made her own stand against what she considered immoral and, in her own way, fought what she considered yet another evil system.

Later, when I kissed her goodbye, she whispered in my ear: 'God should have been a woman,' and I knew she wasn't joking.

At one time Carol Lazar was running a column, a family, a husband, a desk and an out-of-office job at the same time. This was a period when children in Johannesburg required 25-hours-a-day attention. Here is some correspondence on the subject. It occurred in another generation – but some things never change.

Who Said Parties Are Fun?

Dear Melissa's Mommy,

It really is so nice of you to ask Nicky to your dear little girl's seventh birthday party on Saturday late afternoon. She'd love to come. Unfortunately, our Kombi is out of action right now. It's at the garage because I bumped into Mrs Feitelbaum's car as she reversed down Corlett Drive. So I won't be able to lift the 16 little girls to the Bunny Park.

It's a little difficult to fetch Nicky at 9 pm, as we're going to a dinner party – some old friends of ours we haven't seen for six years, ever since they emigrated to London.

And the hostess asked us to be there at 7.30 pm sharp as it's a surprise party.

I've ordered the three dozen rolls but unfortunately I won't be going to the market this week so you'll have to buy a few lettuces at the veggie shop, or ask the kids to bring their own goodies for the bunnies and goats.

I think it's a charming idea asking the little visitors to dress in white and be fairies but do you really think it's practical, I mean with the bunnies, goats and pigs?

We looked everywhere for a Grecian doll. It seems they're impossible to find so eventually we decided to give Melissa a colouring-in book and crayons. If she's not happy she can change them.

Nicky's not too crazy about curry and rice, but don't worry – she can have a hamburger when she gets home.

Cheers,

Carol

Dear Casey's mother,

Jamie would love to come to Casey's disco party.

Of course, he says he's not going to dance; he'd rather climb a tree with Dan and throw candyfloss at everyone. But don't worry, he's got a terrible aim. You know what nine-year-olds are like.

Yes, it probably would bore them to tears playing games.

Oh, I think it's a super idea having a candyfloss machine. It should keep them busy for ages.

I'll pack the braai forks with his soccer ball and the projector. And my husband says please, if possible, don't let the kids operate the projector. Last time they cracked the lens, damaged the sound and lost a reel. Just little things, but very irritating when next you want to use the machine.

Unfortunately Jamie isn't allowed to borrow Barry's records.

Poor old Barry's still trying to scrape the bubble gum off the 'Beach Boys', from the last party.

Jamie hasn't got a glitter shirt or satin pants, so I'm afraid he'll have to wear his tracksuit and joggers.

I'm sorry we won't be able to give Dan, Chris, Simon and Robbie a lift home at 9 pm but as we're going to a dinner party Bob'll have to pop out in between the quiche Lorraine and the duck to fetch Jamie, so he'll be in a bit of a rush.

It's a pity you live out at Halfway House, because the dinner is in Kensington, 40 km away – oh well, it's just one of those things.

Cheers,

Carol

Dear Clothilde's Mom,

Just a few words to say thank you for inviting Ralph to your daughter's 13th birthday party.

What a novel idea having a Roman orgy. It really is unusual. And how fabulous managing to get Bill Haley to come and sing Roman rock to the kids.

Ralph said you wanted to get one of the biggies – Frank Sinatra or Sammy Davis Jnr – but that they were both busy. Oh well. I've packed Ralph's meat in his tog bag, along with his laurel wreath.

They were out of fillet, so I've given him stewing steak. If it's tough, he can chew harder.

I appreciate it's inconvenient for you to run him home at 10.30 pm. Don't worry, it's OK.

We're only going to a dinner party with some old friends we haven't seen for six years, so we can leave early and pop along to fetch him. It doesn't matter if we skip dessert.

He's a little unhappy about wearing a fluffy winter sheet but it's the only one I have, unless he goes along in the fitted drip-dry with the psychedelic design. (Did Romans go for pop art?)

He could wear the lace bedspread in the upstairs cupboard but perhaps it's a bit chilly.

I hope the orgy goes with a bang.

Kind regards,

Carol

Dear Mrs Hodges,

Thank you for inviting Barry to Henrico's 15th party. It's kind of you to say he's a lovely boy, and he'd be an asset to any party – Barry I mean.

My husband and I were very touched by your kind words. And if he'd only learn to eat with a knife and fork, we feel he'd be a sensation.

Yes, he does have a quiet charm. His father says there's nothing to worry about, he'll learn to speak by the time he's 21.

I want you to know I think it's a lovely idea having a 'Riotous Razzle'. It'll be the first one Barry's ever been to.

I don't mean to be difficult, but don't you think that champagne's a little extravagant and that lemonade would do?

I think it's super getting Sol to cater, but Barry's not all that keen on caviar blinis – so perhaps you could ask the chef to knock up a hotdog or two.

No, he's never seen a strip show before and my husband feels he's still a little young. I mean it's not that we want to be over-protective. He can read comics or watch TV in the solarium during the strip.

And don't worry, seeing you're not able to take the kids home at 12.30 am – we'll set the alarm and Rob can stagger out of bed into the cold night air to fetch Barry, Kean and Giuseppe.

Thanks,

Carol

LEGAL HUMOUR

ONE OF *the finest and most delicate of arts – the polished, witty, after-dinner speech – appears to be dying on its feet. Certainly judicial forensic wit, the source of many post-prandial speeches, is languishing.*

When last did you hear of a court-room exchange such as:

Counsel: 'M'Lord, I see I have addressed you for more than an hour, but as this is so complex a case, I must trespass a little further on the Court's time.'

Judge: 'Mr Lushington, you are now trespassing on eternity.'

Prolixity is a favourite target, but there are many others. Because legal forensic wit is confined to the ripostes of learned but eloquent lawyers in earnest argument, it is a rare form of humour. And it is hard to capture because of the difficulty of confirming the precise circumstances and elegant wording of these gems delivered, usually, in the heat of legal battle. Fortunately there is a man dedicated to the task in this country.

Prof. Ellison Kahn, Professor Emeritus of Law at the University of the Witwatersrand, spent years collecting material for his work Law, Life and Laughter *(Juta, Johannesburg, 1991). His collection is culled from books, articles, press reports, unpublished memoirs, letters and stories told to him by the legal fraternity. He meticulously sources all his research from 265 books, law journals, manuscripts and the rest, which often provide him with several versions of the same incident. His book contains some forensic wit, but consists mainly of anecdotes. He has to contend with two realities: the scarcity of judicial forensic wit; and the fact that anecdotes are slippery customers. The best anecdotes are easily appropriated by those not involved in them, and the worst ones are usually exaggerated. But in his painstakingly researched work, 'every person of whom an anecdote is related or a biographical piece is offered is named, if a name has been available …', he explains.*

Our extracts begin with some of the most elusive but oft-repeated anecdotage.

'Mr Interpreter, what *did* the witness say?'
'"Bugger all", your worship.'
'Funny, I could have sworn I saw his lips move.'

(1974) 14 Rhodesian Law Journal 6

'The court takes a very serious view of your case,' said the magistrate. 'This is the fifth pedestrian you have knocked down in seven months.'

'Pardon me,' said the woman motorist with dignity. 'Four. One of them was the same person twice.'

Rand Daily Mail, July 13 1948

The following exchanges took place in Rhodesia (now Zimbabawe):
'After you had been raped, did you show the police the scene of the crime?'

'No, but I showed the doctor.'

Again: 'You have given his lordship your version of the facts, but I must put it to you ...'

'You can put it where you like, Mr Tracey.'

(1974) 14 Rhodesian Law Journal 86

In a Johannesburg newspaper some years ago appeared a report of a crimen injuria case in that city.
Complainant: 'He put his hand up my dress, your worship.'
Prosecutor: 'And did he impair your dignity?'
Complainant: 'No, your worship, he never came near it.'

Rand Daily Mail, September 7 1974

Sam Ellman

Witty figures often attract other people's witticisms, just as figures from Confucius to Winston Churchill are attributed with other people's aphorisms. Sam Ellman, who died in Simon's Town in 1932, was a legendary, beloved character, described by H.H. Morris KC as 'the wittiest and most versatile of all the junior magistrates'. Here are just a sample of the tales told of him:

One day Ellman, feeling the cold, requested the Court constable to turn on the heating apparatus. The constable, being unable to get the heating appliances to function, informed the Court that it apparently was not operating. 'Why, of course,' said Ellman, 'I overlooked the fact that this is a court of "summary" jurisdiction.'

Ellman, becoming impatient, requested the attorney not to take up the time of the Court by irrelevant questions and repetition.

'Surely,' protested the attorney, 'your worship will allow some latitude?'

'I don't mind giving you latitude,' said Ellman, 'it is your longitude that I object to!'

Ellman was once transferred to Germiston, and on the day of his arrival he was called upon to try a case of theft. The defending attorney commenced his opening remarks in somewhat the following fashion: 'Your worship, the first question I am constrained to ask in this case is, where is the *mens rea*? I say, where is the *mens rea*?'

'I am sorry to interrupt you,' said Ellman, 'but to tell you the truth, I only arrived this morning, and I'm a total stranger.'

It had been suggested to Ellman that on his retirement he should write a book of reminiscences. He said that if he did so he would like to name it *Grains of Chaff – Picked up by the Beak.*

Fritz Sonnenberg (attorney of Cape Town), South African Law Times 32–4, 1933

Sam was sent to Witbank, which he said was no place for a white man. He became disagreeable to everyone and within a month he had reached his ambition. He had become the most unpopular man in the district ... The local MPC called on him.

'Mr Ellman, we don't want to do anything behind your back. We are getting up a petition for your removal. Is there anything I can do in the matter?'

'Yes', said Sam, 'bring me the bloody thing. I want to sign it'

H.H. Morris KC, The First Forty Years (1948) 68–70

Mr Justice Ronald (Ronnie) Wordscrambler

Prof. Kahn has given this fictitious name to a former judge, and we shall respect the author's wishes, though others have collected lists of the same judge's famous remarks. His sayings were too rich not to be preserved for posterity. Some of our lists coincided under a single heading: 'Erasmusania'.

Some of his sayings were so apt that one could never be sure whether they were unintentional or deeply inspired. Some were surely said in fun. And some are probably apocryphal – as were many Sam Goldwynisms such as 'Include me out'; 'Any man who goes to a psychiatrist ought to have his head read'; 'In two words: impossible'; and 'A verbal contract isn't worth the paper it's written on'.

Goldwyn must have had great scriptwriters. The South African judge was on his own. Prof. Khan tries – 'probably in many cases unnecessarily' as he admits – to interpret what 'Mr Justice Wordscrambler' intended to say.

Malapropisms

To a friend: 'When you go on the Bench, life becomes circumcised [circumscribed].
Friend: 'You mean a bit cut off?'

As counsel: 'My lord, I now come to my carnal [cardinal] point.'
As counsel: 'Let me illuminate your lordship.'

As a judge, to a colleague: '… the walruses [bulrushes] were ten feet high.'

To a judicial colleague, on the work of the so-called Erasmus Commission on irregularities of the former Dept of Information: 'This is a very contagious [contentious] matter. *(Note from the editors: The judge was right, in one sense. The irregularities affected the State President so badly, he had to resign. And the judge's report contained some glorious prose equating secretive bureaucracy with a black cat in a blacked-out cellar.)*

To a colleague at the Bar: 'We'll get her under the canine [canon] law.'
Colleague: 'That'll serve the bitch right.'

From the Bench: 'Don't let that deturb [? deter or disturb] you.'

From the Bench: 'That would be clear to an outstander [? outsider].'

To a judicial colleague, who arrived late at his party: 'Solly, here's the bar – humiliate yourself.' [? Make yourself at home]

A Word in the Ear

To a judicial colleague: 'You take a piece here and a piece there, and then everything falls into place like a crossword [jigsaw] puzzle.'

To a judicial colleague: 'So during the war you flew to Europe, America, Africa and the East! You must have gone halfway round the bulb.'

To a colleague at the Bar: 'I want my bone [pound] of flesh.'

Of opposing counsel: 'He's barking around [beating about] the bush.'

To a judicial colleague: 'The case was easy fry [meat].'

In an art gallery: 'I love the quiet [still] life.'

Of a witness involved in many matters: 'He had a finger in every tart.'

Conflated Expressions

To a colleague: 'The arrangement is as safe as a house on fire.'

As counsel: 'The plaintiff is now skating on the thin edge of the wedge.'

As counsel: 'What my learned friend says flows down my back like a duck's water.' (cf. Sam Goldwyn: '... like a duck off the water's back'.)

To a friend: 'Since then we have all passed a lot of water under the bridge.'

As a newcomer to the Bar, after hearing Oswald Pirow arguing a case: 'It was wonderful. He spoke with his tongue up his sleeve.'

To a friend: 'I prefer to be a small fish in my own backyard.'

Based in part on Ellison Khan, 'The Seven Lamps of Legal Humour Part 2' 1984 De Rebus 210

H.H. Morris KC

Morris is rapidly becoming a legend. (He was, of course, a 'KC' during the reign of King George VI and a 'QC' when Queen Elizabeth came to the throne – and before South Africa became a republic.) Despite his sometimes forlorn expression, he was undoubtedly one of the wittiest barristers in any court anywhere. There were times, it is said, when his jokes lost him a case ... but his wit also won many.

He may have been weak on law, but his power of breaking witnesses and bending juries was uncanny. He has been described as 'the most famous defender in South African history'.

In Prof. Kahn's book on legal anecdotes more space is devoted to Harry Morris than perhaps to any two or three other legal personalities together. Kahn wrote of Morris that 'one of [his] greatest triumphs was his successful defence in Nairobi of Etonian Sir Delves Broughton, who was charged with the murder of a fellow Etonian, the Earl of Erroll, who had cuckolded him … The trial (May–July, 1941) and its background were the subject of a fascinating book by James Fox, *White Mischief* (1982), on which the film of that name was based. The film, which met with a mixed reception, deviates from fact not only by (a necessary) simplification but also in several important happenings. The trial caused a sensation in exposing the promiscuous and sybaritic mode of existence of a set of debauched and degenerate members of the British aristocracy and their hangers-on, all of whom had settled in Kenya. In his memoirs, Morris makes out that in his view Broughton did not fire the pistol shot that killed Erroll in his motor car … though he does not say that Broughton was innocent …

Morris is believed to have appeared in more courts as counsel for the defence than any other person in Africa. He described the murder hearing in 1931 when the son of a British MP, Richard Louis Mallalieu, was charged with robbing and shooting a taxi driver, as his 'most sensational trial'. In legal precedents it might have been. But many will agree that the trial of Daisy de Melker, found guilty and hanged for poisoning two husbands and her sole surviving son, was more sensational. She probably poisoned at least seven people, including others of her children, and was described by Morris in his memoirs as 'ruthless, remorseless and pitiless'. But even in this trial, certainly in hindsight, he found humour.

Apart from his memoirs in 1948 (*The First Forty Years*), he set out to write about the forensic wit in South African courts. But he abandoned the project because, he said, 'although I have no doubt the stuff exists, the difficulty is to find the man who was present'.

Instead, he resorted to anecdotes from the courts. The tales he collected for his book *In Court and Out of Court* (Central News Agency, South Africa, 1950) 'are founded on fact,' wrote Morris, 'there is no fiction here.'

(Indeed I was in the very courtroom, many years ago, and witnessed Morris's account of the learned judge who, being very deaf, was listening to the evidence on his old-fashioned hearing apparatus. We heard the accused protesting that she wasn't getting a fair trail, 'because the man up there is listening to his radio instead of listening to me'.)

On the subject of deaf judges, there is the other well-sourced anecdote about Charles Gardner, Judge President of the Eastern Districts Local Division, whose deafness – presumably from service as an artillery man in World War I – was legendary. When somebody was asked 'Who's hearing the appeals today?' he replied: 'I don't know, but Charlie Gardner's on the Bench.'

But, more than their entertainment value, the importance of these factual tales gathered by a barrister is their accurate reflection of the mores, the prejudices and the legal practices of the times. It was a time when, for instance, the word 'kaffir' was losing its innocence and being purposely used as a racial insult – as these stories show. It was a time of blatant racial and gender discrimination, not only in South Africa, but also in the United States, Britain and the entire Western world. Morris's time, however, was also a time of pre-apartheid justice. Most judges spent their lives guarding clear, old-fashioned, basic values. Most tried to be fair in an unfair society. The ironic result of this was that, after Morris's time, the jury system had to be abolished in South Africa – in the interests of fairness.

These 'funny stories' demonstrate why.

The following extracts are from H.H. Morris's *In and Out of Court*, which, be warned, is a minefield of old-fashioned political incorrectness.

The Doll

The Judge in his scarlet robe sat motionless on the Bench. A native woman was ushered into the box. After she had been led by the Prosecutor, His Lordship turned his face slowly towards her to ask a question. With a loud shriek the witness fell to the floor of the witness-box. When she came round, the Interpreter asked her what was the matter. 'It is alive, but when I came into Court I thought it was a doll.'

The Marines

The Contractor, who was erecting a house on a farm, had been sued in the Court below for damages caused by a fire-bucket, in working order, which was upset through the carelessness of one of his employees. The countryside was soon ablaze, and an aggrieved farmer, whose crops had been burnt, sued the Contractor for damages. The matter went on appeal before Mr Justice De Waal.

The Court to Counsel: 'Mr Smith, what does the Magistrate mean when he says that the fire-bucket was to windward?' Counsel mumbled that he did not understand nautical terms.

The Judge: 'What you really mean is that you are more at sea than I am.'

Poetic Justice

Sam Ellman was fond of Ponies, Poker and Poetry. The Lady in the case sued on the footing that she had been seduced. In the witness-box she abandoned her declaration and tried to save her face by claiming that she had been raped. She looked like a lady who could be seduced, but not like one who could be raped.

Sam exonerated the Defendant from the crime, but found for the lady in the following lines:

A little she strove, and much repented
And murmuring 'I will ne'er consent' – consented.

The Two Temperance Men

The Temperance Union had brought all its guns to bear on the Evils of Drink. They had been doing so year in and year out, and yet drink remained, and, what is more, it was still an evil. The Licensing Courts refused to be converted. The Evil still had its ally. The destructive effect of drink was emphasised. The world was being ruined by the juice of the grape. All this was too much for me. I rose in my place and reminded the Temperance Union that the destruction of the world was nearly accomplished by Two Teetotallers, Hitler and Mussolini, and that it was saved by Two Hard Drinkers – Churchill and Stalin.

The Referee

It happened on Circuit. The Accused was being tried for attempted rape. The husband was giving evidence. He said that on the night in question he and his wife retired to rest at about ten o'clock. At about midnight he was awakened by the uneasy stirring of the sleeping lady. He then saw the Accused, who was a complete stranger to him, lying on the other side of his wife, attempting to have intercourse with her. The witness said he jumped up and blew his police whistle.

'Why did you blow your whistle?' His Lordship asked.

'Offside,' came in a loud whisper from a Junior Member of the Bar.

Judicial Ignorance

Counsel appeared for one of the parties to an action in which the validity of a rock-drill patent was in dispute. In a masterly opening of his case, which took some hours, he dismantled the drill and explained the function of each part as he did so. He then reassembled the machine. The Court expressed its appreciation of the lucid and instructive presentation of his case.

'But,' said His Lordship, 'that little thing at the bottom. Does it revolve, or does it rotate?'

'That is as Your Lordship pleases.'

Taking the Cow by the Horns

An attorney, who was acting for the defendant in a seduction and affiliation case, found that he could not go on with the trial on the morning of the hearing. He ran round to another attorney with the cover and explained that he had to leave town on urgent business, and asked his colleague to appear for him. He said that it was a very simple case and that he did not think that his client had a hope. The case was called and, to the horror of the deputy, there stepped into the box a lady with whom he had himself been intimate a few years before. When his turn came to cross-examine, he did so with great apprehension. He determined to forestall her.

Said he: 'So you say the defendant was intimate with you?'

'Yes.'

'I suppose you'll next say that I was intimate with you?'

'Of course you were.'

The Magistrate turned to the plaintiff's attorney: 'Mr Jones, for heaven's sake take your client out of the box. I can't believe a word she says.'

That was the end of the case.

The Investigator

Some years ago a cattle dealer disappeared from a village in the Western Transvaal. His affairs were in order. He had been in good health. He had no domestic trouble. Slowly the inhabitants came to the conclusion that he had been murdered for the money which was usually carried about with him. Marshall Square took the matter in hand and sent down its Best Brains.

The Best Brains got busy and interrogated every man, woman and child in that village, and to such good purpose that within six months he had the suspects and the body.

The accused, a man and a woman, were eventually brought to trial before the Circuit Court.

At the trial, after the usual preliminaries, the Prosecutor called the name of the first witness and asked leave to read her evidence. He stated that at a later stage he would call the District Surgeon to depose to the fact that the witness was unable to attend Court. The application was granted and the evidence was read. The same thing happened in the case of the next five witnesses. The District Surgeon then gave evidence to the effect that each of these witnesses was about to become a mother and that none of them could attend these proceedings.

The Accused were convicted. The Court complimented the Best Brains on the very good and effective work he had done.

And so a wise man combined business with pleasure.

Defeating the Ends of Justice

The Plaintiff was suing for damages, which he alleged were caused by his foot catching in the brass nosing of a stairway down which he was walking. During the first morning of the hearing, Counsel suggested an inspection *in loco* at 2.30.

At one o'clock the Judge visited the building. There he found a brawny man with a heavy hammer hammering down the brass nosing.

'Well, my man,' said His Lordship, 'and what are you doing?'

'Well,' said the carpenter, 'a bloke fell down these stairs the other day and broke his leg, and now he is suing my boss for damages. The old Judge is coming to see the place, so I am tidying it up a bit for him.'

Judgments

Mr Justice James FitzPatrick (1816–80), father of Sir Percy FitzPatrick – author of *Jock of the Bushveld* – possessed an uneven temper, short patience and a broad Irish brogue. During an action being tried as to the boundary between two farms, the Attorney-General produced in court a whole armful of ponderous volumes. He told the enquiring judge that they were dictionaries.

'But what for?' persisted the Judge ...

'I am going to quote them on the question of what is a direct line.'

'Well, Mr Attorney,' said the Judge, 'if it's the maning of a direct loine that ye want, just ye look at me, for I'm going in a direct loine to me lunch' – and he went.

Sir Henry Juta KC, Reminiscences of the Western Circuit (1912) 74–5

Mr Justice Israel Goldblatt (1897–1982) recalled that when he was a clerk in South West Africa he replaced a sergeant of the military forces. In one of his files the judge came across a letter sent by the sergeant to the Director of Prisons, enclosing a death warrant 'for favour of execution'.

As a judge, Goldblatt was against executions. He also found that it was easier to decide upon a question of guilt than upon the sentence.

'I came to the conclusion that the only solution was that, for a judge to be able to appreciate the real nature of the punishment he was inflicting, he should previously have undergone it himself. And in discussing this matter with a judge, I went further and suggested that this principle should apply also when a sentence of death by hanging has to be passed.'

I. Goldblatt, Early South West Africa – Bench and Bar (1978) 266

Mr Justice Leopold Greenberg (1885–1964) was a gentleman in the old sense, and a judge with compassion and humour ... In a jury trial [in those days, a full South African jury consisted of nine men] in which he was the judge, the evidence of guilt was clear, and it contained no suggestion that the accused was *non compos mentis*; nevertheless the foreman announced the unanimous verdict of the jury to be 'Not guilty'. Observing a look of surprise on the judge's face, he added hastily, 'on account of insanity'.

'What, all nine of you?' asked the judge.

G.A. Mulligan, 'Retirement of the Hon. Mr Justice Greenberg' (1955) 72 SALJ 1, 1–2

Leaning forward ever so slightly as he speaks, his face more solemn than ever, Mr Justice Greenberg periodically delivers these devastating ironies, and over the years there has now been amassed a whole collection of Greenbergiana ... for instance:

Counsel was arguing the amount of damages to which his client was entitled as a result of the loss of some cattle. Of a certain cow, counsel said its value should be assessed more highly 'because it was in an interesting condition'.

... Mr Justice Greenberg leaned forward slightly, his voice soft and low. 'Interesting to whom?' he asked.

A witness ... turned to the judge and said: 'May the Almighty strike me dead if I am telling a lie.'

Allowing a pause to pass, Judge Greenberg said: 'Until there is a suitable response to this invitation, we have no choice but to proceed with the case.'

[Contrast this response with the attitude of another judge who, when a witness called upon God to be his judge, the bewigged figure on the Bench replied: 'I am the sole authority in this court.']

MADAM & EVE

'FORGIVE ME, *father, for I have sinned. For years I've been paying my maid Eve only R10 for a full day's work,' admits Madam.*

The priest considers this statement from the confessional box and responds: 'Is she available Tuesdays?'

This was the very first strip of their first social commentary in the Madam & Eve *saga, published by the* Weekly Mail. *(The other two appear below.) It poked fun at Johannesburg's white suburbanites, even before most of them voted for a black President. It also poked fun at urban Africans, and South African Indians, and everyone else in the racialist state. And, when racism was 'banned' it continued to laugh with – rather than at – the idiosyncratic attitudes of a very mixed-up people.*

This has proved to be acutely observed and tenderly portrayed 'transition humour' – a powerful instrument in changing social attitudes and encouraging peaceful political solutions.

At first, under the old, already altering as well as faltering political regime, only a few thousand liberally inclined readers saw the paper's illustrated wit each week. The new comic focused mainly on the peculiarly strange mores of a racially divided society. It offered inside jokes to a sophisticated city. The cartoon series was, for many South Africans, their first introduction to the Johannesburg institution of 'the Mealie Lady' and other wonderful characters who wander the city's streets.

A decade later, in 2002, the comic strip was being syndicated to 13 publications and read internationally by more than four million people every day. It became a TV series, and was burgeoning into a Hollywood movie.

More significant for this anthology is the fact that a book entitled Madam & Eve: 10 Wonderful Years *was published to celebrate the first decade of the strip. It reflects not only an era of change, but also a change of one form of humour.*

The 'inside jokes' of Madam & Eve *were first appreciated by 'an outsider', Stephen Francis, who came from America in the late 1980s to visit his mother-in-law. His mother-in-law (at the time) would complain to him about how difficult it was to have a maid, and the maid would whinge to him about 'the madam'. This parochial, domestic relationship fascinated him. He said in an interview, 'I was lucky to come to South Africa with a fresh pair of eyes.' Those who lived their whole lives in a master–servant relationship could 'miss the human poignancy', he reflected.*

It was the poignancy, not the cruelty, on which Francis and his original co-author Dugmore and artist Rico Schacherl focused. The result was a series of comic strips that might not always mirror reality, but which struck chords in several directions, opening jaded eyes and bringing unaccustomed laughter to race relationships.

Over the years the humour and the characters shifted their stances. Madam 'evolved'; so Mother Anderson, an 'outsider' from England, was introduced – short in stature, tall in aggression – whose hobbies were watching TV, drinking gin & tonics, and fighting with Eve and the mealie lady. What glorious fights ensued! Yet there was an interdependence between white and black, privileged and poor, which all the characters respected.

Authors Francis and Rico always aim at portraying Madam & Eve and their cohorts as people living too close to want to fight. The housewife and the 'domestic' and friends and family bicker and criticise and strategise constantly to get one up on the others but, like any close group, there is meant to be unspoken warmth and love.

However, in some of the more potent strips towards the end of the decade, Madam & Eve and their cartoon allies were merely a frame for other satire. There's the strip, for instance, in which a robber is running away clutching the semblance of a colourful, curved blunt instrument. Madam and Eve look on horrified, as Mother Anderson snorts: 'Look, everyone. It's the Rainbow Nation.'

But each week and each year the themes change. There's a September 11 cartoon, for instance, with all the Madam & Eve family standing in line before the slumped figure of the Statue of Liberty, and the remains of the Twin Towers smouldering in the background. The tenth year of the strip reflects – or mocks – issues such as TV's Big Brother, *road rage, Africa's first cosmonaut Mark Shuttleworth, and a host of petty politicians.*

To follow this progression of individual style and national attitudes, we have selected some strips from the authors' own selection of their favourite panels during the decade. The comments below each strip are those of the cartoonists.

Madam's first visit to her 'therapist'. One of our favourite cartoons, the idea came from a dinner party we attended. We figured if you're going to complain about your domestic staff, at least have the decency to make sure they're not in the room serving the food at the time.

This was our very first Madam & Eve cartoon. If you had told us, ten years ago, we'd still be writing and drawing them, we wouldn't have believed you.

Many people ask how we came up with Eve's surname. Quite simply, it was for the punchline. We needed a name that Madam might confuse as a sneeze and 'Sisulu' fit the bill. The cartoon itself was inspired by a story we heard of a 'madam' who employed a domestic worker for years … and never knew her full name.

The first appearance of Eric, Madam's son, and his girlfriend Lizeka. We keep meaning to bring them back. Maybe next week.

We're probably the only country with 11 official languages ... which, for a cartoonist, can be a great source of humour. This has always been one of our favourite strips.

The famous 'free at last' cartoon that inspired the title of our second book. The more things change ... the more they stay the same.

Eve first discovers a second use for her ironing-board. Little did we know that at the time this one cartoon would inspire many, many others.

Don't ask us why. This one just cracks us up every time we read it. We hope Allan Boesak's lawyer feels the same way.

We like this one because it actually happened one afternoon while we were all having a braai. Just kidding.

FRED MAYNE

IN ITS HEYDAY, *long before its demise, that most famous of English humour magazines,* Punch, *put politics second, humour first and favoured a style of languid, elegant laughter. It was an erudite, self-deprecating humour which is supposed to epitomise 'the British'. But it determined the style of many writers around the world and the following writer, Fred Mayne, was one of them.*

Mayne was born in England in 1917 but came to South Africa in his youth and graduated from the University of the Witwatersand after 'an outstanding academic career', according to his publishers of almost 50 years ago. He became a teacher at Parktown Boys' High School in Johannesburg and in 1956 a lecturer in English at the Johannesburg College of Education. We remember Mayne only from one of his readings at the University of the Witwatersand 45 years ago when he came across as a softly spoken, erudite person. He became a lecturer in English at 'Wits', where he was awarded a PhD in 1960 for a thesis on The Wit and Satire of George Bernard Shaw.

He then emigrated to Australia for a short time but returned to Wits University as a senior lecturer in English before finally settling in Canada, where he was professor of English at Victoria University, British Columbia. He retired there in 1980 (Gerald de Villiers, Close to the Sun, *Macmillan).*

Around mid-century he wrote regular humorous articles for the Rand Daily Mail *and the* Sunday Times. *His columns, like those of his successor, A.B. Hughes, became 'the best thing in the paper' for many who had spent years reading nothing except war news, followed by race politics.*

From 1947 Mayne contributed to Punch *and was well represented in a post-World War II anthology –* The Best Humour from Punch. *A collection of his humour was published in an undated book which appeared in the early 1950s titled* The Slaughter of an Innocent: A Book of Laughter *(CNA). The following extract from that book has been shortened.*

My Last Ride on a Horse

It took place in Rhodesia …

The horse I was on was a mare, a special kind of horse. I don't know much about horses as this was the first time I had ever been on one, but I could see that the horse had no business to last another winter. My host told me that I was given the horse because of my inexperience. It was quiet, he explained, and would not toss me off and run me over. I could see at a glance that my host was right. The horse could not toss me off unless I lent it a hand. The saddle, too, was just the thing for a beginner. It had knobs on so that one could not slide off.

I got on, and didn't fall off the other side, and I was facing the right way, because I know what a horse looks like, although I didn't know they went so far down in the middle. Almost immediately I was aware of a sharpish pain underneath somewhere, but I affected not to notice it. The horse offered no resistance. It hadn't any. It looked at me with one eye. The pathos of it all struck me to the heart's core. We were both caught in a web of which we had not shared the making. I felt a shudder. I don't know whether it was I or the horse. I would like to be able to record that I saw contempt or irritation in the horse's eye. Anything would have been better than that look. Its emptiness went straight to my stomach and stayed there. I couldn't help wondering if those Aztec chaps would have thought that I was a god if they had seen me on the horse.

We, the party of three and I, started off. At first I had company and was able to talk about the horse. I noticed a peculiar noise like a fretsaw whenever the horse tried to get air. My host said it was nothing much; it was just broken wind, heaves or roaring – they are all the same. He said the horse used to suffer from strangles, and that frequently ends up in broken wind, heaves or roaring. He also said that three or four grains of arsenic once a day in a mash would cure it. I felt that the dose was too small. He admitted that the horse was not in the best of health. It had an incurable derangement of the optic nerve, which he called glass eye, and when it got tired it suffered from colic or gripes, which is cured by a few ounces of laudanum, with two ounces of turpentine in a pint of linseed oil. It suffered from the ossification of certain cartilages due, so he said, to wearing of high-heeled shoes. It also suffered from corns and saddle galls. These, I knew already, were contagious. Then there was the clicking or forging caused by the horse knocking its feet together as it walked. One way and another it made quite a noise. I asked how old the horse was. He said he could not remember.

We had only gone about a mile when I found that I was going to be alone. The horse gradually gave ground until it was about thirty yards behind the party of three. I tried to force the pace. I made clicking noises in my throat for a few hundred yards, but then found that I couldn't keep it up. Something seemed to be wrong with my throat. I wondered if I had caught the heaves. With the party of three slowly receding I began to feel intense loneliness. I would not have minded solitude; it was the thought of being alone with the horse. I did not want to hit the horse with the little stick which my host provided. I remember reading somewhere that one-horse power represents the amount of work done when 33 000 lb is raised 1 ft in 1 min, and equals 746 watts. I don't know what a watt is, and I am a bit hazy about a lb, but I didn't want to take any chances. It didn't say anything about the age of the horse. I had no qualms on humanitarian grounds. I wasn't feeling so human. Besides, the horse wasn't one either. I began to press my heels gently but firmly into that part of the horse's side which is between the ribs and hips. It turned and looked at me with one of its glass eyes but, beyond that, did nothing. My position was growing desperate. If the party of three got lost the horse might go on walking forever. I didn't want to end my days, or even one of them, on a horse. In rapid succession I hit it with my little stick approximately on the fetlock, the withers, the frog, the gaskin, the hock, the pastern, and the splint bones. Finally, I gave it a crack on the head. This time I did not miss, but it still plodded on. It did not even bother to look at me with one of its glass eyes. I now perceived that I had very little control over the horse. One might even say that it was a runaway horse, only it wasn't running.

I need not have worried about getting lost. The party of three suddenly rounded a bend in the path and were lost from sight. A terrible cry broke from the horse. It was something between a whinny and a neigh, only worse. It sounded rather like my Uncle Samuel, who imitates elephants. I was nearly left behind. I think it must have been the knobs on which I was impaled, and the reins, which I was clutching hard, which took me along. The horse was actually running. I began to regret my wasted youth. I kept on changing knobs. I tried to make it stop by pulling on the reins, but, although it raised its head upwards, sideways, and backwards, its legs did not change pace. It had got the bit under its tooth. Only when we turned the bend and the party of three swam into sight did it resume its normal plod as suddenly as it had stopped it. I was flung against the horse's skull and it took me some time to get back on my knobs. The horse was making an awful noise now. It was roaring like a waterfall.

My host turned and congratulated me on my seat. He asked me why I did not keep up a steady pace instead of proceeding in fits and starts. He asked me if I was enjoying the view. He noticed that I was admiring the distant prospect by the way I was screwing up my eyes. He named the Chimanimani mountains in the distance. They looked a bit like my saddle. He said something else. I could see his lips moving. There was another bend on the path. The horse was getting ready to imitate my Uncle Samuel.

I focused what was left of my mind on one o'clock. By one o'clock I should no longer be on the horse. By one o'clock everything would be the same as it was last night. I might have changed shape a little but it would not be hereditary. Perhaps a lion would eat the horse from under me before one o'clock. I began to scan the bush. The Chimanimani mountains seemed no nearer, but they looked enchanting. I've always been fond of scenery.

By the time we were on the way home I thought my worst troubles were over. I had not gained any control over the horse, but I was growing numb and had adapted myself in some measure. We were approaching a stream and my host, who was now convinced that I was quarrelsome, yelled to me not to allow the horse to drink. We had just passed a bend, so I heard him. The party of three splashed through the stream leading by forty lengths. I thought of stopping the horse, waiting until the party of three disappeared, and then taking the stream at a run; but the horse was not thinking along the same lines. He trudged across the stream and a surge of exultation swept through my upper half. I was nearly through. But just then the horse plunged its face into the stream and began sucking up water like a vacuum cleaner. It had merely been making for the shallow opposite bank so that it could drink without having to hold its head up too high. I heaved at the reins with all my strength, for my host's warning had filled me with a nameless dread. I struck the horse savagely all over with my little stick. My anxiety to stop it drinking caught me unawares. I had relaxed my grip on the reins, and I was watching the receding waters with such intensity that I did not notice the disappearance of the party of three.

They came back for me in the stream, which was gambolling over my withers and between my hocks. I was waiting for it to carry me off to fairyland. They said that they had noticed that I was no longer on the horse. I had noticed it, too, but I was in no hurry to get back there. I was much more comfortable in the stream …

Women Whose Hearts I Have Broken

I take no particular pride in writing this article. I write more in sorrow than in pride. I write to warn other men whose taste for amorous adventure may outrun their finer feelings. I often lie awake at night and think of the women whose hearts I have broken, of the broken lives I have left in my wake, of women I have taken to the Zoo and even to cinemas and then forsaken, of women who have given me up because they loved me too much.

There was Dorothy. Poor little Dorothy. She deserved a better fate. I had spent three pounds, three shillings and four-pence on her when we began to drift apart. It must have been through love of me that she made herself so ill. After only an hour in my company her emotions grew so riotous that she used to get a headache. Later on her headaches became more or less continuous. I only had to ring her up for her to get a headache. I should have stuck by her in spite of her ill health, but I took the easy way out and stopped ringing her up. She got married eventually –

all the women whose hearts I have broken seek to forget the past by getting married – but I often wonder how her husband gets on with all those headaches. He is not, I imagine, so patient as I would have been.

Then came Marjorie. She renounced me for my own sake. She said there was something in her past, which made it impossible for her to marry me. So she renounced me instead. I told her I was not interested in her past – only a little curious. But she was firm. She said she wasn't going to ruin my life by marrying me, much as she would like to. It's true she got married later. I suppose she managed to put her past behind her after all. I met her again after her marriage, but she said she had an appointment and hurried off.

Doris, too, is married now. She could so little do without me that I got into debt taking her out. When she saw that I was getting into debt, she gave me up rather than see me get further into debt. She married a rich man in the end rather than ruin me. I saw her, too, after her marriage, swaddled in furs and bedecked with jewels, doing the bright lights. She was laughing, but I knew she was seeking forgetfulness in a giddy round of pleasure and was laughing to cover up an aching heart. If you had heard that laugh, you would know what I mean. It was the kind of laugh one gives to cover up an aching heart – a kind of hearty laugh.

Elsie was another one who renounced me. She had money, but she felt it would ruin my career if I knew I had her money to fall back on. I told her it would take a great deal to ruin a career like mine, but she said that her money would become a wedge that would drive us apart. I realise now that she was right. Her husband gave up his career years ago, bought himself a seat on the Stock Exchange, and became a poor little piece of flotsam and jetsam with no career worth mentioning. If Elsie had only had the courage of her great love, she would have given her money away to the poor and had me for a husband instead of a stockbroker. It's not as if she loves him either. I saw her the other day in the street talking to a strange man – a man I had never seen before.

I saw Margaret, too, a little while ago. She renounced me because of her mother. There was another man who went to the same church as her mother and had saved her mother from a tram. She married him for her mother's sake. It was fine of her, but I still think her mother should have married him. She was out with her children when I saw her. Despite her light-hearted chatter, there was a misty look in her eyes as she talked to me. I could see that she was pretending to have a cold by the smell of eucalyptus. Suddenly, to relieve her feelings, or to cover up her mounting emotions, she turned round and smacked her little son violently. The poor little fellow, had he but known it, was being smacked because his mother had married the wrong man. He had done nothing wrong except pour a little gravel down the baby's neck.

Ah, women! Why don't you follow your hearts instead of your heads?

NEIL McMAHON

NEIL MCMAHON *is an Australian-born journalist who came to South Africa for a quick look around in 1991 and stayed the better part of ten years – the Chicken Run in reverse. He was, as he says, The One Who Came the Other Way. He covered the transition to democracy for five years as the Cape Town-based correspondent for the* Washington Times *and the* San Francisco Chronicle *before finding a permanent local home at the* Cape Argus *and* Weekend Argus, *where he has been a columnist since 1997, delivering a weekly wry and humorous look at the world around him, the world around you and the world at large. He returned to Sydney in 1999, but continues to offer Sunday morning sermons to Cape Town newspaper readers under the catch-all brief* It's A Mad World.

The first article was written on the occasion of his 30th birthday in Cape Town in 1997.

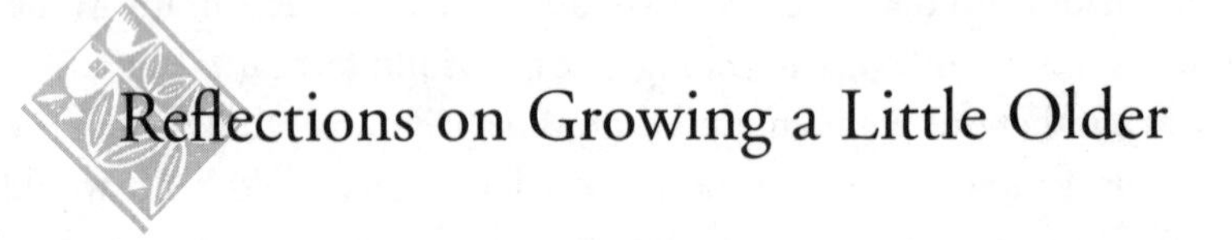

Reflections on Growing a Little Older

My number changes today. That two in front of the nine becomes a three in front of a zero. 3 and 0. Thirty. The 0 I can handle. The 3 I'm still dealing with.

The passing of a decade gives rise to serious reflection and contemplation, a taking of stock as it were. That 3 carries with it a subliminal, but nonetheless powerful message: You Are Not a Child Anymore.

How to cope? Hell, have a party and carry on like a two-year-old. So I threw one at the weekend. It didn't help at all, because I woke on Sunday feeling like the 2 had bypassed the 3 and several other numbers, turning overnight into an 8.

I had memory loss and couldn't walk without assistance. I couldn't speak properly, and had a ringing in my ears which made hearing difficult.

I had only invited 100 intimate friends, as well as several complete strangers, including someone I met in Pick 'n Pay on Saturday morning and a garbage bag salesman (100 for R20) who arrived at 7.30 on Saturday night. I thought he was an early gatecrasher so invited him in for a drink.

He thought it was Christmas. I was glad it wasn't, because this would have involved me having to buy presents for other people and, after spending the equivalent of Winnie Mandela's hat budget for an entire year organising the event, this was out of the question.

It may be better to give than to receive, but then again that may be a load of bollocks. This said, the gift-giving actually got off to a dire start.

My first presents were a large candle and a chocolate cake; they came from different people, but both had pornographic overtones. Things improved later, as guests handed over copious amounts of alcohol, CDs, gift vouchers and several hundred black garbage bags (100 for R20).

Then the music started. Knowing how CDs and tapes can go missing during a party, I had organised a live entertainer (as opposed to a dead one), hoping that, as a fully grown man would not fit in a handbag, or even a standard-sized garbage bag, there was no danger of light-fingered guests wandering off with the music.

Paul Zeman, a singer who was a belly dancer in a previous life, brings these divergent talents together to emerge as a great entertainer.

He also has a high tolerance level for drunkards who believe they can sing better than he can. This is a marvellous quality for him to have because he is also a friend of mine, and has thus had to learn the nuances of playing 'Waltzing Matilda' in preparation for those rare evenings when I am in the crowd, getting drunk and homesick and threatening bodily harm if I am not allowed to sing.

Which I did, though by that point Matilda wasn't waltzing – she was positively staggering into that billabong. I abandoned the stage and (for reasons still unclear to me) my shoes, then joined a conga line through the rain-soaked garden, wearing just socks.

I remember very little after that. I awoke on Sunday morning and considered calling the President and asking that a state of emergency be declared in my living room. Then I decided to be ruthless: I would just throw everything away. But into what? You can never find a black garbage bag when you need one.

I think someone stole my presents!

The following is an extract from a mid-2001 column in which the author bites the accepted butts of Australian hyperbolic humour … but in this case the biter contrives to let himself be bitten.

On the Waterfront

Elsewhere in *The Argus* you might have read the sorry tale of the New Zealand rugby team who turned up at a fancy Waterfront restaurant this past week, vowels askew and wallets bulging, and proceeded to run up a lavish bill. Then, sated by this magnificent repast, these Kiwi scum took their leave without leaving a tip.

As you can imagine, this turn of events left the waiting staff feeling mightily browned off. Surly even. Now, when I lived in Cape Town I was under the impression that behaving as if one was mightily browned off – surly, even – was a condition of employment at fancy Waterfront restaurants, establishments at which I considered it wise to pack a box of flares to attract the attentions of the waiting staff, and a discreet Tupperware container of Nik Naks in case one developed a sudden case of malnutrition while waiting for the food to arrive.

Fortunately I failed to attract attention, for we have now seen what happens when a member of the Waterfront service profession really decides to take umbrage (as opposed to your order, a task rarely performed with such vast enthusiasm).

'Stingy no-hopers,' he called these overfed, overpaid Kiwi rugby players. He went on: 'Six of them came here on Wednesday night and had a fantastic meal, several bottles of red wine, beer, seafood and even cheesecake. The bill came to R897.65, but they did not tip the waiter who served them one cent.'

So far, so spot on. Reading this, I had to concur with his views on those bloody Kiwi swine. Believe me, we know all about those cheapskate New Zealanders here in Sydney. Until quite recently, when the law was changed, one could witness a daily stampede at Sydney airport as the planes from Auckland disgorged their passengers, who would then trample over each other in the race to be the first to collect a social security payment. They would then repair to Bondi Beach to spend their welfare cheques on beer and their time doing absolutely nothing, all at the expense of the Australian taxpayer. The term 'Kiwi dole bludger' is as much a part of the Australian lexicon as 'bugger off', and is quite often employed in the same sentence.

So I am, as I say, in general sympathy and accord with the umbrage taken by the waiting staff over this horrendous incident and broadly share the view that not only do these lumbering New Zealand oafs deserve to lose at rugby, they should probably not be allowed outside the confines of their own country at all if they don't know how to behave properly. Such a development would make us very happy here in Australia, the waiting staff at the Waterfront would be delighted, and ... well, let's face it, who else matters?

In the meantime, to anyone employed at the Waterfront with the misfortune to have a New Zealand customer I would suggest that you stand back at a safe distance, hide anything that might be used as a weapon, and tell them loudly: 'BUGGER OFF'.

Editor's Note: *Sunday Argus* would like to point out that Neil McMahon has been informed that the anonymous Waterfront barman quoted in our report also said: 'This is not a unique experience. We have found that the Australians and the New Zealanders never tip. The Americans, British and South Africans always tip the waiters, but not these chaps from Down Under.'

Contacted for comment, Mr McMahon said: 'I'll give you a tip: never trust an anonymous sauce in a Waterfront restaurant. Now, bugger off.'

Sunday Argus has established that Mr McMahon is an Australian cheapskate who never tipped South African service professionals when he lived here on the shaky grounds that 'we don't have a tipping culture where I come from'. The editor invites outraged Waterfront waiting staff to email him with their thoughts at neilmcmahon@hotmail.com

ZAKES MDA

ZANEMVULA KIZITO GATYENI MDA *has been described as the 'award-winning playwright, novelist, painter, music composer and filmmaker'. Those are some of his labels.*

He has been a professor of literature at the National University of Lesotho, a research fellow at Yale, and a visiting professor at the University of Vermont and the University of the Witwatersrand. Those are some of the signposts in his learning.

But Zakes Mda is more than those. He is a philosopher, prophet, wit and theatrical artist of multiple talents. He also writes theatrical satire – and because several of his plays (and his satire) are now in book form and widely read, we are able to include extracts.

Mda's work is often described as 'surreal', in the style of Dadaism. (Though Rob Amato, a director of his early plays, has cleverly dubbed Mda's unique style as 'Mdadaism'.) There is no space here to represent the complex African surrealism, yet hard-driving logic, which the author uses. Instead we have selected passages of straight satire from You Fool, How Can the Sky Fall? Fools, Bells and the Habit of Eating: Three Satires by Zakes Mda, *introduced by Rob Amato, Witwatersrand University Press, 2002.)*

These extracts are brief because they are less about laughter than about biting satire. It flows from the pen of a black writer parodying a black president and black politicians. In the first scene readers are reminded of the Pope's visit to southern Africa in the 1990s. The President ('The Wise One') is in session with some of his Cabinet Ministers.

Scene One

Minister of Health: Obviously we don't have a quorum. A lot of other honourable ministers are absent …

… Minister of Justice: No need to quarrel about this. You know that when the Wise One is there it is a quorum, even if he is just alone …

… Minister of Agriculture: Remember when the Pope visited our country?

Justice: Who can forget that, my friend? Who can forget that?

President: A private joke about the Holy Father, eh?

Agriculture: Not about the Pope, sir. About the road.

Justice: The dirt road that leads to the racecourse where the Pope addressed the multitudes.

President: Dirt road? There is no dirt road there. I was in the Popemobile with the Pope on that road. It's a tarred road.

Agriculture: Exactly what we mean about the cleverness of the Honourable Minister of Works, sir. When you announced that the pontiff was paying us a holy visit, there was not time nor money to tar the road that leads to the racecourse. And the racecourse was the only open field that was big enough to accommodate the multitudes who were expected to come and see the Holy Father.

President: And so? How did it get tarred?

Justice: It was never tarred, sir. It was just painted black.

Agriculture [*beside himself with laughter*]: And named after the Pope.

Health: And when the rains came, they swept the black paint away. And opened up the gullies. There is no road, sir, and no-one ever told you about this. And the Pope, poor fellow, I'm sure he is sitting over there in the Vatican boasting to his friends, 'Guess what, guys, I have a road in that country. My own road, named after me.' He does not know …

President: And why was I not informed of this?

Justice: We know that the mind of the Wise One is always occupied with heavy matters of state. We didn't want to bother you with petty things …

In the second extract, the Cabinet discusses the Daughters of the Revolution who – believing the revolution has been hijacked by self-interested politicians – are 'demonstrating and polluting this whole city with the stench of filthy ideas', according to the Minister of Agriculture.

The Minister of Justice says the truth is that 'We inherited this revolution from those who did the actual fighting. We now own it.' This leads to a discussion of Truth, eternal or ephemeral, and a view that 'to die for today's truth may be to die for tomorrow's lie.' It is a conclusion which greatly disturbs them.

Scene Two

Minister of Culture: What does this mean as far as the Daughters of the Revolution are concerned?

President: It means theirs was the truth of yesterday when they stood in the line of fire and fought in the revolution. Today we, the inheritors of that revolution, must be resolved to crush them to smithereens. The Daughters of the Revolution are yesterday's news. We are today's.

Culture: My worry, Wise One, is that if we crush them through force of arms overseas newspapers will write about it and that will be a blight on our National Policy of Benevolence. We have put a lot of work into this policy. We are beginning to win over the populace. People are singing about the bountiful benevolence of the leader, the Supreme Commander, the One and Only …

Justice: Except that of course those who sing are on the state payroll. So don't take credit and pretend to the Wise One that they sing because you have effectively done your work as Minister of Culture. However, I do agree that we must find a way to crush these mad women without attracting the unnecessary attention of the world community. Our police have a reputation for brutality already …

President: I have been meaning to talk to the General about this. The police need to do their work as they have done before. They need to suppress uprisings unhindered. But we cannot afford to have the populace thinking that the police are brutal. It goes against the whole idea of benevolence. I want you, General, and you, Minister of Justice, to take immediate action. Buy them new uniforms that are brighter and invoke friendliness. Change their dull militaristic drill to a much more rhythmic one … a much more dancey one … Let the populace see that it's not only the Daughters of the Revolution who know how to dance.

Agriculture: I do not intend to question our great National Policy of Benevolence which, after all, was founded through the wisdom of the Father of the Nation. But I strongly feel that we need a catastrophe to bring our existence to the attention of the world. As long as we are benevolent, as long as there is peace, they will not hear of us. They will not know us.

Culture: Since even the Wise One cannot call upon a natural disaster … an earthquake that kills hundreds, or a flood … maybe we ourselves should do something … should create a catastrophe.

Justice: I have an idea …

Culture: You cannot have an idea. Only his Excellency, the Father of the Nation, can have an idea. You can utter some words about something. They only become an idea when the Wise One thinks they are good enough to adopt and shape into an idea – his idea. That's the first lesson I learnt when I joined this Cabinet.

He laughs proudly at having at last struck a blow against the Minister of Justice, who glares at him with hatred.

Agriculture [*to* Justice]: The son of a bitch has successfully disgraced you in front of his Excellency, my friend.

Justice: My thoughts are that next time the Daughters of the Revolution march at the Market Square we should mow them down with machine guns. That will be a catastrophe that will call the attention of the world to us. They will know of our existence.

Agriculture: Very clever, my friend. Killing two birds with one stone, so to speak. Getting rid of the Daughters of the Revolution, and putting us on the world map.

Culture [*to* Justice]: Your own aged mother is one of the Daughters of the Revolution!

Justice: She is a traitor, and she's none of your business!

Culture: What are we saying? First we say we cannot use force on them because of world opinion. Now we say we are going to use force on them for world opinion.

Justice: Too complicated for your feeble mind. Better you confine yourself to song and dance.

Agriculture: Well, my friend, sometimes these things need elaboration, so that when these decisions are implemented there should be no mistake. I am really asking on behalf of those who will have to implement our decisions.

Culture: Well?

The Ministers of Culture and Agriculture look at the Minister of Justice for the answer, but none is forthcoming. He can only display his confusion.

President [*smiling benevolently at each of them*]: We are the creators of our own little truths, remember? We'll hold a television interview … we'll call the international press … we'll condemn the killings, and make it clear that they contravened our National Policy of Benevolence. We'll tell them that they were by and large self-inflicted by the Daughters of the Revolution themselves, who had disguised themselves as our national army, with the view of calling attention to themselves, and of besmirching the name of this benevolent government.

General: It shall be so.

Justice, Agriculture, Culture: The Wise One is so wise!

JOEL MERVIS

THE BEST-KNOWN *newspaper column in South African history,* The Passing Show, *was almost an afterthought when a new Sunday newspaper was launched in the Transvaal almost a century ago – yet the column lasted nearly a hundred years and came close to being a national institution.*

When the Sunday Times *launched the column on 4 February 1906, the first item under* The Passing Show *title was by no means comic. It was a solemn warning about the danger to health of narrow-necked milk bottles. It was not until the 1920s that the column gave up on parochial current events, and its first fictional, somewhat fishy characters popped up in the form of Gettys B. Haddock and the Snoek family.*

A quarter of a century later The Passing Show *finally took on wild flights of fancy. Its new, zany approach allowed it to lampoon whom and what at whim.*

Joel Mervis (1908–1998), a young barrister turned journalist, began writing The Passing Show *in the mid-1940s and he wrote the column, week in, week out, for the rest of the column's existence and for more than half his lifetime.*

His unique style has an important place in the history of South African humour. He pierced the tensions of the apartheid era almost as effectively and almost as freely as the contemporary political cartoonists were able to do.

Mervis invented the now famous nonexistent newspaper, The Naboomspruit Recorder, *with himself as its former editor, and was able to mock local society and its journalism. But when he became the editor of the* Sunday Times *(1959–1975) – as well as incumbent of* The Passing Show *– he reserved his more subtle satire, and his running political battles, for the main paper. It must be said that, had he not been chief editor, the column would probably have died, for it became increasingly predictable and failed to change with the times. That was the period when Mervis devoted all his considerable energy to writing or rewriting all the main reports of his newspaper, some of them turning from page one onto several pages inside. He then used* The Passing Show *purely for fun, or for lesser, more benign targets.*

Mervis believed – like so many comics before and since – that the more you repeated a joke the funnier it grew. He played repetition to the hilt. For one thing, it saved a lot on material. Take, for instance, Dr Ebenezer Boneash, MA, HFGR. Mervis never forgot to apply the asterisk to Dr Boneash, or the explanation signalled by the * – even though half a million readers knew that MA, HFGR stood for 'May all his finesses go right'.*

In selecting samples of Passing Show *characters, we have sought extracts from Mervis's early columns, between 1945 and 1960. As they became more familiar they became more sophisticated. But they were launched from weird angles off the wall.*

There was Charlie Klopjag, the private eye 'who spoke through narrowed eyes'.

(Everyone knew the character was modelled on Colonel Ulf Boberg, a well-known colonel of the South African CID.)

There was Mrs Dither of Dunkeld, 'fashionably suburbed' and fighting vital issues in South Africa such as the waywardness of city double-decker buses.

There was Dr Boneash, MA HFGR and his scandalous school, Skollypot.*

There was K.C. Taradiddle QC and Mr Justice Fogbound ... and many others whose strange antics should still raise a smile, even though we may have no knowledge of their intended targets.

Mervis's main target, however, apart from the snooping of the Special Branch and the errant behaviour of municipal buses, was the increasing commercialism and strident advertising in all news media, a phenomenon which began in his time in the mid-twentieth century, but whose clamour has reached such a constant background roar that we hardly notice its noise level today.

Mervis deserves to be remembered world-wide for being, if nothing else, the first editor of a commericial newspaper to campaign constantly against advertising.

Dunkeld Bus Club

Mrs Dither of Dunkeld is anxious to form a Dunkeld Bus Club. The objects of the club are Bus Watching, Bus Spotting, Bus Catching. Its chief aim is to find ways and means of avoiding Bus Waiting. The Dunkeld Bus Club, which will also be known as MI5A, will have reciprocity with MI5. There has already been an exchange of letters between Mrs Dither and Sir Percy Sillitoe, in which Mrs Dither undertakes to send food parcels if Sir Percy sends out three of his best men to investigate the mysterious disappearance of the Dunkeld Bus, which is now reported to be suffering from amnesia. Anyone finding a Dunkeld Bus should report the matter to the nearest police station.

Meanwhile, intending members of the Dunkeld Bus Club are invited to apply. Membership will be restricted to persons who are:

On the common roll
Male
Female
Adult
Fashionably suburbed
Bus conductorphobes
Thoroughly maddened by Bus Waiting

Applications should, of course, be accompanied by the usual entrance and subscription fee, which will entitle members to a free copy of Mrs Dither's standard work, *How to Bus Wait*, and its sister volume, *How to Bus Watch*.

MI5A

Every year at this time, when the fields are smothered in yellow petsonias and the gargles twitter in the sombroosh, Mrs Dither of Dunkeld takes a party of bird watchers on a ramble to do some bus watching instead.

'Bus watching', says Mrs Dither, 'is like getting close to Nature, except that you can never get close to a Dunkeld bus (MI5A). It's like that story, if you follow me, "Why is Napoleon like Paul Kruger? Because they both have beards except Napoleon."'

The best time for bus watching is about eight in the morning or five in the afternoon, when buses, in their rich and infinite variety, are on the wheel. The most difficult bus to watch is an MI5A, because of its peculiar habits. It builds its nest in a tram shed near Market Street West and seldom emerges, with the result that it is hardly ever seen. In the nest of an M15A will be found a clutch of bus drivers, slightly mottled, and anything up to five in number.

M15A is the shyest bus on the road, and bus watchers will have to stalk it carefully. The best plan is to wait until it goes to drink at a pothole in Oxford Road, although if the watcher comes too close it will quickly make off into the thick undergrowth of Dunkeld, and even Melrose.

For watching a Dunkeld bus, Mrs Dither recommends a pair of strong field-glasses.

Omnibus Clause

Due, no doubt, to some misunderstanding which will probably be cleared up later, the Dunkeld Bus has received a letter from the Minister of Justice calling upon it to resign from the Omnibus Association, prohibiting it from becoming a member of the Two-piece Movement, and the Uncivil Rights League, and banning it from leaving the Transvaal for two years.

Mrs Dither of Dunkeld was at a loss to explain the ban. 'There must be some mistake,' she said. 'The letter was probably meant for some other bus.'

Do you suffer from hardening of the currencies?
Try Eau de Pippleparrot, the miracle water.
Don't forget, if you want to get your ears to look radiant,
free from decay, and having that refreshingly different glitter,
use Eau de Pippleparrot, the miracle water.

Eau, I Say There

In reply to hundreds of eager requests from thousands of anxious readers who want to know what name I have given my house, I am happy to supply the information.

It is called:

Château de Pippleparrot.

And in further reply to thousands of vulgar critics who say that, for the most part, I talk through my hat, I reply that I have brought to talking through the hat a dignity and status it has seldom enjoyed. Indeed, the way I talk through my hat has given birth to a new phrase in the English language. It is, of course:

Chapeau de Pippleparrot.

Ode to a Nightcap

I'm sorry Sir, sorry Sir,
I'm sorry to trouble you,
But you must try E de P,
The miracle w.

A Point of Etiquette

Dear Sir,

On entering a crowded bus bound for Dunkeld yesterday, I was astonished to see an elephant seated in it. You may think there is nothing surprising in that. Let me hasten to add that I am a lady, and that the elephant did not get up and offer me its seat. I had to stand all the way. Have our manners really gone to the dogs?

Yours, etc., Mrs Dither, of Dunkeld.

Perhaps the elephant was a lady, too – Editor.

The Soft Answer

British civil servants are being taught to write simple, friendly letters – News Item.
Dr Ebenezer Boneash MA, HFGR*, who once worked in the civil service, would have needed no lessons of that kind. He was courtesy itself. Here are some selected examples of letters he wrote:

Sir, – It is with the deepest regret that I must inform you that the supertax you are required to pay is 10 000 pounds, and not 1 000 pounds as stated in my previous letter. It will console you to learn that the person who so carelessly left out the extra nought has been sacked. Wishing you a bigger and better income next year,

Yours,
Ebenezer Boneash MA, HFGR*
p.p. Receiver of Revenue.

* *May all his finesses go right.*

Sir, – There is some talk of your having broken into a bank and stolen 100 000 pounds. This is probably just idle gossip, but nevertheless, I would be extremely grateful if you would be so kind as to appear in court at 9.30 a.m. on the 31st inst. when the whole matter will be gone into. It will be necessary during these proceedings to refer to you as the accused, but I would like to point out that, as far as my department is concerned, this procedure is unavoidable.

Yours,
Ebenezer Boneash, MA, HFGR*
p.p. Attorney-General.

* *May all his finesses go right.*

A subsequent letter to the same person:
Sir, – As you are now to be a guest at one of Her Majesty's institutions for a matter of 15 years, may I extend to you a hearty welcome and express the hope that your stay with us will be most enjoyable? If there is anything we can do to make you comfortable, don't hesitate to let us know. By the way, there is no finer sight than the sunshine streaming through the bars in the early morning.

Yours,
Ebenezer Boneash, MA, HFGR*
p.p. Director of Prisons.

* *May all his finesses go right.*

No Aksent

I am already in zis country from Chairmany twenty years out and I am speaking wizout a trace of English.

The Limit

Chartered Accountant's motto: 'Judge a man by the limited liability company he keeps.'

A Slice off the Withers, Please

The meat shortage reminds me of the terrible meat shortage that occurred when I was editing the *Naboomspruit Recorder*.

Meat was so scarce, one of my subeditors ate my still life of a beef steak painted by Picasso, and then had the impertinence to complain that it was underdone. It would break my heart and yours too if I described the suffering of a meat-starved population, but I do recall that, at the height of the shortage, I was invited to dinner by Mrs Dither of Dunkeld. As I entered her sumptuously appointed mansion, I dashed up to her across the 80-foot lounge and breathlessly exclaimed: 'I'm so hungry I could eat a horse.'

'How fortunate,' mused Mrs Dither.

Poor Kate

Talking of cannibals reminds me of the time my wife Kate and I were captured by the Mbongostingo cannibals. There was a bit of a revolution going on at the time, and the howling mob demonstrated outside the cannibal Queen's palace. 'What's the trouble?' asked the Queen.

'They are hungry,' replied her chief counsellor. 'They have no bread.'

'Then,' said the Queen, 'why don't they eat Kate?'

You Could Have Knocked Me down with a Neutron

When I was editor of the *Naboomspruit Recorder* I decided, for reasons of policy, to launch a bitter attack on a political opponent named Steynium. In place of my usual powerful leader, however, I published this powerful poem:

This awful fellow Steynium
Thinks he's a geranium.
Now if Mynheer Steynium
Thinks he's a geranium
What can he have in his cranium?
It must be uranium!

I got twenty years and was fined 5 000 pounds for giving away an atomic secret.

Miss Naboomspruit of 1951

Owing to an error, this column last week published a photograph over the caption, 'Miss Shot Putt of 1950, entrant in the *Naboomspruit Recorder* Beauty Contest.' Unfortunately the photograph submitted has since proved to be an aerial shot of Johannesburg's new railway station. As the Johannesburg railway station is not eligible for the *Naboomspruit Recorder*'s Beauty Contest, this entry has been disqualified.

One of the thousands, but thousands, of people who have sent in a picture for the contest is a chap named Orpheus, whose girl is a lieutenant in the WAAF. The picture shows both of them and is entitled 'Orpheus with his lieut'.

Someone else writes: 'While sunbathing at the Norwood swimming baths the other day, I rather petulantly pushed aside a half-tanned blonde.' Since our lawyers have been unable to establish any link between this letter and the Beauty Contest, we have re-directed it to the Controller of Hides and Skins.

Don't forget, this Beauty Contest comes to you by courtesy of Hogwash, the reliable shampoo; Cupido, the lipstick that lingers; Treble Amour, the perfume that packs a punch; and Skidaddo, the delicious, refreshing drink that removes indigestion and milk stains from old tennis shoes.

Some of the items above illustrate how Joel Mervis, with his legal training, was able to satirise apartheid law in the crazy style of the Goon Show, *the* Beachcomber *column in the London* Daily Express, *and other humour current in his day. Here is another of Mervis's targets – the Calvinistic-influenced Gambling Act, which forbade church bazaars to hold a lottery. The Government decreed that even a charitable 'raffle' to raise funds for the blind had to be won through skill – not through the evils of gambling.*

With Fogbound J. and K.C. Taradiddle QC, through the Law Reports

When is a Lottery?

Mr Justice Fogbound gave judgment in the matter of Regina v. Naudé, Roos and Pippleparrot. His lordship said:

This prosecution arises out of certain events, which took place during the

'Pippleparrot Half Hour', a radio programme intended to draw attention to the excellence of Eau de Pippleparrot, the miracle water. Incidentally, I have been asked by accused No. 3, J Edgar Pippleparrot, to mention that Eau de Pippleparrot is not merely capable of curing anything from croup to housemaid's knee, but takes the shine out of old blue suits and removes sauce stains from Panama hats.

To revert to the case before us, evidence has been led to show that a competition was held during the Pippleparrot Half Hour. The announcer, it appears, invited listeners to spell CAT. Apart from his telling them that the first letter was 'c', that the last letter was 't' and that the one in the middle was the first letter of the alphabet, listeners were left to work the thing out for themselves. They were invited, furthermore, to send the solution in by letter, and told that the first letter opened containing the correct answer would yield the sender a prize of 10 pounds. Mr Kruisverhoor, for the Crown, contends that the competition required no skill and is a lottery in terms of Transvaal Law 7 of 1890. It will take a great deal to convince me that he is wrong.

Mr K.C. Taradiddle, QC, for the defence, arguing with the vigour and skill which we in this court have for so long admired, maintains that it cannot be a lottery because the competitors have made no monetary contribution. Entrance to the competition is free, he points out, and I was referred to the case of Rex v. Cotterill 1927 C.P.D., at page 48, which says that to constitute a lottery there must be a contribution by competitors.

It is at this point that I doff my wig to the Crown for its cunning ingenuity in charging Tom Naudé and Gideon Roos jointly with Pippleparrot. These two accused are, respectively, the Minister of Posts and Telegraphs and the Director-General of the South African Broadcasting Corporation, and it is common cause that they have given not merely their blessing to the 'Pippleparrot Half Hour', but have also provided the entire machinery and organisation for making such a broadcast possible. The conclusion is therefore inescapable that they are parties to it. Now, while it may be said that Pippleparrot receives no monetary contribution from people who enter the competition to spell CAT, the same certainly cannot be said of the accused, Naudé and Roos.

The accused Roos, in his representative capacity, receives the sum of thirty-five shillings a year from every radio owner – a levy which I would describe as iniquitous were it not that I am not required to comment on it.

As for the accused Naudé, he receives 2d. from every competitor who buys a postage stamp … Indeed, the competitor may well be said to pay 2d, plus a fraction of his licence fee, in a gamble to win 10 pounds. We thus have the odd circumstances of Pippleparrot awarding 10 pounds as a prize, and Naudé (in representative capacity, of course) collecting 250 pounds from the sale of stamps

... If that does not look like a lottery, then I would like to know what does.

There remains one further point raised by Mr Taradiddle, who contended that even if all the accused were parties to the broadcast, it was Pippleparrot alone who gave the prize, that he was the one who got nothing out of it, and that the broadcast could not therefore be a lottery. The law, however, is clear. As Mr Justice Ridley said in Bartlett v. Parker 1912, K.B. at page 497, 'the fact that the person who presents the prizes receives no part of the money contributed does not prevent a scheme from being a lottery'.

In the circumstances, I find all three accused guilty, and sentence each to 20 years or a 10 000 pounds fine.

Mr Taradiddle: The fines will be paid.

Fogbound J: I'm not surprised they can pay, what with all the money they're making out of selling stamps and charging fancy radio licence fees.

Mr Taradiddle: I need hardly remind your lordship that the accused Naudé will in due course sit as a member of the High Court of Parliament. When your lordship's judgment in this case is brought before the High Court on appeal, the accused Naudé will no doubt feel compelled to make some sharp comments on your lordship's findings.

Mr Justice Fogbound grasped his nosegay and tottered from the court, a broken man.

BLOKE MODISANE

MOST OF US *can hazard a definition of 'black humour' – but what is black humour? Rather like white or brown humour in many cases, yet culture often creates differences, and circumstances enforce them.*

Circumstances forged bitter rage in William (Bloke) Modisane as he described his experiences under apartheid and the demolition of his beloved Sophiatown. Sophiatown was a character-filled black 99-year-leasehold suburb of Johannesburg from which the apartheid government, having peremptorily declared all leases null and void, ejected the population, bulldozed the properties and declared it a white freehold area named 'Triomf'.

Modisane never was – and had no intention of being – amusing. Instead, he reminded us how smiling, laughing Africans used their good humour as a weapon against oppression. They also used graffiti and jokes in the same way Poles did under both Nazi and Russian oppression, and in the way Russians themselves did under Stalin.

Modisane's book, published abroad in 1963 (as Blame Me on History, *by Billings and Son, London), was banned locally for its 'incitement and sedition'. The irony is that, under present-day, sometimes overly earnest 'anti-racism' policy, sections of Modisane's writing might qualify for censorship!*

He was one of a team of black writers of the 1950s who helped launch Drum *magazine. As an early black urban intellectual he played host, in his single room in Sophiatown, to people such as Dame Sybil Thorndike, Adlai Stevenson – and to many South African whites who might otherwise never have seen life in the shantytowns and shebeens.*

He died in 1986 in West Germany, aged 63.

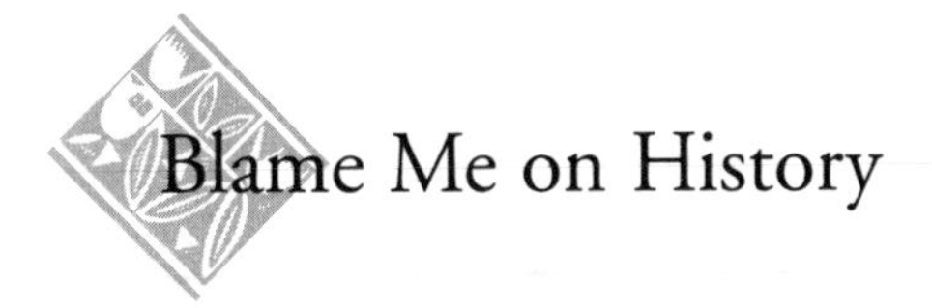

Blame Me on History

I directed my energy to my writing, determined to use it as the weapon for gate-crashing into the worlds which rejected me; my writing showed a studied omission of commitment, the histrionics of tight-fisted protest, and in my first published short story, 'The Dignity of Begging', I created a satirical situation in which I sat back and laughed at the worlds which I rejected. I projected myself into the character of Nathaniel Mokgomare, an educated African capable in any society of earning himself an independent living, but handicapped by being black in a society which has determined that black is the condition of being dependent on white charity, in the same sense that a cripple is dependent for his existence on public charity.

To the handicap of being black I added physical deformity, investing my character with a kind of double indemnity, then confronted him with the realisation of his condition, complete with the stereotyped destiny determined for him; Nathaniel accepts the challenge, deciding that if he is condemned to be a beggar he would become a professional one, with the strict observance of the ethics of the profession. He exploits his deformity, assuming a quality which transfers his demerits to where they finally belong, on the conscience of the over-privileged white public; his eyes plead for human kindness, but sneer behind every 'thank you, *baas*; God bless you, *baas*'.

'The Dignity of Begging' is the reflection of the only possible life – with dignity and sanity – which the African could accept in order to accommodate South Africans; perhaps one of the explanations responsible, among sensitive Africans, for the existence of that phenomenon identified and classified as The Native Mind, a subject which engrosses the attention of the anthropologists, sociologists and psychologists, who have given us such memorable quotes as: 'The natives are always smiling, they're a happy people; how can anybody say they're oppressed and miserable?'

Why not? Even in Shakespeare's time people were known to 'smile and murder whilst they smile'. The Native has to survive his oppressors, he knows that time is on his side, history is on his side, and with time, God will be on his side; the smile policy is one of careless ease, its convenience is contained in the fact that the African cannot at this moment afford to lose his temper, so he must joke about the things which give him most pain. On the main Johannesburg–Orlando road there is a traffic sign on which some African humorist has added a 'very' between the words 'native' and 'cross here'.

very
NATIVES CROSS HERE
^

Until the African loses his sense of humour, he will smile; the Government has not as yet legislated against smiling; in any case, everything else is either treasonable or seditious; if I criticise the Government's racial policies or speak trouble-making lunacies about freedom, liberty, equality and fraternity for the black races, I will be named a Communist; if I should become recalcitrant and angry, lawless and violent, I would be certified as Bestial, Savage and Barbaric. There seems very little left which could be considered appropriate, or safe, except the policy to smile and smile; smiling has its advantages: it has for some time now been discovered that Natives have good healthy teeth, and so white, which is rather baffling when one considers that malnutrition is rampant among them; but it is a proverbial fact that a flashing smile will turn away wrath.

Africans have discovered – and this by way of self-protection – that the white South African is hopelessly and fanatically susceptible to flattery, a weapon which the Africans use with vicious enthusiasm to express their sincerest contempt.

The South African police force attracts to its ranks young Afrikaners recruited from the Platteland for it is perhaps the only employment agency which requires, as a qualification, a minimum of intelligence; I do not, of course wish it to be understood that the force is crawling with country idiots; there are a few urban idiots, not too many intelligent ones and a few English-speaking strays, usually to be found in administrative posts; but the police constable on the beat is invariably Afrikaans, with strong cultural and language ties, stuttering with the historical hatred and fear which the Afrikaner bears the African, yet an African could almost be forgiven anything if he is obsequiously respectful, bowing with servility and speaking in Afrikaans; but heaven help the English-speaking African, because if there is anything the Afrikaner hates more than the English, and the Jews, and the Indians, it is a black Englishman. I would never attempt talking in English to an Afrikaner police constable, not if I know that with Afrikaans I could get him to waive even his prejudice.

The African needs to be a master in the art of chicanery, for only the simple and very proud are arrested on trifling offences, but there is always present the danger of not knowing where to draw the line; white liberals scream their criticisms against Africans, that we bring upon ourselves – by the very nature of our obsequious behaviour – the contempt of the whites, that the canvas smile and the yes-*baas* mentality is sickening. They possibly have a case, but it is a known fact that most people laugh at the *baas*'s jokes; in any case, how many of them could take a 'go to hell' from an African?

NAT NAKASA

THIS TALENTED WRITER *had no reason to be amusing, or happy. His was a wry humour; sad and seeking. The headline on one of his last columns, 'Met with Smiles and Questions', unwittingly reflects the manner in which he met life. Tolerance and compassion were two of his extraordinary strengths in the brutality that was apartheid in his time. Sadly his strengths – those of an ideal model of a South African today – were not enough.*

*Using an appropriate quote, Essop Patel, compiler of Nat Nkasa's works, says: 'He had the ability to see an upside-down situation in an upside-down way' (*The World of Nat Nakasa, *edited by Essop Patel, Ravan Writers Series, 1975).*

Nathaniel Ndazana Nakasa was born in 1937 and educated in Durban. His parental home was the onomatopoeic village of Lusikisiki in Pondoland (its name is derived from the sound of wind in the reeds), but most of his brief adult life was spent in the city of Johannesburg. He was a regular contributor to Golden City Post, *an assistant editor of* Drum, *and later became the first black columnist on the* Rand Daily Mail. *He was the founder and editor of* Classic *magazine, whose objective was to encourage 'those writers with causes to fight for, committed men and women who look at human situations and see tragedy and love, bigotry and commonsense, for what they are'.*

In 1964 Nat Nakasa was awarded a Niemann Fellowship to Harvard University. The authorities, who had tried to deny him a full education in South Africa, denied him a passport to spend a year at Harvard. Instead, he was forced to take a one-way exit permit, leaving him stateless and seemingly without hope of returning.

He found America interesting, but he became, as he anticipated, horribly homesick for his land of sunshine – or, as he might have ironically put it – his 'native' land. Within a few months he was writing for the New York Times *and other newspapers. He penned articles for magazines and appeared in the television film* The Fruit of Fear. *He began work on a biography of the internationally known singer Miriam Makeba, and he attended lectures at Harvard.*

But along the way he lost the gift of laughter. Two days before he committed suicide he told a friend: 'I can't laugh any more – and when I can't laugh, I can't write.'

It was not the insults, oppression and cruelty of apartheid that killed him. It was being banished from Africa. It is ironically macabre that he should refer to his flight to the United States without an exit permit as 'a grave step', for it was the stress of being cut off from his roots which led to his death in 1967. He was not yet 30 years of age.

Are you Bilingual?

I shudder to think what would happen to us if apartheid did not have some comical aspects to it. I hear from a friend that there was once a very fair coloured girl on the Reef – so fair that everyone mistook her for white. In the end she even gave up explaining that she was not white and when she took a new job and received white pay she didn't even bother to protest!

'Are you bilingual?' was the main question she was asked when applying for the job. Innocently she replied 'yes', and the job was hers.

Little did her employers know that when Mary said 'yes' she meant she spoke English and Zulu, the latter being her mother tongue. She knew no Afrikaans.

They're Down to Earth

Give me the South African Police any day. They're down to earth in everything they do. If you swear in the street you are likely to be charged with using obscene language, *aanstoot taal.* No nonsense.

If you make a noise in a police station, you are likely to be told, 'Shut up, man' – '*hou jou bek, jong!*'

Not like those London bobbies I keep reading about. Instead of telling a demonstrator to get a move on, they will ask him to 'proceed, please proceed, sir'.

The limit came this week. One of these bobbies is reported to have told a magistrate that the man who tackled Jomo Kenyatta last week made 'inflammatory observations'. Somebody should prevail upon Her Majesty's Government to get the bobbies to learn some ordinary English – even if it means sending some of them for a course.

Kissing a Banned Girl May Be …

Unwittingly, officialdom is glorifying those things which, in terms of its policy, should be discredited. Our rulers are daily turning our moral and social values upside down and generally causing people to mix them up.

We have now reached a situation, for instance, where to be banned has become a status symbol of considerable value in social and political circles and where a man's worth is judged by the number of friends he claims among the 'banned' and the 'named'.

It is good enough to be able to say, 'That was my pal,' even if you no longer go near the man. And, heaven knows, we have every reason to be scared of guilt by association. After all, our magistrates are now empowered to warn people to desist from engaging in subversive activities without bothering even to outline those activities. Perhaps kissing a banned girl may be aiding and abetting Communism. How do I know?

The new set of status symbols works something like this:

If you were 'in' during the State of Emergency you are sure to get a free drink from the boys in a shebeen.

If you are back from 90-day detention, you can hold the floor for hours without interruption from respectful audiences all over Soweto.

If you know a friend of a friend of a banned man, you aren't doing badly.

If you are actually banned yourself, it becomes your privilege to jump into your neighbour's car and order him to rush you to the police station whenever you are late for reporting at the specific time.

The Myth of Born Musicians

Most communities have their popular myths, which nobody, it seems, can destroy. I can think of two such myths which I find particularly irritating in South Africa. People say, for instance, that music was born in Africa. Others go a step further and say that Africans are born musicians.

It is difficult to know just what this means. I don't see much evidence of a great tradition of worthwhile musical activity to support this myth. It is not Africa which gave us Mozart. On the contrary, I find myself constantly plagued by Africans – those born musicians – bursting into song all over the place and producing some of the most trying sounds.

At the slightest provocation Africa's musicians will volunteer a rendition of 'Nearer my God to Thee' in the train. The worst culprits are to be found on Durban's non-white buses. This is where chaps roll up with their concertinas and violins, mouth-organs and that terrible thing, the accordion. The wailing of these instruments is inflicted regularly on busloads of helpless passengers.

So much for our born musicians.

Then there is another myth, which comes mainly from white suburbia and foreign visitors.

'Africans', these people are always saying, 'are a remarkably patient people.'

How else, they ask, can you explain the smiles on their faces in spite of the colour bar, curfew regulations, pass laws and 300 years of second-class citizenship?

This myth is no doubt inspired by the large numbers of Africans who are always dancing on city pavements, or giggling and chattering away cheerfully at work. But I doubt whether patience has much to do with their smiles or their apparent goodwill. It is not patience which moves me to laugh at the permit raids and the Government's feeble attempts to make apartheid work.

To begin with, apartheid has not only proved a miserable flop; it looks silly as well. For instance, not so long ago, Africans were not allowed to walk on Johannesburg's pavements.

Around the same time, Africans were not allowed to drive motorcars, this being thought to be far too complicated an operation for simple minds. And, until very recently, it was considered that Africans would cause serious trouble if allowed to drink brandy and wines.

Today Africans are not allowed to drink in any hotel in Johannesburg. Yet last week 29 Rhodesian chiefs were allowed all drinking facilities at the only non-white hotel in Johannesburg. While the 'foreign Natives' were there, we, the local 'Bantu', were allowed to drink in the hotel, too. But, God forbid, not after the chiefs had checked out!

It is not patience which one needs to cope with such situations. An ordinary sense of humour does the job.

It would, no doubt, be silly to suggest that Africans will survive all the daily hurts of their experience by laughing them away and waiting for time to overtake them. There must be an explanation why Africans have remained relatively calm while their leaders are confined, banned, detained or imprisoned on conviction.

Having rejected the theory of patience, we must seek the answer elsewhere. My feeling is that, generally speaking, Africans in this country have not yet shown a really fervent interest in their political advancement. Perhaps the oppression we have suffered so long, and the lack of individual initiative produced by our tribalist systems, have prevented us from developing a militant spirit. And I am sure the distractions of urban life, of the bright lights and football matches and American clothes, have had a lot to do with it.

But, ironically, it is also these very aspects of the good life which are whetting African appetites. Africans have tasted enough to make them realise that they are being deprived by apartheid, and it is this which in the long run will make them transcend their present preoccupations and awaken their political fervour.

Yes, There's Too Much Self-Pity

Someone who calls himself 'Group Loyalty' wrote a letter to the Editor this week and said, among other things, that I was 'overcome by self-pity at being a second-class citizen'.

Now I don't know whether self-pity actually overcomes me, but I have a feeling that the writer of this letter is probably right in suggesting that I do in fact suffer from self-pity. This is a weakness I have constantly tried to escape, without, I'm afraid, complete success. It is a weakness that affects a lot of people in situations similar to mine – Negroes, for example, and the rest of the non-white world. These people tend to make a song and dance 'bout 'how we was robbed', as if they were under an anaesthetic when they were robbed.

I think 'Group Loyalty' has a point when he criticises this tendency. I think there is something wrong with people who spend their time mourning about how they are arrested and jailed for petty offences, instead of doing something about it. You see them daily in South African cities, anything up to 20 African men being marched through town because they were found without their passes. They walk in rows displaying meek, self-pitying faces. No civilised Afrikaner, Englishman or Frenchman could be marched along meekly like this wearing that abominable expression which says: 'I am being ill-treated; the world owes me a living.'

'Group Loyalty' must be given his due. I have seen too many Africans who are separated from their wives and families; people who are refused permission to study (yes, there is no place which allows Africans to study engineering in this country), and all they do is pity themselves. It is not for me to say what they ought to do: this country has passed enough laws under which such suggestions could be regarded as incitement. But I am free to say that civilised men like 'Group

Loyalty' would not react with self-pity to some of the laws which this country has passed for Africans – they would do better than that. 'Group Loyalty' also said that my trouble was obvious – 'association with the wrong type of white'. He added: 'If Mr Nakasa took a positive view of the situation, he would move to his tribal area and use his undoubted gifts to uplift his primitive compatriots.' What 'Group Loyalty' overlooks is that, in addition to associating with the 'wrong whites', I also drink (let alone associate) with other people – mine 'boys', street sweepers, flat 'boys' (I have been one myself) and lots of other 'boys'.

Now these 'boys' don't like being called 'boys'. Some are grandfathers from stable homes. Neither do they enjoy being second-class citizens. And, if all were to leave the 'white areas', Johannesburg would come to a standstill. 'Group Loyalty' and his friends would not find it so easy to 'learn self-reliance in *their* own area'.

However, 'Group Loyalty' will be pleased to hear that, though I have not moved to my own tribal area, I have done something about keeping in touch with the ways of 'my people'.

This week, for instance, I was refused a passport to go to take up a scholarship in America. As usual, no reasons were given. I told everyone I met how baffled I was as to why the authorities had done this to me. I even pointed out that I had never been a member of any political organisation – as though it was a crime to be a member of a political party.

While I was self-pitying myself about all this, one of the office drivers came up with the suggestion that I should see an African witchdoctor who would explain it all to me.

And that's what I did. In fact, I went to see two witchdoctors.

The first told me: 'Your way is clear … I can see you want to go to Lourenço Marques. Your way is clear; the only trouble is that there is a fat fellow who wears white clothes where you work and he has been bewitching you.'

Still a little uncertain about why I was refused a passport, I went to see the second witchdoctor.

'My son,' she began, 'your trouble is there are too many girls fighting over you.' (I discarded this as rubbish, because I am always short of girls to take out.)

Then she went on: 'Another thing is that your ancestors are standing in your way. You did not tell them you were leaving.' (Which is absolutely true.)

'Now the white people want to give you the papers you want, but your ancestors, three of them, are causing the commotion. I can see (pointing at two bones) one young white man talking to an elderly one (probably the Minster of the Interior, I thought) and disagreeing. The young man says, 'Give him,' but the old man says, 'No, I won't give him.'

As a solution, the witchdoctor suggested that I slaughter a white goat and things will be fine.

Castles in the Air

Last week, after months of building castles in the air, I was awarded a scholarship to study in America for a year. Normally, I should be giving interviews to newspapers now. I should be saying: This is the happiest moment of my life – like those misguided bridegrooms you find on the social page of the newspapers. At the very least, I should be looking like a cat that has just swallowed a whole lot of cream.

But I dare not – I cannot. For I have just been to the Bantu Affairs Commissioner's Office to apply for a passport. And that was enough to wipe off any smile that might have been developing on my face.

The young white clerk stared through me and said: 'What do you want?' I told him I wanted passport application forms.

'What?'

'The passport forms. I want to go to America.'

'Where?'

'America.'

After this conversation the clerk fished out two forms and warned me to fill in and return them as soon as possible. 'You people like to come here at the last minute and expect everything to be done for you quickly,' he said.

I mumbled some protest and walked out. It seemed odd that I should be accused of wanting to have things done quickly when in fact there are still three months between now and the day I leave in July.

I have now read the forms, which the clerk gave me. One of them carries a word of advice at the bottom. 'You are advised', it says, 'not to finalise any travel arrangements or to deposit fares before you are in possession of your passport, or have been advised of the result of your application.'

This, in other words, is a cold reminder that 'a South African passport may be granted by the Minster of the Interior at his discretion.' Suppose, just suppose, the Honourable Minster does not grant the passport? This is the unholy possibility, which will be driving me slowly round the bend from now on.

Heaven knows, the last thing I want is an exit permit. I've seen enough of my friends leave the country on those things. Some of them are now living as exiles in Europe, England, and America. Nearly all of them write miserable letters reminiscing about the good old days in South Africa. They plead for letters and newspapers from here. They would do anything to be at our mammoth, dance-booze parties, which last anything from two days to a week in the townships.

Life abroad lacks the challenge that faces us in South Africa. After a lifetime of illegal living in the Republic's shebeens, the exiles are suddenly called upon to become respectable, law-abiding citizens. Not a law to break in sight. For my part, it would be an act of providence if I survived under such circumstances. I have broken too many curfew laws and permit regulations to change so easily. Even if I did change, I would miss the experience of illegal living. I would miss the man I met the other day who asked for a loan of my car's windscreen.

'What on earth for?' I asked.

Patiently, over a drink, he explained that his windscreen was scratched and the traffic police had asked him to take his car off the road until he could find another windscreen. Instead of spending R20 on this, he planned to stick my windscreen into his car when going to the testing grounds. He would return it after the test.

This is the life I know, the life I would miss as an exile.

There is only one redeeming feature about exits. It can be quite exciting to arrive in London and face a battery of television cameras with all the thunder and storm which is built-in equipment for political refugees. One friend of mine was so pleased with this prospect that he planned to make directly for the American Embassy on arriving in London.

'I'll tell them to give me a girl promptly,' he said. 'Or else I'm going to ask for one at the Russian Embassy.'

A Native of Nowhere

Some time next week, with my exit permit in my bag, I shall cross the borders of the Republic and immediately part company with my South African citizenship. I shall be doing what some of my friends have called 'taking a grave step'.

For my part, there is nothing grave about it. You needn't even be brave to take the 'step'. It is enough to be young, reckless and ready to squander and gamble your youth away. You may, I dare say, even find the whole business exciting.

According to reliable sources, I shall be classed as a prohibited immigrant if I ever try to return to South Africa. What this means is that self-confessed Europeans are in a position to declare me, an African, a prohibited immigrant, bang on African soil. Nothing intrigues me more.

And the story does not end there. Once out I shall apparently become a stateless person, a wanderer, unless I can find a country to take me in. And that is what I have been trying to achieve in the past few days. I cannot enter America on an exit permit even though I have a scholarship to take up in that country. The Americans will let me in only on a valid passport from a country that is prepared to have me when I leave America.

Apparently, there can be no question of getting the Americans to depart from this, their official policy, unless, perhaps, I moved into the US as a Cuban refugee. For I have read about many Cuban citizens who left their country for the US in that way. But I have ruled this out as something too involved to try. Meanwhile, I have thought of becoming a Zambian, a Nigerian, or a Malawian. But these countries have no embassies in South Africa, so getting their travel documents would take ages.

My best bet may well be to embrace the Jewish faith and procure Israeli citizenship. But again that has its own complications. As an Israeli I may automatically be prohibited entry into Egypt. I may be barred from going to report on any Pan-African conferences that may be held in Cairo in the future.

On the other hand, should I become an Egyptian, I may be expected to declare war on all my Jewish friends – and, Heaven knows, there are many of them. Besides, I don't think I have ever seen an Egyptian, and I have no idea of Egyptian life.

There is some hope, however, that my problems may be solved by the good old Scandinavian countries. I may become the first Scandinavian Pondo in history.

A black Viking! Imagine it!

Finally, if all this doesn't work out, I may be compelled to become a Russian. In this way I might even crash into the limelight as an international statesman. After all, the Russians are known to be very keen on backing an African as the next President of the United Nations. Instead of scouring Africa for a candidate, the Russians might start backing their own African – me.

Having achieved that status, there would be nothing to stop me from rising to the highest office in Russia itself. Who knows? I may wind up as the Prime Minster of the Soviet Union. After all, Dr Verwoerd was born in Holland and he became the Prime Minster of *die Republiek van Suid-Afrika*.

If I should feel homesick while ruling Russia, I could pass a few laws to South-Africanise Russia a little. The first step would be to introduce influx control in Moscow. Get all the native Russians to carry passes and start endorsing them in and out of town. There are enough African and Indian students studying in Russia nowadays to help me carry out my plan. Apartheid all over again! This time with the Russians at the receiving end. Admittedly, this may be described as Afro-Asian minority rule. Others will call it *baasskap*. But we would call it parallel development, or black leadership with justice.

We would introduce the exit-permit system to cut down on the numbers of Russians in the place. At the same time we could bring in millions of Indians and Africans from Bombay, Calcutta, Umtata and Zululand on an immigration scheme – just as South Africa brings in white immigrants by the thousand every month.

We would have to scrap Communism from the start. In fact, I would import South Africa's Suppression of Communism Act lock, stock and barrel. Communism would be an enemy number one. Anybody who opposed my apartheid policies too much would wind up banned or detained.

Unfortunately, all these are mere dreams. For the time being, my future lies in a number of diplomatic bags. Various consuls are trying to see what can be done for me. I hope, when I write next week, it will be as a former South African. As far as I can, I shall try not to interfere with your domestic affairs, let alone meddle with your white or non-white politics.

Met with Smiles and Questions

Travelling without a passport is a hazardous and exhausting business. Having to explain, from airport to airport, over and over again, that the South African Government had refused me a passport but issued me with an exit permit had drained the last bit of energy out of me by the time I landed in New York four weeks ago.

Fortunately, however, the American people are a gay, friendly lot. They greeted me with broad, welcome-into-the-fold smiles, which helped undo some of the tension I felt. Even as I flew from London to New York, the Americans on the plane had been remarkably friendly. 'Say,' the old man behind me had asked, mistaking me for a Negro, 'who won the World Series?'

I had no idea what that was, but we had a friendly conversation nevertheless.

However, I did not like New York – that is, those few parts that I saw. The city has the looks of a great, modern slum. Too many of its tall, redbrick buildings reminded me of Durban's many-storeyed hostels where African men live. The difference is that the New York buildings don't have high wire fencing around them like the 'game reserves' (which is what we used to call them) in Durban. Instead they look more like giant filing cabinets, with people packed neatly inside, many of them doomed never to know the joy of a detached home with a backyard to themselves.

The landlords of the city have apparently been left to make their cash the best way they please. Many of the structures, countless blocks of flats, are without paint on the outside. A lot of the passages and corridors are in a state of perpetual semi-darkness, and few people see the sun rise in the morning. The buildings are so high that they cast gloomy shadows over each other.

Come the night, and New York transforms into a dazzling beauty queen. Instead of the gloomy half-hearted shadows of the day, you get genuine darkness contrasted with the brilliance of a multitude of bright lights. This is when the night prowlers pour into the streets, wrapped in heavy coats, for their share of pub-crawling and party life.

It was to this background that I listened to the Johannesburg trumpeter, Hugh Masekela, blowing Pondo and Swazi tunes in Greenwich Village.

'I wish I could go home,' he said afterwards, 'just to hear the music of the people there – the Pondos, the Zulus and the Shangaans.'

Shortly after that, I had listened to Miriam Makeba's daughter reciting her own poetry and talking about 'the Boers and my people in Johannesburg'.

She obviously longed for home. I wondered if she knew that Bantu Education would have taught her how to weave grass mats instead of learning about the 20th century. She might have grown up into another washerwoman. 'I'm going to be a lawyer,' she said, and I knew there was nothing to stop her.

But I stayed only one weekend in New York. Since then I have seen Boston and nearby Cambridge, where I am now. This is a charming neighbourhood, with lovely old wooden homes that look like homes, not a conglomeration of symmetrical slums.

It will be long before I can write in depth about the people I see around me. For one thing, I spend most of my time at Harvard, which is steeped in the sombre business of education. Like, I suppose, most universities, Harvard is untypical of the 'American way of life'. I could probably spend a year without knowing the full meaning of being black in the United States.

Outside Harvard, people seem to have their own image of South Africa. They look at the scar on my forehead and wonder if it isn't an example of police brutality. So far I have taken the trouble to explain that it was actually the result of a car accident, but I cannot hope to correct many other impressions about South Africa, however exaggerated they may be. It is hardly my job.

People here are startled by the 'wickedness of reserving such ordinary jobs as engine driving for the whites'. They cannot understand the circumstances under which I could remain on speaking terms with Afrikaners in view of their attitudes to black men. And Negroes are filled with despair when they hear that I was expelled from my country because I wanted to go to school abroad.

P.J. O'ROURKE

JUST FOR *a change, here are the views of an outsider looking in – an American in Parys, that sleepy little town poised on the Vaal River between the Free State province and the old Transvaal. He came to look at South Africa at the worst of times – 1986, when the apartheid regime was, at last, more or less boycotted, often isolated, and certainly desperate. It was before the Berlin Wall fell; before the Cold War ended; before most of the world's political attitudes spun nearly 180 degrees.*

He is one of the few chroniclers of human events who survive, quite easily, 180-degree turns in political correctness. All he has to do is shift slightly, to remain an outsider and be able to laugh at the latest fashionable beliefs.

The year of his visit to South Africa was a time when apartheid's men were hinting at dropping a nuclear bomb; of crushing even some of their own wavering supporters; of undermining elected local authorities; of assassinating many of the local figures whose names had been enthusiastically placed on their death wish-lists.

O'Rourke rode above it all. And his style of reportage – so dedicatedly politically incorrect – was a joy for all genuine reporters, if not for committed commentators. O'Rourke's most admirable journalistic feat is that he not only tells another side of the truth … he makes us laugh.

P.J. O'Rourke was born in Toledo, Ohio, graduated from Miami University and went on to read English at Johns Hopkins University in Baltimore. In the early 1970s he wrote for and edited several 'underground' publications, including a Baltimore weekly called, of all things, Harry. *He became managing editor of the* National Lampoon *in 1975, and editor-in-chief in 1978. Later he became a freelance writer for such diverse publications as* Car and Driver, The American Spectator, Playboy, Esquire, Harpers, Rolling Stone *and* Vanity Fair. *He is best known for his caustic books which spare no one, books such as* Parliament of Whores, Give War a Chance *and* Holidays in Hell, *which were bestsellers translated into several languages.*

In Holidays in Hell *(Pan Books, London, 1989) he wrote of a visit to South Africa …*

December 1986

I'd been told South Africa looks like California, and it looks like California – the same tan-to-cancer beaches – the same Granola'd mountains' majesty, the same sub-developed bushveldt. Johannesburg looks like LA. Like LA, it was all built since 1900. Like LA, it's ringed and vectored with expressways. And its best suburb, Hyde Park, looks like Beverly Hills. All the people who live in Hyde Park are white, just like Beverly Hills. And all the people who work there – who cook, sweep and clean the swimming pools – are not white, just like Beverly Hills. The only difference is, the lady who does the laundry carries it on her head.

I was prepared for South Africa to be terrible. But I wasn't prepared for it to be normal. Those petty apartheid signs, NO DOGS OR NON-EUROPEANS, are rare, almost tourist attractions now. There's no colour bar in the big 'international' hotels or their restaurants or nightclubs. Downtown shopping districts are integrated. You see as many black people in coats and ties as you do in Chicago. If I'd really tried, I could have spent my month in South Africa without noticing any hint of trouble except the soldiers all over the place. South Africa is terribly normal. And this is why, I think, we get so emotional about it.

Everywhere you go in the world somebody's raping women, expelling ethnic Chinese, enslaving stone-age tribesmen, shooting Communists, rounding up Jews, kidnapping Americans, setting fire to Sikhs, keeping Catholics out of the country clubs and hunting peasants from helicopters with automatic weapons. The world is built on discrimination of the most horrible kind. The problem with South Africans is that they admit it. They don't say, like the French, 'Algerians have a legal right to live in the sixteenth arrondissement, but they can't afford to.' They don't say, like the Israelis, 'Arabs have a legal right to live in West Jerusalem, but they're afraid to.' They don't say, like the Americans, 'Indians have a legal right to live in Ohio, but, oops, we killed them all.' The South Africans just say, 'Fuck you.' I believe it's right there in their constitution: 'Article IV: Fuck you. We're bigots.' We hate them for this. And we're going to hold indignant demonstrations and make our universities sell all their Kruger rands until the South Africans learn to stand up and lie like white men.

Forty-miles from Johannesburg is Pretoria, the capital of South Africa. It looks like Sacramento with soldiers, like Sacramento will if the Chicanos ever rebel. And on the tallest hill in Pretoria stands the Voortrekker Monument, a 120-foot tower of shit-coloured granite. The Voortrekker Monument's rotunda is decorated with an immense, heroic-scale bas-relief depicting the entire course of the Great Trek from Bible-kissing send-offs in Cape Town to the Battle of Blood River in 1838, when 3 000 Zulu were killed vs. 0 dead Boers.

It was with unmixed feelings about Afrikaners that I climbed the wearyingly dramatic steps to the monument. One stroll through central Pretoria and one walk through the memorial's parking lot were enough to see that they're a no-account people – dumpy women in white ankle socks and flower-print sundresses, skinny, quid-spitting men with hair oil on their heads and gun-nut sideburns.

Their language sounds like a Katzemjammer Kids cartoon: *Die telefoon is in die sitkamer* (the telephone is in the sitting room). *Die dogter ry op 'n trein* (the daughter rides on the train). And their racism is famous for its high degree of international deplorability. Liberal pinkoes, unreconstructed Stalinists, cannibal presidents of emerging nations, and fascist military dictator swine all agree on this point.

Therefore my heart sank when I saw the Great Trek sculpture. It was, God help me, 'Wagon Train' carved in stone. There was no mistaking the pokey oxen, and prairie wagoneers parked in a circle, for a combat-ready camp-out. The gals all had those dopey coal-scuttle bonnets on and brats galore doing curtain calls in their skirts. The fellers all wore Quaker Oats hats and carried muskets long as flagpoles. Horses pranced. Horizons beckoned. Every man jack from Ben Cartwright on down stared off into the sunset with chin uplifted and eyes full of stupid resolve. Every give-me-a-home-where-the-buffalo-roam bromide was there, except the buffalo were zebras, and at that inevitable point in the story where one billion natives attack completely unprovoked, it was Zulus with spears and shields instead of Apaches with bows and arrows. The Zulus were of course doing everything Apaches were always depicted as doing before we discovered Apaches were noble ecologists – skewering babies, clobbering women and getting shot in massive numbers.

South Africa's bigoted, knuckle-headed Boers turned out to be North America's revered pioneer forefathers. And here I was, a good American descendant of same, covered with gore from Indian slaughters and belly stuffed to bursting by the labour of kidnapped slaves, ready to wash up, have a burp and criticise Afrikaners ...

I did see one homeland that worked, beautiful and severe bushveldt taken back from Boer farms and restored to its natural state with blesbok and gemsbok and springbok looking around all antlered and everything and herds of zebra – art deco on the hoof – and packs or gaggles or whatever-they're-called of giraffes (an NBA of giraffes would be the right term). This was, however, a homeland for the animals, the Botsalano Game Park in Bophuthatswana.

Tom Mills and I were riding in a Land-Rover with his wife and two kids when we came right up beside five rhinoceros – four really enormous gigantic ones and a calf that was pretty tremendously huge itself. It's not easy to describe the effect that the first sight of a wild rhino has on a not very brave author from Ohio. It's like taking your four-year-old on a surprise visit to the Mesozoic area. I felt a vaulting thrill combined with some desire to start crying and crawl under the jeep. Tom, in what I felt was an extremely foolhardy move, turned off the engine.

'There are two kinds of rhinos,' said Tom. 'White rhinos are fairly docile. They don't usually bother you. But black rhinos are very nervous and aggressive. They'll charge.'

'These rhinos are grey,' I said.

'White rhinos and black rhinos are actually about the same colour,' said Tom.

'How do you tell them apart?'

'White rhinos have a square upper lip. The black rhino's is pointy.'

I looked at our rhinos. Their upper lips were square, in a pointy sort of way. 'How else do you tell them apart?'

'I forget.'

The rhinos, who are very nearsighted, finally noticed us. They cocked their heads in this Godzilla way they have and began to amble in our direction. A rhinoceros ambles at about 60 m.p.h. There was a movement of brief – but nonetheless high – drama while the Land-Rover engine went ugga-ugga-ugga before it caught.

The rhinos made South Africa more depressing, if that's possible. The big game is disappearing from Africa. Most Africans have never seen a rhino in its natural state (which is a state of mild pique, I believe) any more than we've seen the prairie black with bison. And, to be fair, the white South Africans are the only people on the continent returning any land to the wild. Whatever's going to happen in South Africa will be bad for the rhino, too. And rhinos only occasionally kill for fun and never go to the UN afterwards and say they did it because of American imperialism or communist subversion.

We drank as much as usual that night, sitting outside the tents with Botsalano's game warden. The baboons goofed off in the shrubbery and frogs sounded in the water hole like ten thousand little boys with sticks on an endless picket fence.

The game warden told how the leopard was coming to extinction in South Africa. The leopards used to be hunted as trophies, mostly by Americans and Englishmen. Any farmer who had a leopard shot on his land received a trophy fee of several hundred rand. So whenever a farmer had a leopard around, he was careful to preserve it until some rich guy came looking to decorate the rumpus room. Even if this cost the farmer a few lambs or calves, it was worth it. Then the animal rights people, the 'bunny-huggers' as the warden called them, got legislation passed forbidding the import of all spotted fur, including stuffed heads, into the US and the UK. Now the farmers just shoot the leopards – mothers, cubs and everything – as pests. 'So fucking bloody much for good intentions,' said the warden.

JO-ANNE RICHARDS *is a journalist and the author of three novels. She worked as a reporter and feature writer on the* Evening Post, *the* Cape Times, *the* Sunday Express *and* The Star. *She now lectures in journalism to postgraduate students at Wits.*

Her first novels, The Innocence of Roast Chicken *and* Touching the Lighthouse, *published by Headline, won great reviews. Of her first book, the* Daily Telegraph *said: 'A wise and substantial literary novel.' One critic compared her work to 'an early Doris Lessing'. Her latest,* Sad at the Edges, *was published in mid-2003.*

Her novels are studies of ordinary people trying to live normal lives in an extraordinary society. In this story we find bathos and layers of satire, irony, wit and parodied 'cool', providing a wonderfully decadent insight into contemporary Johannesburg.

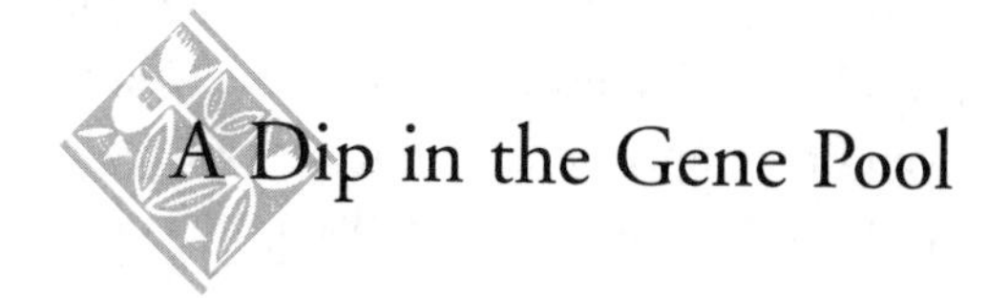

A Dip in the Gene Pool

There was nothing else to be done. It was two in the morning, you see, none of us had had any sleep and my housemate wanted me out of his bed.

It was time to make a list. Mark – my housemate – suggested it in the long-suffering tone he affects in the middle of the night. His partner, Paul, scrabbled on his nightstand for paper and pen without actually opening his eyes. I wrote: REASONS NEVER TO GO OUT WITH MEN AGAIN.

They both sighed. I couldn't do that, they told me.

This was one of life's great decisions, Mark said. And at least, muttered Paul, hand over still-closed eyes, I should be able to approach it with objectivity. I maintained a hurt silence.

Mark swept his eyes heavenward and sighed again. Finally it was decided we should settle for at least the appearance of neutrality. MEN, the list stated.

PROS

1. Making braais 2. Sex 3. Love and Cuddling 4. Babies

Mark sighed again. Okay, that's a start, he said in the annoying tone he used to exhort me to do my best.

'Okay, okay, so I know the braai thing is a little romantic ideal of mine.'

The truth was that no one ever shaped up to my father, squatting beside the open fire, penknife in hand – all sort-of sepia coloured by memory.

'If you meet anyone sepia coloured, doll, avoid him. He's likely to have a serious alcohol problem,' said Paul, while Mark pointed out that boys didn't carry pen-knives nowadays. Très uncool.

We moved on to the sex issue. Mark lost his breath laughing, while Paul had great difficulty maintaining his languid air.

'You told him,' I accused Mark.

'It wasn't exactly hard to pick up the state of your sex life, darling, when The Boy told us that joke about how you find a clitoris? And the answer's "Who cares?" And you said that, coming from him, it lacked a certain irony.'

The Boy was my recent ex-boyfriend. Very recent. He had attained his ex status only six hours before. In fact Mark had just suggested that, before I moved from the house, I ought to borrow his Estée Lauder eye-mask.

The next entry on my list caused so much laughter that I decided to move on to Babies. They stopped laughing. Hhmm, they both said.

'We'll come back to that,' I said. 'Let's get to CONS.'

1. Destroyed self-esteem 2. Misery 3. No olives in your fridge

'Oh my God.' That was Mark. 'It's just occurred to me: you broke up over the olives. I cannot believe you broke up with someone for eating all the olives.'

Paul sat up and stared at Mark. Paul was a chef. Paul took olives very, very seriously.

'Please, please,' I leapt into the breach. 'Don't break up over the olives.'

The Boy had an attractive quiff of blond hair which tended to fall over his forehead when he was trying to be boyish. It was the most attractive thing about him. No, that's not true. He had a couple of attractive qualities.

Anyway, the four of us – Mark, Paul, The Boy and I – had decided to have a dinner party to celebrate passing the mystical three-month relationship barrier.

It was all to do with tedious stuff like sex in the 21st century and the threat of death. If you wanted to wait, he'd regard it as a rejection. Yet you couldn't just sleep with him. You were supposed to be monogamous. So he'd drink all your beer and eat all your olives until, after a respectable three months, and before your CDs had mingled too much, you'd break up.

The Boy lasted three months and three days. The night before our dinner party he had taken me out. Naturally he vetoed my suggestion of quiet and chatty.

Oh no, we had to go to this roof place, where exotic people hung out. The less exotic, like me, stood around saying 'Hey' in a meaningful way. He and his chinas spent much of the evening discussing how cool they were. And how su-bur-ban people were who didn't come here.

Eventually we joined a table of silent Ethiopians, who nodded and said: 'Hey.'

'You see,' they said. 'It's only in places like this you'll meet, like, the real people of the continent.'

I don't think the Ethiopians spoke English. They silently offered us some little sticks. I declined. I like to identify my little sticks before I chew them. After that, I astutely discerned that I could expect nothing further from them.

They let themselves in at eight in the morning. I listened to the clamour of coffee and the assuagement of the Munchies, but I never dreamt they would dare … It was only when Paul, who took olives very, very seriously, donned his apron to make the Chicken Marengo … It was only when he opened the fridge and I saw his hand flutter to his cheek …

Later, I had crept self-pityingly into Mark's bedroom and moaned about men, to which they'd uttered things like 'Mm', or 'I kno-ow'.

It wasn't so much that The Boy was so special or anything. ('I kno-ow.') Deep down I suppose I had known. ('Mm.') And it hadn't really been about the olives. But olives could be a sign, couldn't they?

I didn't know if I could bear it all again. ('Mm.') The endless dispiriting round. I mean, the whole process: the searching, the sussing, the sex thing. ('Oh my God.')

So it had occurred to me that, with our conclusion that men's only advantage was babies, perhaps I should circumvent the whole process by having one. (Silence.) I mean, the only reason women in their '30s rushed around desperately seeking Sam was for that. Wasn't it? (Silence.) Then I could be a whole person who didn't need a relationship. (Absolute silence.)

I realised Mark and Paul were getting into the idea when Paul arrived home with the fluffy hyena. He said babies shouldn't grow up prejudiced. Hyenas had suffered a bad press.

'Oh my God,' muttered Mark. 'Next thing our baby'll be sleeping with a vulture.'

'Whose baby?' I asked.

They told me our baby needed male figures, even if they were, you know, a little camp. And they would make the perfect protectors, the most doting of uncles …

'We think of this baby as ours too,' concluded Paul.

I suggested the first step would be to locate the father of my unconceived child. We made a list.

1. Bruce 2. The boy who plays guitar at the Bassline 3. ?

They didn't like Bruce. Bruce was a press photographer, one of those Old Africa Hands who wore a flak jacket and had white lines around his eyes. He said things like 'Hey Babe'.

I pointed out that Bruce, besides being tall and having perfect eyesight, was bright.

'No one bright stands up to take pictures when bullets are flying,' said Mark.

I mentioned that he had nearly won the Pulitzer Prize.

'No one nearly wins the Pulitzer Prize,' said Paul. 'You win it or you don't.'

'Well, he's macho,' I said. 'Don't you think we need a little balance around here?'

Macho was not genetic, they declared. We'd hire a Sumo wrestler as a child-minder. And not knowing the name of the boy from the Bassline was a small impediment.

That was when I suggested Mark.

'Wait,' yelled Paul. 'Our baby can't be conceived just like that. He or she needs to be welcomed with a Salmon Soufflé.'

They had just told me to put my feet up. I had muttered that I was not yet pregnant. They had also told me coyly that they'd taken themselves for a joint AIDS test.

'It was so romantic,' Mark sighed. I became a little resentful.

The preparation took a long time. Paul went shopping – a tortuous process filled with disappointments (at the poor quality of the salmon) and rekindled excitements (at the thought of crayfish).

Then there were the tarot cards. We were to expect a newcomer. A male newcomer. Paul produced a book of names.

'Aaron?' suggested Mark, starting at the beginning.

'Let's get on with it,' I muttered.

'Wait,' said Paul, and he rushed off for a crystal … wait, and some scented candles. The crystal was for balance and serenity, he said. I needed both.

'Do you want a hot water bottle for your back?' asked Mark. I replied with only slightly gritted teeth (Hey, these crystals work), that I wasn't yet giving birth. And never would at this rate.

After the crayfish soufflé and champagne, followed by herbal tea … ('Coffee's bad for pregnant women.' 'I'm not pregnant.' 'You soon will be.') … we repaired to my bedroom.

'Aren't you going to leave, Paul?' I asked hopefully.

'Why?'

Mark and I gazed at him. Suddenly his hand fluttered to his cheek.

This was how we came to be rushing into old Mr Nathan's all-night pharmacy to beg for syringes. Old Mr Nathan inquired after my acne problem.

'That was adolescence, Mr Nathan,' I enunciated. 'Ad-o-lescence. I'm grown-up now.'

'Are you, dear? What do you need the syringe for?'

'Well, um …'

Mr Nathan explained that because of something called peer pressure, people would sometimes try to get me to take things that would get me into trouble.

So there we were at midnight, sitting disconsolately and syringeless on the kitchen floor. We had finished all the olives.

'It's back to the list then,' I said.

'Perhaps it's just as well,' said Mark. 'You know there's a gay gene.'

'So what,' I said.

'Well, since this is our only shot at the child-thing, I'd like to bank on a couple of grandchildren.'

'Hey Babe.'

I had been right to call him for this assignment, Bruce said. It was best to brief the man who knew the terrain.

'Ja well no fine,' he said. 'When I was in Nigeria …'

'That's riveting, but have you been tested?'

'Sure Babe. I don't shoot blanks … Oh, you mean the other thing? That too.'

I had spent a long time considering underwear. He'd seen quite a few in his time. I couldn't wear the pair that had turned grey in the washing machine. On the other hand, the satin pair I'd bought – oh, just over three months ago now – were a bit frivolous. What if he ripped them off with his teeth. I'd have to say: 'Wait, wait, these are imported. Let me get the old pair.'

Paul had answered the door in his apron. He'd been making soufflé.

Bruce had declined the soufflé and I nearly called it off then and there. Mark, Paul and I had to repair to the kitchen for a team talk.

'Sensitivity', Paul had declared selflessly, 'is not genetic. We'll hire a ballet dancer as a child-minder.'

'What about the Sumo wrestler?'

'We can have a Sumo wrestler and a ballet dancer,' he'd said grandly.

In the bedroom, Bruce unbuttoned his khaki shirt slowly. He ran his hands over his chest just in case I'd missed it. The hair, Babe, the hair – symbol of manhood, emblem of virility.

'Right Babe, let's get this show on the road.'

Nothing happened. I waited. Still nothing happened. I waited a bit more. Men didn't like to be hurried. Perhaps he was gathering the impetus to leap.

Suddenly he did leap, burying his face in my bosom and leaking tears, little sobs breaking from his muscled chest.

'It's just that when I think of my own little *laaitie*. Of never taking my own little guy down the Congo.'

'Perhaps the next one shouldn't be told,' I suggested.

We repaired to the Bassline for a recce. All I could see were Progenitors-in-Prospect. Short-sighted men, tall men, men with bow legs and, boy, there was a predisposition to heart attacks if ever I saw one.

The club was filled with genetic catastrophes. Except for the one nameless man who played guitar. I was just noticing the way those pecs or specs danced across his guitar when Paul pointed out the creativity of the little riff he was playing.

'Aaron can start violin lessons at three,' he said.

I rolled my eyes and told them to bugger off. I wouldn't get far with them hanging around.

But Mark's sister Megan turned up, supported by her over-confident crowd of just-20-somethings. Megan flicked her hair back and asked how come *we* were there. Mark, who can never keep his mouth shut, went and told her.

Megan gave a superior sniff and I was instantly transformed into The Ancient One. I stammered that this was a life choice, not yet a necessity and ... there was still time ...

'Oh sure,' they all chorused. 'We think it's really cool, like for someone of your age.'

Megan thought the guitarist just brilliant. 'I mean it's so clever of you. To pick someone like him in the new South Africa.'

'Why,' cut in Paul. 'Good eyesight?'

'No, like I mean ...'

'Musical?'

'No-o.'

'O-oh, you mean because he's slightly tinted, darling? Well, the fact is, we picked him for aesthetic reasons. The child'll blend so nicely with our pumpkin-coloured walls.'

The upshot was that Megan declared a little more recce was required. She, being the selfless girl she was, would discover all there was to know so I needn't see him more than once.

'You don't want to risk a relationship,' she said, gazing at me in expectation of gratitude.

'Well, it's a tough job ...' muttered Paul, but Mark frowned at him.

'Don't say I never do anything for you,' said Megan as she took up a position to the left of the dais.

I settled into my relaxed life, relatively certain I was committed to nothing for at least three months. In the meantime, the fridge was full of olives, and I began to read *The Alexandria Quartet*.

But things move faster for 20-somethings. I realised this when I arrived home to soufflé. Megan announced that Robert (the last impediment – gone) was just perfect for someone like me.

As it turned out, the fates were with me. My temperature was just right and I had not a zit in sight. So this was it. At last.

There was plenty of time till the Bassline opened. Perhaps I'd just stop off for a cup of coffee. Just to fortify myself. I would probably have to be up all night. I hauled the book from my bag. It would definitely carry me through the first trimester.

'Given up on men?'

He was smallish and wore glasses. Absolutely not on, genetically speaking.

'Why?'

His face dimpled. 'Last time I gave up on women, I read *War and Peace*. A bit clichéd, wasn't it?'

He joined me for coffee. There was still plenty of time, after all. We talked about … well everything. Books and movies and clubs – he enjoyed the roof place, but generally preferred somewhere you could talk.

Suddenly it was 10 o'clock. Probably better to skip the first set, Robert would be more relaxed then anyway.

We switched to wine. It was important not to drink too much caffeine.

He was clever and witty – in every other respect, of course, a minefield of bad heredity. But now that I'd given up men as a romantic option, I could just enjoy the company. Oops, it was past midnight. Maybe it'd be better to get there just before the end. I didn't want to spend the entire night hanging about.

He was telling me he preferred to defer the sex thing while he got to know someone. Funny, when his face dimpled like that … Certainly nice to share a glass of wine with.

He ordered tequila. Well … that was confident. I liked confidence in a friendly companion, if it were balanced by … well, by …

'I just thought tequila would be fun,' he said. Fun, that was it … balanced by fun.

'But don't drink it if you wouldn't like to …' And sensitivity … balanced by sensitivity.

'I'll make sure you get home safely.'

Protectiveness was important.

'It's just that I don't want this to end.' Oh yes, and charm. Charm was essential. It made me wish he wasn't so deeply into deferment.

Oh God, what was I saying? They'd kill me. And Megan had gone to so much trouble. Paul'd made so many soufflés, Mark taken so many temperatures. Oh jeez, it was already too late. The night was gone.

I stared at him and blinked. It must be the tequila. Those genetic shortcomings – what were they again? Um, eyes? But they were such nice eyes. His … his body? But he had a nice way of touching as he talked. And those dimples … Oh God, this was a disaster.

'Do you eat olives?' I asked.

'I don't mind them in food. But I hate them straight from the fridge.'

RICHARD RIVE

YOU ARE *about to relish in the following pages real, rich humour at the expense of mankind's worst follies – race hatred, greed, fanaticism and officious cruelty. Richard Rive's tales about his youth also portray a lot of lust and sloth, and some dishonesty. But in the face of fascism and apartheid these vices are virtually virtues.*

Here is classic humour – wry smiles at the bad roll of life's dice; grins at the pain; laughter at the bullies.

You may be reminded of another classic of comical characterisation – John Steinbeck's Cannery Row *set on the coast below San Francisco. However, it could be claimed that Rive's tale, played out against the looming, bitter fate of District Six, Cape Town, where he was born, has humour and depth beyond the stories of Steinbeck, which so captivated us long ago, if only because of the inhumanity looming behind Rive's comedy.*

Rive hit the funny-bone of truth, 'on the head' (as one of his characters might add). A bang on the funny-bone may amuse uninvolved observers, but for the target it is salutary, shocking and painful. The author does not avoid the pain. Indeed, he wants you to remember nothing else. It is very serious tragi-comedy … the pain; with the bitterness swallowed in laughter.

One thing more. Rive has managed to convey another truth concerning the reality he depicts. It is the exuberance, the effervescence, the sharpness of 'Cape coloured' humour. The author accurately reflects the wit and complexity of it, even though he cannot fully capture it. It is impossible to capture in writing because, like Cockney, it is spontaneous street-theatre played in a language that cannot be put to paper. Richard Rive, who grew up with it in his (funny) bones, has done the next best thing.

However, our difficulty in selecting a representative sample of the work of an author of quality who is dealing with a theme of fundamental importance is that our focus must be on comedy – not tragedy. And in this case the tragedy is ultimately overwhelming. The brief extracts we have chosen, therefore, provide only a fleeting taste of Richard Rive's humour. Enjoy it – but remember it is merely the prelude to his account of the cold-blooded destruction of an entire community.

People moved out of the area before the bulldozers and front-end loaders came. 'Everybody in the District died a little when it was pulled down. Many died spiritually and emotionally. Some like my mother died physically,' the author recalls. Families were scattered … 'None of us went in the same direction.' Although a relatively young man, Richard Rive moved on to live alone in a different, separate group area. He lived with his memories. 'I tried to forget the past but the voices caught up with me… And the voices whispered, "They have done this terrible thing to you, to all of you. Go and see. They have taken your past away." So I went to see.'

He found an empty Hanover Street, with just a few left-over houses standing self-consciously each side. The 'left-overs' resembled 'broken teeth with craters in between where the raw gums showed ... They had taken our past away and left the rubble. They had demolished our spirits and left broken bricks. They had destroyed our community and left dust and memories.'

Back in the 1960s, when the cold-blooded decision to destroy District Six, to throw out all the (coloured) people, was officially announced, one of the editors of this anthology wrote a leader in the Cape Argus *headed 'Monument to White Greed'. It was an angry article. It was deliberately filled with invective against supine whites as well as against a racist government. That's all. We mention it to show the contrast – and the power of humour. The angry editorial contributed a mite, perhaps, to the pressure that prevented property speculators moving onto the prime sites, which lay under rubble for decades after the forced removal of its residents. But anger – even the anger of millions of people – was not enough. Nor was it as effective as Rive's humour – which may never allow us to forget.*

Part One: Morning 1955

I remember those who used to live in District Six ... when I was Tarzan and Batman and could sing 'Rainbow on the River' like Bobby Breen ... We lived in the fourth in a row of five mouldy cottages called 'Buckingham Palace' by the locals. The first, 201, the one farthest from the church as if by design, was a blue-painted House of Pleasure called 'Casbah'. In it lived Mary and The Girls. Next to them at 203, painted bright pink, was 'Winsor Park' (spelt like that), which was occupied by Zoot and The Boys. Then came 205, the cottage of The Jungles, then ours, then at 209 that of Last-Knight the barber, his wife and three daughters. A sprawling open field overgrown with weeds and rusty tin cans separated Buckingham Palace from the church.

Katzen, who was the landlord of Buckingham Palace, had his emporium on the corner of Hanover and Tennant Streets. His shop windows were cluttered with bric-à-brac such as celluloid dolls, huge glass tankards still celebrating the Coronation, rolls of crêpe-de-Chine, gramophones and framed and mounted prints of a violently pink-faced King George VI and Queen Elizabeth. After his premises had been broken into six times in so many weeks, Katzen displayed a notice outside his shop, 'Although Katzen has been burgled again, Katzen will never burgle you!' We all knew that there was no chance of the small, Jewish shopkeeper with his walrus moustache and large feet ever climbing through our back windows to steal our radios, but we also felt that he could rob us in other ways. The thieves always seemed to steal his gramophones and crêpe-de-Chine and patriotically left the prints of King George VI and his queen.

... and I still clearly remember Mary.

In her days of innocence before her personal fall, Mary Bruintjies lived in her own particular Eden, which was a mission station deep in the heart of the Boland. She was young and buxom and known in those days as Baby-face Mary because of her childlike look of artlessness. She was the only daughter of Pastor Adam Bruintjies. During the day she attended the village primary school where she learnt reading and writing, and at night, when she wasn't at Brigade meetings and was playing instead with the boys on the *werf*, she learnt other things which interested her more. Mary had joined the Church Brigade at first to improve her alibis but, such was her dexterity with the baton, that she was soon promoted to drum major over four young bucks who had challenged her for the position. It was the first time in its history that the Brigade had a girl marching at its head doing tricks to dazzle the eye and excite every male onlooker. And when they marched to church on Sunday mornings in full regalia, her father would watch their arrival proudly from the main door.

Her fall was sudden but not entirely unexpected, especially by those in the know. She was caught one Sunday after church parade with the bass-drummer behind a hayrick. What made matters worse was that the bass-drummer was married and he was caught by his wife, who became suspicious when she saw the bass-drum at home without her husband. Both the guilty parties were still in or at least partially out of uniform. The bass-drummer was forced by his wife to leave the Brigade for health reasons and Mary was packed off to Cape Town to continue her formal education in the big city.

This was a grave error of judgement on the part of Pastor Adam Bruintjies. He sent his daughter to stay with his maiden sister in Caledon Street, but the sister was too preoccupied with church affairs to bother about her refractory and unrepentant niece. Mary's formal education progressed slowly once she went to high school but her informal education moved forward apace. She retained an interest in uniforms and joined the local Church Brigade, which was bigger, more splendid and belonged to a more established denomination. Her dexterity with the baton was again such that she was soon marching at the head of far more illustrious and glorious columns than the little mission could ever provide. But she could not confine herself to marching and twirling. This time it was the chief bugler whose wife forced him to resign for health reasons. Mary was also asked to leave the Brigade.

At school her teacher's health and reputation declined suddenly after he had helped her a few times privately with her reading. His wife forced him to give up teaching after-hours, and spoke about it to the principal's wife, who also started worrying about her husband's physical condition. Mary's aunt decided that her niece's formal education should come to an end. After a tremendous row Mary left her aunt's home, got a job in a clothing factory, and as Mary Brown (which sounded better than Mary Bruintjies) moved in with the Knights at 209 Caledon Street, the last house in the row nearest the church.

Mr Joseph Knight, his wife and their three daughters lived in somewhat cramped conditions. His unmarried brother Henry, who was two years older than Joseph, boarded with them. Both were slight, nervous men, with such dark complexions that Joseph was known throughout the District as Last-Knight, and his older brother as Knight-Before-Last. Joseph and his brother ran a barber's shop in Tennant Street, and Joseph was chief churchwarden at St Mark's. His wife revelled in his business position and high ecclesiastical office. With seven persons living in a small cottage, life was a bit crowded and Mary and Knight-Before-Last used to go for long walks up the slopes of Devil's Peak to ease the congestion.

After being caught more than once in compromising positions, on one occasion in the chair of the barber's shop after hours, they decided to get married and hired 201 Caledon Street from Katzen the landlord when it fell vacant. After his initial enthusiasm for his wife had waned and his amazement at her energy had subsided, Knight-Before-Last began to fear for his health. One day, at the very end of his tether he simply took his clothes and ran away and was not seen again in the District for years. Last-Knight went to search for his brother at 201 and, when he came home only the following morning, worn out and happy, his wife accused him of lechery and incest and he was forbidden ever to go back there again.

Although Mary reverted to her former name of Mary Brown, everyone in the District referred to her simply as Mary. There was only one Mary and that was the Madam of the Casbah. She was now on her own but not for long. Soon The Girls started moving in. First came The Butterfly with tattoos on her arms and legs, seeking sanctuary from her common-law husband who used to beat her ... The house was anything but a fortress. A warm, red, welcoming light was fitted over the entrance, and the cottage was officially opened for business.

Mr Zoot September was employed as handyman and general repairman-cum-bouncer. He was on call in case there were problems with which Mary could not cope, and slept in the backroom. Later he and The Boys lived in the cottage next door.

Zoot

Zoot September started life as Milton September. His first name, like those of his brothers Byron and Keats, was given to him by an enthusiastic aunt who had studied poetry at Zonnebloem for her Primary Lower Teachers Certificate and had never recovered from the experience. Milton soon developed a penchant for trouble, from the very first day he attended school at Zonnebloem, where his maiden aunt taught. He became so excited when he first saw the principal, that he peed in his shorts right there in front of the great man himself. When the principal scolded him and his aunt clouted him for this, they set permanently in motion his absolute dislike and disregard for authority and officialdom. By the time he had passed Standard Five he had run away from four schools.

Milton was the youngest of the five boys who lived with their widowed mother in Sterling Street Flats. Once he had settled down at the fifth school, again at Zonnebloem, because he fell in love with his teacher he proved to be an avid reader and could write startling although somewhat unorthodox compositions. He was also found to be good at gymnastics but indifferent to anything else. He began truanting and frequenting Angelo Baptiste's shop near Seven Steps, returning to Zonnebloem only for English composition and physical education.

One day the police arrived at their flat to investigate cases of continuous pilfering from the shop, reported by Mr Baptiste. Milton escaped by climbing over the back wall and for the next three days he lay low and slept in the storeroom of the very shopkeeper who had reported him. Baptiste's losses increased drastically during this period, until the police surprised Milton late one night while he was sleeping under some hessian sacks next to the macaroni. He got off lightly with a hiding which was approved by his mother, administered by a burly sergeant in the charge office.

His skill in physical education now came to the fore and he soon became the best tap-dancer in Sterling Street Flats. His ambition stretched beyond such narrow horizons and he began performing to admiring spectators on the Grand Parade, with his cap strategically placed on the ground in front of him for donations. His dexterity helped when any policeman appeared on the scene. Milton, while tapping, could lean down and without losing his balance scoop up the cap and coins with one deft movement of the arm and hand. He would then run like hell for Castle Bridge. He got away with this strategy countless times until two enterprising policemen put an end to it. While one approached him cautiously, the other waited at Castle Bridge. Late that night he was released into the custody of his long-suffering mother after he had dazzled the officers on duty with a display of tap-dancing and had even sent his cap around for donations.

After he left school voluntarily, to the relief of his teacher aunt, he spent much of his time watching gangster movies in Star Bioscope. Late one afternoon he decided to put his new-found interest into practice. He covered his mouth and nose with a scarf the way James Cagney did in films, borrowed Byron's raincoat and with a realistic toy gun he had pilfered from a stall on the Grand Parade, entered Angelo's shop when he calculated it would be empty of customers. Instead of taking fright and handing over all his takings as they did in the movies, Angelo laughed fit to kill himself and then knocked Milton out cold with a huge bottle of olive oil. Milton was not seriously hurt but found himself behind bars and soaked in oil for the first time in his life. He was found guilty and sent to the local reformatory.

It was while there, since his movements were drastically restricted, that he developed his literary ability. Having the name Milton he was assigned to work in the reform school library and began reading and writing during his spare time. He was on occasions a star turn at concerts and dazzled the spectators with his dextrous footwork, but his real reputation rested on the fact that he wrote highly original and innovative as well as libellous verse. Boys paid him with cigarettes to write poems about warders they disliked and Milton was able to churn these out almost at will. He seemed to know all the unsavoury gossip about everyone. This peculiar upsurge in literary appreciation on the part of his charges soon attracted the attention of the superintendent, and when a few of these poems actually reached his desk he realised that he had a serious problem on his hands. Seldom had he come across such smut, such filth, such libel, rather jaggedly written but highly original. Milton, although he vehemently denied authorship, was placed in the punishment cell for two weeks, and spent his time composing scurrilous poems about the superintendent. After his release from the cell a poem was found pinned to the door of the administration office. It described the superintendent's sexual life in the most embarrassing detail. The superintendent laid down an ultimatum to his superiors: either Milton went or he did. As Milton still had two more years to serve and the authorities were reluctant to release him, the superintendent was granted a transfer to Beaufort West.

Milton proved the power of the pen. No man harmed him with impunity. Defamatory verses flowed from him and were always found posted up in the most strategic places. There was a general sigh of relief from the officials when his sentence was over. The new superintendent, having been forewarned by his predecessor, refused Milton permission to read his valedictory poem to the assembly …

[Later he was sentenced to three years in Roeland Street jail for theft of state property.] Milton's reputation preceded him in prison so that while serving his sentence he was allowed no writing material whatsoever. His mother died during this period and his brothers dispersed in different directions. When Milton came out he was alone in the world, so accepted a job at Mary's and moved into her spare back room. During the day he was general handyman and during the evenings acted as bouncer.

He still practised his dancing on occasions, entertaining The Girls with his fancy footwork. He entered for the annual talent contest at Star Bioscope and, dressed in the latest fashion, the Zoot suit, appeared on stage to do his number. He looked smart in a check suit with padded shoulders, narrow waist, knee-length coat and trousers tapering at the ankles. He wore huge black-and-white Jarmans with dancing-studs knocked into the toes and heels. Mary and The Girls took the evening off to root for him as he jived his way to victory. The compère referred to him glowingly as Zoot, the Jive King of District Six, and the name stuck. The Miltonic era was over …

SAN CHANT

PERHAPS our *most ancient culture is vested in the diminutive San of the dry west whose extinct eastern cousins left South Africa with its wonderful rock art heritage.*

*Alan James (*The First Bushman's Path, *2001) 'reworked' a delightful and probably ancient San chant which had originally been translated by the German-born Cape linguist Wilhelm Bleek in the 19th century and later refined by his daughter Dorothea.*

The poetic song provides a glimpse into the enigmatic lives of these desert-dwelling people. It tells how San mothers invoke the help of older children in distracting babies who are refusing to eat their food. Those who know the San's diet (which includes grubs and scorpions and boiled snakes) may feel they understand the child's problem. Certainly it is easier to understand than the translators' punctuation.

The song in this form is from The New Century of South African Poetry *(introduced and edited by Michael Chapman, Ad Donker, Johannesburg, 2002).*

The Withered-leaf Insect

when the withered-leaf insect walks past the fire
we clap our hands to it so that it nods its head:

we clap to it as it walks past, and we sing to it:

'o withered-leaf insect! Up, up, up, go!'

we want it to nod its head and move its feelers
and therefore we sing to it, we clap our hands to it:

'o withered-leaf insect! Up, up, up, go!'

we sing to it as it walks past nodding its head,

For we want the insect to nod for the young children
So that they will stare at it and swallow their meat:

'we always clap our hands to the withered-leaf insect
so that it will nod its head so that we will laugh,'

the mothers of young children will explain to them,
as the insect walks past the fire nodding its head:

and they will tell the older children to clap for it:

'don't let it burn, keep your hands clapping for it:
let the withered-leaf insect get safely past the fire,'

they will say 'clap for the withered-leaf insect
so that your brothers and sisters keep staring at it,'

And as they clap, the younger children watch it nod
And they swallow the food they were not wanting to eat.

JOHN SCOTT

HERE IS A MAN *with a genial eye, a Shavian beard and a warm heart. In normal circumstances he would be inclined to good humour but, like most South African journalists and writers before him, he lived much of his life in very abnormal times. He was left with little choice but to devote most of his writing to satire.*

Writing – for people in our trade – is quite distinct from reporting.

John Scott spent his early years as a reporter on the Cape Argus *and on the* Windhoek Advertiser *beyond the Namib Desert, and then on the* Cape Times.

His satirical writing began when he became parliamentary correspondent and took over a column, which he maintained for 30 years. What he observed in parliament in the apartheid days angered him so much he left his profession to enter politics and run as a liberal Progressive candidate against a Nationalist (English-speaking) Cabinet Minister. His foray into direct politics resulted in his losing by a margin of only one per cent. He then returned to his newspaper to report on (and write about) the weird events of that time. He knew, as well as anybody, that ridicule and satire, which he wrote daily, were the best ways of dealing with racism. In 2000, a decade after the collapse of the Nationalist government, he became editor of the Cape Times. *He has had five books published and is a winner of the Settlers Award for outstanding journalism.*

The first two of his columns reproduced here are samplings of those written in the 1970s and collected in a book titled The Best of PS *(Don Nelson, Cape Town, 1974). 'PS' was the name of his column at the time and he remarked that "PS" is an attempt to look at life and politics in South Africa from an entirely new perspective – upside down. I find the view is often more illuminating than right way up.'*

The first three columns we've selected were written in the 1970s. The second three appeared in the Cape Times *in the year 2003. This juxtaposition shows that Scott is one of the few writers who have defied humour's fast-ageing process and maintained the same style successfully for a third of a century. This is especially remarkable as his task has been to comment almost daily in the press for all those years on subjects and styles that have changed radically.*

Dancing Dangers

One of the most exciting things a White person can do is dance with a Black person. It wasn't always exciting. People could take it or leave it.

Many believed that dancing was an overrated pastime, whatever their partner's colour, and that it took up valuable time that might otherwise be profitably spent at the bar.

But Mr Peet Pelser, Minister of Justice, changed all that. He decided that racially mixed dancing should be forbidden, like apples in the Garden of Eden.

Now everybody wants to taste a bit of mixed dancing, to see what it's like. I met a man yesterday who said he didn't even mind if his dancing partner was not female, as long as she was Black.

'You mean as long as he is Black,' I corrected him.

'What's the difference?' he replied. 'Both ways, it's living dangerously.'

Mixed eating is not the same thing. Nobody seems to mind very much if people have mixed guests with mixed veg. As long as you've got a permit, you can eat with a Black person until you burst, and no-one will give you a medal for liberalism.

Everybody's doing it, even the Prime Minister. He once ate between two Black women because it was his 'duty'. But a spot of mixed dancing will demonstrate to your friends that you still have a sense of adventure, a yearning for the unknown. We can't all sail yachts round Cape Horn but if we are enterprising enough we might manage a quickstep with a Xhosa, a samba with a Sotho.

I believe a group of *verligtes* ['enlightened' Nationalists] is unhappy about the total ban and would like mixed dancing to be permitted, subject to certain conditions. These are:

1. All mixed dancers must undertake to stay at arm's length away from their partners or one metre apart, whichever is the further. Only under the most exceptional circumstances will cheek-to-cheek dancing be lawful, such as when one partner has to apply the kiss of life to the other partner.
2. The topic of conversation, if any, between mixed dancing partners should be non-political, non-controversial and non-suggestive. It is desirable, but not essential, that they speak different languages and be mutually unintelligible.
3. Before navigating any floor, mixed dancers must prove to the satisfaction of the band-leader, who should be a Government employee, that they have less than 0.08 per cent alcohol in their bloodstreams.
4. Waltzes, quicksteps, foxtrots, sambas, rock, twist, quadrilles, minuets and vastraps are allowed, but mixed dancers will incur severe penalties if they are discovered doing the tango, particularly the last tango, the anti-apartheid polka, the hully-gully and the vasdruk ['hold-tight dancing'].

The feeling is that in addition to these undertakings, preference will be given to applicants who do not actually enjoy mixed dancing, but want to do it through a sense of duty.

It was also suggested that the applicants undergo a smell test, but the idea was dropped as being unfair to those who hadn't had Black nannies to dance attendance on them.

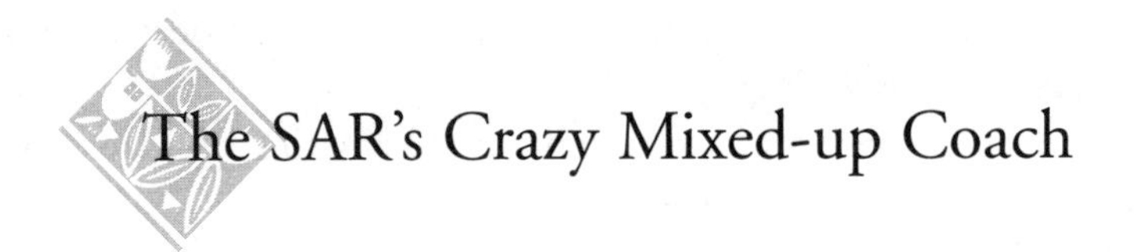

The SAR's Crazy Mixed-up Coach

A few months ago I travelled from Fish Hoek to Cape Town in an integrated railway coach. The Railways deceived me into doing it, and I have never quite forgiven them this insult to my dignity as a White man, even though I was sunburnt at the time.

I had no intention of fraternising with an alien group. I used the White entrance to the station, I bought my ticket at the White ticket office, and I would have crossed the line through the White subway if I was going to Simonstown, which I wasn't.

If everyone was like me, the Railway Police would be out of a job.

Then the train came in and I boarded a middle coach, after first checking carefully to see that my racial qualifications and the coach's racial qualifications coincided.

Our compatibility seemed to be bang-on. But I had not reckoned on a particular railwayman's guile. He had put a 'Whites Only' board at one end of the coach, the end nearest all the other Whites Only coaches. And he put a blue 'Non-Whites Only' board at the other end of the coach, the end nearest all the non-Whites Only coaches.

Such devilish cunning! Perhaps the man was an unwitting tool of the communists. I don't know. But certainly he seemed bent on destroying White civilisation as we know it.

I saw only the Whites Only board, settled myself in a compartment, and looked forward to a happy 50-minute journey in the company of White people. We Whites love one another. Between us there is never any friction, much.

Imagine my consternation when, at subsequent stations, I saw Coloured people in the coach. This was it, the end. They were crashing the barriers, threatening to assimilate me. They looked at me so queerly I wished my tan was darker.

But I refused to move, I knew I was in the right, but didn't know that they also knew they were in the right. We were all in the right. The board-changer was wrong. Maybe he was a Prog [Progressive Party supporter], the only Prog board-changer in South Africa.

At several stations, Whites also boarded the coach. I smiled invitations to them to help shore up our crumbling White defences, for I was on my own, the White Horatius of coach 1007.

But after sudden stricken realisation that there were Coloured people present, the Whites all assumed they had made a mistake in reading the board, and rushed in panic for the inter-coach door.

They showed some pretty nifty footwork, useful any time you have to escape from a plague or a Railway policeman.

Only when the train reached the city did I discover the reason for the integration. Contradictory boards. Blatant defiance of the laws of nature. Some fiend in the Railways had tricked me into becoming an integrated person.

In the Dog Box

Once again people in high places are applying their minds to dogs who go about their proper business.

The Town Clerk of Cape Town, Mr H.G. Heugh, believes that this may not be the appropriate time to fine people R50 for failing to remove forthwith the excrement of dogs who defecate in public places.

He has the support of many dog owners. The main argument of dog owners is that they have no control over the natural functions of their pets, though they wish they had.

Dogs persist in 'going' when they want to go, and not when their owners want them to go. City councillors can kick up as big a stink as they like, but no self-respecting dog will bottle it because of municipal decree.

The problems of enforcing such a regulation are manifold. What man, taking his dog for an evening stroll, will follow it with shovel and dustpan, scoop up haphazard droppings, and carry them round for the rest of the walk?

It could spoil the aesthetic pleasure of watching the sun go down.

Not only that. While the owner is following his dog, a municipal inspector will be required to follow the owner. An organisation far greater than the city's meter-maid brigade will be entirely dependent on 10 000 dogs' bowel movements.

Once an inspector has discovered a dropping, he will be hard pressed to prove it was actually the work of the dog whose owner's footsteps he is dogging. A dedicated owner can usually recognise his own dog's droppings.

If he had finer feelings and respected his dog's privacy, he would avert his eyes. But many owners are either morbidly inquisitive or believe that such information may be useful next time they go to the vet.

So they can tell you, if you let them, the exact shade of colour, the consistency and the 24-hour frequency.

An inspector may leap out of a bush and yell triumphantly: 'I caught you this time. What is that next to the pole?'

The owner will carefully examine the offending pile, and is very likely to reply: 'Sorry, old boy, but I am prepared to swear in a court of law that is not George's.'

George, meanwhile, is wagging his tail in agreement.

Yet another problem is establishing the dog's ownership. It is amazing how many owners are prepared to disown pets temporarily until the danger is passed.

I've seen it happen on Fish Hoek beach repeatedly. The conscientious beach inspector rushes from one person to the next to find out who owns the dogs romping happily but illegally round them. Nobody knows where the dogs come from.

But later the dogs all find they have homes after all, and are seen scrambling into the cars of complete strangers as though they knew them from birth.

We dog-owners are an incorrigible breed. No city council will ever train us. The only answer is to breed a dog that does not drop, at least not in public.

What such a dog does in private will be his own business.

Puppet the Terrier Gets Stuck with Needles

Puppet, the Yorkshire terrier treated with acupuncture and featured in the *Weekend Argus*, wasn't the first local pooch that I know to have had needles stuck all over his back.

Ladies and gentlemen, I give you Josh (actually, you can keep him, but his owners would take great exception), a canine piranha masquerading as a small Maltese poodle. Anyone other than a member of the family approaching nearer than snapping distance is likely to lose a finger. His snarls would put a Rottweiler to flight.

He is without doubt the most bad-tempered little dog in greater Claremont. His family of course dote on him. One of their party tricks is to inform Josh, while cradled in one or other's arms, that he is very tired. He thereupon becomes a limp rag, his head drops to the side, and he shuts his eyes.

'All right, you can wake up now,' they say, and his head jerks back up, his teeth all ready to bare themselves should an unsuspecting visitor be tempted to pat him on the head for his cleverness.

A month or two back his mistress, Jackie, decided that Josh was a bit off-colour. How you can tell this with a dog whose hair is permanently white I don't know. Maybe he wasn't biting as many people as usual. Certainly, said Jackie, 'he wasn't himself', which I would have thought was a good thing.

So she took him off to the 'acuvet'. Somehow the acuvet was able to festoon the poodle's back with needles without requiring major surgery himself, and Josh returned home allegedly much the better for the experience.

Enter my pal Dave, back from work that evening, who asks Jackie how she spent the day. She says she went shopping, had her hair done, got the plumber in and took Josh to have acupuncture.

'You did WHAT?' he exclaims.

Jackie: 'I went shopping, had my hair ...'

Dave: 'No, no, about the Josh and the acupuncture?'

Jackie: 'He's so much better now.'

Dave (always a bottom line man): 'How much did it cost?'

Jackie: 'R400, but it was worth it. He'll probably have to have a second session.'

At this point I will draw a discreet curtain over the remaining dialogue, as recounted to me by Dave, but he is a most accommodating and genial person, and I have no doubt that in the end he realised how important it was for an ancient Chinese procedure to unblock Josh's energy flow.

Cats can have it done, too. One cat clearly fit enough without it, though, is the Theatre on the Bay's resident feline.

On the opening night of *Ghost Stories* last Saturday he prowled among the audience's feet during the first half, and in the second, during the re-enactment of a particularly spooky train ride, mounted the stage and padded behind an apparition in black.

No one watching needed acupuncture needles for a tingling up the spine.

New Laws to Send Johnny Foreigner Packing

Thank goodness some people are still prepared to explain new laws to you, even on condition of anonymity.

Take the new immigration regulations, for instance.

They have just been thrown out of court, with Mangosuthu Buthelezi's legal adviser, Mario Ambrosini, admitting the Home Affairs Department had made a huge mistake.

But he was only referring to the fact that they had not yet been published in the Government Gazette. I would have thought that their contents constituted the huge mistake and that failure to publish them, as required by the constitution, was one of the more sensible things the department did.

Until an anonymous government spokesperson put me straight.

Speaking from KwaZulu-Natal, 'Max' (as he preferred to be called) pointed out the department's motivation in insisting that all foreigners wishing to retire to South Africa or obtain permanent residence should be multimillionaires.

'A lot aren't,' I said. 'What will happen to them?'

'Hard cheese, as we say in Ulundi,' said Max. 'They will have to go back where they came from.'

'But,' I pointed out, 'many own property here and are leading decent lives, contributing to the economy.'

'That's the trouble, there are too many of them,' said Max. 'A lot of them talk funny, even the ones from Britain. Then there are all those from Germany, France, Italy and God knows where. We've got enough languages of our own without having to listen to Eurocentric babble.'

'They also bring skills,' I argued.

'A lot of bloody know-alls,' said Max. 'They judge everything by European standards and expect everything to work, the trains to run on time, the criminals to be caught and the services to be perfect. They are also the first to criticise the government, especially His Excellency the most Honourable Minister of Home Affairs and revered doctor.'

'They would just like to be left in peace,' I said.

'What's more, they are always getting themselves mugged, which leads to bad publicity in overseas newspapers,' said Max.

'If they want to come here without providing monthly income statements by a chartered accountant, they must just spend their money and then go. They only make South Africans jealous.'

'The ones who have enough money to stay will certain attract local envy,' I said.

'There will be too few of them to matter,' said Max.

After that I didn't have the heart to tell Ronaldo, a very friendly Congolese parking attendant from around the corner, that if he wants to stay longer than three months, he will soon have to be earning at least R20 000 a month.

It will put a big strain on the pockets of all of us who support him.

At Least they Haven't Torn up the Runway for Building Blocks Yet

An aviator friend of mine has made light (to coin a pun) of the theft of 15 runway lights from Cape Town International Airport this month.

'Look, at least the main runway itself hasn't been torn up for building blocks yet,' he said, when I expressed concern at the safety aspect of the thefts. Runway lights have also been stolen on three previous occasions in the past year.

'Well, I would keep examining the runway at the N2 end of the airport,' I said. 'There's nothing more unsettling after a long flight than to see the tarmac has disappeared from under you just as you are about to touch down.'

'No Boeings have been illegally removed for their scrap metal, either,' said Bill, continuing to look on the bright and hopefully still illuminated side.

'You'll hardly find a single aircraft window in any of the informal housing surrounding the airport. Not like train windows, which are fitted to many of the more upmarket shacks.'

And he explained to me how security guards have now been posted to protect the lights, which were also being encased in double steel mesh cages.

'I challenge them to get to the lights now,' he said.

'Maybe,' I said, still unconvinced. 'Just be careful the double steel mesh cages don't walk.'

'It's the chaos in the Civil Aviation Authority that worries me more,' said Bill. 'Its chief executive has been suspended and an investigation has uncovered a rat's nest of irregularities within the body responsible for air safety. What's a few runway lights?'

But a contact in the criminal world tells me runway lights are just the start. Thieves are now eyeing the landing gear.

'You know when the northwester is blowing and the planes come low over that hump in the N2 to land? This one gang is wondering if they can't get the wheels and stuff off with a sort of hook on a kite. It'll fetch good money, man.'

'And if the plane crashes?'

'Hey, think of all the scrap metal.'

A security consultant says it's crazy to leave anything close to the N2, especially three banks of five lights each, one on either side of it and the third in the middle.

'Even motorists know that. You never leave your car unattended, or even stationary, and if you have a puncture you drive on the rims until you are out of the no-go area. If I were in charge of aviation I would strip the airport and move it somewhere else.'

'Left to their own devices there are people more than willing to do the first part for you,' I said. 'They'll take it all away on airport luggage trolleys, those that haven't yet been purloined.'

Meanwhile there are some very, very bright lights illuminating the homes of a few lucky families on the Cape Flats. They could practically guide a Boeing down to a place where the airport isn't.

TOM SHARPE

WE WEREN'T *sure about Tom Sharpe, although we acknowledge that as an author of satire aimed at apartheid South Africa he went down very well in Britain. Maybe his goon-like South African policemen with their neurosis about communist saboteurs under every liberal's bed were a little too comic and innocent for those close to the realities at that time.*

His satire can be ghoulish. He had ostriches, fed on gelignite, blowing up in a town centre when, in fact, urban bombs in South Africa and, one supposes, in the United Kingdom were, and still are, too grisly to joke about.

And consider his comic character, Henry Wilt, who indulges in fantasies of murdering his gargantuan, feather-brained wife; fantasies blown to life size when he wrestles with an inflated doll of his wife's proportions and dumps it in a building site excavation – only to be interrogated by the police because his wife actually is missing … 'Sublime orgiastic satire,' said The Guardian. *'I laughed aloud almost continuously,' said the* Sunday Telegraph *of this farce published in the late 1970s.*

After his over-the-top sex-romp 'Wilt' series, published in the mid-1970s, the Mail on Sunday *called him 'the great post-Waugh humorist'. We disagree. But whatever one thinks of Sharpe's humour, in the South African context he cannot be ignored.*

Tom Sharpe *was born in 1928 and educated at Lancing College and Pembroke College, Cambridge, before moving to South Africa in 1951. He was in Natal for ten years as a social worker and a teacher before being deported in 1961.*

His first two light novels are about Natal of that period and the 'indecent exposures' occur in a staid, 'very British' town unsubtly named Piemburg. The author abjures subtlety at all times, though his plots are as complex as any bedroom farce should be.

We have selected a passage from one of his early books, Indecent Exposure *('All good dirty fun,' said the* Daily Telegraph*). It was published in 1973 by Martin Secker & Warburg. The story involves the police second-in-command who is being seduced by the local psychiatrist – she who advises him that his constables can be dissuaded from having sex with 'Bantu women' by showing them life-size pictures of black nudes and then administering electric shocks to their persons. He appoints 12 secret agents to seek out communists in the community and provoke them to commit sabotage, but the secret agents are unknown to each other and each assumes the other 11 are communists …*

Indecent Exposure

Commandant van Heerden was not alone in suffering from the illusion that he was having hallucinations. In Piemburg *Luitenant* Verkramp's efforts to extirpate subversive elements in the body politic were resulting in the appearance of a new and bizarre outbreak of sabotage, this time in the streets of the city. Once again the violence had its origins in the devious nature of the Security Chief's line of communication with his agents.

628461's 'drop' for Thursday was in the Bird Sanctuary. To be precise it was in a garbage can outside the Ostrich Enclosure, a convenient spot from everybody's point of view because it was a perfectly logical place to drop things into, and just the sort of place for a Security Cop disguised as a hobo to get things out of. Every Thursday morning 628461 sauntered through the Bird Sanctuary, bought ice-cream from the vendor and wrapped his message in sticky silver paper and deposited it in the garbage can while ostensibly observing the habits of the ostriches. Every Thursday afternoon Security Konstabel van Rooyen hadn't collected his message and Konstabel van Rooyen had no idea that agent 628461 even existed. All he knew was that *Luitenant* Verkramp had told him to collect sticky pieces of ice-cream paper from the bin and there weren't any.

On the Thursday following the Kommandant's departure, 628461 coded an important message informing Verkramp that he had persuaded the other saboteurs to act in concert for once, with a view to facilitating their arrest while on a job for which they could all be hanged. He had suggested the destruction of the Hluwe Dam, which supplied water for all of Piemburg and half Zululand, and, since no one could blow up a dam by himself, he had urged that they all take part. Much to his surprise all eleven seconded his proposal and went home to code messages to Verkramp warning him to have his men at the dam on Friday night. It was with a sense of considerable relief that he was finally going to get some sleep that 628461 walked to the Bird Sanctuary that Thursday morning to deposit his message. It was with genuine alarm that he observed 378550 following him and with positive consternation became aware as he was buying his ice-cream that 885974 was watching him from the bushes on the other side. 628461 ate his ice-cream outside the hoopoe cage to avoid drawing attention to the garbage can by the Ostrich Enclosure. He ate a second ice-cream half an hour later, staring wearily at the peacocks. Finally after an hour he bought a third Eskimo Pie and walked casually over to the ostriches. Behind him 378550 and 885974 watched his movements with intense curiosity. So did the ostriches. 628461 finished his Eskimo Pie and dropped the silver paper in the garbage can and was just about to leave when he became aware that all his surreptitious efforts had been in vain. With an avidity that came from their having been kept waiting for an hour the ostriches rushed to the fence and poked their heads into the garbage can and one lucky bird swallowed the ice-cream wrapper. 628461 forgot himself.

'Damnation and fuck,' he said. 'They've got it. The bloody things'll eat anything.'

'Got what?' asked 378550, who thought that he was being addressed and glad of the chance to drop his role as shadow.

628461 pulled himself together and looked at 37550 suspiciously.

'You said, "They've got it,"' 378550 repeated.

628461 tried to extricate himself from the situation. 'I said, "I've got it,"' he explained. 'I've got it. They'll eat anything.'

378550 was still puzzled. 'I still don't see it,' he said.

'Well,' said 628461, desperately trying to explain what the omnivorousness of ostriches had to do with his devotion to the cause of world communism, 'I was just thinking that we could get them to eat jelly and let them loose and they'd blow up all over the place.'

378550 looked at him with admiration. 'That's brilliant,' he said. 'Absolutely brilliant.'

'Of course,' 628461 told him, 'we'd have to put the explosive in something watertight first. Get them to swallow it. Fix a fuse and bingo, you've got the perfect sabotage weapon.'

885974, who didn't want to be left out of things in the bushes, came over and joined them.

'French letters,' he suggested when the scheme was put to him. 'Put the gelignite in French letters and tie the ends, that'd keep it watertight.'

An hour later in Florian's café they were discussing this plan with the rest of the saboteurs. 745396 objected on the grounds that ostriches might eat anything but he doubted if even they would be foolish enough to swallow a contraceptive filled with gelignite.

'We'll try it out this afternoon,' said 628461 who felt that 745396 was somehow impugning his loyalty to Marxist-Leninism and the motion was put to the vote. Only 745396 still objected and he was voted down.

While the rest of the group spent the lunch-hour coding messages to Verkramp to warn him that the Hluwe Dam project was cancelled and that he might expect an onslaught of detonating ostriches, 885974, who had thought of French letters in the first place, was deputed to purchase twelve dozen of the best.

'Get Crêpe de Chine,' said 378550, who had had an unfortunate experience with another brand, 'they're guaranteed.'

885974 went into a large chemist's on Market Street and asked the young man behind the counter for twelve dozen 'Crêpe de Chine'.

'Crêpe de Chine?' asked the assistant, who was obviously new to the job. 'We don't sell Crêpe de Chine. You need a haberdashers' for that. This is a chemist shop.'

885974, who was already embarrassed by the quantity he had to ask for, turned very red.

'I know that,' he muttered.

'You sell it in yards,' he said, 'but I'll ask if we have it,' and before 885974 could stop him, had shouted across the shop to a girl who was serving some customers at the counter there.

'This gentleman wants twelve dozen Crêpe de Chine, Sally. We don't sell stuff like that do we?' he asked, and 885974 found himself the object of considerable interest to twelve middle-aged women who knew precisely what he wanted even if the assistant didn't and were amazed at the virility suggested by the number he required.

'Oh for God's sake, never mind,' he muttered and hurried from the shop. In the end he managed to get what he wanted by buying six toothbrushes and two tubes of hair cream at other chemist shops and asking for Durex Fetherlites.

'They seemed more suitable,' he explained when he met the other agents outside the Ostrich Enclosure in the afternoon.

With a unity of purpose noticeably absent from their previous gatherings the agents applied themselves to the business of getting an ostrich to consume high-explosives concealed in a rubber sheath.

'Better try one with sand first,' 628461 suggested, and was presently scooping each into a Durex Fetherlite, an occupation which caused some disgust to a lady who was feeding the ducks on a nearby pond. He waited until she had moved off before offering the contraceptive to the ostrich. The bird took the sheath and spat it out. 628461 got a stick and managed to retrieve the thing from the enclosure. A second attempt was equally unsuccessful and when a third tried to introduce half a pint of latex-covered earth into the bird's digestive system failed, 628461 suggested coating the thing with ice-cream.

'They seemed to like it this morning,' he said. He was getting sick of scrabbling through the fence for obviously well-filled condoms. Finally, after 378550 had bought two ice-creams and a chocolate bar and the sheath had been smeared with ice-cream by itself and chocolate by itself and then with a mixture of the two, the proceedings were interrupted by the arrival of a Sanctuary Warden, fetched by the lady who had been feeding the ducks. 628461, who had just rescued the French letter from the ostriches' enclosure for the eighth time, stuffed it hurriedly into his pocket.

'Are these the men you saw trying to feed the ostriches with foreign matter?' the warden asked.

'Yes, they are,' said the lady emphatically.

The warden turned to 628461.

'Were you trying to induce the bird to digest a quantity of something or other contained in the thing this lady says you were?' he asked.

'Certainly not,' said 628461 indignantly.

'You were too,' said the lady, 'I saw you.'

'I'll ask you to move along,' said the warden.

As the little group moved off 745396 pointed out how right he had been.

'I told you ostriches weren't so dumb,' he said and put 628461's back up still further. He'd just discovered that the sheath in his back pocket had burst.

'I thought you were supposed to get Crêpe de Chines,' he grumbled to 885974, and tried to empty his pocket of earth, chocolate, ice-cream and ostrich droppings.

'What am I going to do with twelve dozen Frenchies?' 885974 asked.

It took 378550 to come up with a solution. 'Popcorn and honey,' he said suddenly.

'What about it?' 628461 asked.

'Coat them with popcorn and honey and I guarantee they'll swallow the things.'

At the first shop they came to, 378550 bought a packet of popcorn and a pot of honey and, taking a contraceptive from 885794, went back to the Bird Sanctuary to try his recipe out.

'Worked like a treat,' he reported ten minutes later. 'Swallowed the thing in one gulp.'

'What do we do when we've filled them all up and set the fuse?' 745396 asked doubtfully.

'Lay a trail of popcorn into the centre of town, of course,' 628461 told him. The group dispersed to collect their stocks of gelignite and that night at nine gathered at the Bird Sanctuary. The sense of mutual suspicion, which had so informed their earlier meetings, had been quite replaced by a genuine camaraderie. Verkramp's agents were beginning to enjoy themselves.

'If this works,' 628461 said, 'there's no reason why we shouldn't try the zoo.'

'I'm damned if I'm feeding contraceptives to the lions,' 745396 said.

'No need to feed them anything,' said 885974, who didn't feel like buying any more French letters. 'They'd be explosive enough on their own.'

If Verkramp's agents were cheerful, the same couldn't be said of their chief. The conviction that something had gone seriously wrong with his plans to end communist subversion had gathered strength with the discovery by the armourer that large stocks of high-explosives and fuses were missing from the police armoury.

He reported his findings or lack of them to *Luitenant* Verkramp. Coming on top of a report by the police bomb-disposal squad that the detonators used in all the explosions were of a type used in the past solely by the South African Police, the armourer's news added weight to Verkramp's slow intuition that he might in some curious way have bitten off more than he could chew. It was an insight he shared with five ostriches in the Bird Sanctuary. What had seemed at the outset a marvellous opportunity to fulfil his ambitions had developed into something from which there was no turning back. Certainly the ostriches viewed it in that light, as the secret agents discovered to their alarm when they released the loaded birds from their enclosure. Gregarious to the last and evidently under the impression that there was more to come in the way of popcorn-coated contraceptives, the five ostriches strode after the agents as the latter headed for town. By the time the mixed herd and flock had reached the end of Market Street the agents were in a state of near panic.

'We'd better break up,' 628461 said anxiously.

'Break up? Break up? We'll fucking disintegrate if those birds don't get the hell out of here,' said 745396, who had never approved of the project from the start and who seemed to have attracted the friendship of an ostrich that weighed at least 300 lbs unloaded and which had a fifteen-minute fuse. The next moment the agents had taken to their heels down the side roads in an effort to shake off the likely consequences of their experiment. Undaunted, the ostriches strode relentlessly and effortlessly behind them. At the corner of Market and Stanger Streets 745396 leapt on to the platform of a moving bus and was appalled to see through the back window the silhouette of his ostrich loping comfortably some yards behind. At the traffic lights at Chapel Street it was still there. 745396 hurled himself off the bus and dashed into the Majestic Cinema, which was showing *Where Eagles Dare.*

'Show's over,' said the Commissionaire in the foyer.

'That's what you think,' said 745396 with his eye on the ostrich, which was peering inquisitively through the glass doors. 'I just want to use the toilet.'

'Down the stairs to the left,' the Commissionaire told him and went out to the pavement to try to move the ostrich on. 745396 went down to the toilet and locked himself in a cubicle and waited for the explosion. He was still there five minutes later when the Commissionaire came down and knocked on the door.

'Is that ostrich anything to do with you?' he asked as 745396 tore paper off the roll to prove he was using the place for its proper purpose.

'No,' said 745396 without conviction.

'Well, you can't leave it outside like that,' the Commissionaire told him, 'it'll interfere with the traffic.'

'You can say that again,' said 745396.

'Say what again?' asked the Commissionaire.

'Nothing,' shouted 745396 frantically. He had reached the end of his tether. So, it appeared, had the ostrich.

'One last question, do you usually –' said the Commissionaire and got no further. An extraordinary sensation of silence hit him, to be followed by a wall of flame and a gigantic bang. As the front of the Majestic Cinema crumbled into the street and the lights went out, agent 745396 slowly slumped on to the cracked seat of the toilet and leant against the wall. He was still there when the rescue workers found him next day, covered in plaster and quite dead.

Throughout the night rumours that Piemburg had been invaded by hordes of self-detonating ostriches spread like wildfire. So did the ostriches. A particularly tragic incident occurred at the offices of the Zululand Wild Life Preservation Society where an ostrich which had been brought in by a bird-lover exploded while being examined by the society's vet.

'I think it's got some sort of gastric disorder,' the man explained. The vet listened to the bird's crop with his stethoscope before making his diagnosis.

'Heartburn,' he said with a finality that was entirely confirmed by the detonation that followed. As the night sky erupted with bricks, mortar, and the assorted remains of both bird-lover and vet, the premises of the Wild Life Preservation Society, historically important and themselves subject to a preservation order by the Piemburg Council, disappeared for ever. Only a plume of smoke and a few large feathers, emblematic of some dissipated Prince of Wales, floated lethargically against the moon.

In his office Acting Kommandant Verkramp listened to the muffled explosions with a growing sense of despair. Whatever else was in ruins, and by the sound of it a large section of the city's shopping centre must be, his own career would shortly join it. In a frantic attempt to allay his alarming suspicions, he had just searched the few messages from his secret agents, only to find there confirmation that his plan if not their efforts had misfired. Agent 378550 had said that the sabotage group consisted of eleven men. Agent 885974 had said the same. So had 628461. There was a terrible congruency about the reports. In each case eleven men reported by his agent. Verkramp added one to eleven and got twelve. He had twelve agents in the field. The conclusion was inescapable and so it seemed were the consequences. Desperately searching for some way out of the mess he had got himself into, *Luitenant* Verkramp rose from the desk and crossed to the window. He was just in time to see a large ostrich loping purposefully down the street. With a muttered curse Verkramp opened the window and peered after the bird. 'This is the end,' he snarled and was astonished to see that at least one of his orders was obeyed. With a violent flash and a blast wave that blew out the window above him, the ostrich disintegrated and Verkramp found himself sitting on the floor of his office with the inescapable conviction that his sanity was impaired.

'Impossible. It can't have been an ostrich,' he muttered, staggering back to the window. Outside, the street was littered with broken glass and, in a bare blackened patch in the middle of the road, two feet were all that remained of the thing that had exploded. Verkramp could see that it had been an ostrich because the feet had only two toes.

In the next twenty minutes *Luitenant* Verkramp acted with maniacal speed. He burnt every file that could connect him with his agents, destroyed their messages and finally, ordering the police armourer to change the lock on the armoury door, left the police station in the Kommandant's black Ford. An hour later, having visited every bar in town, he had run two of his agents to earth drinking to the success of their latest experiment in sabotage in the Criterion Hotel in Verwoerd Street.

'Fuzz,' said 628461 as Verkramp entered the bar. 'Better break up.' 885974 finished his drink and went out. 628461 watched him go and was surprised to see Verkramp follow him out.

'He's making an arrest,' he thought and ordered another beer. A moment later he looked up to find Verkramp glowering down at him.

'Outside,' said Verkramp brusquely. 628461 left his bar stool and went outside and was surprised to find his fellow-saboteur unguarded in the police car.

'I see you've got one of them,' 628461 said to Verkramp, and climbed in beside 885974.

'Them? Them?' Verkramp spluttered hysterically. 'He's not them. He's us.'

'Us?' said 628461, mystified.

'I'm 885974. Who are you?'

'Oh, my God,' said 628461.

Verkramp climbed into the driving seat and stared back malevolently.

'Where are the others?' he hissed.

'The others?'

'The other agents, you idiot,' Verkramp shouted. For the next two hours they searched the bars and cafés while Verkramp fulminated on the evils of sabotaging public utilities and detonating ostriches in a built-up area.

'I send you to infiltrate the communist movement and what do you do?' he shouted. 'Blow up half the bloody town, that's what you do. And you know where that's going to get you, don't you? On the end of the hangman's rope in Pretoria Central.'

'You might have warned us,' said 628461 reproachfully. 'You could have told us there were other agents in the field.'

Verkramp turned purple.

'Warned you?' he screamed. 'I expected you to use your common sense, not go around looking for one another.'

'Well, how the hell were we to know we were all police agents?' 885974 asked.

'I should have thought even idiots like you could tell the difference between a good Afrikaner and a communist Jew.'

885974 thought about this.

'If it's that easy,' he said finally, clinging precariously to some sort of logic, 'I don't see how we're to blame. I mean the communist Jews must be able to see we're good Afrikaners just by looking at us. I mean what's the point of sending out good Afrikaners to look for communist Jews if communist Jews can ...'

'Oh, shut up,' shouted Verkramp, who was beginning to wish he hadn't brought up the subject in the first place.

By midnight seven other agents had been found in various parts of the city and the police car was getting rather crowded.

'What do you want us to do now?' 378550 asked as they drove round the park for the fifth time, looking for the three remaining agents. Verkramp stopped the car.

'I ought to arrest you,' he snarled, 'I ought to let you stand trial for terrorism but ...'

'You won't,' said 885974, who had been giving the matter some thought.

'Why won't I?' Verkramp shouted.

'Because we'll all give evidence that you ordered us to blow up the transformer and the gasometer and the ...'

'I did nothing of the sort. I told you to find the communist saboteurs,' Verkramp yelled.

'Who gave us the keys of the police armoury?' 885974 asked. 'Who supplied the explosives?'

'And what about the messages we sent you?' 628461 asked.

Verkramp stared through the windshield and contemplated a short and nasty future, at the end of which stood the hangman in Pretoria Central Prison.

'All right,' he said. 'What do you want me to do?'

'Get us past the road blocks. Get us down to Durban and give us each 500 rand,' 885974 said, 'and then forget you ever saw us.'

'What about the other three agents?' Verkramp asked.

'That's your problem,' 885974 said. 'You can find them tomorrow.'

They drove back to the police station and Verkramp collected the money and two hours later nine agents climbed out at Durban airport. *Luitenant* Verkramp watched them disappear into the terminal and then drove back to Piemburg.

At the road block on the Durban Road the sergeant waved him through for the second time and made a note of the fact that the Acting Kommandant looked drawn and ill. By four in the morning Verkramp was in bed in his flat staring into the darkness and wondering how he was going to find the other three agents. At seven he got up again and drove down to Florian's café. 885974 had advised him to look for them there. At eleven the Kommandant's car passed through the Durban Road checkpoint yet again and this time the Acting Kommandant had with him two men. By the time he returned, eleven agents had left Piemburg for good. 745396 was in the city morgue, waiting to be identified.

GUS SILBER

APARTHEID'S SURVIVORS *of all races and all persuasions had to stretch their humour to the limit in coping with sudden socio-political change in the 1990s. They loved the new notes of freedom and democracy being circulated, but they worried about the amount of change. Most still do. Many worry that it is merely small change, others feel they've been given too much change. So, for a decade, people avoided the word 'change' and spoke instead of 'transition'.*

Few people – least of all the ardent, sincere, but awfully earnest reformists who planned the transition, with its democratic freedoms and human rights, anticipated the wild, weird chaos that came about.

It was the same elsewhere in the world, of course – from Czechoslovakia to Uzbekistan; from Angola to Zanzibar – after dozens of authoritarian regimes collapsed along with the Berlin Wall. But in South Africa the consequent lawlessness was unbearable unless people could find other things to smile about.

Fortunately the vast majority of those who stayed home and those refugees and expatriates who came home found a lot to smile about, whether wryly, knowingly or uproariously. And almost everybody cherished a great warm feeling about being free at last. It made them want to laugh, even when things went uncomfortably wrong.

Nevertheless, change – or rather 'transition' – particularly when it is unpredictable, uncontrolled and unstoppable, creates immense tension – especially in comic writers.

Gus Silber has probably been the best exponent in touching those nerves, and in anaesthetising them with laughing gas. When 'transition' began, he lived in a little white milieu (if you will pardon the phrase) whose members actually loved and laughed at change. The laughter became infectious, and his writing on the subject became increasingly popular.

Silber is a freelance correspondent, a television scriptwriter and music critic. He describes himself as a 'Jack-of-all-tirades' and counts cabinet ministers, beauty queens, rock 'n' roll stars, and members of the mass democratic movement among the people he has never met. His first book, It Takes Two to Toyi-Toyi: A Survival Guide to the New South Africa, *was published by Penguin in Johannesburg in 1991, just as the African protest dance began to stir up political hopes and fears. A* Sunday Tribune *critic said of his* Toyi-Toyi *collection: 'You'll recognise yourselves in the pages of this book. It's side-splitting, finger-wagging fun – just the kind of medicine seriously sullen South Africans need.'*

The survivors of apartheid – and democracy – needed Gus Silber's medicine so badly that he had to publish another book the following year: Braaivleis of the Vanities: How to Stay Sane in South Africa *(Penguin, Johannesburg, 1992). Here is a taste of those barbecue-burnt offerings.*

All Stressed Up and Nowhere to Go

According to a recent survey specially commissioned for this sentence, nine out of ten South Africans are 'very optimistic' about the future of the country to which they are emigrating.

A further 17 out of 20 said they were adopting a 'wait and see' attitude on the question of whether their emigration visa applications would be approved, while a staggering 92 per cent of people coming out of the pub described themselves as 'confused and uncertain', having forgotten the question they had just been asked.

As these statistics clearly indicate, South Africans of virtually all creeds, cultures, and political perspectives are today caught in the grip of one of the most profound crises of confidence in the country's history.

'I am afraid to say that I have lost all confidence in the history of this country,' said a Professor Emeritus of South African History as he prepared to board his one-way flight to the tropical paradise island of Pago Pago.

And yet, despite the allure of a new life and a brighter future in a land with a stable social and political climate, many South Africans are beginning to realise that the grass is not always greener on the other side of the security fence.

'Staying put in South Africa definitely has its advantages,' argues one South African who is definitely committed to staying put. 'Just the other day, I managed to pick up a complete infrared home security system, plus a hi-fi, video recorder, and leather motorcycle jacket, for an absolute steal. As a result, I am thinking about staying in South Africa even after I have completed my sentence.'

But whatever your personal political convictions, there can be little doubt that staying in South Africa today is a process fraught with stress, tension, frustration, and pent-up fury, as anyone who has ever attempted to query their telephone account will be quick to confirm.

We asked some of South Africa's top decision-makers for their personal tips on combating stress in the current social, political, and economic climate.

'I am in receipt of your faxed request for a personal tip on combating stress in the current social, political, and economic climate,' said one top decision-maker from his office on the top floor of a big glass building in the central business district of Johannesburg.

'Unfortunately, I am not able to reply at the moment, as I have just hurled my facsimile machine out of the window.'

At a power breakfast on the other side of town, a top corporate decision-maker revealed that he could not decide whether to have marmalade or strawberry jam with his white or wholewheat toast. However, he denied allegations that he was suffering from stress induced by the current social, political, and economic climate.

'I am very happy to be in South Africa at this point in time,' he said, spreading marmalade and strawberry jam on his tie, 'as I have just been offered a job in Australia.'

Upgrade Your Home Security System

Thanks to political reforms and advances in home security technology, South Africa is now acknowledged as a world leader in this field, with South African firms supplying systems to several countries that did much better than us at the Olympics.

If you believe that security begins at home, here is a brief guide to some recent innovations designed to prepare you for the transition to a peaceful and democratic South Africa.

The Neighbourhood Watchman. This full-colour, multi-channel closed-circuit in-house video monitor system comes complete with stereo sound, fisheye and zoom lenses, swivel-mounted video-cameras, and professional-quality mixing-desk for instant slow-motion action replay.

While the Neighbourhood Watchman is unlikely to prevent people wearing full-face balaclavas from breaking into your property and liberating your possessions, it could come in very handy if you are ever called on to give evidence in a defamation action involving a former room-mate.

The False Alarm System. It looks like a real alarm, protects like a real alarm, and makes a noise like a real alarm, but don't worry – it's only a false alarm. Primed to emit an ear-piercing signal the moment your cat climbs through the burglar bars or when you press your panic button by mistake while trying to locate your house-keys at two o'clock in the morning, the false alarm system can be linked by radio to the control room of your neighbourhood security company.

For a nominal monthly fee, they will agree not to dispatch any uniformed personnel armed with bazookas and pump-action shotguns to the scene within seconds. This will save you the embarrassment of having to tell them it was only a false alarm, but thanks for coming anyway.

It is recommended that you supplement your false alarm system with a genuine alarm system, in case someone tries to break in and steal your cat.

The Credit Card, the Half-Brick, and the Long Piece of Wire. These items should be carried on your person at all times, in the event that you inadvertently lock yourself out of your house on your way to a pre-breakfast session with your stress-reduction therapist one Monday morning.

In order to retrieve your house and car keys from the fruit bowl on the kitchen table, or the inside pocket of the jacket you decided not to wear at the last minute because it had a dog-print on one of the cuffs, you will be forced to gain entry to your property by means of 'breaking and entering'. Do not be alarmed. Since no one has yet managed to design a home security system that is completely fool-proof, you should be able to do this even if it makes you feel like a complete fool.

First, use the half-brick to create an opening in a small window-pane convenient to the suspected location of your keys. Now hook the long piece of wire around the window-handle. Through careful, patient manipulation, you should be able to force the window open from the inside. Although this will not help you to gain entry, it will at least allow some fresh air to filter into your house through the security bars.

Now try the credit card. Anyone who has ever seen an American detective movie will know that it is possible to open a securely locked door by manoeuvring a credit card between the doorframe and the latch bolt assembly, providing you are an actor in an American detective movie. If not, don't worry. A representative from your neighbourhood security company will be on the scene within minutes, and you will probably be let out on bail in time to telephone your insurance broker, your lawyer, and an after-hours locksmith.

How to Occupy a Government Building

According to the Joint Interim Guidelines for a Peaceful and Democratic Mass Action Campaign, Government buildings in most of the major centres in South Africa may be occupied at any time between 8 am and 9.30 am, 9.45 am and 10.50 am, 11.05 am and 12.30 pm, and 2 pm and 3 pm on any day of the week that does not fall on a public holiday or official stayaway.

No occupation of any kind will be allowed during tea-breaks, coffee-breaks, snack-breaks, chat-breaks, smoke-breaks, work-breaks, cake-breaks and lunch, and any occupying parties who are still in the building at 3.01 pm will be obliged to file for overtime in terms of Civil Service regulations.

Before occupying the Government building of your choice, you will be required to complete a Visitor Application Form at the Security Desk in the foyer. State 'Occupation' under Reason for Visit, 'Occupier' under Occupation, and 'Security guard' under Person to See.

Don't forget to fill in full name, home address, work and home phone, identity number, tax number, nationality, vehicle registration, political affiliation, three credit references, and estimated time and date of filling in form.

Please use non-writing implement provided on end of chain, as all pens and pencils in your possession will have to be surrendered in terms of the blanket provision on carrying pointed objects during a Mass Action Campaign.

When you have completed your form, you will be handed a security sticker, which must be displayed in a prominent position on your forehead at all times during your occupation of the building.

Since your planned action will include sitting in, lying down, stomping along corridors, complaining about the Government, and generally doing everything in your power to obstruct the smooth traffic of bureaucracy, this sticker will play a vital role in distinguishing you from bona fide employees of the Civil Service.

As soon as the other 24 999 participants in the Mass Action Campaign have finished filling in their forms, you may proceed in an orderly fashion towards the glass-enclosed security cubicles.

Press the button once only, and pull the door towards you when the green light flashes. Enter the cubicle, and wait for the orange light to flash before pushing the second door away from you.

If the red light flashes and a high-pitched two-note alarm sounds, do not be alarmed. A security guard will be on the scene within minutes. In the meantime, you may occupy the glass-enclosed security cubicle. For security reasons, no *toyi-toyiing* is permitted in the cubicle, although you are welcome to chant anti-Government slogans once you have finished shouting for help.

Please head directly for the first available lift as soon as you have been released. A marshal will hand you a number.

You are to proceed to this floor when the lift is full.

If the lift does not arrive within 45 minutes of pressing the button, it may mean that the power supply has been disconnected as part of a broad campaign of people's power. Or it may mean that the Civil Service is about to go to lunch.

If this is the case, you will find the self-service cafeteria just below the parking garage on the fourth basement level. After lunch, and a brief occupation of the cafeteria in protest at the quality of Government-subsidised food, please proceed back up the stairs to your designated occupational floor.

Now find something to keep yourself occupied. Examples: filing reports, filing nails, filing cabinets, filing Cabinet Ministers, dancing, chanting, watering plants, planting bugs, reading top-secret letters addressed to 'The Occupant', sending urgent inter-departmental memos, trying to find a pen that works, filling in a requisition form for a pen that works, waiting for an official to accept a petition, trying Mnr Smit in Room 312, trying Mnr Jacobs in Room 624, trying Mnr Van Tonder in Room 225, and applying for a job with the Civil Service.

In the event that the Mass Action Campaign achieves its goals, you may occupy the fourth chair from the left on the east wing of the lower sub-mezzanine level (Requisitions Department). But first, have another cup of tea and a slice of *melktert.*

KEN SMITH

ONE OF THE PROBLEMS *in being a thrice-a-week humour columnist is how to avoid writing about oneself too much. Egocentricity is an occupational disease among columnists and the capital letter 'I' can become conspicuous and irritating. Ken Smith overcame the 'I' problem by inventing a friend – 'Ginger'. Ginger was always in trouble. In fact Ginger was Ken Smith himself.*

Smith was not a bad cartoonist and illustrated his own columns but signed the drawings 'Paish' – his middle name. He had been a reporter briefly in the 1960s, on the Rand Daily Mail *and on* The Star *– but he was a natural humorist and he soon found an outlet in regular columns, appearing under different names at different times over a period of 30 years. Smith, who was amusing company, laughed with people but never at them. He was totally apolitical and so his lightly written columns provided important relief in the newspaper's contents in those tense times. Whether his wacky humour has withstood the test of time is debatable – our own judgement, remembering how we enjoyed his style years ago, is that his humour has been time-damaged. But each to his own judgement.*

In his column he gave the impression of being a stable married man but it was not like that. He married and divorced twice and fathered a son (Simon) and then twins – a boy and a girl who for years spoke to each other in their own very private grunt-like language. All three featured greatly in his columns. He was often without a proper home of his own and once lived in the garage at the house of one of his ex-wives and, for some time, in a Wendy house in a Sandton garden.

Ken ended his days with throat cancer from smoking, but even with his larynx removed and reduced to communicating by scribbling on bits of paper his humour seemed irrepressible. Alas, it was not. One day he discharged himself from hospital, went home and shot himself.

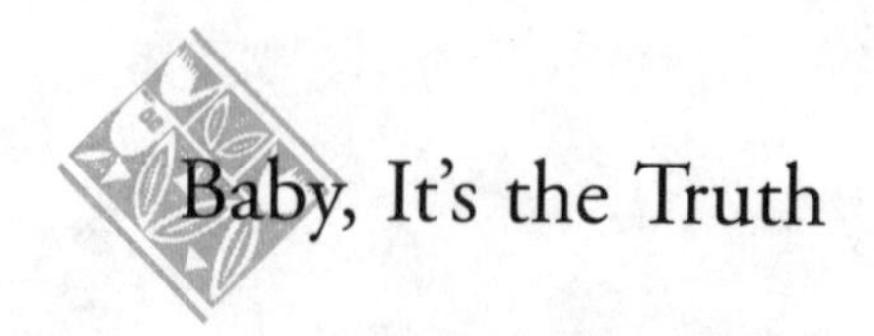

Baby, It's the Truth

According to my old friend Ginger, Interim Chairman of the Mediocrities Club, the trouble is that the modern baby is a different shape to the old type.

They are also, he says, more slippery.

He makes these astounding claims in answer to lively criticism of the manner in which he looked after his niece's baby when she, her husband and Ginger's wife went out to the theatre the other evening.

'Women are all a little touched in the think-box, you know,' he said complacently when I paid him a visit to hear his version of the affair. The truth of the matter is that when they finally got home the baby was fast asleep in a coal scuttle and it was smiling from ear to ear.

'It was the happiest little baby you ever saw in your life. But of course, the women chose to ignore the Big Truth and went into hysterics over the superficialities.'

A disapproving frown crossed his ruddy features. 'Another factor was that they chose to listen to the account given by my nephew, who is only five years old and has no more experience of life than a new-laid egg,' he said.

For example: the nephew says that when the baby woke up and began to cry, Ginger set out to change its nappy. In the course of the ensuing struggle Ginger tossed the baby into the air and caught it just before it hit the floor.

'That', said Ginger severely, 'is simply not true. The truth is that I had rather overdone the baby powder on the bottom bit. The result was that when I gave the dear little mite an affectionate squeeze, it simply popped out of its new nappy and damn nearly went through the ceiling.

'So I was left holding an empty nappy and the baby was left with no visible means of support. I caught it before it went splat on the wall-to-wall and blow me down if it wasn't laughing fit to beat the band.'

This is not mentioned by my nephew, who should have been in bed but was instead observing proceedings from the door of his bedroom.

'As to the fact that the baby was wearing an old cardigan knotted around its middle when the parents returned home, that's easy to explain. I didn't want to take any more chances with one of those new-fangled nappies.'

Ginger beamed broadly and said, 'So I applied Man's ingenuity and tied it up in a nice woolly, warm cardigan instead.'

'And the coal scuttle?' I asked gently.

'So help me,' said Ginger wonderingly, 'It was the only place where it felt comfortable. It went to sleep the minute I put it in there.'

That's one trick Dr Spock never mentioned and perhaps it's just as well.

And one of Ken Smith's final columns:

Life in Ward 566

Like I always say, if you've seen one hospital you've seen them all and personally I can take them or I hate them, which is what I told the Head Bloke when I was clocked in at Ward 566 at the vast new Johannesburg Hospital just before Christmas.

To be absolutely accurate he wasn't actually Head Bloke. He was the Number One in the Ear, Nose and Throat Department where I was admitted to have something pretty drastic done to my vocal cords. The result, allow me to add, of many years of heavy smoking.

This operation is known as a laryngectomy and, as far as the patient is concerned, it has two immediate effects:
(a) He learns how to spell laryngectomy.
(b) He gives up smoking for good.

If you have an ordinary set of nerves and an ordinary approach to personal experimentation it is not possible to smoke a cigarette, pipe, hookah, hubble-bubble, narghile or Woodbine through the hole where your voicebox used to be. In much the same way, if you will permit me to digress, when Gunga Din found himself with a hole where his belt buckle used to be, he found it difficult to distribute water. That, however, is another matter.

So I no longer smoke and when I can talk again I will be a crushing bore on the Evils of Smoking and also, for those who have undergone a laryngectomy, on the Perils of Skin Diving. This Peril I discovered by myself entirely by accident when I trailed off to have my first bath after the operation and, in a thoughtless moment, decided to lie back in the soothing waters.

You only try a trick like that once when your lungs are connected directly to the outside world via an unprotected hole. So, in addition to smoking, I have also given up deep-sea diving and lying back in the bath and have turned my attention to learning how to belch to order.

This sounds like a pretty anti-social thing to do, but that is the only way to talk when the old sound box has gone missing, so I apologise and at present I can only apologise in writing.

Most of the time I communicate by writing things down. This has had the weird effect of enabling me to collect a wall-to-wall record of all my conversations over the past few months, so I have total recall, spelling mistakes and all.

Communicating by means of the written note is not without its hazards. In the bank, for example. Slip a note across to the teller and the next thing you know is that a great hush has fallen upon the institution and you have attracted the keen-eyed attention of the security persons.

Then there are those people who leap to the conclusion that anybody who must write things down to be understood must be deaf as well and they gallantly write down their replies, sometimes at great length and sometimes to such astonishing effect that the purpose of the original question is totally lost.

Telephones present a problem but a simple code enables me to communicate (more or less) with a small group of friends and relatives. One stroke of my silver gong means No, two strokes means Yes.

Well, said an obviously impressed friend who had been told about the code and was phoning for the first time, I must say you're sounding pretty good.

His remark at least gave me a (silent) laugh.

PUBLISHED IN 1958 (Faber and Faber, London), Sylvester Stein's Second Class Taxi *remains one of the few novels that has dealt with South African politics in a genuinely funny (although not flippant) way. Its central character is an engaging black waif called Staffnurse Phofolo.*

Among other adventures he is arrested, sent to work on a farm, becomes involved in 'Congress of Equality' politics, gets a job as chauffeur-cum-servant with a 'liberal' white MP, Professor Hampshire; all this against a background of black protest and boycotts culminating in a bloody confrontation which uncannily foreshadowed Sharpeville two years later.

This first extract introduces Staffnurse, who acquired his singular name because his mother named him after the most important person at hand – the midwife at the clinic where he was born. The other extract describes an unorthodox driving lesson.

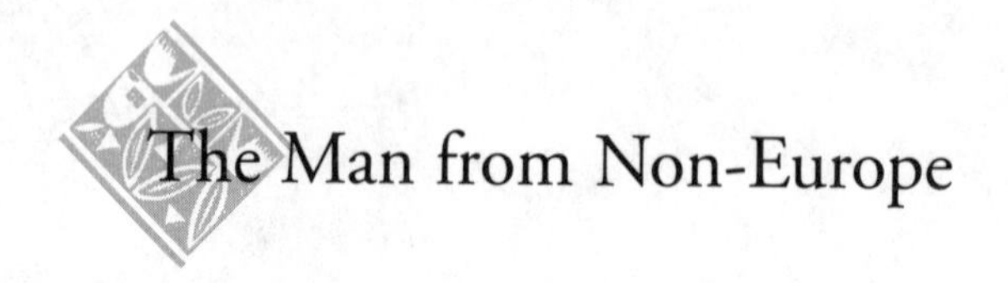

The Man from Non-Europe

Staffnurse puzzled the police at the charge office by being able to produce no papers at all, not even a forged pass.

'Name, then,' growled the policeman, a Constable Kees van Tonder.

'Staffnurse Phofolo, baas.'

'What race?'

'African,' said Staffnurse, very pleased with himself at remembering to use this new designation, and hoping the policeman would be as pleased.

Constable van Tonder looked up aghast at this subversive nonsense, snapped 'Non-European,' and grunted that if he had his way he would put him down as a plain bleddy kaffir, and in fact would be inclined to greater accuracy by entering 'bleddy Baboon'.

'Where from?'

'Non-Europe,' said Staffnurse accommodatingly, wanting to correct the bad impression he had made.

Driving Lesson

Staffnurse was about to go up solo for the first time.

The Coca-Cola man had taken him through a course of driving lessons on the Common at Green Point and was now serenely repeating his instructions to his pupil. 'Don't frighten, fellow, I never ever gone and lost one single pedestrian yet, with my students. Patience, fellow. Don't worry for the pollismen and the traffic cops too much.'

He sat beside Staffnurse, who was driving cautiously, bent into a hunch over the wheel. From the Common through the one-way streets to the centre of town. The old canvas sign, 'Quick-Time Driving School', flapped at the back of Coca-Cola's elephantine eight-seater Buick.

'It's of course much necessary you don't fright, boy,' said Coca-Cola. 'Hey, use footclutch, you damnfool,' he shouted at Staffnurse, as the car jerked up to a robot, 'I tell you, of course, left footclutch before you brake.'

Staffnurse and the Buick reared nervously at the shouting. Coca-Cola howled again. Staffnurse stopped the car in half its length leaving Coca-Cola's ears to flap forward with the motion and the back seat to crash on to the floor behind them. Coca-Cola bellowed: 'FOOT-CLUTCH, not brake, you DAMNFOOL. You doan know how to clutch after eight damnfool lessons, you amazing damnfool.' He pulled his pants up around his waist, tightened his teeth, and said to himself: 'Patience, fellow, that's how we teach this driving art, by the way. Patience some more.'

'Amazing,' boiled Coca-Cola away to himself as Staffnurse carried on through the traffic. 'Mind you, amazing!'

'My method', he turned to Staffnurse to boast, 'never ever got one pedestrian killed off. My method, that's still secret, boy, until you get your ticket. But my good self teaches 'em to drive solo quicker than anyone in this town.'

'Dual Control College?' he laughed; 'Money-back Motors?' he laughed again. 'Doan make me laugh,' he warned Staffnurse. 'I send the boys on the streets after half that amount lessons.'

'Now,' he said. 'Will yours truly turn up kindly into the Parade?'

'My method for stopping braking', said Coca-Cola, 'is I switch 'em off. I disconnect you, my student friend, from the brakes, yah.' He snapped a link out of a wire on the floor near the driver's seat.

'No brakes now. Don't make no mistakes also.'

Staffnurse looked at him terrified.

'DOAN LOOK HERE, LOOK WHERE YOU DRIVE, MY FRIEN."

Staffnurse looked back quickly, swerved around a traffic cop, and picked his way along at ten miles an hour.

'Now,' said Coca-Cola, 'my ever-loving self jumps out and leaves you to swim alone, by the way. Good luck.' He swung open his door on the passenger's side and vaulted out. 'Keep going, of course,' he called, 'you on your own now, boy. Mind the pollismen and the coffie traps.'

Staffnurse steered for the edge of the Parade while Coca-Cola ran along behind him shouting. Staffnurse tried to stop her, couldn't make out how to do so without brakes. He tried to take his foot off the accelerator, but she started bucking again. Coca-Cola screamed at him from behind: 'Revvle her up my friend, revvle her up,' and off he went again, cantering through the crowds.

At the other end of the square he hadn't left enough room to turn around in, so had to make for the exit-way instead and shot through, into a stream of traffic on the road.

Then at last he discovered the mechanism of the clutch, and pushed it almost through the floor. The Buick floated to a stop right in the middle of the broad main road, while the rest of the traffic continued to flow past and around it in two streams. Staffnurse started thinking quickly about a heart-shaped swimming-bath full of ginger beer. Up came Coca-Cola riding on the running-board of an elderly fruit lorry, to rescue him.

'That's it, boy,' he was saying, 'that's it, revvle her up and run. Never mind the pollisman. Amazing! Very amazing work from yours truly. I can say, mind you, of course, I'm pleased with such amazing work from yourself.'

Staffnurse tried to smile, failed, tried again, failed again, and said in a squeaky voice instead: 'Okay.'

'My method', said Coca-Cola, 'is quick-time, all right. I think you nearly ready to take off now.'

MARIANNE THAMM

Marianne Thamm is a journalist, writer and columnist who lives in Cape Town where she has 'a great view of a busy street'. Indeed she has an excellent view of some of the peculiarities of South Africa's many peoples. Her perspective prompted her to write The How-to-be a South African Handbook, *published by our publishers, Double Storey. They describe the handbook as 'an essential survivor's guide for visitors and confused locals who want to make sense of South African life in the 21st century'. The handbook is clever enough to confuse you even more. Here are some samples – not in the sequence published in the guide.*

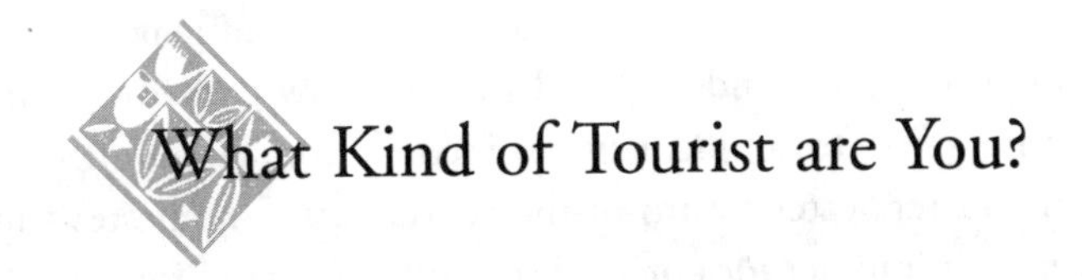

What Kind of Tourist are You?

Roots Tourist

Visitors, mostly from the USA, who would like to get in touch with their African roots. They are often overcome with emotion upon alighting on African soil and will immediately buy clothes that they believe reflect their true African identity. This makes them stand out from locals, who tend to prefer American designer labels.

The Big Fiver

Usually wealthy Europeans and Americans who fly straight into game parks, where they pay a fortune to experience Africa as a big-screen Hollywood epic. They arrive looking like celluloid neo-colonials kitted out in khaki, wearing retro pith helmets and bearing trunks full of Imodium, bottled water and herbal mosquito repellent.

The Yob

Likely to be a British or European tourist who has discovered that a strong currency can buy several weeks' worth of luxury and debauchery somewhere in the 'developing world'.

Yobs don't care where they end up as long as it's low cost, alcohol is freely available and they can buy cheap souvenirs on the way out. Yobs (if you don't hear them first) are often identifiable by the crusty, pink sores from too many unprotected hours spent tanning in the merciless South African sun. Favoured yob outfits are undone floral Hawaiian shirts with shiny running shorts and plastic beach thongs.

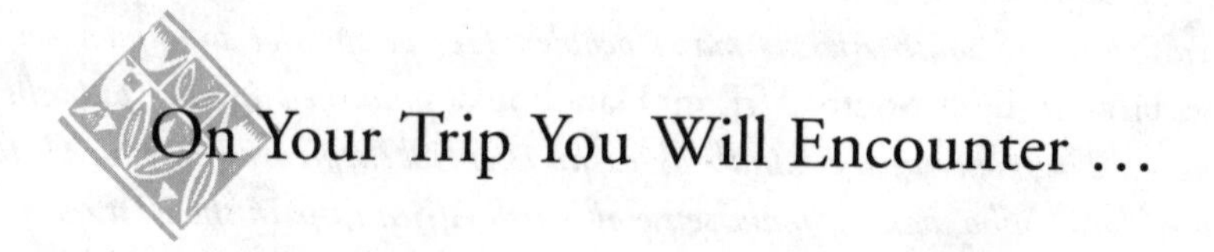

On Your Trip You Will Encounter …

The Rural Guesthouse Proprietor

Often a divorced, former city dweller who has had enough of making her fortune in the advertising or insurance industry and who has now packed up and headed off in search of rural bliss. To supplement her income from clever offshore investments, she buys and renovates a turn-of-the-century rural homestead in a half-horse town, turning it into her idea of a private country retreat for tourists. Using local decor magazines as inspiration, she will try out a variety of styles. She usually adorns the rooms with floral prints, voluminous curtains and bedspreads, and places small hand-made, local crafts including clay guinea fowl on side-tables and cistern tops.

She has never really adjusted to the solitude of rural life and views you, the guest, as a long-lost friend who has just popped round to catch up on the last twenty years of news. From the moment of your arrival you will not know peace, as the proprietor will insist on 'entertaining' you with the story of her life and other amazing South African tales.

Do not be alarmed if she bursts into your bedroom unannounced, bearing a tray of tea and breakfast. Best ploy to get rid of her is to tell her you are in a witness protection programme and that it may be extremely dangerous for her to interact with you. If that fails, pretend to be hard of hearing.

The Visitors' Book

South Africans like to have a record of the private thoughts or inane musings of guests, and for this reason many of us keep a visitors' book. It is ubiquitous in this country: you will find versions of it placed visibly at the exit or entrance to museums, libraries, guesthouses, art galleries and hotels. You will even find one at the top of Table Mountain. Ignore it.

The Craft Market

Hundreds of self-help craft centres have sprung up in townships and villages offering employment to talented locals who make anything from beaded handbags to cellphone covers. It is here that you will encounter some of the shrewdest businesswomen or -men in the country. Do not try and bargain down prices – otherwise you will have to endure much tongue clicking and looks of mild scorn. It is considered impolite to bargain when you are clearly loaded with cash.

The Self-driver

A very brave sort of tourist who feels confident enough to tackle South Africa's highways alone in a hired car. Some are never seen again, as our road signs can be very misleading. What may have started off as a journey to the airport could end up on the borders of Zimbabwe. Those who have lived to tell the tale swear this is one of the most thrilling ways of seeing the country.

The Hitchhiker

One of the most enduring myths in South Africa is that of the killer hitchhiker who roams the countryside waiting to catch a ride with his next victim. If you don't like the look of that crowd of Sunday school kids stranded on the side of the road, don't stop. Generally go with your instincts.

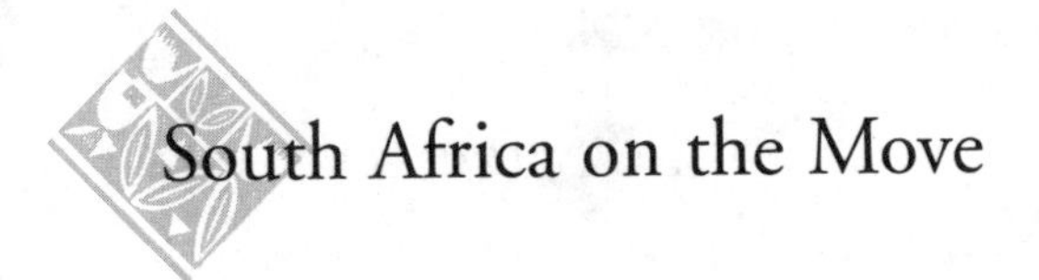

South Africa on the Move

Passengers

Those travelling in minibus taxis have learned to master the difficult psychological trick of dissociation. Their vacant look means they are relaxing on their own inner beaches while the taxi driver plays Russian roulette with their lives. Minibus taxi passengers have come to terms with the fact that life is cheap but that the taxi fare is even cheaper.

As more and more passengers are sardined inside, you will get very, very close to your fellow travellers and may even be able to tell their collar sizes by the time you get out.

Accidents

If you are involved in a collision, don't say anything. South Africans always blame someone else for an accident, and being polite about it (even if you are to blame) will cost you dearly. Play dumb and never admit that the fault is yours. Say you speak only Spanish.

Police seldom bother to attend the scenes of accidents. They're not considered a priority even though more people die on South African roads than anywhere else.

You will have to find your own way to the police station to report the matter if you need a case number for insurance purposes. If someone with no insurance has collided with you – and that means about 80 per cent of the vehicles on South African roads – then you can be sure that the name, address and telephone number scribbled down will be false.

Taking down the number plate won't help either. How do you think you're going to trace him? The cops? Nah, they don't even know how to switch on their computers.

The only South Africans who respond with remarkable swiftness after a collision are tow-truck drivers, who appear miraculously out of nowhere while the engine's still hissing, having themselves caused several accidents on the way to rescue you!

They are not angels of mercy. Tow-truck drivers are known to wrench vehicles up even before the ambulance has arrived. Tell them you don't have any money, and then you'll see just how quickly they drop your wreck.

The Street

The Mobile Vendor

Usually solicits business at traffic intersections and has a selection of only four types of goods on offer – black bin-liners, plastic coat-hangers, flags or giant, Chinese-made plastic toys. Years of sluggish sales have not deterred this most tenacious of salespersons.

The Flag

Although it has only been around since the liberation of the country in the mid-1990s, South Africans are very proud of our new flag. You'll see it on condoms and underwear (the Y being particularly well placed). If you're going to wear the flag, remember the red bit goes at the top.

We do of course expect all visitors to be able to pronounce the motto '!Ke e: /xarra //ke' ('diverse people unite') on our coat of arms.

The Informal Parking Attendant

Believes he is offering a unique and special service by leaping out into the road and directing you to the parking bay you spotted long before he popped up in your rear-view mirror.

He will wave his arms like a windmill and whistle while he guides you into the space that you would have been quite capable of navigating all by yourself. For this, the car guard will expect to be tipped. Ignore him at your peril. Touching up paint scratches can be costly.

In some areas this highly sought-after job has been semi-regulated. Crafty middlemen exploit the car guards, forcing whoever gets there first in the morning to hire a garish neon bib. This, the operator believes, gives the enterprise an air of legitimacy.

The Formal Parking Attendant

In an attempt to discourage hustlers, car guards, pickpockets and other informal businesspersons from operating in the streets, some South African cities have opted to follow the American model of the 'central improvement district' (CID). The result is that now you get doubly ripped off: once by the officially appointed, uniformed parking assistants, who are tasked with reloading special parking cards which you are required to purchase; and once by the unofficial parking attendant, who has not been in the least bit deterred by the CID's supposed 'anti-hustling' regulations.

The Hawker

The South African street hawker or vendor can be found in almost every city, suburb and street in the country and will sell you anything from fruit to a triple bypass. You will also be able to purchase cigarettes, get a haircut, have your tyres replaced, an exhaust fitted or even a windshield repaired.

All business is strictly cash and no receipts will be issued. Fortunately you don't have to pay VAT either.

The hawker is a vital cog in the big wheel that is known formally as the 'informal sector' in the country. South Africans are extremely resilient and cunning when it comes to trying to earn a relatively honest living (except for paying taxes).

How We Are

South African Intellectuals

You can immediately single out the South African intellectual by the questions he or she asks. For example, if someone comes up to you and begins their conversation with 'Who is an African?', you know you have come across a South African intellectual.

South African intellectuals come in many shapes and sizes. They often enjoy drinking wine, writing poetry, listening to jazz and talking deep into the night. They are troubled souls who seldom get a satisfactory answer to any of the questions that plague them.

South African Excuses

'The Devil made me do it.'
'I am sorry, I won't do it again.'
'I never accepted the bribe.'
'I didn't know it was a bribe.'
'What bribe?'
'I'm sorry, she doesn't work here anymore.'
'I'm sorry, we lost the invoice/cheque/application.'
'It's a gay plot.'
'It's an Indian plot.'
'It's a white plot.'
'It's an Africanist plot.
'It's a Xhosa plot.'
'It's a Zulu plot.'
'It's an Afrikaner plot.'
'It's an English plot.'
'It's a working class plot.'
'It's a middle class plot.'
'Are you talking to me?'

CAN THEMBA

TO IDENTIFY *with this author one needs to know only that his friends named his small, humble home in Sophiatown 'The House of Truth' and that his guests were expected to rail against snobbery, orthodoxy, custom, officialdom and anything that smacked of the formal. The host would often pass out from drink at some stage of the night or next day … and often so would his hard-living guests, mainly black writers and journalists. It was the style, brother. The life-style. You lived as hard as you could when a prisoner in your own land.*

Can Themba was a highly educated, highly respected member of his community. In his innocent youth he won a scholarship to university and graduated with a first-class degree in English. He became a teacher, but wanted only to be a writer. Then he won first prize in a short story competition in Drum *magazine. He turned to journalism and later became associate editor of* Drum, *then* Golden City Post. *Though he was one of a famous band of black journalistic pioneers of the 1950s and 1960s, he was never really a newspaperman. He was a writer.*

In 1963 he went, with his family, into exile in neighbouring Swaziland. He died five years later, aged 43. As Essop Patel, editor of his collected works, says in a preface to The World of Can Themba *(Ravan, Braamfontein, 1985): 'My sons will discover that Can Themba, like Nat Nakasa, sacrificed himself for his people. They had no real business to die so young.'*

Girls in High-heel Shoes

The modern African Miss. She's city-slick and sophisticated. She's smart. She's delicate and unselfconscious in the way she handles men, the home and life. And that's been achieved in less than fifty years, for fifty years ago she was content to sit in the sunshine of mud walls and on dung-smeared floors.

And, because of new jobs – not just kitchen chores – jobs in factories, in department stores, clerical jobs, secretarial jobs, social welfare jobs, nursing jobs, teaching jobs, the Modern Miss has got her red-painted talons on to more money than she has seen before.

More money has meant a more elegant way of living. At first she was gaudy and brash, and flourished her newly-won freedom and funds in the colourful manner of the prostitute and brazen flirt. Grey old heads shook themselves sadly.

But soon she learned grace and poise and finesse. True, this brought brand-new problems for her man. This creature was talking back, was catty and gossipy, was asking for nylon stockings, was going to 'nice-time parties' at holy hours of the night and returning at unholy hours of the day, good heavens! She was even reading disturbing books!

Even the domestic servant was speaking English with an un-African accent, which I can only blame her mistress for. But she was a lovely dream. In the home she looked like the delightful things that they put in magazines. And when one's educated friends were present, she could hold her own in the conversation argument and with dignity. You sat back and looked in wonder at this woman, not long out of the loin-cloth, now draped in python gowns and making her point with a long cigarette holder.

True again, she now talks about those unheard of things: divorce, abortion, feminine rights, and mere males. But, well understood and treated square, she's a lovely feline, stimulating to the mind, satisfying to the creature desires, at once an ornament and an ordeal. Some people hazard marriage with them, then grin and bear it. Others just have their fling with them.

And she's a woman of the world. Whereas in the days gone by she didn't think much beyond the kraal walls, she now imagines herself as a Lena Horne, a Vijayalakshmi Pandit, or a Madame Chiang Kai-shek. Only thirty years ago she never thought of marrying anybody outside her tribe, now she writes romantic pen-pal letters to men in Ghana and Nigeria.

Perhaps the crassness and immaturity that inevitably goes with swift development brought a knotty crudeness to the way women adapted themselves to the new situation. But they're arriving in style. To us men it means a new attitude, a new factor in our calculation of the problem of the black man and himself.

But we're not going to make it sociological. We're going to grin at the tricky packet of femininity, while we try to solve it. But we realise that the Modern Miss is catching up with modern times and with us. God save us when she by-passes her man.

But nevertheless I thank the Bigshot for bringing her in line with modern times and fashions. The other day I went to Mapokkerstad, about 35 miles north of Pretoria. The village was lovely with the houses painted in varying colours, styles and designs. The women there went in for natural beauty, with frank breasts jutting out like promontories. It was very romantic, just the sedative for jaded, city nerves.

But the thought came to me that the shattering silence would get me down, and I would panic back to the near-thing life of Sophiatown and some loud-mouthed, bewitching girl. The wonderful girl of my dreams.

HARVEY TYSON

LAURENCE GANDAR, *editor-in-chief of the* Rand Daily Mail *in the 1960s, said almost anybody could write straight-forward stuff – but with humorous writing it was different. This really was a remarkable gift, he said, and very few people had it.*

One of the few was the editor-in-chief of Gandar's main rival newspaper, The Star *– Harvey Tyson. I knew him for most of his newspaper career. He rarely took himself seriously and never for long; not even when the Special Branch was tapping his phone and bugging the office and planting spies in the Reporters' Room (as the secret police did throughout most of his time). Nor did he take death threats seriously, not even when his name was found to be on an apartheid assassin's hit list.*

During the 1970s, when the apartheid government broadcast a daily propaganda programme, euphemistically named Current Affairs, The Star *ran a counter-column called* Undercurrent Affairs. *Harvey, then assistant editor, adopted it and continued to write it when he took over as editor-in-chief of* The Star*'s stable of newspapers in 1974. I watched the column move from being mainly a tirade against the government to becoming a brilliant mockery of it and, gradually, a sometimes pure humour column in which nobody was the victim. His humour is the rollicking kind – a modern version of Jerome K. Jerome – as demonstrated in the latter stages of* Undercurrent Affairs. *(It was at this point he found he was on a hit list, and decided it was because of his jokes.) His humour was often about his own sometimes hair-raising exploits, driving for instance in the annual Roof of Africa Rally across the snowy mountain fastness of Lesotho on nightmare tracks, or golfing or sailing or visiting some remote part of the globe. He became something of an intrepid explorer towards the end of his career, visiting Samarkand, canoeing in the Amazon jungle, climbing (aged 67) the Great Breach route up Mount Kilimanjaro.*

Tyson can be seriously funny, yet he is essentially a political animal. He lived through, and reported on, the entire 43-year-life of apartheid and was in the parliamentary Press Gallery for years covering dramatic times in South Africa's history.

The apartheid government hauled Tyson into court many times – not that this made him unique among newspapermen. But he was never absent from court when one of his staff was facing trial for testing the apartheid laws to the limit. It was difficult being funny in such times.

Tyson was born in Johannesburg, destined for the church, but 'called to the Bar, where I fell among journalists'. Forty years later, journalists gave him a medal for 'fighting for press freedom'.

He wrote Editors under Fire *(Random House, 1991), a report on the South African press under stress – but he was soon back to humour again.* Walk on the Wild Side *was a hilarious but sometimes very poignant account of some of his adventures in the outdoors, in South Africa and abroad. This was followed by* The Itch of the Twitch, *which entrenched Tyson as a humorist. Literary critic Jennifer Cruys-Williams said his yarns were 'as South African as Oom Schalk (of Herman Charles Bosman fame), but a great deal more polished'.* The Itch of the Twitch *was a romp, filled with irreverence, crazy adventures and hilarious episodes of birding.*

Here are three of his romps – written during the era of freedom and excitement in the mid-1990s. The first is from a weekly Star *column he also wrote, called* Off the Wall, *the second appeared in* The Humerus, *the humour section of* diversions *magazine, and the third is an extract from a chapter on golf in* A Walk of the Wild Side *(Struik Publishers, 1995).*

– J.C.

Kill the Whales

Those of us who, for sins in a previous life, were condemned to write newspaper editorials and anti-apartheid comment pieces for years and years, often found ourselves plumbing the depths to find subjects to write about in light columns which were not concerned with apartheid, racism, torture or – looking on the bright side – redistribution of wealth. Once, in search of an issue of deep gravitas outside of these constants, I found myself embroiled in a debate with readers concerning the weight of whale dung.

Research had shown that in fact whale dung ends up weightless, because it is absorbed by the vast volumes of water which necessarily surround it. My advice, all the way from America, was that although a big whale dispenses three tons of waste a day, the waste is in liquid form and has no more substance or depth than the stuff they put out on the TV and radio waves.

But you know what newspaper readers are like. They contradict everything you say. One regular wit from Randburg, for instance, questioned the very satisfactory solution (in both senses) to the problem.

'Never!' claimed this pseudo mass expert from Randburg when I announced the facts of nature. 'Whale droppings are so heavy you can't imagine. Scientific research shows', he says … (an instant give-away) … 'that fish have evolved their slim bodylines to easily dodge' (he even splits infinitives) 'easily to dodge falling whale matter, but the poor old crabs on the sea floor have not been clever enough to avoid having their squashed-flat appearance.'

Superficially logical, I suppose. But, deep down, lower than shark … er … I know it's not so.

Whatever the solution, we need to be grateful that whales don't fly.

The other problem with whales is that they eat too much. They are helping to destroy our environment.

While whales are gobbling up most of this planet's plankton, humanity has thoughtlessly opened the environment envelope, thus allowing in nasty sun's rays that seek out and destroy the smarter plankton who have managed to evade the whales.

Heaven knows what happens if the Earth (I mean of course the ocean) runs out of plankton. We need to keep even some of the slowest-witted plankton who don't really deserve to evolve.

That is why, for almost a decade, I have been trying to launch a 'Save the Plankton – Kill the Whales' campaign.

But it's tough being on the side of the small battalions. And no piece of plankton is as lovable and cuddly as a killer whale.

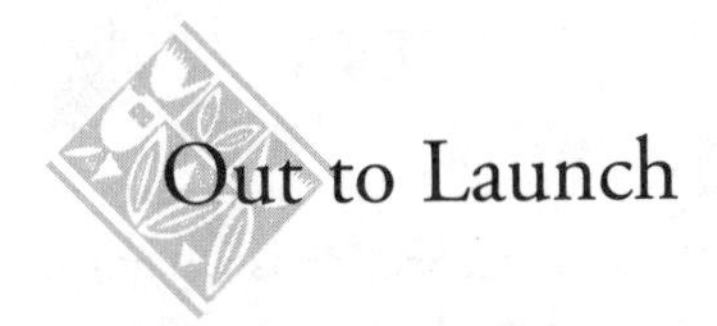

Out to Launch

Starting a voyage, even in a relatively small six-berth yacht, is like launching a new magazine. It's all too frantic for a romantic. You wonder why you ever got involved. And then it gets worse.

Let me tell you about the time I set out to sail in search of the Western Isles. Well, I was actually looking for Robben Island, Dassen Island and that other one outside of Saldanha Bay – all stepping stones to a pub on a wharf somewhere up the coast. I had hired a yacht, and summoned a crew, and believed that was all that was required until I was able to don my braid cap and be piped aboard.

But then all sorts of fiddly details came down on me – more ghastly work than can be envisaged even for a global journey. And we hadn't left harbour yet. That's why I say it's like launching a magazine. The seemingly simple exercise of getting going is beset with crises.

For evidence, look at the initial entries in our log, covering only the first few hours of the start of our voyage.

Dawn. Day One. (Note: Find out the date and fill it in when we get back.)

Nine hundred hours. The good ship *Venus* lies beside a green-slimed floating jetty at the foot of a precarious gangplank. The wife of the yacht's temporary 'owner' clambers down the gangway in her high heels, negotiates some spiked wires and slime-slippery floating planks and is pulled aboard for inspection. She pronounces it too small. She declares that its undetectable motion in this furthest corner of the harbour has made her sea-sick; and that *Venus* is likely to sink if we let go the string holding it to the jetty-planks. She wishes us fair seas and a fond farewell.

But *Venus* is by no means small. A single glance of my practical nautical eye establishes that the good ship is two-tenths of a third of a furlong in length (or two-thirds of a chain), and that she has an impressively high pole in the middle with lots of ropes and sticks sticking out. She also has a satisfactory amount of electronic gadgetry below decks. I hit my head against the bulkhead and, in suitably salty terms, declare her seaworthy.

Only later do we discover how dangerously wrong first impressions can be. It is revealed too late, for instance, that the screen in the saloon isn't a TV set, so necessary for watching Australian cricket at dawn, and cowboy movies in the dogwatch. It is just a bleeping radar thing. And when I call up the Port Captain: '*Venus* here. *Venus. Venus. Venus.* Do you read me? Come in, Port Captain. Over!', the instrument I am using is found to be totally under-powered. In fact it turns out to be a ventilation spout. Our skipper has installed the radio in the stove somewhere.

Another serious deficiency: I cannot find a yard-arm for the sun to come over.

Ten hundred hours. The skipper arrives. He is a navigational instructor, author of nautical works and well-known yachtsman, who has insisted on joining the cruise because, at the end of it, he wants his boat back.

Before we cast off and set sail, elaborate preparations are necessary. To avoid the tedious business of stowing things, I call for volunteers for the especially delicate task of cleaning the decks.

'Hoses Up! Ho-o-oses U-up! …'

The haunting cry floats across the bay. There is no answer. Sailors cower in their berths. I issue the command again. Silence.

Could this be mutiny? Already?

Finally, the brave captain responds. 'You'll find the hose connected to a water tap on the quay. Just swab down the deck, will you?'

I discover I have volunteered to do the job myself, and execute this responsibility with dash and skill. So efficiently, that the jet of water hits the saloon table downstairs no more than thrice. So well, that I am elected to do the job anywhere in the Southern Hemisphere, whenever the whole crew can get ashore, and wherever a freshwater tap is available. Fortunately there appear to be only two such taps (with hose) on the West Coast of Africa, for it is backbreaking work; specialist work, which prevents the hose-handler doing any other job aboard ship except opening bottles.

Twelve hundred hours. After a tedious but complex period of fiddling about with ropes and strings and untying knots and things, we cast off ('give berth', as we sailors say). We drift across the harbour about 100 yards … maybe even further, perhaps 100 metres, and tie up at another wharf, where there is a great deal of fiddling with ropes and strings and tying knots and things.

Glad to be ashore again, some of us hurry to the welcoming doors of the Royal Cape Yacht Club. Others go shopping. After a visit to the Yacht Club I buy some tough leather gloves, designed for handling steel halyards, but also necessary for tender hands which will have to open bottles for days to come.

Meanwhile our skipper has pumped 165 litres of fuel aboard, and we cast off once more … after much fiddling about with ropes, and so on.

Thirteen hundred hours. We motor 50 metres from the wharf, and are turning the boat's sharp end towards the sea when a fat bearded observer in a well-oiled peaked cap cries out from the shore: 'Hey, Skipper! Your water! Mind your water!'

'Mind your own business!' I call back, for I firmly believe that the personal plumbing of any man and woman aboard, including our skipper, is his or her own affair.

But the skipper is galvanised. 'Cut engine!' he yells at all of us, and clambers, distraught, on deck.

Suddenly we are powerless in a timeless morass. We are adrift among a forest of masts lining a channel as busy as Adderley Street, filled with puttering motor boats. One of the putt-putts nudges us back to the wharf, where the captain and bearded figure prod the innards of *Venus* until they find a wodge of nylon which has been sucked into her engine's water-cooling system.

'It was quick of you to spot the dry exhaust,' our skipper thanks the Ancient Mariner. 'Another five minutes and we would have burnt out, and ended the voyage.'

I too showed appreciation, where those without marine engineering experience might have been puzzled.

'Why should a yacht with such vast sails need an engine?' I hear you think. 'Is this not a sailing ship on a sailing trip?'

'Ah yes!' I reply, chewing the baccy and sticking out the jib. 'But how can you travel with no engine to heat the fridge to cool the beer?'

Our skipper is right. We wouldn't have got as far as the outer breakwater of Cape Town docks. As it is, we ran into other problems, too petty and too heartbreaking to enter in this log.

Nineteen hundred hours. Wind increasing. Waves suddenly sick-making as we round the end of the harbour outer wall and fall among the Atlantic rollers in Table Bay. Someone (no good blaming me) has forgotten to load, or bring, or even buy many of the vital vittles. Frantic check shows we are not short of liquids. Nevertheless, skipper orders a turn-about and we make for our original berth to indulge in much tying of ropes and things.

Twenty-one hundred hours. This is the life; enjoying the sea, and the sky, the swaying masts, and the happy clink of cutlery in a Waterfront café.

We sail at dawn …

The way we have begun this venture reminds me of a magazine I once launched.

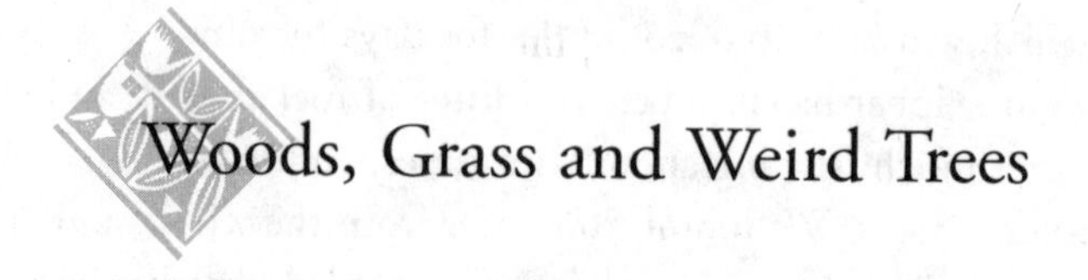

Woods, Grass and Weird Trees

In *Cry, the Beloved Country* Alan Paton wrote of the rich soil of Natal's hills, where the grass sings. The grass sings in the hills beyond Ixopo and, in late summer, it stands tall; tall as a Number One Wood. Ben tells me he once played golf somewhere in those Ixopo hills – though unlike all other golfers, he cannot quite remember where. Ben does not stand tall, and fortunately, he does not sing – not so that anyone would recognise it as such. Anyway, there he was, among the chuckling streams and the tall-standing hills, and the singing grass (and vice versa) with an infant caddie about half Ben's non-standing-tall height.

In this unpredictable pursuit named Golf, Ben did the predictable. He hit his first ball straight over the fairway, into the tall-standing, singing grass. He and his caddy went in search. After the stipulated five-minute hunt, which Ben invariably stretches to 15 minutes, he and his caddie went in search of each other. They were going round in circles, unable to hear each other above, or even below, the singing grass. After anxious aeons, first the one, then the other staggered onto the open fairway, where they held a heartfelt reunion. Ben delivered his usual lecture to his caddie about 'keeping your eye on the ball', and then magnanimously agreed to declare it lost and start again.

'Hand me my Number One Wood, caddie, and another ball.'

It was at this point, I assume, that the two of them stared at each other with a wild surmise – just as the poet, as well as golfer P.G. Wodehouse, remembered stout Cortez staring for the first time at the Pacific. Both Ben and his little helper knew instinctively at that moment that the Number One Wood, and all the other clubs, and the bag, and the necessarily large reserve of balls, were lying somewhere in the singing grass. The equipment was found eventually, but not before the sun started sinking in the west, and not before Ben had to be dissuaded from setting the singing grass on fire.

I cannot vouch for Ben's tale – indeed I positively refuse to vouch for it – but I was present at another strange ball-hunting incident at a golf course high in the hills – and ravines – at Kloof, above Durban. In those days there was a private shooting range right in the middle of the golf course, so that one would tend to tense up, waiting to hit one's ball in an anticipated lull between the rifle-shots which echoed around those non-singing hills. Inevitably one would fail to synchronise with the invisible target-shooters, and as the guns went off one would slice into the rough. I was mesmerised by a weird, witch-like tree which lurked on the edge of the fairway, and sure enough my slice sent my ball flying into its encompassing branches like a cuckoo to some other bird's nest.

'See where it fell, caddie?'

'It never came out, suh.'

'What do you mean "never came out"?'

'It's stuck in the tree.'

'You can't be serious. How can it stick in the tree?'

But he was serious. And it apparently *was* stuck in the tree, though there was no way of seeing it. The caddie threw a half-brick into the cloying pine-needles – and it never came down. Half impatiently, half amusedly, I threw my club at the tree to shake its foliage and bring down my ball. The club stuck in the tree. We could see the club's shaft, three metres above us, pointing at the sky. It was the only visible item so far gobbled up by the tree. We threw three stones into the tree. Two came down.

'I think it's full,' I said.

'Not!' said the caddie.

He was taking me seriously.

'Oh well, better shin up there, caddie, and get the club. A bit of a shake may also bring the ball down.'

'Not!' he said.

And nothing would make him. Eventually we had to summon help and a ladder from the faraway clubhouse so that I could go up and retrieve my five-iron.

'I swear this tree must practise catching bullets from old Field's rifle-range over there,' I told the caddie master. He too took this quite seriously.

You see how much mystery and romance and adventure there is in golf? Golf also has a fascinating chemistry. You can watch it at work every time a golfer consults his caddie – or himself – about which club to use for a particular shot. Each time it appears to be the most important decision of his life. Usually he proceeds to duff the shot, then snarl at his caddie – or himself: 'I said I should have used a wedge, not a four-iron.' And the chemistry really bubbles when you hold out your hand for your caddie to pass you your five-iron, and neither he nor the five-iron is there.

In my case, I found both of them on the side of the fairway beside a stream. Moosa was trying to stun some fish, and hoick them out of the water with my club.

'You can't use my five-iron to fish with!' I exploded ... which began an ugly argument. He finally had to apologise and back down. I then gave him a little lecture: 'For that kind of fishing you should use a wedge, because it has a sharper edge for hitting, and a wider blade for scooping.'

He had to agree.

Choice of club is fundamental. The options are wide, and growing wider and more confusing.

There is, for instance, a relatively new golf-club available which is a bastardisation of irons and metal woods (the metal wood itself being, not only a bastard – as many a golfer has been heard to mutter – but also a contradiction in terms, an oxymoron, as golfers like to describe their opponents). The latest in-between club is called a driving-iron, and boasts an ultra-heavy blade. You should have one of these in your bag. It is the very best club yet invented for driving off burglars, *skebengas* who try to mug you, and for use in scoring against others in the compulsory-redistribution-of-wealth industry. But remember, the driving-iron with its extra-long shaft is designed for the great outdoors. I find that for defence in the confines of the home, a sawn-off putter is the best club. And on the green, it's the only club to use when you are really on your knees.

I find the sand-wedge, as opposed to the wedge, is the best club for snakes. The sand-wedge's combination of a heavy edge and flat blade allows you to thump aggressive cobras on the head, or lift lazy puff-adders and put them back in the bush where they belong. Never touch a mole-snake with anything but a three-wood. Mole-snakes are harmless lovable creatures that will cling round a cosy, rounded wood, but are easily frightened off by an iron. Make sure the mole-snake to whom you offer your club isn't a mamba. They look the same, but their temperaments are as different as those of a non-playing buddhist and a golfer who has hit three successive balls into the water. Give mambas and hydrophobic golfers a wide berth ...

PIETER-DIRK UYS

HERE IS A SATIRIST *who is the embodiment of the fear, expressed in one of the introductions to this book, that top humorists are deserting the written word to take to the boards, radio waves, television, audio-disc or web.*

Pieter-Dirk Uys uses all these media. As a personality – or rather a multiplicity of donned personalities – he shocks his audiences into bursts of laughter; he mixes satire with buffoonery; he produces forensic wit among music-hall winks, and he parodies even satirists.

The pity is you will find only traces of his talents in his writing. A flat page is too limiting for him – and even more so for her, his alter ego, *whom he invented in order to mock apartheid – Evita Bezuidenhout, the homeless ambassador to a long-vanished apartheid 'Homeland' named Bapetikosweti. Evita, and all of Uys's characters, need room to flaunt their clothes, taunt their audiences, and time their knowing smiles.*

He once floored a gathering of the world press with his imitations and parodies of world-famous figures. No one is safe from his barbs, so that when he suddenly turned into the spitting image of Winnie Mandela and parodied her rantings, he offended several white editors from northern Europe – who thought it tasteless to mock a black politician!

Astonishingly, Pieter-Dirk Uys gets a bit earnest himself when he sheds his make-up and picks up a pen. However, if you have enjoyed one of his one-man or one-woman shows anywhere in the world, watched him on television or seen one of his videos, you appreciate more the words he puts to paper. His record is prodigious. He has:

- *scripted and directed more than 50 revues in theatres around the globe*
- *starred in, scripted and produced nearly 30 TV films and videos*
- *entered the audiotape business with a CD called* Truth Omissions, *and*
- *written more than 20 books and plays.*

His novel-writing might appear to contradict the fear that Uys leads the modern trend of humorists forsaking the written word, but most of his books are really scripts in disguise, or scripts in the making: theatre reviews with glorious titles like Farce about Uys.

Yet he has managed to write countless articles and weekly and monthly columns for newspapers and magazines in South Africa and abroad. Not bad for a boykie *from the backveld, as he might say.*

Satire is his whole career – but he was one of the first to complain, loudly, that apartheid out-satirised his efforts. He countered by publishing a book of quotes of State President P.W. Botha at the moment when the apartheid leader reached the apogee of authoritarianism in South Africa. P.W. Botha: In His Own Words *(Penguin, 1987) carried quotes from P.W.'s speeches, such as: 'Never in the history of this country have so few people done so much for so many without acknowledgement by the international community.' Sad, really.*

Uys lives in Darling (a 90-minute drive north of Cape Town) and has converted its disused railway station into a theatre-restaurant. There's also Uys's museum of Afrikaner kitsch there, which displays tin trays depicting heroic Voortrekker battles against hordes of Zulu; a bust of Verwoerd with a light bulb on top of his head; and framed pictures of pioneer women in huge white kappies clutching their sturdy little children to their voluminous skirts and staring resolutely into a distant veld bristling with menace.

Uys, surely the most irreverent Afrikaner of them all, has a little garden with gnomes (of course) and faded plastic flowers stuck in the ground.

Do the local Afrikaners resent this mockery? When, one day, Uys experienced a power failure and could not cook for his theatre-restaurant, the local aunties got to hear about his predicament and arrived with ready-cooked meals.

Uys's philosophy is to make people laugh at themselves. The people who needed that therapy the most were his own folk and it is significant that Uys's satirical shows have become more and more popular among Afrikaners. His penmanship may not match his other talents, but it is no exaggeration to say his merciless wit played a role in helping white South Africans come to terms with their situation and eventually agree to share power.

The following piece, which exposes an interesting guilt complex, is from the Johannesburg-based Sunday Times *in 1995.*

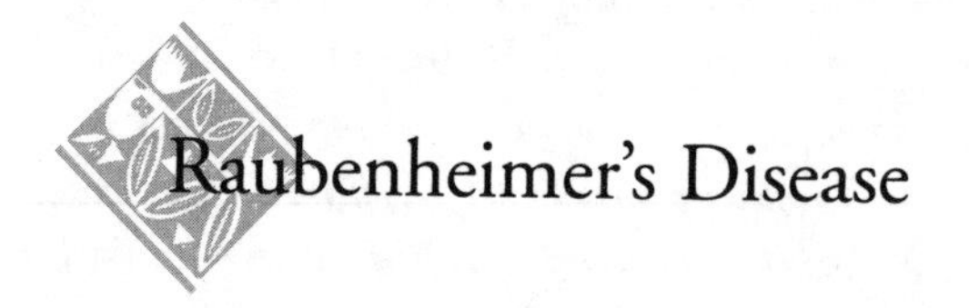

Raubenheimer's Disease

There is an old Afrikaner ailment that seems to have hit epidemic proportions here in this most southern African Land of Rising Hope. It's called Raubenheimer's Disease, only related to the infamous Alzheimer's in that no one remembers nothing! It was first noticed after the Boer War, when the British Empire was nearly forced to its knees by our boer guerrillas in the mist.

The khaki brigades copyrighted that type of warfare and exposed it to various skirmishes from Bosnia to Afghanistan with great success, while the Brits introduced the civilised world to their new concept of the concentration camp. It has also in various ways been an inspiration to others.

When the Boer War ended there was great hatred and grumbling against the British overlords, but by 1910 the Afrikaner found himself in a newly formed

Union, blueprinted by the compromise of those of the Cape Colony (Union Jack) and the two ex-boer republics.

Raubenheimer's Disease was spotted for the first time on the day of Union, 31st May 1910, in a small dusty dorp on the wide plains of the Karoo, where Farmer Raubenheimer, having just lost his farm to fire and his family to famine, suddenly started speaking English and singing 'God Save the King!'. He seemed to have completely forgotten the reason for the pain of his past. This merciful amnesia made it possible for him to live side by side with his bloody enemy in peace. He even married again, a young English girl, and they had three sons and called them after various recent British kings. Some of his bitter neighbours swore that Farmer Raubenheimer had in fact lost his marbles.

It is said that since then all Afrikaners have been born with a trace of Raubenheimer's Disease. In decent company it was just whispered that these strange bearded and braided *volk* knew how to be able to adapt and not to die. ['Adapt or die' was the famous exhortation of President P.W. Botha.] 'Damn pragmatic' and 'bloody unbalanced' were more often used to explain the strange ways by which Afrikaners turned their other cheek and then whipped around, guns ablazing. We Afrikaners have always been great artists in absorbing. No, call it stealing.

We would take something from another people, maybe a Dutch language and unrecognisably beat it up to become Afrikaans. Or take a democratic Westminster system of government to bleed dry of its truth. Even legitimise an inbred sense of racial madness, give it an official Afrikaans name that the English spelt apart-hate, weave it into the statue books 'democratically' and end up in the smelly corner of the world's classroom with a skunk's tail pinned to our backs.

No more.

Some Afrikaners who swore bloody revenge on a democratically elected non-racial, non-sexist government are swopping fond stories of World Cup [Rugby] Celebration barbecue-braais with their new non-white neighbours. Former terrorists and old fascists are comrades-in-arms beer-in-hand. A cloudburst over a squatter camp is no longer the fault of bad Nationalist politics, only bad weather.

Amnesties and amnesias seem to go hand in hand. There are now more free men on the street and in parliament with blood on their hands than in the jails. Politically-motivated crimes which range from mass killings to messy murders have a cut-off date, which means that if you blasted our enemies away before then, you're OK.

Herr Hitler would've had an easy way out here.

'Adolf Hitler, you are accused of the murder of millions!'

'Nein, it was all just politically motivated!'

... When South Africa got rid of apartheid as Germany got rid of Nazism, did the world look beyond the celebration and the masses all shouting in unity? If you did, you couldn't help noticing that relatively well-educated, relatively civilised, relatively pleasant groups of white Christians and Jews took this most beautiful country in the world and so successfully utterly and completely scorched its earth, and nearly got away with it! And then turned round with a smile at the edge of the cliff and handed the only parachute to the former enemy.

I think I started with a question. I really can't remember the answer. Just call it a touch of Raubenheimer's Disease.

There's No Place Like Home

London is having a hangover after a heatwave. Grey and stuffy, with dirty woolly clouds pressing down on the drab red roofs of the location-houses that clutter the narrow streets like impenetrable walls. So many cars parked helter-skelter, one wheel on the sidewalk. Which means the wheelchair-lady can't go for a ride and the big truck can't use the road for a shortcut.

Every time I see this megatropolis there seem to be more automobiles. As if the mother of them all sits somewhere deep in the bowels of the earth and breeds Unos and Fiats and Fords. It is whispered fearfully that one day a red bus will take a wrong turn in Earls Court and instantly the entire London will be caught in a paralysing gridlock. No one will be able to turn left, right or centre. Sounds like British politics.

I lived here as a student for four years up to 1973. It was here where I realised with a shock that I was criminally wrong. Not just me, but everyone I thought was right. The stern teacher who told me that whites were better. The pompous dominee who promised that whites were best. The fat-cat society that showed that whites were all. Here in London, I learnt the hard way. People didn't like me! I was an Afrikaner! What did that mean?

Soon the truth sat in my mouth like bitter mouthwash at a dentist. I had been running down a road that ended nowhere. I was hauled back from the edge of the cliff by life in London. And during the last 20 years, I have been back so often that it feels like Home to me too. There are familiar faces and places that I remember well from those days when I arrived here fresh from four years' University and a lifetime of sunshine and being a local Clifton beach blond.

My first bedsit was in Kilburn, just down the road from the Tricycle Theatre, where I am doing my show at the moment. I lived upstairs in one room in an old cold house owned by Mr and Mrs Northwood. She made it very clear that she saw me as a close relative to Hitler. Me being a boer and suppressing those poor blacks. It became one of the first of many similar epitaphs I was to collect from the residents of the moral high ground of this strange and irritating island.

I also met my first friend in London who wasn't white! I invited him back to my place for a beer. Revolutionary me! We tiptoed through the cluttered hallway of the Northwood Castle, up the steep stairs and into the freezing kitchen, where the beers were standing on the icy windowsill, frozen. The next morning my landlady called me aside. 'Peter, dear,' she said, 'you know how we feel about all the things you boers do in South Africa?'

Here it comes again, I thought.

'But really, we don't want blacks in our house. We'll have none of that, all right, dear?'

'HEY, MAN, VAN DER MERWE ...'

'EVERY NATION has its van der Merwe,' say the compilers of a collection of van der Merwe jokes – 'whether disguised as Paddy, the double-talking Irishman, Taffy, the cunning Welshman, or Jock, the pecuniary Scot. He's a miraculous amalgam of all that makes each nationality what it is, and every man is the richer for being able to laugh at himself.'

They wrote that in the dark and distant 1970s, and added: 'It is a tribute to the strength of character of South Africans that our Everyman (van der Merwe) is so well defined, so universally known, and so widely loved.'

More accurately, van der Merwe jokes – or Irish or Polish jokes or, for that matter, the South African Indian community's Patel jokes – reflect how different types of people are perceived by others. Invariably they depict the target as, at best, slow or at worst stupid or parsimonious – but, these days, there's a distinct note of affection involved and, most of the time, no real harm meant.

When Jan van Riebeeck arrived in Table Bay in 1652, an ancestor of the South African van der Merwes was on board. In modern times, according to Dominee C.P. van der Merwe's research and calculations, the family name probably outnumbers all others among whites in Africa. A comic character, the butt in fact of Afrikaans humour, became 'van der Merwe' in the 19th century, and blossomed into national popularity via Afrikaans radio after World War II. So far, so good. A community is able to laugh at itself. They see their comic character as racist and stupid – and he becomes the victim of their own ridicule.

But political and racial sensitivities have always been close to the surface in South Africa's multicultural society, and it was not long before die Engelse (the 'English') were thought to be laughing at the 'stupid Afrikaner' – or joining in laughter at other races, which to an extent they were. Indeed the racial jokes (centred on blacks) became bitter – the worst of them, ironically, originating from America's Deep South – and progression into stark racism was stemmed only during the dramatic political change of heart in the late 1980s and 1990s.

The compilers of the 1975 Van der Merwe book were able to write: 'Van der Merwe ... is not simply a mindless bigot. Rather he is subject to the love-hate relationship with Blacks which so many [white] South Africans have. It is a relationship born out of the common understanding of Africa and of the land, coupled with the fear of racial domination. We make no apologies for including a few racial jokes, for they reflect an essential side of the character ...'

But if their book had appeared a few years later they would have needed to make those apologies, for the van der Merwe jokes moved beyond humour and infringed on race hate. Neither the compilers of Van, nor our own review, go that route.

A Bit Slow

At a board meeting a new director broke the ice with a van der Merwe joke. All the other directors laughed – except one.

Oh dear, thought the new member, and asked the scowling company director: 'Excuse me, but is your name van der Merwe?'

'Yes it is,' snapped the other.

'Well, I do apologise. I'm truly sorry. I'll tell the joke again – slowly.'

Van der Merwe met a beautiful girl in the woods.
'I'm game,' she said, so he shot her.
(Editor's note: Drawn-out versions of this joke have gone round the world. As hunting wild game is a national sport here, it could be original ... though the word play is in English.)

Van der Merwe phoned Johannesburg airport and asked the switchboard:
'How long does it take to fly to London?'
'Just a minute, sir,' said the telephonist.
'Thank you very much,' said van der Merwe, putting down the phone.

Origins Obvious – Definitely Home-Made

Van der Merwe was elected mayor of Kakamas and was thrilled with the title. He brooked no criticism of his town. One day he met the mayor of Lichtenburg, who was equally pleased with himself and proud of his *dorp*. Inevitably their bragging turned to argument, until the Mayor of Lichtenburg said:

'Mr Mayor of Kakamas, let me tell you, I am often known as the 'Lig' [Light] of Lichtenburg. What, may I ask, do people call you?' [*Kak* in Afrikaans is 'shit'.]

Van der Merwe went down to the once narrowly Calvinistic Free State to watch a skydiving demo one weekend. Tragedy struck.

Three parachutists jumped – and one after the other, as each chute failed, they plunged to their deaths.

After a long, horrified silence, people began to ask each other what could cause such a tragic chain of coincidences. Only van der Merwe was unperturbed.

'Hey, man, it's obvious. Nothing opens in the Free State on a Sunday.'

Much attention is given to the Bible in South Africa and much of public life was, until recently, dominated by it; from behaviour on the Sabbath to naming of places – for instance, there are at least two local River Niles that never get to Egypt.

With all his biblical background, van der Merwe was actually able to become a finalist in the $64 000 television quiz in America.

'Now for the final question,' said the quiz master ... 'Where was Jesus Christ born?'

Van der Merwe hesitated. 'Bloemfontein,' he said.

'Wrong. The correct answer is Bethlehem.'

'Yuss!' said van der Merwe. 'I knew it was in the Free State.'

Kaalkop [bald-headed] van der Merwe grew increasingly embarrassed about his name as he grew older. He took a friend's advice, and officially changed it.

'What have you changed it to?'

'Ja, no. Now you must call me Kaalkop Swanepoel.'

Race Relations

On a visit to the land of the English, van der Merwe was taken by a friend to see Oxford University. In a student cafeteria, while jostling with a tray, he bumped into an African and unthinkingly reacted:

'Hey, man – can't you see where you're going, piccanin?'

To his dismay the black man burst into tears.

'Look, I didn't hurt you!'

'No – but you've made me so homesick.'

Van der Merwe and his friend were wandering around London when they stopped to watch some men working in the street.

'Twelve people for a little job like this!' said van der Merwe. 'Man, just give me six "boys" [African labourers] and I could do it by myself.'

When the Americans first landed on the moon, Neil Armstrong found, much to his surprise, that the South Africans had got there first. Sitting on a rock in his space suit, looking bored, was van der Merwe.

'How long have you been here?' asked Armstrong.

'Ag, about five days.'

'Well, why don't you build yourself a shelter and make yourself a little more comfortable?'

'No, well, I'm waiting for my boys.'

Some playful Frenchman got van der Merwe into a corner at a party, and asked him whether having sex was regarded as work or play in South Africa. Van der Merwe thought about it for a while, and then hesitantly answered that it was play.

'Why did you take so long to make up your mind, Van?'

'We-ell,' said van der Merwe, 'it must be play, because if it was work, we'd get our Blacks to do it for us.'

The Joke's on Him

In the late 1980s, when the white Nationalist government began to break down its segregationist policy, it was defied by a racist group of town councillors in Boksburg. Instead of taking down the apartheid signs, they put up a fence around Boksburg Lake with new signs shouting 'Whites Only'. The following joke was soon going the rounds.

Shortly after the race laws were reinforced at Boksburg Lake, Councillor van der Merwe was killed instantly and tragically in a motor accident. Sannie, his wife, was distraught. She wanted, somehow, to hear some parting words, to find some meaning in the tragedy. At last she made contact with van der Merwe through a spiritual medium.

'Van? Is that you!'

'Yes, my *skat*.'

'But where are you? I worry about you.'

'I'm fine, *skattie*, I'm in a wonderful world. There are no blacks here. It's very quiet.'

'No blacks in Heaven, Van?'

'I'm not in heaven. I'm a duck on Boksburg Lake.'

IRIS VAUGHAN

IF YOU ARE *very young, you are unlikely to find Iris Vaughan's diary funny. But, as Iris points out several times in her writing, grown-ups forget wot chilren no. So now that modern adults are about as grown-up as people can get, they have lost the wonderment most children enjoy, and instead find amusement in the perspectives and childlike observations of Iris's 100-year-old diary. It was published for the first time in* Outspan, *the nationally popular magazine of the mid-20th century. It was reprinted by Stormberg Publishers in 2002 – for at least the fourth time.*

We find it difficult to accept that all of this diary is genuine. The story of the tok-toks, for instance, which is one of our selected extracts below, seems too well-rounded to be a child's tale. Did some grown-up change a few words, perhaps? Or did Mom – enjoying the humour and her daughter's views on Pop, the 'savige' magistrate of the Eastern Cape in the late 19th century – do a little adult editing? It is not possible to tell.

What we do know is that our friend and colleague, the late Charles Barry, who edited Outspan *magazine nearly 50 years ago, had the same reservations then as we do now. But soon he had proof that the diary was genuine – even if an unidentified grown-up did possibly try a little editing. Certainly the style and spelling changed as the family 'got a shift on' from Cradock, to Maraisburg, to Adelaide, Fort Beaufort and places in between.*

Charles Barry wrote:

'When Mrs Niland submitted the manuscript of Iris Vaughan's Diary to Outspan for consideration, I thought it was one of two things – a clever hoax, or a major literary find.

'There was never any doubt in my mind that the diary was readable, immensely readable. But was it, in fact, the work of a young girl? (She was ten years old when she wrote about the Boer War.)

'We published a few instalments and waited for the public to react. We did not wait long. Letters poured in from delighted readers. And in these letters was the confirmation we were seeking. People from all over Southern Africa who had not seen Iris Vaughan since childhood remembered vividly the events she described. They also remembered that she spent much of her time writing a diary.

'Thus we were able to prove the Diary was genuine; and thus we were able to say confidently that it was a major literary find. I see no reason to change that view.'

And never in all the years we knew him had we reason to doubt Charles Barry's editorial judgement.

Iris Vaughan's Diary

My Diry Diray Diery

Today is my birthday. I am going to write a diry a diray a diery Book. Pop told me I could. He gave me this fat book. It was a government book, but it is mine now. I shall write here in the loft and hide my book in the old box with straw where no one can see it. Every one should have a diery. Becos life is too hard with the things one must say to be perlite and the things one must not say to lie. This is something I can never get right. If I say you are an ugly old man, that is bad manners, and if I say you are not an ugly old man I am telling a lie and not speaking the truth, the whole truth and nothing but the truth so help me God. That is what the peopel say in the witnes box when they are at a case in the courthouse. When they say this it is a great sin to tell a lie. Pop says to the witnes who is to speak about the prisoner what you are to say is the truth the whole truth and nothing but the truth, and the witnes says so Help me God. Then he tells the truth and is not punished. But in our house it is not like that. The other day when Mr. O was eating with us he said You are my little sweethart, and I said NO and he said Why not and I said So help me God becos you are such an ugly old man with hair on your face. For that I was sent to bed without any more dinner even jelly and had a good jawing about perliteness. All the time I said I was only telling the truth Mom said Nonsense. You are just a rude little girl. So Pop said you have a diary and write all the truth in it and when you cant speak the truth its better to hold your tongue. That is why I am writing. Charles said it is all too much trubbel. Dont evertalk and you wont be punished. But my tongue is an unruly member Pop says and will cawse me to suffer much being a female.

Tok Tokkies

There are tok tokkies. They are the knocking kind beetle. One day I had two toks in my room and Charles had 2 in his room. In the night when all was asleep the toks got out and started to walk, the wives looking for the husbands which were mixed up. The wives have a brown spot on their stumick. When they cant find them the husbands stands still and knock with his stumick on the ground and the wives knock back. That night they knocked so loud on the floor Mom woke up and said Cecil, wake up someone is knocking, and Pop got up and looked at the back door and at the front but no one was there. Then he went to bed and said Patty you dreaming and blew out the candle. When all was quiet the toks knocked again and Mom said whose dreaming now, and Pop said someone is playing the fool and he went to the back door and Mom went to front but no one. Mom said this house is haunted. Pop said Rot and Mom said Mrs Oost told me an old woman died of hunger in this house when her peopel went to nagmaal and forgot her. Pop said old woman be damned, ghosts dont knock. But the toks went on knocking and Pop said Iris and Charles are you making this noise, becos if you dont stop I'll tan your bottoms for you. Then we all sat quiet to listen and Charles said 'It is only the toks look there they are behind the door', and we saw them knocking loudly with their stomachs on the floor Pop said, My God, who would have guessed these dam beetles knew about morse code in their secks life. Then he threw them out and we all went to sleep.

God, the Devil and his Fork and Fire

This is the first time we will go to Church and really learn about God. In Maraisburg was only the Dutch church and we did not learn about God. Only sometimes Pop read us out of the Childs Bible about Moses and David and other old men. All had beards. Solomon was the wisest becos he had so many wives and learnt to keep alive for 200 years. That was becos God liked him. I asked Pop why he does not have many wives and he said God forbid, and told me not to ask silly questions. This Church has a choir where singing peopel sit. They have to bellow very loudly to help all the other peopel who sit in the benches to sing strange songs called salms and chant. Not easy to do, becos sometimes they go so fast you cant get your breath and then so slow you far in front of everyone of the choir. I would not like to sit in that choir, becos of everyone looking at you. If your garter came down you would have great troubel to get it up with all staring. We have all got the red prayer books. We look in them but dont know what it is all about. Charles has the best seat by the window and is putting his name on it with a knife.

The parsons name is Damp. He is young but bald. He has not a wife he is a bacheldor and comes often to our house. He is very strange sometimes. Charles says he is not right, but Hester our cook, says who is not right, all have a little mad in them. Mom says no one would think Pop was a parson's son with his savige temper and his swearing. He does not swear when Mr. Damp comes. Mr. Damp says he is going to make Christians of us. He says 'you all little heathens not knowing about God and Church. You will go to Sunday school.' I said 'what is Sunday school' and he said it is the nicest place.

Florence and I had new white muslin with daisies round our hats. Charles had a suit which scrached him. He hates scraching clothes. Coot went to Church but when plate time came she had to sit down. Charles says some boys at the back dont put their tickeys in the plate just pretent to and keep them. Thats cheating God …

When the Bishop comes a big boy is to get confirmation. He is Mark Raine. He is very clever and asking Mr. Damp so many things about God that Mr. Damp gets savige. Pop is now the chief warder man in Church taking the plate round to ask for money. On Sunday all must go. Some in morning some at nite putting on of best clothes and hats. In Church men take off hats women keep on hats. Pop puts on his tail coat and best black bouler hat. On other days he wears his old bouler hat. The other nite the lamp hanging over the front seat was going up high and making smoke. Mr. Damp was preeching a long sermon in the pullpit, and made signs to Pop to put it out and Pop must go and stand on High bak of seats and shaking backwards and sidewards becos tops are thin to stand on and coat tails flying and he not being able to reach lamp and nearly falling over backwards and much laughing was going on we laughed much too, and then Pop got his savige look and got slowly down and came and sat in his place and Mom was red in the face and just left the lamp with long smoke coming out and Pop said let the dam thing burn I not braking my neck for it, and then the dam thing went out which was lucky for all …

… I think Mr. Damp is indeed a horrid man. When he saw our photo he said she looks like Alice in wonderland with her long neck and Charles looks like a chesire cat with its grin going away. I wished I belonged to Mr. Makles church. He only pats you on the head and says Lassie girl, never about how you are looking.

I found a pictur of the devil in a book in the libery. He has horns and a pointed tail like dragon flames coming out of his mouth and a long fork. Mr. Damp says God sees all you do. All your sins are written down in a big book for jugement day like stealing and glutony and swearing and lying. Florence says if you just take a few is that stealing. Becos of the peaches. I said God must be a very busy watching all in the whole world like how does He do it. I would never like to be Him. Mr. Damp says we all impossible. We told Coot about the devil and his fork and fire and how he poked you in it and about absalom hanging up by his hair on a tree and we showed her the picturs of the childs bible Pop bought us and she got a night mare … Why mare?

Dr. Room the school inspector has been. He has just got a wife. Teacher said he hoped he would be kinder to all pupils now he has a wife. It isnt always so. He went to Germany to find her. He has a very long head and blue eyes with big glasses. He looks very fierce but he is better than Mr. Raymond but not very much. He snaps. You can see he does not know about children yet.

Dancing

It is the first time we have seen the dance … The wals is a strange thing. The men hold the ladies round the middle and turn very fast one way then they turn very fast the other way. This is called reversing. It makes us giddy to watch this thing. Those who cant do the turning just push the lady down the room backwards. I wonder how she never hits the pillars that hold the roof up. It is a dangeros way of having fun this dancing. The most dangerous is the LANCERS why lancers. Lancers are horse soldiers. The lancers made a lot of noise stamping and clapping their hands and shouting at ladies in the center. They ran in and out holding hands and bowing to each other with one hand on the stumick and some of the ladys were swung high and nearly fell down. When they finished the men wiping the sweat off their faces. We went home after the lancers. It is just across the road not far to walk. Pop [staying at home to look after the youngest] was savige becos we so late. He said what an hour to be staying out at night. We said we saw lancers. I said, Pop why do they call them lancers he said being very savige, because the prancing like cavelry horse and screeching like hoeligans no civilised man will make such an idiot of himself. Mom said that just becos you cant do them I am going again next month becos Mrs. Simms and I have to be lady Pat for the dance and I am shaperoening Miss Maud and Miss minnie. Why Lady Pat? I must ask when Pop not in rage. Pop said Dam the Lady Pat and then we all went to bed.

Good and Bad

This has not been a good week at school. Charles and I both got punishings and it was not fair. All becos of doing that honesty is the best policy … I always have to help Charles with his homework or he would be getting a caning every day at school. I do it badly then no one will know. He had to do an essay on George Washington. The teacher reads the story in school 3 times and gives you the hard words to copy down. Then you must come home and write it in your exercise book. But Charles did not rember what the story about G. Wash was about becos he was not listening trying to make his christmas bees go back in the match box. So I guessed and told him what to write. He wrote 'G. Wash greatest words were I cant tell lie father I choped down your cherry tree and his father must have been a different kind of father to ours becos he praised George up but if I choped down the tree in our back yard my father would get out his strap when I told him I cant tell a lie I choped down your tree. This shows that honesty is not always the best policy becos it depends on your fathers and mothers.' Charles said it was a very good essay. But when we came to school the story about G. Wash was not a bit like that and Mr. Pat said who helped you to write this and Charles would not say But Mr. Pat guessed and said Iris did you help to write this and I was like G. Wash I said yes I did. Charles got caned and I got kept in becos Mr. Pat said we were trying to be smart. Charles said it just shows all peopel are not like G. Washes father. When you tell the truth in Adelaide all you get is not praising but a caning which shows that honesty is not the best policy. It is a lie. Charles says from now when it suits he will tell lies becos anyway you mite not get found out, and anyway if you are found out or tell truth you get caned anyway. It is all too much for me. I have not decide yet what policy I must do.

PETER WILHELM

THIS AUTHOR *has built a reputation as a top journalist, a novelist, a short story writer, a critic, a poet and an essayist. The variety of his styles, the volume of his writing, and the versatility of his output demonstrate how complex his superficially retiring nature is.*

His writings range over many themes from savagely satirical to tenderly delicate. His column Up Front *in the* Financial Mail *(South African equivalent of* The Economist*) is celebrated for its sardonic humour. There's a Hogarthian cynicism in his columns, cooked in satire and, mercifully, garnished with humour.*

Peter Wilhelm was born in Cape Town in 1936, spent his early years at a rural mission station, and became a teacher. He drifted into journalism. His first book, LM and Other Stories, *was published in the 1970s by Ravan – shortly after they had published J.M. Coetzee's first book,* Dusklands. *Wilhelm became one of Ravan's favourite authors, and in 1977 they published his first novel,* The Dark Wood, *followed by his volume of poems,* White Flowers, *and a second collection of stories,* At the End of the War.

As Peter Randall, head of Ravan Press, said in an introduction to Wilhelm's collection of columns, The State We're In *(Ravan Press, Randburg, 1999): 'Thank God that he has not succumbed to ennui, anomie, alcohol, political correctness, lechery or fatigue, and that he continues to enrich and enliven our lives.'*

Wilhelm's columns are so engorged and frenetic that it is difficult to select anything 'typical'. We have simply dipped into his turn-of-the-century collection for random samples. Topicality is a problem, for it fades in months, so we have deleted – with the potent instruments of the computer – some of the columnist's now obscure topical references.

Not with a Whimper

Not so long ago, when I first visited London, I lodged with an excruciatingly prim landlady called Mrs Smee. There was a Mr Smee, a furtive stockbroker with a ferociously nicotined moustache. I seldom saw him except late at night when I would meet him padding with intent towards the fabled glories of the Swedish *au pair*'s room. This 'inappropriate contact' was understandable, since Mrs Smee had all the allure of a desiccated hedgehog. She spent her days seeking to poison squirrels.

Whenever the Royal Family appeared on TV she would rasp at me: 'I'll not hear a word said against them, young man!' She must have thought I was an Australian.

It must therefore have come as a terrible shock to Mrs Smee to learn that shit has been falling out of the sky on to Windsor Castle – once even while Her Majesty and Prince Philip were watching a polo match.

An official report by the celestial-poo-watching Civil Aviation Authority states: 'Numerous brown, foul-smelling pellets fell into the area.' The castle is directly below the flight path of Heathrow-bound jets, but the CAA denies that the airliners were dumping on the royals. However, a spokesman did admit that 'if somebody calls us, we have to go and take a look at it.' The outcome of this forensic 'look' is unreported. Perhaps the 'brown pellets' raining down were surplus beefburgers served on the flight out from Abu Dhabi. That would certainly baffle chemists seeking to distinguish them from faeces, as passengers know.

More probable is that the CAA is lying. As I have suggested before, to eliminate falsehood from all public discourse would undermine the very basis of civil society.

I have before me Bill Clinton's address to the American people on the Monica crises. Apart from its lack of resemblance to the Gettysburg Address, it is resonant with true Nixonian unction. Clearly Clinton heeded his lawyers, who told him, in effect, to deny that evil-smelling brown pellets were raining down on the White House. What if he had chosen to tell the truth? The speech might have sounded like this:

'My fellow Americans – this afternoon in this room, from this chair, I testified before the Office of the Independent Counsel and the grand jury. I answered their probes with quivering wattles and a powerful desire to swig from the bottle of Old Granddad I keep in case of snakebite. And golly! They sure got personal! How would all you good folks out there in Intercourse, Pennsylvania, like being cross-examined about the misdeeds of your willy?

'Anyway, though my little head always leaps in before my big head can stop it, I told them that what I did was inappropriate. I mean, I don't know how Monica and her Mom are going to get that DNA out of her party frock in time for the prom.

'I suffered a critical lapse in judgement, even though Monica's teeth are pretty white and much straighter than Paula Jones's before she got them flossed and fixed. So it wasn't much of a lapse. It wasn't as if I pushed the wrong button and nuked Tel Aviv. I really deserve to keep this job.

'Right now, I intend to watch *Armageddon* in secluded quality time with Hillary, Chelsea and my adorable poodle, little Muffie. If they don't go on hugging me in public, I'll have Muffie put to sleep on the Larry King show. The President must be allowed to do his job without obnoxious flak from geeks who've probably never even spent an hour in a motel. Accordingly, as of 7 pm tonight, I've ordered a first strike against Lesotho. So bye now, and go easy on the Viagra.'

Mrs Smee would not have been amused. But perhaps, that alone should have encouraged Bill to go out with a bang.

Will Claudia Sleep with Enrique?

Once asked what she wanted most in life, Madame de Gaulle replied, 'A penis,' which prompted the General to correct her: 'It's "'appiness," my dear.' I wonder what those cunning frog-leg-guzzlers would make of the findings of one Michael Argyle of Oxford University who, after a stupefying 11 years of research, claims to have drawn up a list of what makes people happy or unhappy.

Argyle informs us that watching soap operas, getting married, going to church, joining in team sports and having friends will lead to happiness. Surely 11 years is sufficient to discover all kinds of important things like pink quarks and fearsome discontinuities in the fossil record? Argyle's research seems not so much scientific as the kind of thing you hear down at the local when some *wuss* bursts into spontaneous *dronkverdriet* because he hasn't been home for three days. 'I love my wife!' he blubbers into his floozie's blouse.

I once got married in the Johannesburg Magistrate's Court, where a sign helpfully pointed you towards WHITE MARRIAGES AND BANTU MENTAL PATIENTS. How prophetic! But that was in a previous life. Never get married in places like that; go to a sympathetic or cynical church even though you belong to an ultra-secret cult of Moloch or Baal. The worst that can happen, as opposed to being mistaken for a BANTU MENTAL PATIENT and hauled off in leg-irons, is the social agony when some lout breaks wind at a deeply inappropriate moment, just as you stutter, 'I d-d-d-do!'

Such gremlin factors undercut the bald assertion that marriage is a happiness cocoon. It is an immutable law that in all human affairs things will go wrong. What makes all governments stupid is their childlike belief in legislating for happiness – making you stop smoking, giving you a house, curbing greenhouse gas emissions. They should have known better long ago, discarding such idealism with Noddy, Big Ears, Lenin, and Mr Plod the Policeman.

As for watching soap operas, who gives a toss when 'Brooke tells Ridge to leave before the police arrive; Claudia tells Hunter that it was Enrique who shot Grant; and Enrique wonders if Claudia will sleep with him'? Argyle cautions: 'The results have been most perplexing. People who watch soap operas seem to gain a great deal of happiness from that. One theory is that they make imaginary friends.'

These imaginary friends – with crappy-hippie names like Ridge, River, Storm, Sky and Mountain – have some advantages over real friends. You don't have to offer them a drink, explain where the Waterfront is, send them outside to smoke, or worry about any sexual tension when you all get together in your private Holodeck, like the one on the starship *Enterprise*.

But, I must caution, if you watch too much soap opera, you will take on that pallid, trembling, sweating, sly appearance which the Victorians attributed to self-abuse. And if you have too many imaginary chums you won't have room for real ones. Frankly, Argyle's research looks dodgy. I imagine he spent his 11 years in the Cuttlefish & Roadkill, a faux-pubby boozer somewhere in far-off Willesden Green.

Watching sport – on TV, of course – is the favourite recreation of our males. It enables them to perform simultaneously other happy duties, glugging beer or scratching in unsociable places. I don't know what the wives do then, so again Argyle seems to be proffering a half-truth. And he skirts one hugely important factor in well-being – the amassing of vast sums of money, without which you will be unable to buy 'appiness, let alone compensatory comforts such as champagne and cigars.

A Rainbow over Signal Hill

At the end of a fractious political year, ordinary folk wish simply to put aside everyday concerns and relax in front of 'the little bioscope', to see our great sports teams grinding their ghastly foreign opponents into dust.

Few elements of our public life are as important as rugby, cricket, soccer, golf – and even mountaineering with all its controversy [over a Sunday newspaper-sponsored, gender- and race-diversified team dispatched to Mount Everest]. The tragedy is that when the teams flounder or lose, a colossal depression sets in: a dark night of the national soul. Introspection saps the fragile ties of self-esteem.

The time has come to move away from wimpismo, to reanimate national pride through a new, challenging venture. To this end, I am proposing myself as team leader for the all-South African Ascent of Signal Hill.

I alone am psychologically fit for this task. My military record speaks for itself. I was troop leader in the Florida Lake Sea Scouts and once knew how to tie a reef knot. And ever since my dog ate the TV remote, the repeated exercise of straining up from my armchair and shuffling over to the set to change channels has kept me in prime physical condition.

The team will be chosen on the basis of ability to pay me money, as well as ethnic diversity, and will have to undergo strenuous training before assaulting the arduous trail winding from the Cape Town Waterfront to the summit of the famous hill, an astonishing 350 metres above sea level.

In that rarefied atmosphere, facing the grim reality of low-flying seagulls and slavering purple-arsed baboons, one wrong step could mean standing on a slumbering mole snake or rabid dassie.

The composition of the expedition must reflect all hues of our rainbow nation. It must also be gender correct, and any blondes – or, indeed, brunettes – who want to participate are invited to meet me on the kelpy rocks below the Sea Point Pool so that I can assess their ability to laugh at my jokes. If, in the possession of uncontrollable mirth, they lose their balance, they must go back to shopping, sobbing into their handbags.

Stamina will be built up by hop-skip-and-jump races across the fabulous dunes: a punishing course through eggshells, seashells, squids' eyes, generalised crumble, huge pipes of seaweed with minuscule crabs scuttling over them, the heady scent of ozone, piles of indeterminate jellyfish, beached whales, rusty fishhooks and the detritus of wild moonlit parties. We will all 'bond'.

Further training will including trekking from the provincial Legislature – past the gauntlet of official post-lunch lurches – up Long Street to the public baths without once staring into the windows of a sex shop or second-hand bookshop.

My proposed route to the summit will be the classic 'hookers' parade' along Lower Main Road to Upper Main Road, stopping at each shebeen on the way for the all-important rehydration essential to survival in these desolate regions, savaged by inflated house prices and bitter southeasters that often cause the inexperienced to fall down and remain on the pavement for days, just like winos, backpackers and feral children who subsist in the hostile terrain.

At all times, the risk of being approached by beggars for money for glue, or tourists for directions to the IMAX cinema, will be high. But surely no sacrifice is too great if we are to forge a new nation fit for the demands and opportunities of the 19th century.

Let Them Eat Prozac

Before I climb into my hyper-spatial module and flee to the rings of Uranus to escape more facetious columns about Viagra, I venture one final prediction. To wit, this overblown substance – the oysters and champagne of senescent geeks – will soon be banned. Why? Because, inexorably, it will feature in the obituaries of politicians and wired celebrities like George Michael, whom I suspect of ripping out his Viagra drip in an evil obsession with going arse-over-tip in LA.

Already, I note, a number of people have been reported dead after snorting this loathsome and unnatural substance. Doubtless they are so astonished at any semblance of life below their eyebrows that they immediately pop their clogs. And just watch feminists react to the first Viagra Rape Trial. They will detonate.

One could blame the pharmaceutical industry for exploiting human weakness. Viagra is one of those 'magic-bullet' drugs like Prozac and Virodene, which implausibly appear to offer happiness, immortality and the three-hour orgasm – the great trinity of modern hope. One rationale is if this celestial promise is validated, the need for large sums of money to fund welfare, health and education simply falls away.

Is this the panacea being pursued by South Africa's most illustrious female social Ministers with hyphenated names? I refer of course to Dr Nkosazana Dlamini-Zuma, Sankie Mthembi-Mahanyele, and Geraldine Fraser-Moleketi. Why are they hyphenated? It's too much of a coincidence. Surely they all belong to some underground coven, meeting in secret bunkers to natter about quick fixes for the perpetually disadvantaged.

Together they might well serve fiscal prudence by coalescing their ministries, seeking out and funding magic chemicals for the masses. Thus, if Virodene works … Aids will disappear. Those without housing or whose welfare cheques have been stolen by the postman can console themselves with incessant Viagran bonking in cardboard boxes; and cold, grey, rainy days turn rosy with just a soupçon of Prozac.

… The blessed-out multitudes will laugh merrily at such minor inconveniences as being washed away by winter rain; the unacceptably grainy reception of soccer matches on TV sets powered by naked wires draped over Eskom pylons; and even the vile intrusions of pollsters demanding to know why they are beginning to suspect [political Opposition leader] Tony Leon is cute. They will never revolt!

This cheery fantasy depends on the pills working, and not being stolen before they trickle down …

BUGS WILMOT

THIS AUTHOR *of a book on East Cape 'colonial' English is not so much a writer as a collector. Indeed, Brian Wilmot's nickname and by-line arise from the fact that he is an entomologist who once collected bugs before collecting the title of Director of the Albany Museum and then director of the National Festival of Science, Engineering and Technology. As a pastime he collected samples of the sayings of a community of English-speaking people who are distinct and unique. Their humour is peculiar in the correct sense. Therefore it is not easily appreciated by outsiders who fail to understand their colloquialisms, their agricultural jargon or their history.*

They are unusually concerned about their unsettled history, for they are the descendants of the 1820 British Settlers, and they live at the very heart of 'Settler Country' on the old Kaffrarian Frontier, between the Great Fish and Bushman rivers. They are the farming folk of Lower Albany, and they affect an exaggerated bucolic air when their cousins come down from that great seat of learning, Grahamstown – 'the City of Saints' – only a few miles away.

Bathurst may be described as the lower-case capital of Lower Albany. Until quite recently, it consisted of little more than a picturesque Anglican stone church, a village common and agricultural showground, a village hall, a cricket field and a pub, 'The Pig and Whistle'.

Very English, you might think. Wrong. Very, very, peculiarly South African, for the Bathurst people have, in a period of nearly two centuries, developed an amalgam of English, Xhosa and Afrikaans spoken nowhere else on Earth. Of course, elements of their 'dialect' spread to the rest of the country when the East Cape settlers were involved in the diamond and gold rushes and other pioneering efforts of the 19th century. Traces of their style also entered politics, and their beneficial influence on language is reflected in the fact they have been leaders of the cause of freedom of the press since the 1820s. In the 21st century, some of their colloquialisms have become part of a current television series.

(Wilmot, one of the 1820 Settler Wilmots, offers an example of their style of language – that amalgam – which, in British Settlers' typically languid speech, would read: 'Kwek'u ... but ... the dam ... is ... dry-y-y ... swaer.' (Kwek'u *is a Xhosa exclamation, and* swaer *is the Afrikaans term for 'brother-in-law', meaning* boet, *which is 'brother', and expands into cousin, friend, fellow and even 'hullo, stranger'.)*

In our day, if you drove past the 'The Pig', which the locals never did – they always went in – they would summon you in for a beer. Many beers. No argument. You couldn't even pay for a drink.

Pub talk was about the 'p-i-i-n-es' (pineapple fields) and the 'she-e-e-ep', and similar farming matters – but mainly it was about huntin', fishin' and cricket, always dis-

cussed in slow measure and usually with a deft, humorous twist at the end of it.

Wilmot offers this exercise in how to practise their slo-o-ow, flat form of speech:

The Bradfields, the Timms and the Taarrs
Are very close neighbo'rs of aars.
They live with their Ox'n
And sleep with their socks'n
An' they've done so for yaarrs and yaarrs.

What is almost impossible to remember about these farmers as they indulge in their special form of repartee is that nearly all were well educated at institutions based on the English public school; many have university degrees; and most have travelled often to London, and as occasional tourists or business people visiting Europe, North America, Australasia and the Orient. Yet, at home, they scorn their English manners and standard English, preferring a local laid-back style and a unique set of figures of speech.

Some of their metaphors were illustrated and published in the local Grocott's Daily Mail *for the edification of the professors and their colleagues in Grahamstown. Here are a few of the ones that Bugs Wilmot and Gerhard Marx published in a booklet –* L.A. Lore: The Lighter Side of Life in Lower Albany *(Albany Museum, 1992). 'I published one or two, and amused farmers sent me the rest,' says Bugs.*

'The rains were so bad down there in the Coombs that the only way old man Dixon could reap his 'taties was with a throw-net just before they went over the weir.'

'Take those cattle to stock-fair in town? Impossible, *swaer*. Those beggars are so hungry in this drought that if I stop at a robot [traffic light] they're off the truck and trying to eat the green light.'

First farmer: 'In this drought my sheep are so small I'm tying them in bunches and selling them like carrots.'
Second farmer: 'Boet, my sheep are so small you can put a whole one on a sandwich and the legs don't even stick out the sides.'
Third farmer: 'Our sheep are so thin we just fax them to the abattoir.'

'That guy on the box drives a golf ball further than I go on holiday.'

Cricket umpire: 'Sorry, Jimmy, but the ball was missing the leg stump.'
Wicket-keeper: 'You're right, *swaer*, but it would have knocked hell out of the middle stump!'

'Ask old Uncle Aubin when he was born and he'll tell you it was a Tuesday.'

'Man, that nort' wind's bin blowing so bad, the only thing from my farm old Eric hasn't got on his place now is the title-deeds.'

The farmers were complaining about the lack of maintenance of the roads by the local council. The farmer from Salem said: 'I hit that donkey in the road with my truck. I didn't see it because it was hiding in one of the corrugations.'

This was confirmed by a farmer from Coombs. 'The other night I picked up a pair of ears in the headlights. I thought it was just 'nother dumb *mvundla* (hare) … but the pot-hole in the road was so big that the ears sticking out were of a ruddy donkey! … This 's serious [if] we are gonna have to pay to put reflectors on the ears of all our animals.'

Jack Ansley, describing to a guest how to get to his farm at Clumber, concluded by saying, 'An' when you get to the house, just kick on the door.'

'Why did you tell him to kick the door instead of knocking?' asked a third party later.

'Hell, *swaer*,' said Jack looking puzzled, 'you don't think he's coming empty-handed, do you?'

When challenged for subscribing to the belief that water-tortoises seen away from water are a sign of impending rain, the farmer retorted: 'Those li'l beggars don't talk, so those li'l beggars don't lie!'

'My wife's having a hell of a time in this drought; every time she throws the dish-water onto the garden the windmills come running.'

'Old Leonard's dogs are so *maer* [thin] he has to tie knots in their tails to keep them out of the chicken run.'

'*Mfondin*', the dam's so low now you can lip-read the bass.'

'Eric's lands are so wet he has to use a prawn-pump to lift his chicory.'

'Quiet, you ask! Look 'ere, *swaer*, this car is a luxury job – as quiet as a mouse wearing *tackies* [tennis shoes].'

'Parties are *mooi* [lovely], but if there's two things that can spoil them it's food and music.'

'Those farms down by the New Years River are so steep even the baboons use walking sticks.'

'I'm telling you, boet, it's so hot at Carlisle Bridge in February that dikkop eggs, laid in the mornin', hatch the same day.'

'That chap's so cheerful he don't look better 'n a long drink of sour-milk.'

'I'm telling you, boet, there's more ways of killing a cat than drowning it in a pound of butter.'

'The Bushman River's so dry you have to dust the bass off before you put them in the pan.'

'He's as nervous as a long-tailed cat in a roomful of rocking chairs.'

'Man, business is so quiet these days you can hear the turnover dropping.'

ZAPIRO

JONATHAN SHAPIRO, *who is the pen and the talent as well as the brains and the wit behind 'Zapiro', must rank among the top political cartoonists in the world as the 21st century begins. He has the advantage of observing and caricaturing a society that has gone through bewildering change and is still not quite sure what is happening.*

He has also had the luck of being able to concentrate his cartooning on extraordinary characters such as Mandela and Tutu as well as on egregious operators such as Mugabe and Terre'Blanche.

Zapiro lampoons politicians and personalities without favour, although you can see his sympathies lie with the underdog, for he likes to bite the ones on top. Often in his cartoons you can discern history as well as wit. For instance, in a single cartoon he once depicted with a few brilliant strokes five of apartheid's most notorious leaders from Malan to P.W. Botha. They're standing in hell as the regime collapses.

Verwoerd: 'It took us 40 years to build apartheid, and they try to undo it in 100 days!'

Vorster: 'Bleddy cheek.'

Jonathan Shapiro was awarded a Fulbright Scholarship and studied at the School of Media Arts in New York. He has had exhibitions in Cape Town and New York, and his work appears in international as well as South African newspapers and journals.

Here are some recent samples.

Trevor Potter
AND THE PHILOSOPHER'S STONE
THEY SAY THIS STONE TURNS BASE METALS TO GOLD!
Hogwarts MAGIC FOR BEGINNERS
The Rand
©ZAPIRO SUN TIMES 25-11-01

6 April 1652
©ZAPIRO M&G 4·4·02
"WELL, THERE GOES THE NEIGHBOURHOOD!"

CAN I GET BACK TO YOU? I'M IN THE MIDDLE OF SOMETHING.
A TYPICAL DAY IN THE LIFE OF WINNIE MADIKIZELA-MANDELA
ZAPIRO
17-7-02 SOWETAN

SANDF
TO COUNTER REPORTS THAT OUR TROOPS ARE TOO FAT, WE WILL HOLD AN INSPECTION.
LEKOTA
TROOPS! ROLL OUT!
I CAN'T STAND IT!..
LEKOTA
19-7-02 SOWETAN
ZAPIRO

Acknowledgements

A book of this nature, considering the time it has taken, would be economically impossible if the editors were obliged to pay royalties on all the work quoted, and to our relief all but two publishers and all but one author waived fees. We therefore thank Pan Macmillan, Penguin and Secker & Warburg as well as Independent Newspapers and the *Sunday Times* in Johannesburg for allowing us to quote gratis from works published by them.

We appreciated the helpful advice of Ann Smith and Dr David Medalie of the University of the Witwatersrand's Department of English. The editors wish to thank Ben Maclennan for permission to dig into his collection of newspaper cuttings reflecting the weirdness of apartheid; Les Aupiais for permission to quote her articles; the late Arnold Benjamin for his generosity in giving us his ideas (for he had, years ago, contemplated writing something similar); and Doc Bikitsha for his uproarious reminiscences and allowing us to quote his work. We are grateful for the help of Darrel Bristow-Bovey and for his allowing us free access to his columns. *The Star* library was unstinting in its help – allowing us, among other things, access to the Herman Charles Bosman clippings files. David Bullard gave us access to his *Sunday Times* columns and allowed us to dip into his book of columns. Jonathan Shapiro, better known as Zapiro, was especially helpful with all elements of this collection of humour. Dr Chris Ellis allowed us free rein with his material as did Sue McGuinness, his publisher (Sue McGuinness Communications, Johannesburg). We were particularly appreciative of the generosity of Gus Ferguson in allowing us to use his verses and charming drawings, and Gordon Forbes and his publishers, Penguin, for allowing us to reprint from his two highly popular books. The extract from Christopher Hope's *Darkest England* (1996) is reprinted with kind permission of Rogers, Coleridge & White Ltd, 20 Powis Mews, London W11 1JN. Arthur Goldstuck was generous with his time and material, as was South African novelist Jenny Hobbs. We tried our best to find relatives of A.B. Hughes but failed; the same with Joel Mervis and Dr Fred Mayne (whom we traced to Canada before the trail became cold). We would welcome hearing from relatives or friends. Professor Ellison Kahn was generous not only in allowing us to quote from his books but in offering advice. We thank Carol Lazar and Neil McMahon for permission to quote their columns. We thank Ad Donker (Jonathan Ball) for permission to reprint Bloke Modisane's work, *Blame Me on History*; as well as *The World of Nat Nakasa* (edited by Essop Patel),

The World of Can Themba (edited by Essop Patel) and Peter Wilhelm's *The State We're In* (all three quoted from by permission of Ravan Press). We thank Jo-Anne Richards. David Philip and New Africa Books permitted us to quote from Richard Rive's *Buckingham Palace, District Six* and Gus Ferguson's *Stressed–Unstressed.* Columnist John Scott was very helpful as was the Cape Times for whom he writes. Gus Silber gave us carte blanche with his humorous writing. We thank the Witwatersrand University Press for allowing us to use extracts from Zakes Mda's play *You Fool, How Can the Sky Fall?* We are indebted to Secker & Warburg for permission to quote from Tom Sharpe's *Indecent Exposure.* Sylvester Stein, now living in London, was generous both in his advice and in allowing us to quote from *Second Class Taxi* (Faber and Faber). Pieter-Dirk Uys generously gave us access to his journalistic efforts. The Albany Museum gave us permission to quote from Dr Brian Wilmot's *L.A. Lore: The Lighter Side of Life in Lower Albany.*

Every effort has been made to trace and acknowledge copyright holders. Should any mistake or omission have been made, the publishers and compilers apologise and will correct it in the next impression.